Doctrines
of
GRACE

An Attempt at a Comprehensive Scriptural Look at the Salvational Doctrines of Grace

Chad Staerkel

ISBN 978-1-63874-351-4 (paperback)
ISBN 978-1-63874-352-1 (digital)

Christian Faith Publishing, Inc.
832 Park Avenue
Meadville, PA 16335
www.christianfaithpublishing.com

Printed in the United States of America

Contents

Preface

First of all, I want to start off by saying that I take very little if any credit at all, personally, for the writing of this book, other than being used as a vessel by God in order to type this book out into print. With hesitancy of disclosing my personal prayers offered to God, whenever I sat down to study and work on this book, I did not do so until after praying something similar to this: "Dear Lord, I pray that as I sit down to continue working on this book that You be with me and give me the words to speak, that this would be the message You want spoken. I pray that You use me merely as the fingers on the keyboard and that this book would be Your words, not mine. Lord, guide me, lead me, and even more so, teach me as we go through this process. Reveal to me what it is that You want to be said, and most importantly, I pray that every single word of this book would be truthful to Your Word and Gospel.

"God, I have zero desire to print anything that contradicts or departs from or supersedes Your Biblical Truth. I do not desire that this book would take the place of or supplant Your Word in any way but that it would merely act as a compliment to It and would point and draw people to dig deeper into Your Word for themselves and closer in their relationship with You. I firmly believe that You have led me into this project, and I pray that You continue to lead me through the completion of it.

"Let everything in this book be spoken in accordance with Your Biblical Truth. Do not let me type anything that is contradictory to Your Word. And, Lord, I pray that You would use this book to lead others closer to You, to point them to Your Word and to dig deeper into Your Word for themselves, to learn more about You, to draw closer to You, to know Your infinite love and grace and mercy, and to praise You, worship You, and that all glory may be lifted up to You!"

However, in saying this, in no way am I implying that this should be held parallel to the perfectly inerrant and fully inspired Word of God! I am just a servant and child of God. Everything good in me is from God. The only thing I have ever personally accomplished is putting Christ on the cross. I have often felt inadequate, but often, God uses those who are. Gideon, for example. I hold no official formal training or theological degree. I am merely a fellow believer in and follower of Christ who felt God strongly leading me into the task of this project, resulting in this book, through certain personal situations and life experiences and deep studies, trying to draw closer to Him, and to learn as much as I can about our holy and precious, gracious, merciful, and loving God.

After a few years of collecting and compiling the, might I say, "outline" for this book for personal reasons as just a collection of Scriptures on each individual topic spoken of in this book along with excerpts from books of other authors, I sat, somewhat perplexed, wondering what it was all for, and that is when I strongly felt God nudge me saying, "Well, you've already basically prepared the entire outline. Put it into book form!" So began the task.

Also, I can confidently say that during the typing of this book, while "in the moment," I can honestly say that there were numerous times I ended up typing something that when I had looked back over it, it blew my mind and was a thought or statement that I had never heard or thought of previously and at times don't even remember writing in the first place and therefore firmly believe it was God's words spoken through me.

I lift this book up as a gift of praise to God as I believe it was given as a gift down to me. And though I pray it will become a gift to many others, I will forever be content with whatever God decides to do with it, whether one or a million people ever read it. I just pray that whoever does read it will be led and feel a great desire to draw closer to God, to dig deeper into His Word, and to grow stronger in their relationship with Jesus Christ, our Lord and Savior! To God be ALL the glory!

Most of the verses quoted in this book were usually taken from the ESV translation, unless otherwise stated. You will also find that I capitalize every single noun and pronoun associated with God, His Word, and His Kingdom. Conversely, I will never capitalize the name of the enemy, even if his name or his pronoun comes at the beginning of a sentence. This is not a typo. I just refuse to offer him capitalization.

1

In the Beginning...

"In the beginning, God"—the first four words of the Bible. So profound! Just four words yet so incredibly packed with the most important information you need to know. First, God was there. He is preexistent. He was at the beginning before there was anything. No other piece of literature makes this claim. No other person or being makes this claim. According to this very important first verse, God was the only Person, place, or thing present at the very beginning. He is the sole Author of these moments of beginning. As God Himself states in Revelation 1:8, 21:6, 22:13, "I AM the Alpha and Omega, the First and the Last, the Beginning and the End."

But Who is this God? What can we know about Him? The prophet Jeremiah calls Him "The Lord Who is the habitation of righteousness" (Jer. 50:7 NASB). That is quite an exceptional description of God! The late acclaimed pastor/theologian A. W. Tozer states the seriousness of these concerns:

> What comes to our minds when we think about God is the most important thing about us. The most portentous fact about any man is what he in his deep heart conceives God to be like. Without doubt, the mightiest thought the mind can entertain is the thought of God, and the weightiest word in any language is its word

for God. That our idea of God correspond as nearly as possible to the true being of God is of immense importance to us: that He *is*; what He is *like*; and what we as moral beings must *do* about Him. The man who comes to a right belief about God is relieved of ten thousand temporal problems.[1]

So Who is He?

To expand a little further on this first verse of the Bible, "In the beginning, God created the heavens and the earth" (Gen. 1:1). This is the origin of everything. "In the beginning" (time: the starting point as we know it), God created (God the Creator: the "Who did it") the heavens (space) and the earth (matter). Time, space, and matter making up the entire universe and the name of the Person Who created it all.

In the original written Hebrew of Genesis 1:1, God is named as "Elohim." Besides also possessing other great qualities, Hebrew is a unique and detailed language in that it is pictographic. When we take a look at the word *Elohim* in the original ancient Hebrew, we see a very detailed description of what Elohim means and are given a glimpse of Who God is. The Hebrew letters that spell the name Elohim are *aleph, lamed, hey, yod,* and *mem.* The first letter, *aleph,* is a picture of an ox head and means "the strong leader." *Lamed* is pictured as a shepherd's staff and means "the one who has control and the one that speaks with authority." *Hey* is pictured as a man lifting his hands up to Heaven, signifying that true revelation comes from Heaven alone, and it means "to reveal." *Yod* is pictured as a hand and it means "to work, a mighty deed, or to make something." *Mem* is pictured as and means "water." So if we summarize the translation of Elohim, we are given Aleph, The Strong Leader, Who is God the Father. Lamed, The One Who speaks with authority, Who is God the Son. Hey, The One Who Reveals, Who is the Holy Spirit. Yod, does a mighty work with His hands that separates. Mem, the waters from the water.

So we see that the name Elohim reveals not only the three Persons in the Trinity, but it also reveals the essence of His creative work. Elohim is God the Father, God the Son, and God the Holy Spirit doing a mighty work of separating the waters from the waters in order that we might have an earthly home (cf. Gen. 1:6–10). God revealed His name as Elohim so that every time you considered His name, you would be reminded that it was He Who created the Heavens and the earth:

> In the traditional Jewish view, Elohim is the name of God as the Creator and Judge of the universe (Gen. 1:1–2:4a). In the second narration of the creation story (Gen. 2:4b-ff) the name of God is revealed as the sacred name of "YHVH" or "Yahweh" (from the Semitic root that means "To Be") and expresses the idea of God's closeness to humans.[2]

But let's get back to the name Elohim in verse 1. *El* is the basic form name for the Almighty God meaning "strength, might or power," describing the God of Israel.

> The "-im" ending, as used in Elohim, denotes a plural masculine noun. Most of the time, however, when the noun is used for the true God it has singular masculine verbs, which is contrary to the rules of Hebrew grammar, which is the case here in Genesis 1:1. When used of the True God, 'Elohim' denotes what is called by linguists as a plural of majesty, honor or fullness. That is, He is GOD in the fullest sense of the word. He is 'GOD of gods' or literally, 'ELOHIM of elohim' (Deuteronomy 10:17, Psalm 136:2).[3]

In this name, Elohim, we see that we have a plural noun of fullness, and continuing on in Genesis 1:1, we read "God created" or in the Hebrew "*Elohim bara.*" The Hebrew word here used for "created" is *bara* which literally means to "create from nothing" (cf. Heb. 11:3) and is a singular verb. So we see that we have a plural noun with a singular verb, which is a footprint of the Trinity, the Triune God, Three in One—both plural and singular—God the Father, Son, and Holy Spirit.

In the very beginning, we are introduced to our Triune God Almighty. To us, this is a paradox. How can one be three and three be one? We cannot grasp how this works, but I personally do not want a god that I can fully understand. I do not want a god that is at my level because then he is of no more use to me in a salvational sense than any of you. I want the True God Who is so far beyond me and so much more grand and amazing than I can ever comprehend.

This issue of the Triune Godhead we simply have to take in faith. A. W. Tozer wrote this, speaking of the Trinity:

> Our sincerest effort to grasp the incomprehensible mystery of the Trinity must remain forever futile, and only by deepest reverence can it be saved from actual presumption. We think more loftily of God by knowing that He is incomprehensible, and above our understanding, than by conceiving Him under any image, and creature beauty, according to our rude understanding.[4]

There's no way to explain it and no way to comprehend it and there is no way to depict it. We do not understand how three equals one and one equals three. We can only accept God at His Word, knowing that He is the Almighty and glorious One Who does know all, Who created all, Who was before all, and therefore is above all. However, if it does help even the slightest bit, the best analogy that I've heard is that of water. H2O can be found as ice, liquid, or vapor, but it is all still water. But obviously, that analogy still infinitely pales in comparison to the Triune nature of our infinite God Who is all three at once—Trinity in Unity.

> The Persons of the Godhead, being One, have one will. They always work together, and never one smallest act is done by One without the instant acquiescence of the other two. Every act of God is accomplished by the Trinity in Unity. Throughout the Scriptures the three Persons are shown to act in harmonious unity in all the mighty works that are wrought throughout the universe. In the work of Creation (Gen. 1:1; Col. 1:16; Job. 26:13; Ps. 104:30), the Incarnation (Matt. 3:16–17; Luke 1:35), the Atonement (Heb. 9:14), the Resurrection (Acts 2:32; John 10:17–18; Rom. 1:4), the Salvation of man (1 Pet. 1:2), and the Indwelling of the Christian man's soul is said to be by the Father, the Son, and the Holy Spirit (John 14:15–23).[5]

Fourteenth-century English troubadour, Richard Rolle, stated, "Verily, God is of infinite greatness, more than we can think;… unknowable by created things; and can never be comprehended by us as He is in Himself."[6]

"God can be known only as the Holy Spirit performs in the seeking heart an act of self-disclosure."[7]

God is simply infinitely far beyond our feeble abilities to fully comprehend fully. "When we try to imagine what God is like we must of necessity use that-which-is-not-God as the raw material for our minds to work on; hence whatever we visualize God to be, He is not, for we have constructed our image out of that which He has made and what He has made is not God. He is indeed incomprehensible."[8]

To elaborate even more on Genesis 1:1, the HCSB Study Bible states:

> This opening verse of the Bible, seven words in the Hebrew, establishes seven key truths upon which the rest of the Bible is based. First, God exists. The essential first step in pleasing God is recognizing His existence (Heb. 11:6). Second, God existed before there was a universe and will exist after the universe perishes (Heb. 1:10–12). Third, God is the main Character in the Bible. He is the subject of the first verb in the Bible (in fact, He is the subject of more verbs than any other character) and performs a wider variety of activities than any other being in the Bible. Fourth, as Creator God has done what no human being could ever do; in its active form the Hebrew verb *bara'*, meaning "to create," never has a human subject. Thus *bara'* signifies a work that is uniquely God's. Fifth, God is mysterious; though the Hebrew word for God is plural, the verb form of which "God" is the subject is singular. This is perhaps a subtle allusion to God's Trinitarian nature: He is three divine Persons in one divine essence. Sixth, God is the Creator of Heaven and earth. He doesn't just modify pre-existing matter but calls matter into being out of nothing (Ps. 33:6, 9; Heb. 11:3). Seventh, God is not dependent on the universe, but the universe is totally dependent on God (Heb. 1:3).

He was there in the beginning. He was the only Person or thing in the beginning. He created everything else in the universe from nothing. Therefore, He is the sole Author and Authority of everything else that is to come, beginning to end. And if you cannot accept this, you will have an incredibly large problem with the rest of what the Bible says.

In this book, I am writing mainly to those who already know Christ as their Lord and Savior. If you are not a Christian believer and do not have faith in Jesus Christ as your Savior, this book may be a little over your head and hard to understand or fully grasp. However, please feel free to continue, for God may help lead you to an understanding.

I am not going to spend much time on Creation versus evolution, apologetics, or the origins of things in this book. That is another whole topic that is a mountain of books in itself that other authors have written extensively about. This book is mainly going to deal with doctrinal topics such as salvation, election, eternal security, grace, mercy, agape love, original sin, baptism, works, law, and the like. The purpose for this first short chapter is mainly just to express the foundation of Who God is, which could also become a mountain of books in itself.

Initially, He is our Creator, our Maker, and therefore the Ruler and Judge of the universe. He made it all from nothing (Gen. 1:1), and He holds it all together (Col. 1:17, Heb. 1:1–4). He is the sole Author and Authority of everything, and since "All Scripture is God-breathed and profitable for teaching, for reproof, for correction, and for training in righteousness, that the man of God may be complete, equipped for every good work" (2 Tim. 3:16), we can trust His Word in faith and should base our lives according to the words of our Creator.

We have also mentioned that God is infinite.

> When we say that God is infinite we mean that He knows no bounds. Whatever God is and all that God is, He is without limit. He is measureless. He is above all this, outside of it, beyond it. All that He is He is without growth or addition or development. Nothing in God is less or more, or large or small. He is what He is in Himself, without qualifying thought or word. He is sim-

ply God. Because God's nature is infinite, everything that flows out of it is infinite also. His love
is measureless. It is more: it is boundless. It has
no bounds because it is not a thing but a facet
of the essential nature of God. His love is something He *is*, and because He is infinite that love
can enfold the whole created world in itself and
have room for ten thousand times ten thousand
worlds beside. There may be, and I believe there
surely are, other aspects of God's essential being
which He has not revealed even to His ransomed
and Spirit-illuminated children, but it is enough
to know that God is God. It is obviously impossible for a limited mind to grasp the Unlimited.[9]

Third-century Roman theologian Novatian wrote "For God is
greater than (the created) mind itself. His greatness cannot be conceived. He is greater than all language, and no statement can express
Him."[10]

Lastly, to build just a little bit more of a foundation for the rest
of this book, I will touch a bit more on the Creation. In six literal
twenty-four-hour days, starting at the beginning of time, God created the entire universe out of nothing. Time itself was part of that
creation. God is eternal. He is not bound by time. As those previously stated verses in Revelation say, He has no beginning and no
end. He is the One Who always was, is, and will be (Rev. 1:8).

Time is a created dimension that we, as part of the Creation,
along with the rest of the universe, are bound by. Time, space, and
matter are all part of His Creation from nothing into existence. We
are all bound by these things, yet He sits completely outside of them,
controls them, and can affect them in any way if He chooses (i.e.,
miracles). Furthermore, He created everything in the universe perfectly to His preference.

On the sixth day of Creation, God looked and "saw everything
that He had made, and behold, it was very good" (Gen. 1:31). In the
Hebrew, the word for "very" is *mod*, which means "wholly, greatly,

exceedingly, up to abundance, to a great degree;" and the Hebrew word used for "good" is *tov*, which means "good in the widest sense, best."

The Amplified Bible (which tries to portray the detail of the Hebrew and Greek texts that gets somewhat lost in the English translations) reads like this, "God saw everything that He had made, and behold, it was very good and He validated it, or approved of it, completely." God created everything perfect. If there was any kind of death, decay, sin, pain, struggle, strife, disorder, conflict, wickedness, unrighteousness, evil, or immorality, He could not have said that everything was "very good." He would not have approved of it completely. It was all created perfect, started off perfect, and it wasn't until we screwed it up via sin that death, decay, evil, suffering, and disorder came about, which led to our need for a Savior.

Thankfully for us, God is a God of love (1 John 4:8, 16), and He sent and provided for us a way of redemption through His Son Who became the propitiation for our sins (John 3:16; 1 John 4:9–10, 14). He created the beginning, and He also created the way of salvation.

2

Original Sin/Total Depravity of Man

To truly grasp the need for salvation, we need to first fully understand our predicament and therefore our necessity for redemption. Now I realize that both these terms, *salvation* and *redemption*, may be foreign to you, but before I explain these terms, we need to start at the beginning. If you do not understand the crime, you will not understand the penalty. If you do not realize that a punishment is deserved, you will not realize that a remedy is desirable or necessary. If you do not understand the need for justice, you will not appreciate the immense gift of God's grace and mercy.

I will start this off much like Paul did in the Epistle to the Romans. We must first realize, acknowledge, and establish our dilemma, our predicament, and the wretched state that we find ourselves in. Sadly, many do not even realize they are in need, yet we are all in the same sinking ship. In the letter to the Romans, Paul spends the first three chapters hammering away on the fact that we are all entirely and desperately lost and in need of a Savior as he culminates in chapter 3, verse 23, where he states, "For there is no distinction: for ALL have sinned and fall short of the glory of God."

Before we dive deeper into this, what is sin? Ken Willig, in his book entitled *The Free Gift*, on page 35, defined it like this:

> Sin can be defined as a spirit of independence from God, doing what we want to do

regardless of God's laws. The essence of sin is to choose to do my will instead of God's will. This self-will can surface in active rebellion against God, or passive indifference to Him.

Many scholars and theologians regard Romans as the most comprehensive statement of the Gospel in the entire Bible.[1] Some call it "The Gospel according to Paul." The outline Paul forms starts with a doctrinal blueprint of faith which starts with the most complete diagnosis of sin found in the Bible. Starting at verse 18 of chapter 1, he unleashes a tirade against the pagan man, the man who does not know Christ, the non-Christian.

For the wrath of God is revealed from Heaven against all ungodliness and unrighteousness of men, who by their unrighteousness suppress the truth. For what can be known about God is plain to them, because God has shown it to them. For His invisible attributes, namely, His eternal power and divine nature, have been clearly perceived, ever since the Creation of the world, in the things that have been made. So they are without excuse. For although they knew God, they did not honor Him as God or give thanks to Him, but they became futile in their thinking, and their foolish hearts were darkened. Claiming to be wise, they became fools, and exchanged the glory of the immortal God for images resembling mortal man and birds and animals and creeping things. Therefore God gave them up in the lusts of their hearts to impurity, to the dishonoring of their bodies among themselves, because they exchanged the truth about God for a lie and worshipped and served the creature rather than the Creator, Who is blessed forever! Amen.

Whether a person has ever heard of the name of Jesus Christ or not, they are still "without excuse" as for "what can be known about God is plain to them because God has shown it to them. For His invisible attributes, namely His eternal power and divine nature, have been clearly perceived, ever since the Creation of the world, in the things that have been made" (vv. 19–20). Pagan man is responsible.

Paul continues:

> For this reason God gave them up to dishonorable passions. For their women exchanged natural relations for those contrary to nature; and the men likewise gave up natural relations with women and were consumed with passion for one another, men committing shameful acts with men and receiving in themselves the due penalty for their error. And since they did not see fit to acknowledge God, God gave them up to a debased mind to do what ought not to be done. They were filled with all manner of unrighteousness, evil, covetousness, malice. They are full of envy, murder, strife, deceit, maliciousness. They are gossips, slanderers, haters of God, insolent, haughty, boastful, inventors of evil, disobedient to parents, foolish, faithless, heartless, ruthless. Though they know God's righteous decree that those who practice such things deserve to die, they not only do them but give approval to those who practice them. (vv. 26–32)

Pagan man, the non-Christian, is lost and dead without a Savior. Again, "they are without excuse."

Paul then continues in his denunciation and shifts his focus to the moral man, the person who thinks they're "good enough" or at least better than others. He starts chapter 2 by saying:

> Therefore you have no excuse, O man, every one of you who judges. For in passing judg-

ment on another you condemn yourself, because you, the judge, practice the very same things. We know that the judgment of God rightly falls on those who practice such things. Do you suppose, O man—you who judge those who practice such things and yet do them yourself—that you will escape the judgment of God? Or do you presume on the riches of His kindness and forbearance and patience, not knowing that God's kindness is meant to lead you to repentance? But because of your hard and impenitent heart you are storing up wrath for yourself on the day of wrath when God's righteous judgment will be revealed.

He continues in vs 8 and following:

[F]or those who are self-seeking and do not obey the truth, but obey unrighteousness, there will be wrath and fury. There will be tribulation and distress for every human being who does evil, the Jew first and also the Greek...for God shows no partiality.

And in verses 15–16:

They show that the work of the law is written on their hearts, while their conscience also bears witness, and their conflicting thoughts accuse or even excuse them on that day when, according to my gospel, God judges the secrets of men by Christ Jesus.

No one can hide. No one is immune to God's judgment. God knows all our secrets. And when Christ preached the Sermon on the

Mount, He even escalated the standards. In Matthew 5:21–22, He stated:

> You have heard it said, "You shall not murder," but I say to you that everyone who is angry with his brother will be liable to judgment; whoever insults his brother will be liable to the council; and whoever says "You fool!" will be liable to the hell of fire.

And in Matthew 5:27–28 Jesus said, "You have heard it said, 'You shall not commit adultery,' but I say to you that everyone who looks at a woman with lustful intent has already committed adultery with her in his heart." Jesus is saying that:

> [E]ven anger is enough to overstep the mark. Anger is always an attack on the brother's life, for it refuses to let him live and aims at his destruction. Anger is an offense against both God and our neighbor. Every idle word which we think so little of betrays our lack of respect for our neighbor, and shows that we place ourselves on a pinnacle above him and value our own lives higher than his. The angry word is a blow struck at our brother, a stab at his heart; it seeks to hit, to hurt and to destroy. A deliberate insult is even worse, for we are then openly disgracing our brother in the eyes of the world, and causing others to despise him. With our hearts burning with hatred, we seek to annihilate his moral and material existence. We are passing judgment on him, and that is murder. And the murderer will himself be judged. When a man gets angry with his brother and swears at him, when he publicly insults or slanders him, he is guilty of murder and forfeits his relationship to God. He erects a

barrier not only between himself and his brother, but also between himself and God.[2]

And "lust is impure because it is unbelief. Instead of trusting to the unseen, we prefer the tangible fruits of desire, and so we fall from the path of discipleship and lose touch with Jesus."[3]

So it doesn't just depend on the full assault of murder or fornication but goes all the way to the core in the heart, of basic anger, hatred, ill-will, slander, and simple lust and impure thoughts which are all in themselves damning, and all of mankind has been guilty of these to some degree. Paul goes on throughout the rest of chapter 2 of Romans to drive this point home. No matter how good and righteous you think you are, you are no better than anyone else. And no one is exempt from the judgment of God.

Paul continues after his omission of pagan man and moral man and turns his focus onto the religious man. Today, the term *religion* usually caries a bit of a different meaning:

> Religion can be defined as "belief in God or gods to be worshipped, usually expressed in conduct and ritual" or "any specific system of belief, worship, etc., often involving a code of ethics." To put it briefly, religion is a set of beliefs and rituals that claim to get a person in a right relationship with God. The most common misconception about religion is that Christianity is just another religion like Islam, Judaism, Hinduism, etc. Sadly, many who claim to be adherents of Christianity do practice Christianity as if it were a religion. To many, Christianity is nothing more than a set of rules and rituals that a person has to observe in order to go to Heaven after death. That is not true Christianity. True Christianity is not a religion; rather, it is having a right relationship with God by receiving Jesus Christ as the Savior-Messiah, by grace through faith. Yes,

Christianity does have "rituals" to observe (e.g., baptism and communion). Yes, Christianity does have "rules" to follow (e.g., do not murder, love one another, etc.). However, these rituals and rules are not the essence of Christianity. The rituals and rules of Christianity are the result of salvation. When we receive salvation through Jesus Christ, we are baptized as a proclamation of that faith. We observe communion in remembrance of Christ's sacrifice. We follow a list of dos and don'ts out of love for God and gratitude for what He has done. Religion can be a false method of having a relationship with God. Religion tends to substitute the heartless observance of rituals for a genuine relationship with God. Religion can be valuable in the sense that it points to the fact that there is a God and that we are somehow accountable to Him, yet the only true value of religion is its ability to point out that we have fallen short and are in need of a Savior. Jesus Christ is the fulfillment of religion, and spirituality. Jesus is the One to Whom we are accountable and to Whom true religion points. Jesus is the One to Whom we need to connect and the One to Whom true spirituality points.[4]

Alistair Begg from Truth For Life Ministries explains it like this:

Within the framework of an externalized religion people are constantly thinking "It's about me, it's about what I do, it's about how well I do it." Religion is all about how well I do. Christianity is about the wonder of what Christ has done! So that a real Christian is always saying, "Oh how the grace of God amazes me! Because I, in myself, am unworthy, and even vile!"[5]

Biblical author, Timothy Keller, writes in his book, *The Reason for God*, these words on the subject:

> There is, then, a great gulf between the understanding that God accepts us because of our efforts and the understanding that God accepts us because of what Jesus has done. Religion operates on the principle "I obey—therefore I am accepted by God." But the operating principle of the Gospel is "I am accepted by God through what Christ has done—therefore I obey." The primary difference is that of motivation. In religion, we try to obey the divine standards out of fear. In the Gospel, the motivation is one of gratitude for the blessing we have already received because of Christ. While the moralist is forced into obedience, motivated by fear of rejection, a Christian rushes into obedience, motivated by a desire to please and resemble the One Who gave His life for us.

True Christianity is a relationship with Christ, not a religion. Religion is man's attempt to right himself with God, which you simply cannot do. You can never be "good enough" or "perform well enough" to be holy and righteous in your own merit. You must instead have a relationship with the One Who can bring you before God and declare you innocent of sin only on His behalf.

So Paul, starting at verse 17 of chapter 2, continues on to the third and last person type, that of the religious man and uses the Jew as the exemplar of religious man and lays claim that religion in itself is bankrupt also. Even to those who knew God, it was not enough for them to simply work and live in prideful obedience. Paul says:

> But if you call yourself a Jew and rely on the law and boast in God and know His will and approve what is excellent, because you are

instructed from the law; and if you are sure that you yourself are a guide to the blind, a light to those who are in darkness, an instructor of the foolish, a teacher of children, having in the law the embodiment of knowledge and truth—you then who teach others, do you not teach yourself? While you preach against stealing, do you steal? You who say that one must not commit adultery, do you commit adultery? You who abhor idols, do you rob temples? You who boast in the law dishonor God by breaking the law. For as it is written, "The name of God is blasphemed among the Gentiles because of you."

"Paul is making sure that there are no misconceptions on the part of his Jewish readers, who had their pride rooted in their Law and culture."[6]

I am reminded of a story in John chapter 8 where the Pharisees, "the Jewish elite who were distinguished by strict observance of the traditional and written law and commonly held to have pretensions to superior sanctity"[7] in verse 3:

[B]rought a woman who had been caught in adultery, and placed her in the midst and said to Jesus, "Teacher, this woman has been caught in the act of adultery. Now in the Law Moses commanded us to stone such women. So what do You say?" This they said to test Him, that they might have some charge to bring against Him... Jesus said to them, "Let he who is without sin cast the first stone." When they heard this, they went away one by one, beginning with the older ones, and Jesus was left alone with the woman standing before Him. Jesus stood and said to her, "Woman, where are they? Has no one condemned you?" She said, "No one, Lord." And

Jesus said, "Neither do I condemn you; go, and from now on sin no more."

The Pharisees, pretending to be holy and righteous themselves, looking to condemn this woman for her sins, and looking to test Jesus and bring a charge against Him in order to condemn Him also were slapped with the cold hard reality that despite their dedication and servitude to the Law of Moses, they themselves are still sinful and unholy. Jesus also emphasized this during the Sermon on the Mount in Matthew chapter 5 when He said, "Unless your righteousness _exceeds_ that of the scribes and the Pharisees, you shall not enter the Kingdom of God" (v. 20). As good as they thought they were, it wasn't good enough.

Paul then goes into a section starting at verse 25 where he minimizes the effect of circumcision, a ritual the Jews held in high, salvational regard ever since the time of Moses:

> For circumcision indeed is of value if you obey the law, but if you break the law, your circumcision becomes uncircumcision. So if a man who is uncircumcised keeps the precepts of the law, will not his uncircumcision be regarded as circumcision? Then he who is physically uncircumcised but keeps the law will condemn you who have the written code and circumcision but break the law. For no one is a Jew who is merely one outwardly, nor is circumcision outward and physical. But a Jew is one inwardly, and circumcision is a matter of the heart, by the Spirit, not by the letter. His praise is not from man but from God.

In other words, "the outward rite is of value only when it reflects the inner reality of a heart separated from sin unto God. Salvation results from the work of God's Spirit in the heart, not mere external efforts to conform to His law."[8]

Paul then culminates his exposition of the depravity of all men when he makes his way through chapter 3. Sealing his dismission of the religious man in the form of the Jew, he says in verse 9, "What then? Are we Jews any better off? No, not at all. For we have already charged that all, both Jews and Greeks, are under sin," He then ties these first couple chapters together and continues:

> As it is written, "None are righteous, no, not one; no one understands; no one seeks for God. All have turned aside; together they have become worthless; no one does good, not even one. Their throat is an open grave; they use their tongues to deceive. The venom of asps is under their lips. Their mouth is full of curses and bitterness. Their feet are swift to shed blood; in their paths are ruin and misery, and the way of peace they have not known. There is no fear of God before their eyes."

He then throws in one last dismissal on justification by obedience of the law by saying in verse 20, "For by works of the law no human being will be justified in His sight, since through the law comes knowledge of sin."

Did you catch that? The law or even obedience to it does not offer justification. It only offers knowledge of sin. It only makes the sin known. It does not offer relief from the sin. It makes sin known, but it cannot save. The law cannot save. "Doing perfectly what God's moral law requires is impossible, so that every person is cursed by that inability."[9]

Paul then climaxes his comprehensive statement of sin and the depravity of man by saying in verse 23, "For there is no distinction: for ALL have sinned and fall short of the glory of God." I'd say that's pretty straightforward. So to summarize a little bit, Paul just spent the good part of three chapters hammering away at the fact that "all have sinned and fall short of the glory of God."

I do not see a single exception to this being presented here. Not one example of someone who has bypassed this is given here or anywhere in all of Scripture. Besides Christ Himself, every other human being on this planet, past, present, and future is guilty of sin. It is inherent. It is inescapable. And to any who ignore or even deny this intrinsic doctrine, it is dangerously destructive. It is one of the most basic and even easily visible doctrines of Christianity.

Babies cry and are naughty without being taught to be so because we are all born with the propensity to sin. We are all born with an original rootage of selfishness. We all immediately want what we want, whether that coincides with God's law, or desires or will, or not. We are all inherently selfish, prideful, and sinful, horribly depraved, wretched, and fallen. And also completely hopeless on our own.

At several other places in the book of Romans, Paul continues preaching the issue of original sin and the depravity of man. In Romans 5:12, he tells us, "Therefore, just as sin entered the world through one man, and death through sin, and in this way death came to all men, because all sinned." Through the one sin of Adam, which we will touch on in just a second, all were now sinful. Later in the same chapter, verses 15–19, he continues:

> For if many died through one man's trespass...like the result of that one man's sin. For the judgment following one trespass brought condemnation...for if, because of one man's trespass, death reigned through that one man... therefore, as one trespass led to condemnation for all men... For as by the one man's disobedience the many were made sinners.

How many times does he have to repeat it to get his point across? In Romans 6:20 and 23, he explains our predicament, "when you were slaves to sin, you were free from righteousness...for the wages of sin is death." In Ezekiel chapter 18, we find a quick phrase that exactly coincides with this. Verse 4 says, "The soul who sins shall die." And in chapter 7 of Romans, Paul rails on himself and his personal propensity to sin. Romans 7:14, 18, and 24 follows, "I am of the flesh, sold under sin…for I know that nothing good dwells in me, that is, in my flesh… O wretched man that I am! Who will deliver me from this body of death?"

This is the Apostle Paul speaking! The Pharisee of pharisees. Arguably the greatest apostle that ever lived, the man who penned about half of the entire New Testament, talking about how wretched he is! Even he was not immune to sin's presence. Following that up in Romans chapter 8:5, 7–8:

> [T]hose who live according to the flesh set their minds on the things of the flesh…the mind that is set on the flesh is hostile to God, for it does not submit to God's law; indeed, it cannot. Those who are in the flesh cannot please God.

We will deal more with the role of the law in the following chapter, but the big picture here is the doctrine of original sin and the total depravity of man. Pastor/Teacher John MacArthur from Grace to You Ministries defines it like this:

> Total depravity is man's universal inability and unwillingness to come to God. He is both unable and unwilling. No man seeks after God nor does any man have any capacity to come to God. He has no interest in God. He is far more interested in what satan can give him in this life. All men are both unable and unwilling to offer anything worthy to God that in any sense could please God or cause God to bless them. The doctrine of total depravity is where all understandings of the doctrines of grace have to start. Man can do nothing.[10]

Total depravity says that we are ultimately and utterly helpless and hopeless in and of ourselves. Without God, we are entirely lost, spiritually dead, and by ourselves, we cannot please Him. We cannot right ourselves with Him. In every sense of the word, we NEED Him!

To broaden this and to step outside of the book of Romans, let's go back to the beginning. Sin entered humanity in the Garden of Eden, in Genesis chapter 3, at the fall of man. Like we have already spoken about, God created the entire universe perfectly. There was no death, decay, evil, sin, etc., and man was included in this. We were created holy and righteous, just as God is holy and righteous, and therefore, Adam and Eve dwelled in perfect fellowship with God. All of Creation was made with a Godly perfection. God Himself "walked through the garden" (Gen. 3:8), and they were at times in the direct presence of God Himself, seemingly in even a physical sense.

Since God said on day six of Creation that everything that He had created was "very good" (Gen. 1:31), and we are not given any other dates until the birth of Seth when Adam was 130 years old (we do not know the dates of Cain and Abel), we reason that the fall of satan and the other demons from Heaven could have happened at any time between day six and up to more than a hundred years after day six, maybe even just prior to the time of Genesis 3:1, although it would've been before the time period of Cain and Abel, since that narrative includes the sin of murder and lying and pride.

You can cross reference Ezekiel 28:16–19 and Isaiah 14:12–15 to understand a bit of satan's fall from Heaven, but to put it simply, he was part of Creation. he was created as the head of the angels, and once his pride got in the way, he desired to supplant God on the throne, and so because of his pride and rebellion to worshipping the only and One True God, he was cast out of Heaven along with, as some believe, as many as a third of all the other angels who shared in his rebellious desires and natures.

This fallenness of the angel realm did not immediately and directly affect the human race. It wasn't until the serpent, that is satan, visited Eve in the Garden of Eden in Genesis 3:1 and deceived her, and Adam, likewise, into breaking the one command that God had placed against them in the garden, "you shall not eat of the tree of the knowledge of good and evil" (Gen. 2:17) that sin had entered into the human race in Genesis 3:6. And since God had placed man in dominion over all of Creation, once man had sinned and destroyed the perfect holy union with God, God placed a curse of death and decay over all of the creation. As Romans 8:20ff tells us:

> For the creation was subjected to futility, not willingly, but because of Him Who subjected it...its bondage to corruption... For we know that the whole creation has been groaning together in the pains of childbirth until now.

Man didn't just fall, but all of creation was placed under this curse as well. The Law of Entropy had now begun. The Second Law of Thermodynamics, the Law of Decay, started at this very moment. Everything in all of creation now had a certain ending point to its lifespan. Man, animals, plant-life, earth, stars, galaxies, all of creation was now in decay.

To dwell a little bit more in this narrative of the fall of man and the birth of sin and death, let's spend a little more time looking at this text. When satan first came to Eve in the form of a serpent, his first words were, "Did God really say, 'You shall not eat of any tree in the garden?'"

Here we already see the deceptive nature. We already see that satan has twisted the words of God, trying to insinuate doubt which could then lead to unbelief and disobedience. What God actually said was verse 2:16, "You may surely eat of every tree in the garden, but you shall not eat of the tree of the knowledge of good and evil, for in the day that you eat of it you shall surely die."

So Eve corrects satan by saying in verse 3:2ff, "We may eat of the fruit of the trees in the garden, but God said, 'You shall not eat of the fruit of the tree that is in the midst of the garden" but then she adds for reasons unknown, "neither shall you touch it," which was not part of God's original command, "lest you die."

Despite that quizzical addition by Eve of God's command, so far so good. She hasn't fallen into sin yet. But satan wasn't finished yet. "But the serpent said to the woman, 'You will not surely die. For God knows that when you eat of it your eyes will be opened, and you will be like God, knowing good and evil.'"

So after satan failed with his attempt at "Did God really say," he essentially followed it up with trying to place more doubt by suggesting, "Did God really mean? Surely He meant something else?" as he continued to try to get Eve to distort God's Word and maybe tried to appeal to her sense of pride. That is when the entire downfall of man begun.

> When the woman saw that the tree was good for food, and that it was a delight to the eyes, and that the tree was desired to make one wise, she took of its fruit and ate, and she also gave some to her husband who was with her, and he ate. Then the eyes of both were opened, and they knew that they were naked.

Initially, sin entered into the human race through the sin of Eve and then became finalized in the sin of Adam as the head of mankind. Immediately, Adam and Eve knew they had done wrong. Up until this point, they lived in perfect holy union with God; they had no need for clothes because they were created perfect by God in a perfect universe with no presence of sin, lust, shame, embarrassment, etc. They lived in their "birthday suits," working the land, dwelling in the presence of God—all was "very good." They were also believed to have had some type of clothing of "light" prior to the fall, which would've made the realization that they had done wrong even more obvious to them.[11]

This also marks the very first act of religion. As we discussed earlier, religion is man's attempt to right himself with God. What did Adam and Eve do when they realized they had sinned? "They sewed fig leaves together and made themselves loincloths." They covered their nakedness. They tried to cover their fallenness. They tried to correct their wrongdoings. They tried to right themselves with God. But even worse, when "they heard the sound of the Lord God walking in the garden in the cool of the day, the man and the woman hid themselves from the presence of the Lord God," they hid themselves from their Creator God Who just moments before they shared perfect and holy union and fellowship with; but now they were filled with shame and despair. They hid themselves from God, but God sought for them!

> But the Lord called to the man and said to him, "Where are you?" And he said, "I heard the sound of You in the garden, and I was afraid, because I was naked, and I hid myself." God said, "Who told you that you were naked? Have you eaten of the tree of which I commanded you not to eat?" The man said, "The woman whom You gave to be with me, she gave me fruit of the tree, and I ate." Then the Lord God said to the woman, "What is this that you have done?' The woman said, 'The serpent deceived me, and I ate."

Notice that both of them tried to shift the blame. Adam first basically shifted the blame to God for "the woman whom You gave to be with me," then shifted the blame over to Eve. Then when asked, Eve shifted the blame toward the serpent. Neither one of them took responsibility for their own actions, tried apologizing, confessing, or repenting of what they had done. The full sin nature was now present.

God proceeded by cursing satan, the serpent, but then also made the first promise of the coming Messiah Redeemer and promised satan's destruction through Him (Gen. 3:15). God then placed a curse over woman, man, and the rest of creation (Gen. 3:16–19). After placing this curse on mankind, He foreshadowed another message of the coming Savior-Messiah by making for them "garments of skins and clothed them" (Gen. 3:21). These were not like the fig leaves that Adam and Eve sewed together themselves. They were skins of animals which means that blood was shed to make these skins. A sacrificial death was made to cover them. This was a symbol of the sacrificial Lamb that was to come in the substitute of Christ. This was the first act of sacrificial grace—all done by God! God's grace trumped man's futile and pathetic attempt at religion.

After doing this, in verse 3:22,

> The Lord God said, "Behold, the man has become like one of Us in knowing good and evil. Now, lest he reach out his hand and take also of the fruit of the tree of life and eat, and live forever." Therefore the Lord God sent him out from the Garden of Eden…and placed the cherubim and a flaming sword that turned every way to guard the way to the tree of life.

A quick point here: if original sin and total depravity were not true, why did God cast out Adam and Eve from the garden of Eden (Gen. 3:23–24), and then have "placed a cherubim and a flaming sword that turned every way to guard the way to the tree of life" so that no one ever could return to the garden? If Cain and Abel and Seth, etc., were not born in sin, then why wouldn't they have a chance at returning to the garden where the tree of life was? Sin, sadly, was here to stay. The entire human race was now affected by the sin nature which is inherited through our forefathers.

> G. K. Chesterton in his book Orthodoxy, p. 15, states, "Certain new theologians dispute original sin, which is the only part of Christian theology which can really be proved." There is a dark side to humanity. God's light reveals everything about us, including our dark side. Yet we tend to run away from the light. One way to expose the lie that man is really basically good, is to look at communism. Based on the notion that man will work toward the common good (or at least per-

fectible through law and evolution), communism has been the greatest failure to those under its ideology. The evidence of man's sinful nature is overwhelming, as world history cries out to this truth. Anthropologists tell us that one-third of all humans who ever lived died at the hands of other humans. In the twentieth century alone, the most advanced ("enlightened") in all history, well over 100 million people have been murdered by their own governments (Russia, Germany, China, Cambodia, etc.). Every day the newspaper headlines prove the truth of man's sinful nature. Ninety-nine percent of Americans will be a victim of theft at least once. John Stott notes that every house in America not only has a door, but a lock as well. "The plain truth is that a right knowledge of sin lies at the root of all saving Christianity. Without it such doctrines as justification, conversion, sanctification, are 'words and names' which convey no meaning to the mind. The first thing, therefore, that God does when He makes anyone a new creature in Christ, is to send light into his heart, and show him that he is a guilty sinner."[12]

Biblical author Ken Willig, in his book titled *The Free Gift*, puts it like this:

Everyone is born with an innate propensity to sin. Sinning is not an acquired habit. We are not sinners because we sin—we sin because we are sinners. Everyone is born spiritually dead and must have a spiritual rebirth in order to have fellowship with God. This comes from accepting God's free gift of Jesus Christ as our Redeemer.[13]

Despite the passages already discussed in Romans and Genesis, there are numerous other passages throughout the Bible that teach about our fallenness and depravity. Leading up to the flood in the time of Noah, in Genesis chapter 6 verse 5, "The Lord saw that the wickedness of man was great on the earth, and that every intention of the thoughts of his heart was only evil continually." That's a pretty strong statement. Not just every thought, but "every *intention* of the thoughts of his heart was only evil continually!"

By the time of the flood of Noah, only about 1,600 years had passed since the Creation, and now every intention of the thoughts of man's heart were only evil continually, which led to the Lord feeling regret for even creating them and bringing them into being, so much so that He planned to wipe all of them off the face of the earth and cleanse the earth of this overwhelming evil and sickness that had plagued His fallen creation. He created them perfectly, but He also created them with free will so they would not just be mindless robots and real true love could be possible; however, with free will also comes the potential of disobedience and rebellion which led to the point we have here.

In a little over 1,600 years, the entire earth had become populated by an overwhelming evil population. All except for eight people. Verse 8 tells us:

> But Noah found favor in the eyes of the Lord... Noah was a righteous man, blameless in his generation. Noah walked with God. And Noah had three sons, Shem, Ham and Japheth. Now the earth was corrupt in God's sight, and the earth was filled with violence. And God saw the earth, and behold, it was corrupt, for all flesh had corrupted their way on the earth. And God said to Noah, "I have determined to make an end of all flesh, for the earth is filled with violence through them. Behold I will destroy them with the earth."

God then instructed Noah to build a massive ark, and said,

> "For behold, I will bring a flood of waters
> upon the earth to destroy all the flesh in which
> is the breath of life under Heaven. Everything
> that is on the earth shall die. But I will estab-
> lish My covenant with you, and you shall come
> into the ark, you, your sons, your wife, and your
> son's wives with you. And every living thing of all
> flesh, you shall bring two of each kind into the
> ark to keep them alive with you. They shall be
> male and female."

Continuing into chapter 7, God then said, "Go into the ark, you and all your household, for I have seen that you are righteous before me in this generation." Now please do not misinterpret this. God is not calling Noah perfect. Noah was sinful, but He did follow the Lord. He was obedient to God (though not perfectly). He "walked with God." Noah and his immediate family, wife, sons, and son's wives were the only ones who acknowledged God in this fallen and evil time of the world. Hence, they are the only ones He saved from this judgment of justice. God cleansed the entire world of this overwhelming evil, including men and women, girls and boys of all ages, except for the eight people of Noah's family and enough animals of each kind to repopulate the world.

Sadly, though, original sin and the depravity of man had permeated creation by this point so that even after the flood had subsided, God once again stated, "the intentions of man's heart is evil from his youth," though He vowed "I will never again curse the ground because of man...neither will I ever again strike down every living creature as I have done" (Gen. 8:21). So, once again, even after this cleansing of the earth, God saw and knew that man's heart was still evil entirely. The sin nature was and is still present in all of us.

In 1 Kings 8:46, we also read, "If they sin against You—for there is no one who does not sin—and You are angry with them." This passage was quoted by King Solomon in a prayer of dedication for the Temple of God in which he was entreating God to hear His people and forgive them when they pray to Him and repent. King Solomon, the wisest man to ever live, his wisdom being a direct gift he received from God (1 Kings 3:12), plainly says, "For there is no one who does not sin." He includes no age constraints in this statement. Second Chronicles 6:36 repeats the same statement, "If they sin against You—for there is no one who does not sin—and You are angry with them."

In the narrative of Job, we find a few other mentions toward the overall depravity of mankind. In Job 4:7 (NASB) we read, "Whoever perished being innocent? Or where were the upright destroyed?" This was spoken by a friend of Job's named Eliphaz, explaining that innocent people do not get destroyed and perish for being upright. Then in verse 17, he adds, "Can mortal man be in the right before God? Can a man be pure before his Maker?" Clearly, he is implying the impossibilities of these statements. Man is wretched and cannot, by himself, make himself pure once again before God. Mankind as a whole is wretched and fallen, impure, and unjust!

In Job 14:1ff, we hear from Job himself, "Man who is born of a woman is few of days and full of trouble. He comes out like a flower and withers… Who can bring a clean thing out of an unclean? There is not one." Job is acknowledging that all men are sinners and unclean and full of trouble from the time of birth. Sure, Job 1:1 calls Job a blameless and upright man, but that does not mean he is sinless. The context tells us that he feared God and put his trust in Him. Why would you fear God if you were sinless and had nothing to fear? Again, the context is telling us, "Job faithfully lived a God-honoring, sincere life of integrity and consistency personally, maritally and parentally."[14]

Also, in the next chapter, we read, "What is man, that he can be pure? Or he who is born of a woman, that he can be righteous" (15:14)? This is again Eliphaz, Job's friend, speaking, acknowledging that man is sinful and cannot be righteous, even from birth. And also, later in the book of Job, another friend of his, Bildad, speaks in 25:4 and 6, "How then can man be in the right before God? How can he who is born of woman be pure? How much less man, who is a maggot, and the son of man, who is a worm!" Wow! That's pretty blunt. Man is wretched from birth. He is a maggot!

The beautiful and poetic book of Psalms is no hiding place for the depravity of man either. Psalm 14:1–3 is pretty straight to the point:

> The fool says in his heart, "There is no God." They are corrupt, they do abominable deeds, there is none who does good. The Lord looks down from Heaven on the children of man, to see if there are any who understand, who seek after God. They have all turned aside; together they have become corrupt; there is none who does good, not even one.

"The 'alls' and the 'nones' of these lines make the indictments universally applicable."[15]

Psalm 53:1–3 is almost an identical copy of Psalm 14:

> The fool says in his heart, "There is no God." They are corrupt, they do abominable iniquity, there is none who does good. God looks down from Heaven on the children of man, to see if there are any who understand, who seek after God. They have all fallen away; together they have become corrupt; there is none who does good, not even one.

Psalm 143:2 couldn't be any more to the point either, "for no one living is righteous before You."

And one of the most evident passages for total depravity in the entire Bible, which is found in Psalms, is found in King David's Psalm 51 verse 5, "Surely I was sinful from birth, sinful from the time my mother conceived me." And this is King David, a man that God Himself called "a man after My Own heart" (1 Sam. 13:14; Acts 13:22).

Again, do not misinterpret this either. God is not saying that David is perfect and sinless as God is. He was acknowledging that David's heart was devoted to God fully. David was still a sinner as is plainly evident in 2 Samuel chapter 11 when he cheats on his own wife and commits adultery with another married woman and then has her husband murdered so that he could cover up her resulting pregnancy; however, God saw his heart. He wasn't sinless and perfect, but his heart was toward God. It stands to point, though, that we are sinful from the time of conception! Because of the fallen nature of man, sin is transferred through the seed in the womb at the moment of conception, not just the moment of birth.

In the book of Proverbs, known as the "Book of Wisdom," mostly written by King Solomon, we read in 20:9, "Who can say, I have made my heart pure; I am clean from my sin?" He is saying that no one is clean from sin, and that no one can make himself pure. Proverbs 22:15 tells us, "Folly is bound up in the heart of a child." Foolishness is a byproduct of sin, not holiness and righteousness, and it is present in each one of us, even to the youngest child.

In the book of Ecclesiastes, also written by King Solomon, in chapter 7 verse 20, it reads, "Surely there is not a righteous man on earth who does good and never sins." You can't get much more straight forward than that. Solomon is being blunt and telling us that there is not a single person on this earth—past, present, future—that has not a single sin and is therefore good and perfect. No one! The meaning of the word *surely* that starts off this verse, in the original Hebrew, carries a sense of certainty along with it. You could substitute it by saying, "Yes, indeed!" And notice there are no age constraints here either.

From the highly venerated Prophet Isaiah, we read in 48:8, "From before birth you were called a rebel." Here we have another verse that puts depravity before even birth. A righteous and sinless man is not called a rebel.

From the highly respected Prophet Jeremiah, we also find some evidence of this. In Jeremiah 13:23, it does not quite state the issue of depravity and original sin, but we find a teaching that we cannot change ourselves. "Can the Ethiopian change his skin or the leopard his spots? Then also you can do good who are accustomed to do evil."

John MacArthur explains, "The vivid analogy assumes that sinners cannot change their sinful natures. Only God can change their hearts."[16] Henry Morris states, "Only a miraculous regeneration can change man's heart and nature."[17]

A little bit later in Jeremiah 17:9, we read, "The heart is deceitful above all things and is desperately sick; who can understand it?" So we see from Jeremiah that our hearts are deceitful and desperately sick and that we cannot do anything to even understand it by and of ourselves.

Lamentations reminds us that we are entirely deserving of punishment and have no grounds for questioning regarding our punishment due to our sin nature. In 3:39 (AMP), we are told, "Why should any living mortal, or any man, complain [of punishment] in view of his sins?"

From the Prophet Micah, we read in 7:2, "The Godly person has perished from the land, and there is no upright person among men. All of them lie in wait for bloodshed; each of them hunts the other with a net."

Moving on into the New Testament, in the Gospel of Mark, we find in 7:21–22, "For from within, out of the heart of man, come evil thoughts, sexual immorality, theft, murder, adultery, coveting, wickedness, deceit, sensuality, envy, slander, pride, foolishness." Just like Jeremiah told us, the heart is sick.

The Gospel of John tells us more. We see in John 5:40, "You refuse to come to Me that you may have life." These people Jesus was preaching to were seeking eternal life yet they were not willing to trust the only possible Source of that eternal life. In John 6:63, Jesus tells us, "It is the Spirit that gives life; the flesh is no help at all." Until you have the Spirit, you are lost! And if you are lost? John 8:42–44:

> If God were your Father, you would love
> Me, for I came from God and I Am here. I came
> not of My Own accord, but He sent Me. Why
> do you not understand what I say? It is because

> you cannot bear to hear My Word. You are of
> your father the devil, and your will is to do your
> father's desires.

In John 9:34, we see that even the Pharisees understood the issue of being sinful from birth when they scolded a blind man who had been healed and received his sight from Jesus, "You were born in utter sin, and would you teach us?"

John 15:4–5 says, "The branch cannot bear fruit by itself, unless it abides in the vine, neither can you, unless you abide in Me...apart from Me you can do nothing." Unless you are in Christ, you cannot do good. Period.

Let's move into the epistles. In 1 Corinthians Paul continues in 1:18, "The word of the cross is folly to those who are perishing, but to those who are being saved it is the power of God." Chapter 2:14 says, "the natural person does not accept the things of the Spirit of God, for they are folly to him, and he is not able to understand them." And in 1 Corinthians 15:21–22, we see, "For as by a man came death, by a Man has come also the resurrection of the dead. For as in Adam all die, so also in Christ shall all be made alive." This issue of all men dying through the sin of Adam we have already touched on back in Romans chapter 5.

In 2 Corinthians, we do not receive any rest either. In 4:4, we read, "The god of this world has blinded the minds of them who do not believe, to keep them from seeing the light of the Gospel of the glory of Christ." We are depraved from the beginning, but satan also works to blind our eyes so as not to see the light of the Gospel.

And on into Ephesians, Paul continues this teaching. In 2:1–3, 12–13, he says:

> You were dead in trespasses and sins...follow-
> ing the course of this world, following the prince
> of the power of the air...we all once lived in the
> passions of our flesh, carrying out the desires of the
> body and the mind, and were by nature children
> of wrath, like the rest of mankind... Remember

that you were at that time separated from Christ, alienated from the commonwealth of Israel and strangers to the covenants of promise, having no hope and without God in the world. But now in Christ Jesus you who once were far off have been brought near by the blood of Christ.

And in chapter 4:18, "They are darkened in their understanding, alienated from the life of God...due to their hardness of heart." Because of the depth of depravity in the human heart, all sinners spurn the goodness of God.

In Colossians 2:13, we find, "You who were dead in your trespasses and the uncircumcision of your flesh." We were all dead in our trespasses at one point and still are if without Christ.

In 2 Timothy 2:26, Paul pleads that we "may come to our senses and escape the snare of the devil, after being captured by him to do his will." Until we are saved by Christ, we belong to the devil and are slaves of evil.

Titus 3:3 tells us, "For we ourselves were once foolish, disobedient, led astray, slaves to various passions and pleasures, passing our days in malice and envy, hated by others and hating one another." Again, we use to be slaves of unrighteousness, partaking in all sorts of evil.

In 1 Peter 1:18, we read, "You were ransomed from the futile ways inherited from your forefathers." This verse, though not directly but through referencing, is speaking of our fallen sinful nature that we inherit through our forefathers. Just like David confessed that we are sinful from the time our mothers conceived us, we are born into sin as we all have inherited that sinful and fallen spiritually dead nature of our forefathers all the way back to Adam.

The Apostle John tells us in his first letter in 1 John 1:8 and 10, "If we say we have no sin, we deceive ourselves, and the truth is not in us... If we say we have not sinned, we make Him a liar, and His Word is not in us." By saying that original sin and total depravity are not true Biblically, it is calling God a liar because we have all been sinful from conception.

Finally, in the book of Revelation, the prophetic book of the end of times, we are given a telling bit of information concerning the entirety of mankind. In chapter 5, verses 3–4, we read:

> And no one in Heaven or on the earth or under the earth was able to open the scroll or to look into it. Then I [the Apostle John] began to weep loudly because no one was found worthy to open the scroll or to look into it.

Now I realize this is a bit more abstract on the surface so let's dig into it. The book of Revelation is also known as the Revelation of Jesus Christ and is the foretelling of the future events of the end of the world. Jesus Himself took the Apostle John, "the one whom Jesus loved" (cf. the gospel of John), whom He spent close time with during His three-and-a-half-year ministry here on earth and showed him a vision of what was to come. Here in chapter 5, we come to a part of the vision where John sees God seated on the throne of Heaven, holding in His right hand "a scroll written within and on the back, sealed with seven seals."

> This is typical of various kinds of contracts in the ancient world, including deeds, marriage contracts, rental and lease agreements, and wills. The inside of the scroll contained all the details of the contract, and the outside—or back—contained a summary of the document. In this case it is the title deed to the earth.[18]

This was the title deed to the earth and all its inhabitants which Adam forfeited when he fell the entirety of humankind into sin. John then saw "a strong angel proclaiming with a loud voice, 'Who is worthy to open the scroll and break its seals?'"

> In accordance with ancient legal custom, the deed was inscribed in full on the inside of the

scroll with enough information on its backside to indicate the land involved and the rightful owner who had purchased it. It was then sealed and deposited somewhere for preservation and record and could only be opened by the owner when he arrived to take possession. The ultimate Owner of the earth is its Creator (Ps. 24:1); only He has the right to deed it to anyone, and He did give Adam dominion over it (Gen. 1:26–28). satan, however, usurped that dominion when Adam sinned and died, and now "the whole world lies in the power of the evil one" (1 John 5:19).[19]

So when the great angel asked, "Who is worthy to open the scroll and break its seals?" we are then brought to verse 3 which again says, "And no one in Heaven or on the earth or under the earth was able to open the book or to look into it."

After Christ created the universe, He gave Adam the title deed to the earth and gave him dominion over the entirety of earth, including all creatures, but he forfeited that right and privilege to satan when satan tricked him into sin, and throughout the entirety of human history, as shown in verse 3, not a single soul, dead or alive, has ever become worthy of receiving back that scroll/title deed as verse 4 says, "No one was found worthy to open the scroll or look into it." The redeemer of the scroll of the title deed of the lost world must be either God the original Creator and Owner or a kinsman—that is, a man, not an angel or demon—and he had to be sinless. A sinful man cannot redeem sinful humanity. Wrong cannot correct wrong. Evil cannot redeem evil.

And in verse 4, John "began to weep loudly ('sobbed convulsively' in the Greek) because no one was found worthy." John knew what this meant. Without a kinsman, the earth had no redeemer to reclaim the title deed of the earth back from satan, and it was destined for hell and destruction. There wasn't a single person dead or alive in Heaven, on earth, or under the earth that was worthy, that was sinless, who could open the scroll and redeem mankind, and so John wept convulsively!

Just then, in verse 5, we read, "Weep no more; behold, the Lion of the tribe of Judah, the Root of David, has conquered, so that He can open the scroll and its seven seals." Jesus Christ alone, Who was true Man and perfectly sinless and also true God and the Creator of the universe, is the only One found throughout the entirety of Creation and mankind's history that is worthy, i.e., sinless, holy, righteous, and perfect to redeem and restore mankind. Not a single man or woman who has ever walked this planet can be the same. We are all fallen, wretched, and unworthy. We are all depraved.

Renowned theologian and pastor Charles Spurgeon touches on the issue of depravity by saying:

> Men are in a restless pursuit after satisfaction in earthly things. They will exhaust themselves in the deceitful delights of sin, and, finding them all to be vanity and emptiness, they will become very perplexed and disappointed. But they will continue their fruitless search. Though wearied, they still stagger forward under the influence of spiritual madness, and though there is no result to be reached except that of everlasting disappointment, yet they press forward. They have no forethought for their eternal state; the present hour absorbs them. They turn to another and another of earth's broken cisterns, hoping to find water where not a drop was ever discovered yet.

John Piper of Desiring God Ministries provides a very profound and deep thought when he says:

> That it should take the death of the Son of God, the fact that it took that much, to atone for my sin, ought to show me that I was in such bad shape that I can't bring any resources up out of myself to make a contribution to that salvation.

Wow! There's power in that statement! If what it took to bring about salvation for us was Jesus Christ, Who was true God Himself, the Creator of the universe, to enter into this world as a humble and lowly servant, Who "had no form or majesty that we should look at Him, and no beauty that we should desire Him" (Isa. 53:2), was born in a dirty feeding trough for farm animals, lived a life of humble servitude, and then suffered what was arguably the most torturous and brutal death endured by any human throughout all of history (the only reason He even made it to the cross was because He was God; any other human would have died during the relentless beating He received in the Praetorium [Isaiah 50:6, 52:14]; the only reason He made it to the cross is because He had a job to finish), all of this in order to save us by enduring all of this and then rising victoriously from the grave. If it took THAT much to redeem us from our sins, that ought to show us how insanely depraved and wretched we were to demand such an incomprehensible punishment to bring justice to our souls!

And to follow this up, it should also show us that we have absolutely zero ability in and of ourselves to offer anything in merit or addition or contribution to the sacrifice Christ made on our behalf to reconcile us to God. It took God Himself to remedy this condition. We are far too feeble to do anything to contribute to the resolution of it.

Noted Christian New Testament Greek scholar and professor, Kenneth Wuest tells us, referring to the first few verses of John 3:

> The teaching here is that human kind in their depraved and sinful condition cannot be improved. Reformation will not change them into a fit subject for the Kingdom of God. The flesh, our nature, is incurably wicked and cannot by any process be changed so as to produce a religious life. What that person needs, Jesus says, is a new nature, a spiritual nature which will produce a life pleasing to God and which will be a life fit for the Kingdom of God. We need a spiritual

intervention that is nothing less than a new birth. We don't need reformation, we need transformation. We need the Gospel of Jesus Christ, and without the Gospel of Jesus Christ to transform our lives from darkness to light we are without hope. There's no cure apart from the Gospel of Jesus Christ. The new birth is a spiritual event or even a spiritual mystery. It's beyond our ability to logically process. But it produces an undeniable reality when we experience this transformation. We don't get it by good works or religious discipline, because if that was the way, Nicodemus would've had it. It's not by acknowledging and believing that Jesus is a good teacher. It's not by acceptance of certain theological information. We don't get it by just right information, we don't get it by being religious or astute in religiosity. Jesus says they love darkness and hate the light (John 3:19–20).

Romans 3:11 says, "There are none who seek after God." Some people claim to seek God, but they are not seeking God, they are seeking all the stuff God might want. They want peace, they want relief from guilt, they want happiness, joy, they want all the benefits, but let's not say they're seeking the God of all the universe, because in and of ourselves we cannot seek. That's why we need Jesus to seek us out. You wanna be seeker friendly, turn the tables. It's Jesus who sought you. It's Jesus Who came after you. It's Jesus Who rescued you, when you were dead in sin and trespasses. Sometimes we use the analogy, we need to throw the gospel lifeline, we're flailing around in the ocean. My friend, you are dead on the bottom of the ocean. Jesus plunged in to the depth of your sin and rescued you and hauled you back to shore and gave you mouth to mouth resuscitation, otherwise you would have rotted dead in your sin and gone straight to hell without Christ. Jesus is the Light seeking us out. We are not born a little good and a lot bad, we are not born with just a little flicker, we are dead. If Jesus wouldn't have turned on the light I wouldn't be here. Like the blind man, "Look guys, I don't know. All I do know is that I was blind and now I see." All I know is that I was lost and now I'm found (John 9:25).[20]

This issue of original sin and the total depravity of man is a very serious one and should be a very undeniable one. We are all inherently lost without the help of a Savior and wretched from the time of conception, and all understandings of the doctrines of grace must stem from this. The whole of Christianity is based on this as part of its foundation. From the first sin of Adam, the entire human race was plunged into depravity and inherited the cursed and sinful nature. This same concept of inheritance is also found in Hebrews 7:9–10, where we read, "One might even say that Levi himself, who receives tithes, paid tithes through Abraham, for he was still in the loins of his ancestor when Melchizedek met him." Levi, who was not even conceived yet, paid tithes through Abraham through this same type of ancestral inheritance.

Let's stretch this concept out to show just how absurd it is to deny this doctrine. If you were to hold that original sin was not valid doctrine, that man is not inherently evil from birth or conception, then by default, you would have to hold to the belief that someone could possibly and plausibly perhaps carry through and accomplish living a perfectly sinless life since, after all, they are born without sin and therefore perfect, which therefore would mean they would not even need Christ as their Savior; or you could even say that that person was equal with Christ at that point. They would not even need or deserve to die at all because they have started life sinless, done no wrong, and lived perfectly.

If you hold that the doctrine of original sin is not valid doctrine, then you at least have to hold to the belief that this is at least possible for someone to fulfill in their life. They might even be able to enter into Heaven at that point and say, "Move over, Jesus! There's two of us now and I deserve a seat at the throne too." That is absolutely absurd!

We are all conceived into sin (Ps. 51:5; Isa. 48:8) and therefore born into sin (Job 14:1, 15:14, 25:4–6; John 9:34). We are all sinful and destined for hell unless God brings us back to life, and we accept Jesus Christ as our Lord and Savior as our substitute. By the fall of Adam and Eve, we all became sinful and dead (Rom. 5:12; 1 Cor. 15:21–22). We are all born dead. We are all born in need of a Savior. If we are not born with original sin, if we are not born in total depravity, then why are there abortions or miscarriages? Why do fetuses/infants die if they are not sinful and therefore perfect? Why would the perfect and innocent die in the womb?

Some people still try to argue against the doctrine of original sin, and one of the main verses that is used to try to refute it is Ezekiel 18:20 which states:

> The soul who sins shall die. The son shall not suffer for the iniquity of the father, nor the father suffer for the iniquity of the son. The righteousness of the righteous shall be upon himself, and the wickedness of the wicked shall be upon himself.

This verse is also reflected in two different verses that are virtually mirror images of each other. They are found in 2 Kings 14:6 and 2 Chronicles 25:4, and they both go on to say, "[T]he fathers shall not be put to death for the sons, nor the sons be put to death for the fathers; but each shall be put to death for his own sin."

These verses are by no means claiming anything against the doctrine of original sin. This verse is talking about a father and a son, one of whom, and then vice versa, sins, worships idols, rapes, oppresses, robs, steals, murders, etc., and that the other of the two who is already living shall not suffer for his family members sins. For example, if I go and murder someone tomorrow, my father will not be thrown in prison for my offense, and neither would I be thrown in prison, if the tables were turned, for his offense.

The one committing the offense would be the one put in prison. But that has NOTHING to do with "ORIGINAL SIN!" That has nothing to do with being born into depravity and inheriting a sin nature! This verse is not in any way saying that the son was born perfect into this world and is without sin and therefore without the need of a Savior. We are ALL born into sin! We are ALL born with a sinful nature and are born with an innate propensity to sin! No one here on earth is better or worse than any other in the department of sin. We are all equally dead in sin. We are ALL born with the need for Christ as our Savior! John MacArthur describes it like this:

> We are not dead because of sin, we are dead because we were born sinful. We are not dead because we commit sin, we don't commit a sin and then die, we are born dead…that's WHY we sin. I'm not a liar because I told a lie, I told a lie in the first place because in my heart I'm a liar. We are dead, and that deadness functions in sinfulness.

Some people may then combat against this by saying something like, "What then? Are babies who are aborted or die prior to or during childbirth all sent to hell?" Praise God, NO! This is where the doctrine of the Age of Accountability or the Age of Innocence comes into play.[21] The Age of Accountability/Innocence teaches that a child is not responsible for his or her salvation until that child is old enough and mature enough to understand his or her depravity and need for a Savior and is able to make an understood and conscious decision to devote and surrender their life to Christ, for Him to take their place and redeem them through His work on the cross. A newborn infant has no capacity to understand these things. It has no real idea that it is even alive. It is simply trying to survive, almost entirely by the efforts of the parents, completely clueless to what is going on in this new overwhelming world outside of the dark and enclosed womb, which is also a very vivid picture of our own lives before and after salvation. It has no comprehension of its own sinful nature or need for a Savior and couldn't possibly make any sort of eternal-minded thought or decision on its own.

If a child dies before this age of accountability, or during the age of innocence, that child is held by God and brought to Heaven by the grace and mercy of our Heavenly Father. This is the only silver lining on the disgusting issue of abortion and other child murders and the disheartening issue of miscarriages and stillbirths. Those helpless children are all saved and resting in Heaven, saved by the grace and mercy of our infinitely loving Father! Praise God!

Do not misunderstand this, though. That does not make them sinless. They still possess the nasty sin nature and its depravity and are in need of a Savior like the rest of the human race. They just, at this point, do not have the capacity in themselves yet to understand Him, the need for Him, nor are they able to make that conscious decision yet to acknowledge Him and surrender to Him. This would also, most likely, graciously apply to the mentally handicapped who also cannot comprehend these things and make a conscious eternal-minded decision regarding their sin and deliverance by Christ alone.

The one passage that seems to identify with this topic more than any other is 2 Samuel 12:21–23. The context of these verses is that King David committed adultery with Bathsheba, with a resulting pregnancy. The prophet Nathan was sent by the Lord to inform David that, because of his sin, the Lord would take the child in death. David responded to this by grieving and praying for the child. But once the child was taken, David's mourning ended. David's servants were surprised to hear this. They said to King David, "What is this thing that you have done? While the child was alive, you fasted and wept; but when the child died, you arose and ate food."

David's response was, "While the child was still alive, I fasted and wept; for I said, 'Who knows, the LORD may be gracious to me, that the child may live.' But now he has died; why should I fast? Can I bring him back again? I shall go to him, but he will not return to me."

David's response indicates that those who are unable to have the capacity to believe are safe in the Lord. David said that he could go to the child but could not bring the child back to him. Also, and just as important, David seemed to be comforted by this knowledge. In other words, David seemed to be saying that he would see his baby son (in Heaven), though he could not bring him back.[22]

Another illustration of this is described by John MacArthur in a Q&A that he was giving when he was asked to speak on this very topic of babies that die. He mentioned that there are several instances where the Bible supports this and said:

One that just jumps out at me is when the Old Testament prophets are talking about offering babies to Molech, which of course is what was required to satiate or pacify Molech and keep him from harming you, you offered your baby alive on an altar and incinerated the baby. The comment of the Bible on that is that it's the killing of the innocents, the killing of the innocents. The Bible is very reluctant to identify people as innocent unless they actually are. That's one very interesting thing. You have pagan parents, you have idol worshipping parents offering a child to a pagan god, and yet in the context of that bizarre

kind of paganism there is God's designation that
these are innocents. There are a lot of passages
like that that give a very strong testimony to the
fact that God gathers those little ones to Himself,
and that then is, in itself, an illustration of salvation by grace, because they could obviously do
nothing to gain that. And born in sin and fallen
they would have to be saved by grace, and grace
alone.[23, 24]

To sum all of this up, we are ALL sinful, from the time of conception (Ps. 51:5, Isa. 48:8) as we have all inherited this sinful flesh
from our forefathers all the way back to Adam (1 Pet. 1:18). We are
all deserving of death, and all of us, including some children still in
the womb, will and do die, and that is the required sentence for all
who are sinful (Rom. 6:23). There are NO exceptions to this in all
of Scripture. ZERO! All of mankind is sinful and deserving of death
(Rom. 3:23). That is our predicament. And none of us have the ability in ourselves to come to God (John 15:4–5).

3

The Law

So we just ever so briefly touched on the law earlier in the last chapter, but let's get more into it here. When most Jews/ Christians refer to the Law, they are usually largely referring to the Ten Commandments of Exodus 20 and Deuteronomy 5, which are:

1. You shall have no other gods before Me.
2. You shall not make idols or worship them.
3. You shall not take the name of the Lord your God in vain.
4. Remember the Sabbath day, to keep it holy.
5. Honor your father and mother.
6. You shall not murder.
7. You shall not commit adultery.
8. You shall not steal.
9. You shall not bear false witness against your neighbor (lie).
10. You shall not covet.

This is known as part of the Mosaic Law as Moses was the one who brought it to the Israelites from the direct hand of God. God Himself wrote these Ten Commandments upon two stone tablets as the authoritative law man was to follow.

"The Mosaic Law was given specifically to
the nation of Israel (Ex. 19; Lev. 26:46; Rom.

9:4). It was made up of three parts: the Ten Commandments, the ordinances, and the worship system, which included the priesthood, the tabernacle, the offerings, and the festivals (Ex. 20–40; Lev. 1–7, 23). The purpose of the Mosaic Law was to accomplish the following:

(1) Reveal the holy character of the eternal God to the nation of Israel (Lev. 19:2, 20:7–8).

(2) Set apart the nation of Israel as distinct from all the other nations (Ex. 19:5).

(3) Reveal the sinfulness of man (cf. Galatians 3:19). Although the Law was good and holy (Rom. 7:12), it did not provide salvation for the nation of Israel. "No one will be declared righteous in God's sight by the works of the law; rather, through the law we become conscious of our sin" (Rom. 3:20; cf. Acts 13:38–39).

(4) Provide forgiveness through the sacrifice/offerings (Lev. 1–7) for the people who had faith in the Lord in the nation of Israel.

(5) Provide a way of worship for the community of faith through the yearly feasts (Lev. 23).

(6) Provide God's direction for the physical and spiritual health of the nation (Ex. 21–23; Deut. 6:4–19; Psalm 119:97–104).

(7) Cause people, after Christ came, to see that they couldn't keep the Law but needed to accept Christ as personal Savior, for He had fulfilled the Law in

His life and paid the penalty for our breaking it in His death, burial, and bodily resurrection (Gal. 3:24; Rom. 10:4). The believer in Christ has the very righteousness of the Law fulfilled in him as he obeys the Holy Spirit Who lives within him (Rom. 8:4).

The purpose of the Mosaic Law raises these questions: "Are you trusting in yourself to keep all the Ten Commandments all the time (which you can't do)?" OR "Have you made the choice to accept Jesus as your Savior, realizing that He has fulfilled all the commandments all the time for you, even paying your penalty for breaking them?"[1]

Then there is also what's known as the Levitical Law.

The Levites were the descendants of Levi, one of Jacob's twelve children. Moses was of the tribe of Levi, and when God delivered the Law to him on Mount Sinai, He marked the Levites as the tribe responsible for the primary religious duties in the nation. They were made priests, singers, and caretakers in the worship of God. In calling it the Levitical Law, we acknowledge that God revealed the Law through Moses, a Levite, and that God appointed the Levites as the religious leaders of Israel. The same Law is sometimes called "Mosaic" because it was given through Moses, and it is also referred to as the "Old Covenant," because it is part of God's promise to Abraham and his descendants.

To discover God's purpose in the Law, we must first look at its inception and the things

God said to Moses about it. When Moses and the people arrived at Mount Sinai, God said, "Now if you obey Me fully and keep My covenant, then out of all nations you will be My treasured possession. Although the whole earth is Mine, you will be for Me a kingdom of priests and a holy nation" (Ex. 19:5–6). The first mention of the Law to the nation was as a covenant—a legal agreement between God and the people He chose. The Israelites were required to obey it *fully* if they were to receive its benefits.

God began His introduction to the Law with the Ten Commandments, but the entire Law encompasses 613 commandments as detailed in the rest of the books of Moses. Jesus summarized the Law as having two emphases: love for God and love for neighbors (Matt. 22:37–39). These emphases can be easily seen in the Ten Commandments: the first four commands focus on our relation to God, and the remainder focus on interpersonal relations. If we think that is the whole purpose of the Law, though, we miss an important element. Many of the individual commands give detailed instruction on how God was to be worshipped and how the people were to live their lives. As we will see, it is in those fine details that love was either shown or withheld.

For hundreds of years, the Israelites lived under the Levitical Law, sometimes obeying it but more often failing to follow God's commands. Much of Old Testament history deals with the punishments Israel received for their disobedience. When Jesus Christ came, He said that He did not "come to abolish the Law or the Prophets...but to fulfill them" (Matt. 5:17). In the Sermon on the Mount, Jesus took the Law to a higher level, applying it to the thoughts and intents of the heart. This perspective significantly diminishes our ability to keep the Law.

The apostle Paul gives us insight into God's purpose for the Law in his letter to the Galatians. In Galatians 3:10, he says, "All who rely on observing the law are under a curse, for it is written: 'Cursed is everyone who does not continue to do everything written in the Book of the Law.'" The fine details show up again—if we don't keep *every* command perfectly, we are condemned (see Jas. 2:10). In Galatians 3:19, Paul asks, "What, then, was the purpose of the law? It was added because of transgressions until the Seed to Whom the promise referred had come."

And in verse 21, "Is the law then contrary to the promises of God? Certainly not! For if a law had been given that could give life, then righteousness would indeed be by the law."

What does all this mean? Verse 24 clarifies: "The law was put in charge to lead us to Christ that we might be justified by faith."

The Law pointed out our sinfulness, proved our inability to keep our end of the covenant, made us prisoners in our guilt, and showed our need of a Savior. The purpose of the Law is also revealed in Romans 3:19–20 as producing a consciousness of sin and holding the world "accountable to God." Paul even goes so far as to say he would not have known what sin was except by the Law (Rom. 7:7).

The Levitical Law did its job well, pointing out the sinfulness of mankind and condemning us for it. But as powerful as it was in that regard, it was powerless in another way. Hebrews 7:18–19 tells us that the old Law was set aside "because it was weak and useless (for the law made nothing perfect)." The Law had no way of changing our sinful nature. We needed something better to accomplish that. In fact, Hebrews goes on to say that the Law was "only a shadow of the good things that are coming—not the realities themselves. For this reason, it can never...make perfect those who draw near to worship" (Heb. 10:1).

God's desire has always been to have fellowship with mankind, but our sin prevented that. He gave the Law to set a standard of holiness and, at the same time, to show that we could never meet that standard on our own. That's why Jesus Christ had to come—to fulfill all the righteous requirements of the Law *on our behalf* and then to take the punishment of violating that Law, also on our behalf.

Paul wrote in Galatians 2:16 that we are not justified "by observing the law, but by faith in Jesus Christ." When we receive God's forgiveness through our confession of faith in Jesus's sacrificial death, the Law is fulfilled for us, and "there is no longer any sacrifice for sin" (Heb. 10:18). The Law's condemnation does not fall on us because "the law of the Spirit of life set me free from the law of sin and death" (Rom. 8:2)."[2]

The problem with the Laws, Mosaic and Levitical, is that many people believe that it is through obedience to them that you "earn," "receive," "deserve" or even "merit" salvation and your way to Heaven. This is absolutely not true! As Romans 3:20 tells us, "For by works of the law no human being will be justified in His sight, since through the law comes knowledge of sin."

We were all born sinful as we saw in the previous chapter, and therefore, we are all incapable of fulfilling God's moral law perfectly, which is what is demanded for true holiness and righteousness. To be in the presence of God's perfect holiness, He demands perfect holiness, and we are all cursed by the complete inability to do so (depravity). The law simply makes sin known. It does not offer relief from that sin; therefore, the law has absolutely zero ability to save you, unless you were to fulfill it perfectly, which none of us are able to do since we are born dead.

Paul restates the fact that the law makes sin known in Romans 7:7–8 where he says, "If it had not been for the law, I would not have known sin." He continues, "But sin, seizing an opportunity through the commandment, produced in me all kinds of covetousness. For apart from the law, sin lies dead." Wait a minute. Did he just say the law produced sin? He takes this even further and says in Romans 4:15, "For the law brings wrath, but where there is no law there is no transgression." And in 5:20, he says that, "Now the law came in to increase the trespass." And in 7:13, "Did that which was good (the law), then, bring death to me? By no means! It was sin, producing death in me through what is good (the law), in order that sin might be shown to be sin, and through the commandment might become sinful beyond measure." That's pretty heavy!

Let's dissect this a little bit. So we find in these passages that even though the law itself is considered good, the law produces and increases sin in us! How can this be? The law itself is good, created by our holy and righteous God, but it cannot save. It merely makes sin known. It makes us aware of exactly what sin is. You could say that it gives each sin a name, what's good and what's bad, and from that knowledge of sin, our fallen and sinful nature, sin living in us continues to heap more on top of it.

In 2 Corinthians chapter 3 verse 7, we even see Paul calling the Law the "ministry of death, carved in letters on stone." And he says the same thing, again back in Romans 7:9–10, "Once I was alive apart from the Law; but when the commandment came, sin sprang to life and I died. I found that the very commandment that was intended to bring life actually brought death."

Ken Willig describes it like this:

> Allow me to dispel a myth: God did not give us the Ten Commandments or the Law to provide a way to salvation—that is, to show us what we must do to save ourselves. The purpose of God's law is to prove to us that we cannot do all that it says and that we are all sinners in need of a Savior. Its purpose is to show us the imperfection that separates us from God, and then to lead us to Christ so that we will put our faith in Him (cf. Gal. 3:19, 24). The primary function of the law is that of a mirror. The law reflects the righteousness of God and reveals our own sinfulness. By studying the law, we recognize our ever-present sin and our need for forgiveness. False teachers deceive us into thinking that God gave us the law as a means to save ourselves, but God gave us the law to prove us sinners (cf. Rom. 3:20). So, no one—not anyone—can earn his or her salvation through the law, through trying to meet its demands of do's and don'ts (cf. Gal. 3:10, 11, 23). God's good law defines that which is sinful and creates death for us (cf. Rom. 7:9–10). No matter how well anyone keeps the law, when we break one point of it, we are guilty of breaking all of it (cf. Jas. 2:10). If it were possible to get to Heaven—to gain salvation and to be justified before God—by following rules and traditions, or through a religious do-it-yourself system of do's and don'ts to merit salvation, then Christ died for nothing (cf. Gal. 2:21)![3]

Author and pastor, Ray Pritchard, president of Keep Believing Ministries, explains it this way:

> In this we see the simplicity of Christianity when compared with the religions of the world.

Religion is spelled with two letters—D-O. Religion is a list of things people think they have to do in order to be accepted by God— go to church, give money, keep the Ten Commandments, be baptized, pray every day, and do good works. The list is endless. It's always DO… DO… DO. If you wanna go to Heaven, you're going to do something and keep on doing it until the day you die. Christianity is spelled with four letters—D-O-N-E. Christianity is not based on what we do but upon what Jesus Christ has already done. If you wanna go to Heaven, you don't have to do anything; you just have to trust in what Jesus Christ has already done for you. That's the whole difference—Do versus Done. Either you do it yourself or you believe that Jesus Christ has already done it for you.[4]

Galatians says in chapter 3 verse 11, "Now it is evident that no one is justified before God by the law, for 'the just shall live by faith.'" Paul is saying that it is plainly obvious that we are not saved by obedience to the law. And in chapter 5 verse 4, Paul says, "You who are trying to be justified by law have been alienated from Christ; you have fallen away from grace." If you are trying to become justified or found righteous by obedience to the law, you have fallen away from the beautiful grace of God and you have become estranged and even hostile to Christ. Rest in God, not in the law.

Paul hammers this in detail in Philippians 3, starting at verse 3:

For we are the circumcision, who worship by the Spirit of God and glory in Christ Jesus and put no confidence in the flesh—though I myself have reason for confidence in the flesh also. If anyone else thinks he has reason for confidence in the flesh, I have more: circumcised on the eighth day, of the people of Israel, of the tribe of Benjamin, a Hebrew of Hebrews; as to the law, a Pharisee; as to zeal, a persecutor of the church; as to righteousness under the law, blameless. But whatever gain I had, I counted as loss for the sake of Christ. Indeed, I count everything as loss because of the surpassing worth of knowing Christ Jesus my Lord. For His sake I have suffered the loss of all things and count them as rubbish, in order that I may gain Christ and be found in Him, not having a righteousness of my own that comes from the law, but that which comes through faith in Christ, the righteousness from God that depends on faith—that I may know Him and the power of His resurrection, and may share His sufferings, becoming like Him in His death, that by any means possible I may attain the resurrection from the dead. Not that I have already obtained this or am already perfect, but I press on to make it my own, because Christ Jesus has made me His Own.

Paul is saying that if anyone has reason to boast in his works or in his flesh, it would be himself, yet he would throw it all away and count it all as loss and rubbish in order to gain Christ and be found in Him and to know Him and the power of His resurrection. All of his accomplishments in the flesh and according to the law were worthless.

The writer of Hebrews backs this up. In Hebrews 7:18–19, we read, "For on the one hand, a former commandment is set aside because of its weakness and uselessness (for the law made nothing perfect)." The law has made nothing perfect! On the other hand, it can and does show you exactly how painfully imperfect you are! It shows you just how many sins you've committed, lists them all, and names them all.

Hebrews 10:1–3 follows that by saying:

> For since the law has but a shadow of the good things to come instead of the true form of these realities, it can never, by the same sacrifices that are continually offered every year, make perfect those who draw near. Otherwise, would they not have ceased to be offered, since the worshippers, having once been cleansed, would no longer have any consciousness of sins? But in these sacrifices there is a reminder of sins every year.

The wording of this may be a little difficult, so let's look at a different translation to open it up a little better. The New Living Translation says it like this:

> The old system under Moses was only a shadow, a dim preview of good things to come, not the good things themselves. The sacrifices under that system were repeated again and again, year after year, but they were never able to provide perfect cleansing for those who came to worship. If they could have provided perfect cleansing, the sacrifices would have stopped, for the worshippers would have been purified once for all time, and their feelings of guilt would have disappeared. But instead, those sacrifices reminded them of their sins year after year.

Again, the law and less than total perfect obedience to it can never make you perfect. It is simply the shadow or the image of what is to be done, not the action or inaction itself. It is a picture of what true holiness looks like and also shows us what the sin in us looks like.

In 1 Timothy chapter 1, we see more of this. Starting in verse 8, "Now we know that the law is good, if one uses it lawfully," which no one except for Christ Himself has been able to do. Therefore, the law has a different purpose for the entire rest of the human race. It was never meant to be a system or means to self-righteousness but instead a mirror toward self-condemnation and conviction, leading to repentance and surrender, pleading to God for mercy.

Continuing into verse 9, "Understanding this, that the law is not laid down for the just but for the lawless and disobedient," which we just touched on, "for the ungodly and sinners, for the unholy and profane, for those who strike their fathers and mothers, for murderers, the sexually immoral, men who practice homosexuality, enslavers, liars, perjurers, and whatever else is contrary to sound doctrine, in accordance with the Gospel of the glory of the blessed God." The law was never meant for the righteous but for the wretched and sinful and desperately unrighteous, which includes all of us, to show them their need for a Savior.

Continuing on this, the law is one solid whole, and in order to be perfect and be saved by the law, you would have to keep the entire law perfectly. As James 2:10 tells us, "For whoever keeps the whole law but fails in one point has become accountable for all of it." If you commit just one slip up, one fault, one selfish intent, one lie, one sin, or even one failure to do right, you are guilty of breaking the entire law! Galatians 3:2–3 tells us, "All who rely on observing the law are under a curse, for it is written: 'Cursed is everyone who does not continue to do *everything* written in the Book of the Law." Can you honestly say that you have never broken even just one little sin? One little white lie? One ill thought or intent? One failure to do what is right? No one can! Besides Christ, no human that has ever walked this planet can say that. We are all guilty and deserve justice and punishment.

John MacArthur states it this way:

> Every other religion in the world except true Christianity says man can and must do something. There are only two religions in the world. Divine accomplishment and human achievement. Divine accomplishment is true

Biblical Christianity and every other religion is some form of human achievement.[5]

Those who do believe they can achieve salvation by obedience and "works of the law" are known as "self-righteous." They believe they can achieve righteousness by their own intents and merits or "works." This is simply and truly nonbiblical. John Piper of Desiring God ministries defines "works" as "the warfare of righteousness un-empowered by faith in the satisfying, liberating promises of God."

Jumping back into the Old Testament, there is an excellent and very telling lesson on this found in the very first chapter of the prophet Isaiah. The book of Isaiah starts off with kind of a court-room vision in which the Lord is the plaintiff and the nation of Israel is the defendant.[6] Instead of responding to God's ultimate care and provision for them, the people had failed to give Him the loving obedience that is His due and that belongs to God. God intended Israel to be a channel of blessing to the nations, but because of their incessant rebellion, He calls upon the nations to look upon Israel's shame.

Despite their disobedience, though, the physical descendants of Abraham are still God's chosen people. Keep that in mind. So God speaks to them through Isaiah the prophet. Verse 11:

> What to Me is the multitude of your sacrifices? says the Lord. I have had enough of burnt offerings of rams and the fat of well-fed beasts; I do not delight in the blood of bulls, or of lambs, or of goats. When you come to appear before Me, who has required of you this trampling of the courts? Bring no more vain offerings; incense is an abomination to Me. New moon and Sabbath and the calling of convocations—I cannot endure iniquity and solemn assembly. Your new moons and appointed feasts My soul hates; they have become a burden to Me; I Am weary of bearing them. When you spread out your hands, I will hide My eyes from you; even though you make

many prayers, I will not listen; your hands are full of blood. Wash yourselves; make yourselves clean; remove the evil of your deeds from before your eyes; cease to do evil, learn to do good; seek justice, correct oppression; bring justice to the fatherless, plead the widow's cause.

What is God saying here? He's saying that He hates the religiosity of His people. With their multitude of sacrifices, offerings, assemblies, feasts, even their prayers, He says, "I have had enough! I do not delight in them. They are an abomination to Me. My soul hates them. They are a burden to Me. I Am tired of bearing them. I will hide My eyes from you, I will not listen." And we see this exact same thing proclaimed in Psalm 40 verse 6. "In sacrifice and offering You have not delighted, but You have given me an open ear. Burnt offering and sin offering You have not required." God simply does not delight in our mere religiosity.

As we just mentioned, all the religions of the world are all centered on a form of self-righteousness, a list of dos and don'ts—I must do this, I must perform a certain way. I must be "good enough." Religion is man's pathetic and failed attempt to right himself with God. We are all sinners and have fallen short of the absolute perfection, holiness, and glory of God (Rom. 3:23). And ever since the fall of man, all of us have been utterly hopeless to remedy this situation on our own. Religion is our attempt at righting this massive eternal wrong which has been done, but of course, none of us have the infinitely large ability to do this. To dwell with a holy and perfect God, we need to be holy and perfect also, which we certainly are completely incapable of doing, no matter how strong our religiosity is.

So we see here in these verses in Isaiah that the nation of Israel was seemingly very diligent in their religiosity and most likely felt very secure in their practices and in their position with God. We also see here in Isaiah that the outward evidence of the emptiness of their ritualism was the presence of evil works and the absence of good works, their constant rebellion, and it is impossible to doubt the Lord's total aversion to their hypocritical religion. God found all of these sacrifices meaningless and even abhorrent if the offer failed in obedience to His laws.

We also see in Ezekiel 33:13 where we read:

> Though I say to the righteous that he shall surely live, yet if he trusts in his righteousness and does injustice, none of his righteous deeds shall be remembered, but in his injustice that he has done he shall die.

Again, unless you keep the law perfectly, which is impossible, even just one sin will condemn you against the entirety of the whole law. It will render useless every "good" thing that you have ever done. Adam and Eve lived for how many years in perfect holy fellowship and union with God, and then one error, one disobedience, one sin destroyed that flawless union and brought death and decay not just to themselves, but the whole of creation. Paul tells us in Romans 9:31–32, "Israel who pursued a law that would lead to righteousness did not succeed in reaching the law. Why? Because they did not pursue it by faith, but as if it were based on works."

In his letter to the Galatians, Paul plainly tells us at the end of 2:16 that "by works of the law no one will be justified." In the following chapter, in 3:10–11, he says, "Let me ask you only this: Did you receive the Spirit by works of the law or by hearing with faith? Are you so foolish? Having begun by the Spirit, are you now being perfected by the flesh?" This is a series of rhetorical questions implying that "You can't possibly be so ignorant as to think that you have received the Spirit, and therefore salvation, by works of the law, can you?" Paul is showing how absurd that line of thinking really is. Martin Luther has said, "The most damnable and pernicious heresy that has ever plagued the mind of man is that somehow he can make himself good enough to deserve to live forever with an all-holy God."

John Piper states,

> The stumbling block of the cross (1 Cor. 1:23), the thing that makes it so offensive, is that

it means that in ourselves we are utterly helpless (Rom. 5:6, 8) and can't do anything to enhance our justification or sanctification. Paul said in Gal. 5:11, "If I preach circumcision...the stumbling block of the cross has been removed." If we believe that by being circumcised or doing any other work of law (tithing, going to church, teaching Sunday school), we can add to the work of Christ, then we are bewitched and do not understand the Gospel. If I add anything to what Christ has achieved on the cross, to help ingratiate me with God, I make the stumbling block of the cross vanish. Or as Galatians 2:21 states, "I nullify the grace of God and make Christ to have died in vain."[7]

So we see that God's law is never made null and void, but if God's holy law, given to us through the Torah, the first five books of the Bible, also known as the Pentateuch, which were largely written by Moses, did not bring salvation, since man was incapable of keeping it perfectly (total depravity) which is demanded in front of the perfect holiness of God, but instead was brought to show sin to be sin (Rom. 7:13) and to know sin (Rom. 3:20) and define sin (Rom. 7:7–11), therefore increasing sin (Rom. 5:20; 6:19), how could any other form of obedience to lesser laws/rituals/rites/ceremonies/acts/obedience lead to salvation, seeing as we are all sinful and incapable of living sinless and perfect lives of obedience even once reborn (Rom. 7:14–24)?

Let me ask that one more time without some of the clutter: If God's holy law did not bring salvation, since man was incapable of keeping it perfectly (total depravity) but instead was brought to show sin to be sin and to know sin and define sin, therefore increasing sin, how could any other form of obedience to lesser laws/rituals/rites/ceremonies/acts/obedience lead to salvation, seeing as we are all sinful and incapable of living sinless and perfect lives of obedience even once reborn? The law reveals man's utter sinfulness, inability to save himself, and his desperate need of a Savior—it was never intended to be the way of salvation (cf Rom. 7:1–13).

Obedience does not and cannot lead to salvation since prior to salvation, we are totally depraved and hopelessly sinful and incapable of pleasing God pre-redeemed, pre-justified, pre-cleansed, pre-re-born (Rom. 8:8, 13). Commentator Chuck Missler from Koinonia House ministries says, "Obedience has no part in salvation. Salvation does not come by obedience. Paul spent a large portion of Romans teaching that the law merely defines sin, obedience to it does not provide salvation." Obedience comes from a life redeemed (Rom. 1:5–6, 6:17, 7:4, 15,18, 16:26; Eph. 2:10; Ti. 2:11–12). Obedience is fruit of the Spirit in the life of the reborn. We will hit on this in much more detail in a later chapter.

Obedience comes from a converted, thankful, and repentant heart that finally understands what was desperately lost, what has been found, what price has been paid, by what extreme sacrifice, at what extreme cost, without any self-input, all as a gracious and merciful and free gift (Rom. 5:15, 16, 17, 6:23) by an infinitely loving Father and Creator Who was previously unknown to us (Rom. 5:6, 8, 10; Eph. 2:4–5). Before and without His work inside of us "all our [so-called] righteous deeds are like filthy rags" (Isa. 64:6).

Romans 5:8 and 10 says, "but God shows His love for us in that while we were still sinners, Christ died for us...while we were enemies we were reconciled to God by the death of His Son." This shows us that we did not do any good things in order to be saved. We did not work to receive salvation. We did not obey to receive salvation. We did not do anything "good" prior to being saved and reconciled to God. While we were still sinners and enemies of God, Christ died for us and saved us and reconciled us. Ephesians 2:4–5 takes this just a step further and tells us that, "But God, being rich in mercy, because of His great love with which He loved us, even when we were dead in our transgressions, made us alive together with Christ (by grace you have been saved)."

We weren't just sinners or enemies; we were dead! And dead men cannot bring themselves back to life. This is all God's work done within us out of His gracious love for us. It is not by any of our own merit or by any act, ritual, obedience, checklist, ceremony, or work of our own that we are saved by Christ. We are reconciled to Him entirely by His doing.

So if we are so utterly depraved from the start and have no capacity to "works" our way, "obey" our way, "earn" our way, how do we get saved? How do we avoid judgment? How do we reach Heaven? How do we obtain or appropriate this reconciliation to God?

Before we answer that, let's touch shortly on a few terms and definitions and concepts that will help bring this together. First of all, let's touch on justice. God is a holy and righteous and just God. Justice means that when a wrong is committed, a just and appropriate and deserving punishment or penalty is demanded against the wrongdoer to reconcile the two parties involved. When we sin against God—or in our case, are born with a sinful nature—a reconciliation has to take place before we can have a relationship with Him. We have already determined that we can't do this ourselves. So how does it happen? We also already lightly touched on the fact that Jesus Christ did it all for us at the cross, which we will touch on in more depth in a later chapter, but how does it become applied to us?

As a quick illustration, let's use the setting of the courtroom. If a person were to murder a beloved family member of yours, you would demand appropriate justice for this crime. If in the court of law the judge listened to the case and then determined, "I find the defendant guilty of murder and I order him to pay $100 as restitution," that would not be justice. The penalty does not fit the crime.

Now without getting into a debate over whether or not the death penalty should be instituted, the penalty should be to a degree that is of a severity corresponding to the offense. For the intentional taking of someone's life, a proper sentence or penalty would be many years in prison or the death penalty or something of a much greater and fitting severity than $100 fine. To illustrate justice being served let us say that the just judge this time makes the ruling, "I find the defendant guilty of first-degree murder, and I order him to die in accordance with the death penalty" or twenty-thirty years in prison—something like that. Though this does not bring your loved one back from the dead, you at least have some sense of justice being served for a violent and horrible wrong being done. To state it easily, justice is getting what you do deserve.

Now let's touch on mercy and grace. Though they are loosely similar, they are quite different. To put it simply, mercy is not getting what you do deserve. Grace, on the other hand, is getting what you do not deserve. In that same courtroom illustration, let's this time put it in a little better perspective to illustrate our condition before God. Let us now put ourselves on trial.

We stand before the just Judge, God. His ruling comes down, "I find you guilty of countless sins against My law, Word and will. You have disobeyed Me, rebelled against Me, lived a life completely contrary from Me and failed to do what I commanded from you. I hereby sentence you to eternal death for all of your wretched wrong-doings and your entire unrighteous life of sin."

(Now some of you may try and say, "Well, I'm not that bad, I'm a pretty good person, I never killed anyone." We already touched on Matthew 5 where Jesus said in the Sermon on the Mount that gossip and hatred of your brother is the same in God's eye as murder.)

In making this ruling, God remains just. We "have all sinned and fall short of the glory of God" (Rom. 3:23), and therefore God is just in making that judgment. We have all sinned against God to great severity; therefore, we all deserve a great and severe penalty.

Enter Jesus Christ! Jesus Christ has entered the courtroom of God and has made a plea in our stead. Jesus Christ took our place and bore our punishment as our propitiation or substitution, which means that He suffered what we deserved in order to appease the justice of God and reconcile us to Him. This is mercy. We did not receive what we deserved. Christ took it for us. The other side of the coin is this: once Jesus has sufficiently paid our price, served justice, appeased the courts, ransomed and reconciled us to God and justi-fied us in the face of God, He then gives us eternal life with Him in Heaven. This is grace. We will receive what we do not deserve. This is entirely His gift to us through His amazing grace! We do not deserve it, but because of His eternal and infinite love for us, He gives it to us as a free gift! How glorious is our Lord and Savior!

Let's take this courtroom analogy just one step further to show the more true reality of the entirety of our situation. Imagine the same scenario, but in the courtroom, we are actually present as only a dead corpse! And when Jesus is pleading in our defense and offers Himself as our substitution, God looks at Christ's perfect fulfillment and offers our justification through His substitution and raises us back to life in His redeemed image! We were not sitting there alive, pleading our own case, pleading good things that we have done, begging for forgiveness, or even witnessing this trial taking place! The Bible calls us dead in our trespasses (Eph. 2:4–5) and only by grace (Eph. 2:5, 8) and Christ's substitution are we redeemed, made holy and righteous.

So what we are looking for is called justification.

> Being justified is a legal or judicial declaration of righteousness. Justification has two parts: 1) Being declared free of blame, acquitted of sin—not guilty. Believers are justified because Jesus Christ personally assumed the guilt for our sin on the cross; 2) God declares the person righteous, that is, placed in a position of right-standing with Him. A person may not be made righteous by his own personal behavior, no matter how good, or by the declaration of any other human being.[8]

The question remains, though: how do we receive or obtain this amazing gift of grace from the substitution Christ made in our place? How do we appropriate this reconciliation with God? How do we become justified?

To recap a little and to transition into that answer, let's look again at Galatians 2:16–19:

> Know that a man is not justified by observing the law, but by faith in Jesus Christ. So we, too, have put our faith in Christ Jesus that we

may be justified by faith in Christ and not by observing the law, because by observing the law no one will be justified.

First of all, this passage specifically says, "A man is not justified by observing the law, but by faith in Jesus Christ." Three times in this verse, Paul declares that salvation is only through faith in Christ and not by law. But to look at it deeper, what is another way that you could say "observing the law?" I suppose another way to say that would be "obedience" as the NLT puts it as "obeying the law." Acts of obedience DO NOT save you! "Know that no man is justified by observing the law (obedience), but by faith in Jesus Christ" or "By observing the law (obedience), no one will be justified." You do not nor could you obey in order to be saved (Isa. 64:6, Rom. 9:16)! You obey and become obedient once you are and BECAUSE you are saved and reborn and have a new heart for Jesus and live according to His Word (Eph. 2:10), and we'll get into that more later also. Keeping the law is an unacceptable means of salvation because the root of sinfulness is in the fallenness of man's heart, not just in his actions. The law served as a mirror to reveal sin, not to be a cure for it.

Pastor Kris Langham describes it beautifully like this in his audio commentary to chapter 7 of Romans.

> What the law does is show me that I'm bad. "Before I started reading the Bible I thought, I was a really good person, better than most people anyway. I was proud of it. Then I started in the Bible and found out that pride was a sin. But finding out it's a sin doesn't take away the sin. In fact, it can make it worse. See, the law says, 'Don't look,' and sin says, 'Look at what?' The law says, 'Don't open that box,' and sin says, 'What's in it? Whatever it is, I think I want it.' See, the law is like a scale. It doesn't make you fat, it just tells you when you are fat. Or for me,

a watch. It doesn't make me late, it just tells me that I am late. A lot. The scale is good. The watch is good. And the law is good. But I am not. The law was necessary to convince me that I'm bad. The law is the diagnostic but it's not the cure."[9]

Ken Willig says:

> Salvation is not a payday for how well we have lived our lives. We cannot earn grace or our salvation—not through any amount of works, deeds, actions—no matter how good, religious or humanitarian they may be (Rom. 4:4–5). Salvation—justification before God and entrance to Heaven—cannot be earned by good deeds, praying, charitable giving, being an exemplary humanitarian, or anything else. The audacity of believing that Jesus's perfect life, passion, death upon the cross, and resurrection was not sufficient payment for salvation is deplorable and embarrassing. I can do nothing for God. He needs nothing from me. I cannot improve upon His perfect free gift of His Son, Jesus Christ. Salvation is a free gift given to you and me when we place our faith and trust in Jesus Christ as our Redeemer, and make Jesus the Lord of our lives. Our right relationship with God, our righteousness, and our entrance into Heaven, is through Jesus Christ alone (cf. Acts 17:24–25). So it is not through the commandments, traditions, works or anything else, but through trusting in Jesus Christ only as my Savior, that I have eternal life. Everlasting life becomes mine only through the acceptance of the unearned gift of His unconditional love— through believing that He died to pay the penalty for all my sins: past, present, future.[10]

4

God's Sovereignty: Foreknowledge/
Predestination/Election/Chosen/Called

To begin to explain this burning question of "How do I receive salvation or become reconciled to God in order to be able to enjoy eternity with Him?" let's go back to the beginning, and even pre-Genesis. Beginning to touch on this subject a bit, Alistair Begg says:

> So much religion doesn't actually begin with God at all. It pays scant reference to God. Most of the time when you have anything in the magazines or the media about religion it's usually about the search for God, and we're supposed to believe that everybody in the universe is actually out there looking for God. They just can't find Him. They've been looking all over the place, and this is the story of religion, that man is just trying to find God wherever He is. But when you read the Bible it's the absolute reverse of that. The Bible begins with God calling out to man. The Bible begins with God taking the initiative with man, and it is God here Who has blessed us with every spiritual blessing in the Lord Jesus

Christ. In fact, when you look at the verbs, you can see how important they are. In verse 3 (*of Ephesians 1*), He has blessed us. In verse 4, He chose us. In verse 5, He predestined us. In verse 8, the riches of His grace He lavished upon us. And when you go from the verbs to the nouns, it is God's will, it is God's plan, it is God's purpose. It is unmistakable. It is impossible to miss this. And if God is the source of this blessing, you will notice also the sphere of this blessing. He's blessed us in Christ with every spiritual blessing in the Heavenly places.[1]

This excerpt was taken from a sermon that Pastor Alistair preached on the first few verses of Ephesians. Ephesians 1:3–5 states:

> Blessed be the God and Father of our Lord Jesus Christ, Who has blessed us in Christ with every spiritual blessing in the Heavenly places, even as He chose us in Him before the foundation of the world, that we should be holy and blameless before Him. In love He predestined us for adoption as sons through Jesus Christ, according to the purpose of His will.

And Ephesians 1:11 states, "In Him we obtained an inheritance, having been predestined according to the purpose of Him Who works all things according to the counsel of His will."

The issues we are going to address in this chapter are called foreknowledge, predestination, election, and being chosen or called—all loosely connected. Before we begin digging deep, might I add that:

> No doctrine is more loved and more resented at the same time than the doctrine of eternal election—divine, sovereign choice; predestination. In fact, there are those who suggest

that this doctrine is actually devilish. Rationally and emotionally it seems unfair and destructive of free will and human autonomy and choice. And I can understand those feelings because they're very human. We think everything should depend on us. This is part of the pride of our fallenness. But ultimately, according to Scripture, it's not our reason, nor our sentiment, nor our feelings, nor our desires that determine what is true; God has already determined that. And it is further unacceptable to make God in our image, to design Him to fit our own ideas of what He should be, and what He should do, and what He should not do. Still there are also those who are bold enough to be undisturbed by an all-out attack on the doctrine of sovereign, saving grace, the doctrine of election. Making your own, perhaps more comfortable, more rational, more human god, twisting your own instincts about God, is essentially an assault on Him, and it misrepresents Him. And such misrepresentation of God, simply stated, corrupts our understanding; therefore corrupts our worship, corrupts our service, and can be not just ignorant, but even blasphemous.[2]

So let's put our own opinions and desires aside, hold to the integrity of Scripture, and look deeply into this and see what Scripture tells us on this subject; we will see that "Scripture is unambiguous about this; and maybe even more importantly, it is unembarrassed about it."[3]

John MacArthur writes a beautiful devotion on this very topic of predestination and election in his year-long devotional book, entitled *Drawing Near*, that I think will help kick this chapter off and get us started.

Praising God for Your Election

"Having been predestined according to [God's] purpose Who works all things after the counsel of His will" (Eph. 1:11).

In Ephesians 1:4 Paul says that God "chose us in [Christ] before the foundation of the world, that we should be holy and blameless before Him." In verse 11 he reiterates that marvelous truth by affirming that believers have been predestined to salvation according to God's Own purpose and will.

Many reject the teaching that God chose (predestined) believers to salvation. They think believers chose God. In one sense they're right: salvation involves an act of the will in turning from sin to embrace Christ. But the issue in predestination goes deeper than that. It's a question of initiative. Did God choose you on the basis of your faith in Him or did He, by choosing you, enable you to respond in faith?

The answer is clear in Scripture. Romans 3:11 says that no one seeks for God on his own. Unregenerate people have no capacity to understand spiritual truth. It's all foolishness to them (1 Cor. 2:14). They are spiritually dead (Eph. 2:1), blind (2 Cor. 4:4), and ignorant (Eph. 4:18).

How can people in that condition initiate saving faith? They can't! That's why Jesus said, "No one can come to Me, unless the Father Who sent Me draws him... All that the Father gives Me shall come to Me, and the one who comes to Me I will certainly not cast out" (John 6:37, 44). Paul added, "God, Who has saved us, and called us with a holy calling, not according to our works, but according to His Own purpose and grace which was granted us in Christ Jesus from all eternity" (2 Tim. 1:9).

God took the initiative. He chose you and gave you saving faith (Eph. 2:8–9). Rejoice in that truth. Rest in His power to conform all things to His will. Draw strength and assurance from His promise never to let you go (John 10:27–29). Then live each day as God's elected one by shunning sin and following after holiness.

Praise God for placing His love upon you and granting you salvation.[4]

Pastor John MacArthur makes a few great points here. There are many Christians who believe that it is man who chooses God as their Savior, and we will get more into the subject of free will in the next couple chapters, but when you go deeper and further back before us, before we even existed, it is ultimately God Who initiates. God does not choose us because of our faith and belief in Him or because of some obedience to Him, He knew us from the beginning, He predestined us, He chose us before the foundations of the earth, before Genesis 1:1, and it is only because of His choosing of us that we are enabled to respond to Him in faith. Without God's divine call sinful man has no desire for the things of God as stated in 1 Corinthians 2:14, "The natural person does not accept the things of the Spirit of God, for they are folly to him, and he is not able to understand them because they are spiritually discerned."

And to expound on what Pastor John says above, in John chapter 6, several times in Jesus's Own words, He tells us in verses 37, 39, 44, and 64–65, "All that the Father gives to Me will come to Me, and whoever comes to Me I will never cast out...all that He has given Me... No one comes to Me unless the Father Who sent Me draws him... This is why I told you that no one can come to Me unless it is granted him by the Father." Plain and simple, you cannot choose or come to God unless you are first called and chosen by Him. He initiates.

Some may say to this, "Well, that's totally not fair! And that's even evil of God to not call someone and not allow them to come to Him!" In response to this I'd like to look at Romans chapter 9 starting at verse 10:

> When Rebekah had conceived children by one man, our forefather Isaac, though they were not yet born and had done nothing either good or bad—in order that God's purpose of election might continue, not because of works but because of Him Who calls—she was told, "The older will serve the younger." As it is written, "Jacob I loved, but Esau I hated."

Before I continue, so you don't get the wrong idea about the last part of this passage, this is quoted from Malachi 1:2–3.

> Actual emotional hatred for Esau and his offspring is not the point here. Malachi, who wrote this declaration more than 1,500 years after their deaths, was looking back at these two men—and by extension the nations (Israel and Edom) that came from their loins. God chose one for divine blessing and protection, and the other He left to divine judgment.[5]

He was referring to their legacies or lineages, not emotional hatred toward the person of Esau.

Continuing on in Romans 9, Paul then asks,

> "Is there injustice on God's part? By no means! For He says to Moses, 'I will have mercy on whom I have mercy, and I will have compassion on whom I have compassion'" (Ex. 33:19). So then it depends not on human will or exertion, but on God, Who has mercy. For the Scripture

says to Pharaoh, "For this very purpose I have raised you up, that I might show My power in you, and that My name might be proclaimed in all the earth" (Ex. 9:16). So then He has mercy on whom He wills, and He hardens whomever He wills.

And here he poses virtually the same question we just asked and then adds a rebuttal to that question.

You will say to me then, "Why does He still find fault? For who can resist His will?" But who are you, O man, to answer back to God? Will what is molded say to its molder, "Why have you made me like this?" Has the potter no right over the clay, to make out of the same lump one vessel for honorable use and another for dishonorable use? What if God, desiring to show His wrath and to make known His power, has endured with much patience vessels of wrath prepared for destruction, in order to make known the riches of His glory for vessels of mercy, which He has prepared beforehand for glory—even us whom He has called, not from the Jews only but also from the Gentiles?

Twice here, Paul first quotes God when He said to Moses, "I will have mercy on whom I have mercy, and I will have compassion on whom I have compassion," and then Paul himself explains that God "has mercy on whom He wills, and He hardens whomever He wills." It is God's prerogative. He created everything (Gen. 1:1) and controls everything (Heb. 1:3) and His will is perfect (Rom. 12:2), even though we may not understand it or have questions sometimes.

Now I realize that this may not be sufficient enough of an answer for some of you. You still may be asking, "Well, how is it fair that He chooses some and not others?" Like I said in chapter 1, I don't want a god that I can fully understand. Who are we (the clay) to question the Creator of the universe (the Potter)? God is sovereign and divine. He dwells in and sees the eternal. His ways and mind are FAR above ours. We cannot begin to grasp the infinite realms of God.

God is love (1 John 4:16). He is the God of all grace (1 Pet. 5:10) and His ways are perfect (Ps. 18:30), even if we don't understand them. Pastor Laurian Lazarescu from Seraphim Fellowship in Jesus Christ and Trinity Evangelical Free Church of Boise ID says this on the topic, "He did not choose Israel for their size and certainly not for their obedience (or lack thereof), He just chose them as His chosen people. It was simply His choice. His children are not chosen based on their future performance, He chooses whom He will and we will be forever amazed. Nevertheless, in Heaven we will understand."

Nonetheless, you might try to rest assured in this: 1 Timothy 2:4 tells us that, "God our Savior desires all people to be saved and to come to the knowledge of the truth." Although:

> The Greek word for "desires" here is not that which normally expresses God's will of decree (His eternal purpose), but God's will of desire. There is a distinction between God's desire and His eternal saving purpose, which must transcend His desires. God does not want men to sin. He hates sin with all of His being (Ps. 5:4, 45:7); thus, He hates its consequences—eternal wickedness in hell.
>
> God does not want people to remain wicked forever in eternal remorse and hatred of Himself. Yet, God, for His Own glory, and to manifest that glory in wrath, chose to endure "vessels...prepared for destruction for the supreme fulfillment of His will" (Rom. 9:22). In His eternal purpose, He chose only the elect out of the world (John 17:6) and passed over the rest, leaving them to the consequences of their sin, unbelief and rejec-

tion of Christ (cf. Rom. 1:18–32). Ultimately, God's choices are determined by His sovereign eternal purpose, not His desires.[6]

We also might read in 2 Peter 3:9, "The Lord is not slow to fulfill His promise as some count slowness, but is patient toward you, not wishing that any should perish, but that all should reach repentance." But again, we should not try to find unwarranted peace in this verse either as:

> The "any" here must refer to those whom the Lord has chosen and will call to complete the redeemed, i.e., the "you." Since the whole passage is about God's destroying the wicked, His patience is not so He can save all of them, but so that He can receive His Own. He can't be waiting for everyone to be saved, since the emphasis is that He will destroy the world and the ungodly. Those who do perish and go to hell, go because they are depraved and worthy only of hell and have rejected the only remedy, Jesus Christ, not because they were created for hell and predetermined to go there. The path to damnation is the path of a non-repentant heart; it is the path of one who rejects the person and provision of Jesus Christ and holds on to sin (cf. Isa. 55:1; Jer. 13:17; Ezek. 18:32; Matt. 11:28, 23:37; Luke 13:3; John 3:16, 8:21, 24; 1 Tim. 2:3–4; Rev. 22:17).[7]

Alistair Begg offers a bit of response to this issue:

> The Source is in God and the sphere is in the Heavenly realms. Inevitably we then ask the question, "Why did He choose me?" We're always looking for an answer or reason, in our-

selves, as to why it is that we have been made a part of God's amazing grace. But there is no answer in that. "Why did He choose me?" The answer is because He loved you. "Yea but why did He love me?" The answer is because He loved you! Deuteronomy 7:7, "The Lord set His love on you and chose you, because the Lord loves you." Why did He choose me? Because He loved me. Why did He love me? Because He loved me. People may then say, it's rather unjust, isn't it? No! Porshia in Merchant of Venice (*Shakespearean play*) says, "Though justice be thy plea consider this, that in the course of justice none of us should see salvation, we do but pray for mercy." For in the course of justice none of us should see salvation. Why would He ever choose any of us? If justice was served, we all deserve condemnation. Why would He choose any? It's a mystery. And it's because of His love. "For God so loved the world that He gave His one and only Son, that whoever believes in Him should not perish but have eternal life' (John 3:16)."[8]

Reverend Eric Alexander, who preached in the Church of Scotland for over fifty years, says this:

The doctrine of election is a Biblical doctrine. It is right there in the Bible. You can't read your Bible without dealing with it. It is Biblical. Secondly, it is difficult. That's why so many people have so many problems. And thirdly, it is profitable. Embracing the doctrine of election is not then to become for us a banner under which we march, nor is it a bomb to be dropped on people, but rather it is a bastion for our souls. Then we bow down in the amazing awareness of the fact that we are who we are in Christ because before the dawn of time He set His affection upon us in His Son.[9]

Whether you tend to find these doctrines challenging or not, they are clearly Biblically taught and true. God foreknew, predestined, and elected those who would be saved and chose them and called them to Himself. Before the foundations of the world, God already knew all. You cannot come to Him and accept Him without His first calling you. This is not to say that He forces anyone or only chose those whom He knew would accept Him; however, as Jesus states in John 6:37, 44, "No one can come to Me, unless the Father Who sent Me draws him... All that the Father gives Me shall come to Me, and the one who comes to Me I will certainly not cast out." Let's look at more from Scripture.

God's sovereign election is not just something that is found in the New Testament, we can find several teachings of it in the Old Testament as well. Starting off in Deuteronomy 7:6, we read, "For you are a people holy to the Lord your God. The Lord your God has chosen you to be a people for His treasured possession, out of all the peoples who are on the face of the earth." Even from the beginning, God has chosen a group of people out of the entirety of mankind, to be His Own. A few of the Psalms reiterate this same sentiment. Psalm 105:43 refers to Israel as His chosen ones. Psalm 135:4 says, "For the Lord has chosen Jacob for Himself, Israel as His Own possession." God chooses whom He wills.

In Psalm 22:10, King David shows us that "Upon You I was cast from my birth; and from my mother's womb You have been my God." Clearly, still inside the womb, David had zero knowledge or ability in order to do this with any intentionality or decisive purpose of his own. This was all entirely the work of God Himself in David's life.

The Prophet Isaiah tells us in 42:1, 6:

Behold My servant, Whom I uphold; My
elect, in Whom My soul delights, I have put My

Spirit upon Him, He will bring forth justice to the nations... I Am the Lord, I have called You in righteousness, I will take You by the hand and keep You, I will give You as a covenant for the people, a Light for the nations.

Here God the Father is speaking, and though He is speaking about His Son, Jesus, the issue of His sovereign will, call, and control is still in view. Isaiah also says in the words of Jesus in 49:1, 5, "The Lord called Me from the womb, from the body of My mother He named My name... He Who formed Me from the womb to be His servant." Now you may say that this doesn't apply the same because, of course, Jesus the Messiah was prophesied about from Genesis 3 at the time of the fall of man; however, it does still focus on God's foreknowledge and sovereign overall plan. Let's begin to move on toward us nonetheless.

In Isaiah 43:10–12, God is again speaking through the Prophet Isaiah but this time is speaking in regards to the people of Israel:

"You are My witnesses," declares the Lord, "and My servant whom I have chosen, that you may know and believe Me and understand that I Am He. Before Me no god was formed, nor shall there be any after Me. I declared and saved and proclaimed, when there was no strange god among you; and you are My witnesses," declares the Lord, "and I Am God."

God sovereignly selected them and chose them as His chosen people and nation to be His witnesses so that they may believe in Him, and He granted them the knowledge to truly understand exactly Who He is; that He is the Creator and Lord over all. He chose them, made Himself known, saved them, and proclaimed His Own glory through them.

In Jeremiah 1:5, we read of God's sovereign call and election of the prophet Jeremiah, just as we have seen previously in the life of David, "Before I formed you in the womb I knew you, and before you were born I consecrated you; I appointed you a prophet to the nations." This speaks of God's foreknowledge and selection of Jeremiah as His chosen prophet before Jeremiah was even conceived in the womb.

Moving into the New Testament, the Apostle Matthew shows us a few things about these topics. In Matthew 9:13, he quotes Jesus as saying, "For I came not to call the righteous, but sinners." Jesus came to call each one of us who does not try and save himself by the law. In Matthew 11:27, we read more of Jesus's words, "All things have been handed over to Me by My Father, and no one knows the Son except the Father, and no one knows the Father except the Son and anyone whom the Son chooses to reveal Him." You simply cannot know the Father unless Jesus first chooses to reveal Him to you.

In Matthew 13:11, when Jesus was speaking to the apostles on why He speaks to others in parables, He answers, "to you it has been given to know the secrets of the Kingdom of Heaven, but to them it has not been given." And as is common in the gospels, these words are mirrored in Luke 10:22, "All things have been handed over to Me by My Father, and no one knows Who the Son is except the Father, or Who the Father is except the Son and anyone whom the Son chooses to reveal Him." Jesus chose who would understand these things and who wouldn't. And to those who were chosen, He spoke of in Matthew 25:34, while prophesying of the final judgment, "Come you who are blessed by My Father, inherit the Kingdom prepared for you from the foundation of the world." He has chosen us from the beginning and has prepared for us an inheritance from the beginning. You can rest assured that there are not going to be any vacant inheritances of people who God foreknew, predestined, elected, and called that will not be there to inherit.

The Apostle John has much to teach us about these topics. In John 3:27, John the Baptist plainly says, "A person cannot receive even one thing unless it is given him from Heaven." In this exact context, John is referring specifically about ministry opportunity, but it encompasses all things.

John 13:18 says, quoting Jesus, "I Am not speaking of all of you; I know whom I have chosen." John 15:16, 19 says, "You did not choose Me, but I chose you and appointed you that you should go and bear fruit and that your fruit should abide, so that whatever you ask the Father in My name, He may give it to you." In these last two sets of passages Jesus is speaking of the twelve apostles and making it clear that there be no misconception that He sovereignly chose them; they did not choose Him.

In John 10, starting at verse 24, we read of an instance where:

> [T]he Jews gathered around Jesus and said to Him, "How long will you keep us in suspense? If you are the Christ, tell us plainly." Jesus answered them, "I told you, and you do not believe. The works that I do in My Father's name bear witness about Me, but you do not believe because you are not part of My sheep."

The point here is that you cannot believe in the things of God unless you are already His. And how do you become His? Jesus continues:

> My sheep hear My voice, and I know them, and they follow Me. I give them eternal life, and they will never perish, and no one will snatch them out of My hand. My Father, Who has given them to Me, is greater than all, and no one is able to snatch them out of the Father's hand. I and the Father are One.

Here Jesus plainly says, "I give them eternal life... My Father... has given them to me." Jesus reiterates this same statement seven times during a prayer where He prays directly to the Father expressing His infinite love for us and His perfect obedience to the Father in chapter 17 in verses 2, 6, 9, 11, 12, 24, and 26:

> You have given Me authority over all flesh, to give eternal life to <u>all whom You have given</u>

> Me…the people <u>whom You gave Me</u> out of the world. Yours they were, and You <u>gave them to Me</u>, and they have kept Your Word…for those <u>whom You have given Me</u>, for they are Yours… Holy Father, keep them in Your name, <u>which You have given Me</u>… I have kept them in Your name, <u>which You have given Me</u>…<u>whom You have given Me.</u>

Then He follows it up with this phrase, "<u>I made known to them Your name</u>, and I will continue to make it known." He also expresses this same sentiment one more time in 18:9, "Of those <u>whom You gave Me</u> I have lost not one." This is a direct face-to-face communion of the Son and the Father where Jesus prays for Himself, the apostles and all NT believers, and praises God the Father for the sentimental "gift" that the Father gave to Him, emphasized by the reiteration. We were given to Jesus by the Father; this was the Father's giving and the Son's receiving; we had no part in making this transaction come to be or come to pass. We are made His by Him.

The Book of Acts gives us a little insight into this as well. In Acts 2:39, Peter is referring to the promise of forgiveness and the gift of the Holy Spirit when he says, "For the promise is for you and your children and for all who are far off, everyone who the Lord our God calls to Himself." What he is saying is that this promise, this gift, is for those who God calls to Himself; anyone and everyone, no matter who you are or where you're from, but God does the calling, and He's calling you to Himself. And shortly after that in 2:47 we read, "And the Lord added to their number day by day those who were being saved." Here, it is saying that God is the one that was adding people who were saved to their numbers. He once again receives all the credit.

And to follow that up, we read in chapter 13:48 that, "as many as were appointed to eternal life believed." It is only those who are already appointed for eternal life by God Himself that are the ones who come to believe. We can't come to Him unless He first appoints us to be able to come to Him. This is "one of Scripture's clearest statements on the sovereignty of God in salvation. God chooses man for salvation, not the opposite."[10]

Paul speaks extensively on God's calling of believers in Romans where he starts by mentioning his own calling in the very first verse of the Letter. "Paul, a servant of Christ Jesus, a called apostle, set apart for the Gospel of God." The Greek word used here for "called" is the adjective, *kletos*, which means, "divinely selected and appointed; or invited by God in the proclamation of the Gospel to obtain eternal salvation in the Kingdom through Christ."[11]

He then continues speaking of the beloved and elected of God in 1:6–7, "You who are called to belong to Jesus Christ, to all those in Rome beloved of God and called to be saints." Here, the Greek word *kletos* is also being used. This is an effectual call from God to His elect sinners resulting in salvation. Not just an offer or invitation, but an effectual call resulting in relationship.

In Romans 8:28, Paul presents us with a beautiful promise that we can always use to find great comfort in, but for the purpose here, just pay attention to the "who:" "And we know that all things work for the good of those who love Him, for those who are called according to His purpose." We are not only called but we are called for His purpose. And, again, this is the word *kletos*, speaking of the effectual call made by God leading to salvation.

The following set of verses is one of the most beautiful and complete passages regarding many of the doctrines of grace, starting with predestination and ending in the realms of Heaven. Romans 8:29–30 reads:

> For those whom He foreknew He also pre-destined to be conformed to the image of His Son… And those whom He predestined He also called, those whom He called He also justified, those whom He justified He also glorified.

From the very start and all the way to the finish, it is all God's work done for us and in us. He initiated it, and He will complete it. We will greatly dissect this verse in a later chapter, there is SO much packed into these two verses. He also says a few verses later in v. 33, "Who shall bring any charge against God's elect? It is God Who justifies." Again, it is God's election and work that saves us. In Romans 9:23–24, we see that, "He has prepared beforehand for glory—even us whom He has called." God has predestined, preordained, and called us from beforehand for His glory. It is all His preexistent choice.

Romans 11:28–29 shows us another aspect of this beautiful truth, "[B]ut as regards election, they are beloved for the sake of their forefathers. For the gifts and the calling of God are irrevocable." This gift of God, His effectual call, this time—*klesis* in the Greek, the noun form of kletos, basically having the same meaning of "a divine invitation to embrace salvation of God"—is an irrevocable gift from God. It is an effectual call. We are virtually and basically helpless against its invitation, and it cannot and will not be taken away from us by anyone, including God Himself.

Paul carries this teaching on into the epistles as well. He follows in Galatians chapter 1 verses 6 and 15, "[H]im Who called you in the grace of Christ... But when He Who had set me apart before I was born, and Who called me by His grace." Here we again see that God has chosen us from the beginning, predestined before we were even born, all by His amazing grace. In verse 6, Paul is talking about and to the Galatians who are the "called" by God. In verse 15, he is referring to himself and speaking of his conversion. He details of his former life of Pharisaic obedience and persecution of the church of God, trying to utterly destroy it. It was only by Christ's intervention and calling in Paul's life that he was brought into the truth and into a relationship with Christ when his life was completely turned around because God set him apart even before he was born, and he was supernaturally and spiritually transformed into a totally surrendered and devout servant of Christ who was now entirely eager to spread the Word of the Gospel to the rest of the world.

This was not Paul's decision or an act of obedience; this was entirely done by the grace of God. God Himself turned the strictest Pharisee and persecutor of the followers of Christ into one of the greatest apostles and teachers of the Gospel of Christ that has ever lived, entirely done by His grace, as he mentions in verse 16, "[He] was pleased to reveal His Son to me, in order that I might preach Him among the Gentiles." Throughout all of Scripture, Paul never takes credit for this transformation. It was all of God's election and call and grace.

Paul continues on into the letter to the Ephesians in the first chapter starting at verse 3:

> Blessed be the God and Father of our Lord Jesus Christ, Who has blessed us in Christ with every spiritual blessing in the Heavenly places, even as He chose us in Him before the foundation of the world, that we should be holy and blameless before Him. In love He predestined us for adoption as sons through Jesus Christ, according to the purpose of His will, to the praise of His glorious grace, with which He has blessed us in the Beloved. In Him we have redemption through His blood, the forgiveness of our trespasses, according to the riches of His grace, which He lavished upon us, in all wisdom and insight making known to us the mystery of His will, according to His purpose, which He set forth in Christ as a plan for the fullness of time, to unite all things in Him, things in Heaven and on earth. In Him we have obtained an inheritance, having been predestined according to the purpose of Him Who works all things according to the counsel of His will, so that we who were the first to hope in Christ might be to the praise of His glory.

These are very straightforward passages proclaiming all that is God's work and will to bring us to Him. He "blessed us in Christ with every spiritual blessing."

"He chose us in Him before the foundation of the world."

"He predestined us for adoption…according to the purpose of His will."

"In Him, we have redemption through His blood, the forgiveness of our trespasses, according to the riches of His grace, which He lavished upon us."

He made "known to us the mystery of His will, according to His purpose."

And "In Him we have obtained (past tense) an inheritance, having been predestined (past tense) according to the purpose of Him Who works all things according to the counsel of His Own will."

Before the foundation of the world, He chose us and predestined us to be His blessed and adopted children to be redeemed by His blood, all according to His will and His grace. "The Church is marked off from the world not by special privilege, but by the gracious election and calling of God."[12] God has orchestrated all of this ever since even before time began, before He created any of us, and brought us to Him. Also an important point to make here is that "God did not base our predestination on His ability to foresee our decision to accept Christ, but simply according to 'the counsel of His Own will.'"[13]

The next couple verses in Ephesians touch on our part or responsibility in all of this, but we will touch on that in the next couple of chapters. Here we are focusing on God's initial will and work in all of this, which is also reiterated in Ephesians chapter 2 verse 10, "For we are His workmanship, created in Christ Jesus for good works, which God prepared beforehand, that we should walk in them." We are His workmanship, created before time, for God's purpose.

To the Philippians, Paul also explains this in Philippians 1:6, "I am sure of this, that He Who began a good work in you will bring it to completion at the day of Jesus Christ." Again, we see here that it is God Who not only begins this work in us but also finishes it.

In the first letter to the Thessalonians, Paul says in 1:4–5:

> For we know, brothers loved by God, that
> He has chosen you, because our Gospel came
> to you not only in word, but also in power and

in the Holy Spirit and with full conviction; just
as you know what kind of men we proved to be
among you for your sake.

How do you know that God chose them?
Here's the proof: the Gospel came. It came with
power. It came with the Holy Spirit. It came
with conviction. And as a result of it, verse 6,
"You became imitators of us and of the Lord."
The Gospel came and transformed them so that
they imitated the behavior of the apostle and the
Lord Himself. Verse 7 says, "So that you became
an example to all believers." God chose them
in time. He brought that eternal choice to fru-
ition by bringing the Gospel to them in power
through the Holy Spirit with full conviction, so
that they were saved, became imitators of Christ
and examples to all believers.[14]

In 2:12 of Paul's first letter, he continues, "We exhorted each
one of you and encouraged you and charged you to walk in a manner
worthy of God, Who calls you into His Own Kingdom and glory."
We are only able to enter the Kingdom of God if He has called us
into His Own Kingdom and glory.

In the second letter to the Thessalonians, Paul says in chapter 2
verses 13–14, "God chose you as the firstfruits to be saved, through
sanctification by the Spirit and belief in the truth. To this He called
you through our Gospel, so that you may obtain the glory of our
Lord Jesus Christ." He chose you and called you to be saved.

And in his second letter to Timothy, we read in chapter 1, verse
9, "God, Who saved us and called us to a holy calling, not because
of our works but because of His Own purpose and grace, which He
gave us in Christ Jesus before the ages began." Paul never budges
from this teaching. It is always the same. God, before the ages began,
saves us and calls us, not because of anything that we have done but

because of His Own purpose and grace. It is His work, not ours. You cannot find anything different in Paul's teachings.

In 2:10, Paul continues, "I endure all things for the sake of the elect. I do all things for the sake of the chosen to obtain salvation." In essence, Paul was defining his ministry by saying, "Everything I do in my ministry is geared toward bringing the Gospel to the elect and chosen of God."

In Paul's letter to Titus, in 1:1–3, we also see this taught:

> Paul, a servant of God and an apostle of Jesus Christ, for the sake of the faith of God's elect and their knowledge of the truth, which accords with godliness, in hope of eternal life, which God, Who never lies, promised before the ages began and at the proper time manifested in His Word through the preaching with which I have been entrusted by the command of God our Savior.

God's promises to His elect are from before the ages began.

The writer of Hebrews also gives us some insight into these topics. We see in 2:10 and 12:2, "For it is fitting that He, for Whom and by Whom all things exist, in bringing many sons to glory, should make the Founder of their salvation perfect through suffering" and "looking to Jesus, the Founder and Perfecter of our faith." In these verses, we see that Jesus is both the Founder of our faith and our salvation and then also the Perfecter of our faith, which mirrors what Paul taught us in Philippians 1:6. From the beginning to the end, it is all His work in us.

We also see in 4:3 that "His works have been finished since the creation of the world." "The spiritual rest that God gives is not something that is incomplete or unfinished. It is a rest that is based upon a finished work that God purposed in eternity past."[15] The plan of salvation and also those who would be saved were all predestined before the foundation of the world.

In 9:15, we also learn that, "Therefore He is the Mediator of a new covenant, so that those who are called might receive the promised eternal inheritance." We see here that those whom God calls—which in the Greek used here is *kaleo* which again refers to the effectual call related to salvation—might receive the promised eternal inheritance. The "might receive" used here in the Greek is *lambano* which means to "take or lay hold of; to take what is one's own; of that which when taken is not let go." The Greek for "promise" is *epaggelia* which means "announcement or promised good or blessing." So we see that God effectually calls us, and through this call, we take hold of the promised or announced blessing of our eternal inheritance which, when taken, is not let go.

James 1:18 gives us a bit of a look at this also, "Of His Own will He brought us forth by the Word of Truth, that we should be a kind of firstfruits of His creatures." It is by His will that we are brought forth as firstfruits. In 2:5, it reads, "Has not God chosen those who are poor in the world to be rich in faith and heirs of the Kingdom?" Again, God chooses who will inherit His Kingdom.

Peter teaches us quite a bit also in his letters. In his first letter, he shows us in chapter 1, starting with verse 1:

> Peter, an apostle of Jesus Christ, to those who are elect exiles of the Dispersion in Pontus, Galatia, Cappadocia, Asia and Bithynia, according to the foreknowledge of God the Father, in the sanctification of the Spirit, for the obedience to Jesus Christ and for the sprinkling of His blood.

Peter is saying that he is an apostle of Jesus Christ chosen by God to be set apart from sin to obey Jesus Christ. Continuing on into verses 3ff, 15, and 20ff, he writes:

> Blessed be the God and Father of our Lord and Savior Jesus Christ! According to His great mercy, He has caused us to be born again to a

living hope through the resurrection of Jesus
Christ from the dead, to an inheritance that is
imperishable, undefiled, and unfading, kept in
Heaven for you, who by God's power are being
guarded through faith for a salvation ready to be
revealed in the last time…as He Who called you
is holy, you also be holy in all your conduct…
He [Christ] was foreknown before the foundation of the world but was made manifest in the
last times for the sake of you who through Him
are believers in God, Who raised Him from the
dead and gave Him glory, so that your faith and
hope are in God.

In these verses, we see that it is purely because of God's great
mercy that He caused us to be born again through Christ to an eternal inheritance that cannot be taken away and that the entire Gospel
of Christ and salvation was present in God's foreknowledge before
the foundation of the world. We also see in 2:21, 3:9, and 5:10 that
we are called by Him which again is the Greek word *kaleo* which as
always in the New Testament epistles refers to the effectual call to
salvation which is more than just an invitation; it is a call that has
as its effect being finalized in a salvational relationship with Christ.

We read in 2:21, "For to this you have been called, because
Christ also suffered for you, leaving you an example, so that you
might follow in His steps." Here we see that our call to salvation may
and usually does result in some trials, persecution, and hardships, but
just as Christ was our example, we may follow in His footsteps and
shine in His image during these moments.

In 3:9, it reads, "Do not repay evil for evil or reviling for reviling, but on the contrary, bless, for to this you were called, that you
may obtain a blessing." Here we learn that again, just as Christ is our
example, we are to bless others just as Christ has blessed us and to
forgive others as Christ has forgiven us instead of looking for retribu-
tion toward those who have wronged us.

And verse 5:10 kind of tells us the outcome of this, "And after you have suffered a little while, the God of all grace, Who has called you to His eternal glory in Christ, will Himself restore, confirm, strengthen, and establish you." God Himself will perform the restoration and secure the place of those who are called in Christ.

We also read of this effectual calling in 1:3–4 of Peter's second letter, "His divine power has granted to us all things that pertain to life and godliness, through the knowledge of Him Who called us to His Own glory and excellence, by which He has granted to us His precious and very great promises, so that through them you may become partakers of the divine nature." It is only through His effectual call that we are brought into possession of these divine truths.

Jude also makes mention of those who are effectually called in his short epistle in verse 1 "to those who are called, beloved in God the Father and kept for Christ," making mention that those who are effectually called to salvation are the beloved of God and kept secure for Christ. Again, the word used for "called" is *kletos*; the Greek word used for "beloved" is the verb *agapao* which finds it's root in the noun *agape* which is the unconditional, charitable, and sacrificial love of God; and the word for "kept" used here is *tereo* which means "take care of; guard; to keep, to reserve."

We also see evidently in the final book of the Bible John's prophetic book of Revelation, in 13:8 and 17:8, that God's election of His children was made in eternity past before the foundations of the world were even created and that the names of those who would be entered into the Book of Life were written in before the foundations of the world; and those whose names would not be written into the Book of Life would also be determined and excluded from the Book of Life before the foundations of the world. Both God's election of His children and God's rejection of those who would reject Him and would not know Him were foreknown before the beginning. In 13:8, "Everyone whose name has not been written before the foundation of the world in the Book of Life of the Lamb Who was slain." In 17:8, "The dwellers on earth whose names have not been written in the Book of Life from the foundation of the world."

This is not to say though that God predestined some to destruction. Those whose names are not in the Book of Life are excluded according to their own demerit. Romans 1:18–25 shows us that everyone knows God, and it is only those who choose to reject God that are destined to hell and destruction. If man rejects God, then God, in turn, rejects man.

Sovereign, divine election is all throughout redemptive history, it is the way God operates. And we know this, we instinctively know this. All true Christians know this. No one congratulates himself for his salvation. We all thank God. We all give Him praise and glory for saving us. We all understand the wretched fallenness of our hearts prior to salvation that we were unwilling and unable to change. His power came upon us by sovereign decree, and made us willing and made us able to do what we were neither willing nor able to do. We all know this. We don't congratulate ourselves, we thank God for our salvation. Also, we pray to God for the salvation of others. If this is something people do on their own, why are we bothering to talk to God about it? Why are we pouring out our hearts in intercessory prayer for the lost? And even though it is the work of God, we were never forced. None of us were dragged kicking and screaming to the cross, to the Kingdom. God moved on our wills and we willed to abandon our sin, we willed to turn to Christ, we willed to repent. We willed to believe, we desired to believe; we desired to turn from sin. We desired from the heart to love Christ. We honestly felt the conviction of sin and righteousness and judgment, so that each of us desired to repent and longed to believe, and cried out to the Lord to save us and forgive us and give us eternal life. But all that willingness and all that acceptance of the Gospel was because God made us willing. He made us willing by giving us life, regeneration.[16]

John MacArthur sums this up, speaking of John 17:

> Go to verse 6 and look at this phrase: "They were Yours. They were Yours."
>
> Who? "The men You gave Me. The men to whom I've manifested Your name; they were the ones You gave Me out of the world; they were Yours."
>
> Let me talk about that. "Before they were ever converted, before they were ever called, before they ever knew anything, before they ever believed, they were Yours—past tense—they were Yours." It's really a stunning statement.
>
> "They were in the world, and You gave them to Me out of the world, but they were Yours even when they were in the world."
>
> What is the world? The world is the evil anti-God, anti-Christ, satanically ruled system of evil and sin, composed of demons and all the unredeemed human beings who oppose God, who belong to satan, and who live in the kingdom of darkness. Within the realm of darkness, there are some sinners who belong to God. "They were Yours—"Were, not are, were"—even when they were in the world, they were Yours, and You gave them to Me out of the world."
>
> Back in chapter 15 and verse 18, our Lord said earlier that night, "If the world hates you, you know that it has hated Me before it hated you. If you were of the world, the world would love its own; but because you're not of the world,

but I chose you out of the world, because of this the world hates you."

"You were in the world. I chose you out of the world. God delivered you out of the world. When you were still in the world lost in sin, and darkness, and death, and ignorance, you were still God's. You were God's." Powerful reality.

In the thirteenth chapter of Acts, there's an illustration of this as Paul is ministering— Paul along with his companion Barnabas—and in the thirteenth chapter, they're on their early missionary journey. It says in verse 48, "When the Gentiles heard this," they heard from Isaiah that the Messiah was a Light to the nations, the Gentiles; bring salvation to the ends of the earth. "When the Gentiles heard this, they began rejoicing and glorifying the word of the Lord"—listen to this—"and as many as had been appointed to eternal life believed."

Did you get that? "As many as had been appointed to eternal life believed." They had been appointed to eternal life, that's why they believed. They had been appointed to eternal life before they believed.

Look at the 18th chapter of the book of Acts, and again, the ministry of Paul. The Lord comes to Paul in Corinth, down in verse 9, "And the Lord said to Paul in the night by a vision, 'Do not be afraid. Go on speaking; do not be silent,'" no matter what the threats were.

There were some serious threats earlier in the chapter. "Go on; for I Am with you, and no man will attack you in order to harm you, for I have many people in this city." There were people in the city of Corinth who belonged to Christ, who belonged to God. They were still in the world, in the darkness, in the ignorance of sin, but they belonged to God. How did they become God's? Ephesians 1:4 says, "He chose us before the foundation of the world, that we would be holy and blameless before Him."

Colossians 3:12 says, "We are those who have been chosen of God, holy and beloved."

Back to Ephesians 1:5–6, "He predestined us to adoption as sons through Jesus Christ to Himself, according to the kind intention of His will, to the praise of the glory of His grace, which He freely bestowed on us in the Beloved." Verse 11, "Predestined according to His purpose Who works all things after the counsel of His Own will, to the praise of His Own glory."

So God, for His Own glory, made an uninfluenced choice. He chose some people and they are His, even though they are not yet saved. They were predestined for justification, they were predestined for adoption, they were predestined for Heaven because they were chosen by God.

In 2 Thessalonians 2, verse 13, Paul says, "We should always give thanks to God for you, brethren beloved, because God has chosen you from the beginning for salvation." Those who believe in the Son of God, those who accepted the ministry of Jesus and believe in Him, did so because they are God's. They've always been God's. They were God's before there was a creation.

Revelation 13:8, 17:8, "Their names were written in the Book of Life before the foundation of the world."

Did you get that? "Their names were written in the Book of Life before the foundation of the world." God chose them before He ever created them. God wrote their names down. And Revelation 20:15 says, "If anyone's name was not found written in the Book of Life, he's thrown in the lake of fire."

"They were Yours; You gave them to Me, You gave them to Me." This is not new to us in the Gospel of John. Go back to chapter 6. Much earlier in our Lord's ministry, He made it clear to the disciples that anyone who came to salvation was a gift from the Father. Listen to John 6:37, "All that the Father gives Me will come to Me, and the one who comes to Me I will certainly not cast out, or reject." Verse 39, "This is the will of Him Who sent Me, that of all that He has given Me I lose none, but raise it up on the last day." Verse 40, "This is the will of My Father, that everyone who beholds the Son and believes in Him will have eternal life, and I Myself will raise him up on the last day."

In verse 44, "No one can come to Me unless the Father Who sent Me draws him; and I will raise Him up on the last day." And we've learned this through the years, the Father chooses; the Father writes names down before creation. There are people throughout all of human history who are born sinners in the world, engulfed in sin, spiritually dead and blind and ignorant, but they are God's; and in God's time, He plucks them out of the world, then they become love gifts to His Son. The Father chooses, the Father gives; the Son receives, the Son keeps, and the Son raises, and no one is lost. It's as if the Father gives a gift and it's up to the Son to protect the gift and bring that one to glory; that's John 6. "All that the Father gives to Me come to Me. My job is

to receive and not reject. My job is to guard and
keep and raise them all in the end to glory."

That then is the much more work of Christ,
the work of getting all of us through all the vicissitudes and issues of life, and all the battles with
sin and doubts and fears, to get us all to glory.
That's His intercessory, mediatorial ministry.
"You gave them to Me, and I'm going to get them
to glory."[17]

For some, this is sometimes still a challenging doctrine, but be
aware: it is entirely Biblically true doctrine, and "uncertainty about
election can only arise from some kind of self-righteousness."[18]
Uncertainty in election and predestination can only arise due to a
belief that you self-righteously have some degree of making yourself righteous before God; that you have some action-based influence on God's final decision concerning your holiness. This is simply
not true! As we have already touched on in Romans 5:6, 8, 10, and
Ephesians 2:5, when we were still weak, still sinners, still enemies of
God, and therefore still dead in our trespasses, Christ died for us, the
ungodly, so that we may be reconciled to God by the death of His
Son and justified by His blood, making us alive together with Christ.
It was all His work done for us while we were still lost and dead. As
Charles Spurgeon quips, "I'm glad God chose me before I was born.
Because if He saw me now He might change His mind!"

The benefits of this doctrine are so stagger-
ing as to be beyond words, but let me make an
attempt. The doctrine of sovereign election is the
most pride-crushing doctrine. It is pride-crushing because it's all of God. Spurgeon said, "I
know nothing, nothing again that is more humbling than this doctrine of election. I have sometimes fallen down before it when endeavoring
to understand it. But when I came near it, and
the one thought possessed me, God has from the

beginning chosen you unto salvation, I was staggered by the mighty thought and from the dizzy elevation came down my soul, broken, saying, 'Lord, I am nothing. I am less than worthy. Why me? Why me?'" Pride-crushing truth produces thanksgiving at its highest level.

Secondly, it is the most God-exalting doctrine. It gives all the glory to God. It declares that choice, regeneration, calling, faith, repentance, reconciliation, adoption, sanctification and glorification are all the work of God, Who, according to Psalm 110:3, made us willing in the day of His power, so that we all say, "Not unto us, O Lord, not unto us; but to Thy name give glory."

Thirdly, it is the most joy-producing doctrine. It brings the ultimate supreme joy. There's no hope of salvation apart from sovereign choice by God. Psalm 65:4 says, "Blessed is the man whom You choose and cause to approach You, that he may dwell in Your courts." What joy that God has set His love on us from eternity past and guaranteed it into eternity future. "I have loved you with an everlasting love" (Jer. 31:3).

It is the most privilege-granting doctrine. It grants us incomprehensible blessings, Ephesians 1:3, "Blessed with all spiritual blessings in the heavenlies in Christ Jesus," all spiritual blessings.

It is the most holiness prompting doctrine. It compels us to live holy. It is a holy calling. Again, Spurgeon said, "Nothing under the gracious influence of the Holy Spirit can make a Christian more holy than the thought that he is chosen. Shall I sin"—says Spurgeon—"after God has chosen me? Shall I transgress after such love? Shall I go astray after so much lovingkindness and tender mercy? No, my God. Since You have chosen me, I will love You, I will live for You. I will give myself to You, to You forever, solemnly consent to do Your service."

And finally, it is the most strength-giving doctrine. It makes us be at peace with every situation. And that's sort of where Paul lands at the end of the second chapter of 2 Thessalonians. "We should always give thanks to God for you, because God has chosen you for salvation, sanctification, calling, to gain the glory of our Lord Jesus Christ."[19]

What would you expect to see in the lives of the people who were laid hold of by this? We shouldn't expect to see a lot of bravado. A lot of talking about ourselves. A lot of explaining our Christian faith, always beginning in first person singular. But rather the explanation of our Christian faith that begins in the third person singular. It is not that I did this, but that He did that. How is it that you come to be here tonight? Push back through your whole journey. Push back and back and back, further and further. How far back can you go? I tell you eventually, you bow down on your knees and say, "This is the mystery of Godliness. That God in Christ reached out and laid hold of me." If our being in Christ is anchored in eternity then we have every reason to be confident that He will see us safely through time and bring us back into His eternal presence. Safe in the arms of Jesus, safe in His tender care.[20]

5

God's Sovereignty versus Man's Responsibility/Divine Election versus Free Will

If you were to now skip ahead to chapter 6, you would probably rule me out as a double-sided lunatic who can't pick which side of the fence to stay on. As I expressed at the end of the last chapter, I said that there are still some who have a problem resting in the doctrine of predestination and election, largely due to some self-righteous view that they themselves are responsible for their own salvation in part or in whole. In a negative sense, they may believe that they have done certain things in order to earn it or deserve it, that they have appropriated their own salvation in part or in whole by their own action, obedience, or merit. Or in a more positive sense, they may hold to the belief that though their actions and obedience played no part in it, they still made the decision in faith on their own while denying the predestined election of God.

This idea of man's choice or man's responsibility is also known as the issue of free will. A couple of the most common and straightforward passages that are used regarding this topic are found in the book of Acts and the letter to the Romans which reiterate each other by saying, "For everyone who calls upon the name of the Lord will be saved." Jeremiah 29:13 also backs this up, spoken from God's viewpoint, "You will seek Me and find Me, when you seek Me with all of your heart." Deuteronomy 4:29 says almost the exact same thing but from a second-person point of view, "You will seek the Lord your God and you will find Him, if you search after Him with all your heart and with all your soul." First Chronicles 28:9 and 2 Chronicles 15:2 both also reiterate these statements by saying, "If you seek Him, He will be found by you," and then they both add "but if you forsake Him, He will forsake you (2 Chron.)/ He will cast you off forever (1 Chron.)." And also, in 2 Chronicles 7:14, we are told, "If My people, who bear My name, will humble themselves, and pray and seek My face and turn from their wicked ways, then I will hear from Heaven and will forgive their sins and heal their land."

That all seems pretty straightforward and air-tight, but how do we associate that with everything we just studied in chapter 4? Well, first of all, both of those first two passages, Acts 2:21 and Romans 10:13, are quoted from the book of Joel chapter 2 verse 32 which fully reads, "And it shall come to pass that everyone who calls on the name of the Lord shall be saved. For in Mount Zion and in Jerusalem there shall be those who escape, as the Lord has said, and among the survivors shall be those whom the Lord calls." Wait a minute; that seems to contradict itself. The first part of that passage says, "Whoever calls on the name of the Lord," and the second half says "those whom the Lord calls." Which one is it?

Alistair Begg explains it this way:

> How then, have these blessings become ours? The answer is in vs 4 *(of Ephesians 1)*, "that He chose us in Him, that is in Christ, before the foundation of the world." In other words, our election in Christ is not some kind of historical afterthought. Actually, it is a resolve that goes all the way back into pre-eternity, into eternity before Creation. When you come to all this someone almost always inevitably says, "But wait a minute, I was the one that decided." What do you say to that?

You say, "Yes of course you did decide, but you never would have been able to decide if God did not first have decided on you before the creation of the world." So that when you push back and back and back, you eventually push back into the eternal councils of the will of God. How then do you reconcile eternal election, which God has done predestinating us to be conformed to the image of His Son, how do you reconcile that to the responsibility and the responsible action and decision of man? Some people say that you believe either in the sovereignty of God and reject the notion of man's responsibility, or you propound the responsibility and freedom of man and reject the sovereignty of God.

That's a bad idea. Someone else might say that you are to collapse the two of them into one another. So that you sort of believe in sovereignty and you sort of believe in responsibility and you sort of amalgamate them in that way. And what you are left with is a theological dog's breakfast. You can't do anything with it at all. It doesn't work or make sense. Well then, what are we going to do? Well, you believe both things. Because both things are taught. You believe them in their entirety. You don't believe them partially. You believe them entirely. Reconciling the fact that they are friends. Spurgeon was asked how he reconciles these things, and he said, "I don't. There is no need to reconcile friends."

So there is no need to spend much time toying with this as an intellectual exercise. Stott said, "It is not likely that we should discover a simple solution to a problem which has baffled the best brains of Christendom for centuries." The answer lies in God Himself. It is an antimony. They are

two self-existent truths that sit side by side, both
entirely true and yet, from a human perspective,
ultimately irreconcilable. That's why it calls for
us to bow down in wonder.[1]

Many people, as well as many great theologians, over the ages
have been challenged by the seemingly paradoxical issue of election/
predestination versus free will; or in other words, God's sovereignty
versus human responsibility. Many try to take one side or the other,
or worse yet, try to haphazardly, and might I add destructively, amalgamate the two, usually resulting in some form of incoherent mess or
mixture of the two. Both predestination—or commonly also known
as election as they are very similar in definition—and free will are
both found to be equally Biblical and equally true doctrines in the
Scriptures. This seems to be a complete paradox, you might say. But
who are we to question God's mind which is far beyond our capacity?

I personally do not want a god that I can completely understand. I do not want a god who is at my level because then, ultimately, what good is he to me? We have a God Who is infinitely
above all of Creation and therefore there are going to be things that
are incomprehensible and even paradoxical to us and that our feeble
minds cannot wrap our heads around. Just as we read from Scripture,
from Deuteronomy 29:29, "The secret things belong to the Lord our
God." And in Psalm 139:6, "Such knowledge is too wonderful for
me; it is high; I cannot attain it."

Also, in Romans 11:33–35, we see, "Oh, the depths of the
riches and wisdom and knowledge of God! How unsearchable are
His judgements and how inscrutable His ways!"

"For who has known the mind of the Lord, or who has been His
counselor (Isa. 40:13)?"

"Or who has given a gift to Him that he might be repaid (Job
41:11)?'"

There are many things about the Almighty, powerful, and
omniscient God that we simply cannot grasp and fathom with our
feeble minds. He is infinite and eternal and all-knowing; we are feeble, fickle, and sinfully fallen. Maybe Adam and Eve understood

these things when they were still in their created perfectness before the fall, but none of us are anywhere near that reality anymore, and we have to realize there are things that are true with God that we may not be able to even come close to fully grasping, but we take God's perfect knowledge and control in faith and trust that what He tells us in His Word is His pure and complete truth.

Both these doctrines are intrinsically found and taught as solid Biblical truth in the Scriptures without explanation or apology. And to raise a bit of thought, let me point out, do you believe in the Trinity? God the Father, Son, and Holy Spirit—one God, three in one. It also is beyond our mental capacity to fully grasp and understand that. How can three be one? One be three? But we unwaveringly accept it as Biblical and Spiritual truth in faith.

Ultimately, it is God's decision and calling that saves us (John 15:16; Acts 2:39, 13:48; Rom. 9:10–16; Heb. 12:2), but we have to accept (Acts 2:21, 13:48; Rom. 10:13; Joel 2:32 and John 6:37 show both sides of this topic), but you cannot do it without Him first drawing you and granting you the ability to come to Him (John 6:44, 65), which in itself is also a complete gift of God's grace (Eph. 2:8–10). It is our paradox, not God's!

John MacArthur explains the paradox in this way:

> But let me read, we left off our discussion of the conversation between Jesus and Nicodemus in the opening ten verses *(of John 3)* where Jesus talks to him about being born again, born from above. And we talked about the new birth. We talked about being born from above. It's a work of God; it's a divine work, a work of sovereign grace and sovereign power. It's a monergistic, unilateral work of God that's not a synthetic work where you have God participating with man. It's not some kind of coalescing of the will and power of man, with the will and power of God. It's a singular work of God by which He comes down from Heaven, irresistibly brings a

call—we call it an effectual call on the heart of a sinner—draws that sinner to Himself, regenerates that sinner, and then justifies that sinner, sanctifies that sinner and then glorifies that sinner *(Romans 8:29–30)*. It's a work of God. The new birth being born from above, in the very illustration of birth, makes the point because no one participates in his own birth. You didn't participate in your physical birth; you didn't participate in your spiritual birth. It is a work of God, a divine, creative miracle.

Salvation is not by grace and works, it is by grace alone—*sola gratia*. And it is appropriated not by works or any effort of man, but *sola fide*, "by faith alone" and for the final *sola, soli Deo gloria*, for "the glory of God alone."

So we're looking at *sola fide*, the aspect of salvation that declares that one is saved by faith alone, not by faith and works, "for by grace are you saved through faith, it is not of works." That's Ephesians 2:8 and 9. It is not of works. It is by faith alone. Or Romans 3, "No one is justified by behavior, by the deeds of the Law." Or Romans 4, "Abraham is justified by faith and not by works." Or Romans 10, "One is saved by believing in the resurrection of Christ and acknowledging His Lordship." The Word of God is crystal clear on that. I read earlier from Hebrews 10 an Old Testament statement, "The just shall live by faith." That is to say, justification comes by faith and faith alone. And we all know something of the history of that. That was the great discovery that Martin Luther made that launched the Reformation. And he was kind of the trigger point to get it rolling, and it roared against the Roman Catholic Church and Protestantism, named as a protest against Catholicism, was born and the true Gospel was recovered. Salvation comes by faith alone, not by faith plus works—by faith alone.

That is what John is saying in verses 11 to 21. He is telling Nicodemus and beyond Nicodemus using those plural pronouns, "I say to all of you," that is to anybody else who was standing there with Nicodemus, including His Own disciples, "And I say to all who will ever read this that you will be saved only by faith." Verse 15, "Whoever believes will have eternal life." Verse 16, "Whoever believes will not perish but have eternal life." Verse 18, "He who believes is not judged." It is about believing. It is about faith and faith alone.

This is consistent with John's purpose. If you remember, John gave his purpose at the end of his letter, John 20:31, "These have been written," meaning the entire Letter, the entire Gospel, "These have been written so that you may believe that Jesus is the Christ, the Son of God, and that believing you may have life in His name." John consistently says eternal life, that is, the forgiveness of sins, reconciliation to God, the hope of Heaven comes to those who believe. It is by faith alone.

Now what is so fascinating about this is the fact that it comes on the heels of verses 1 to 10. Just think about this. Jesus is talking to a non-believer. He's talking to a man who is in a defective, heretical, apostate religion. He is desiring to bring that man to a knowledge of the truth and consequently He says to him three times in this conversation, down through verse 11, "Truly, truly," which is a way of saying, "In contrast to all the error that fills your mind, error which you have learned and then taught as *the* teacher in Israel, "I want to tell you the truth. And the first truth I want you to understand is that salvation is a divine work that God does from Heaven down, that doesn't depend on you." We saw that. It's absolutely crystal clear in verses 1 to 10.

And then without any explanation, without any transition, our Lord takes the next part of the conversation, turns it into a monologue and says this, "Anyone can be saved who believes," and explains that in these verses. Anyone can be saved who believes. So on the one hand you have the doctrine of divine sovereignty. On the other hand you have the doctrine of human faith, human belief, or human responsibility. There are warnings that I just read you. If you don't believe, you'll be condemned. If you don't believe, you'll be judged, which means that if you don't believe, you're responsible for your unbelief, you will be held guilty, and you will be punished. This is human responsibility. Consequently, you need to believe. You need to believe and in believing in the Lord Jesus Christ the Son of God, you will not perish; you will have eternal life. So here is human responsibility, both negatively and positively. You will bear the full weight of judgment if you refuse to believe. On the other hand, if you will believe, eternal life waits for you no matter who you are.

So you have then as clear a presentation of sovereign salvation in verses 1 to 10 as anywhere in Scripture, and right against it you have a clear presentation of human responsibility. And the question that if I don't answer today, you will be asking in every verse, is how do those two things fit together? I've done questions and answers through the years in every place I've ever gone in the world, and every time there is an open question and answer session, I am asked this question: "How can salvation be solely a work of God and me be held responsible for believing or not believing? How can those two go together?"

Now I want to say this to you, first of all. Most people in doing evangelism would avoid that question all together, assuming that Christians who have been Christians for a long time don't even like to face that question. They would do everything they could to keep a non-believer in the dark about it, and they would be doing exactly the opposite of what Jesus did. Jesus is talking to a non-believer and He presents to him the twin parallel truths of divine sovereignty in salvation and human responsibility, and He does it at the very beginning of the conversation. This is a work of God, solely a work of God, but you will be held responsible if you do not believe, and you are called to believe and eternal life awaits you if you will believe. Those are twin truths that run parallel.

May I tell you? They will always run parallel. They will always run parallel. They will never come together. They will never intersect. They will never be diminished; legitimately, they are what they are. The fact that you don't understand how they go together only proves that you're less than you should be. It doesn't say anything about God. Your inability to harmonize those things is a reflection of your fallenness, my fallenness. People ask me all the time, "How do you harmonize those?" And my answer is, "I don't. I can't." They can't be harmonized in the human mind.

But realize this, you are a puny mind and so am I, and collectively we are puny compared to the infinite, vast, limitless mind of God. All I can tell you is that in the Word of God, these truths run parallel. And the answer is to believe them both with all your heart. And the one, divine sovereignty, will inform your worship and the other, human responsibility, will motivate your evangelism.

How could we be saying these things about you must believe, if you believe you can be saved, and make that square with what we already know about divine sovereignty in salvation? How do those things come together? They don't. I say it again, they are parallel truths, they are both true. I've been around a long time and I have seen every imaginable, every conceivable effort to harmonize those things done by people, well-intentioned people, very gifted people, well-known preachers, theologians, writers, commentators who tried to harmonize it. Anybody whoever tries to harmonize those two things destroys one or the other of them, or both of them. You can't change them, you can't tamper with them. You must be content to believe them both.

Now how can I help you to deal with that? I can't harmonize it. I can't bring it all together. I can't solve your dilemma. I can't answer the apparent paradox. So what am I left with? I want to make you comfortable with your inability not to get it. Okay? That's my objective. I just want you to be completely happy that you don't get it. Just put you to rest, stop fighting that. I want you to be comfortable with the fact that, wow, you just might not understand something. I know that's a big pill to swallow because of human pride, but get over it and be content not to get it.

Now I want you to understand that when the Bible deals with these things, it doesn't explain itself. It isn't self-conscious. These things are stated in Scripture as parallel realities and never really explained or harmonized because they both exist. And the fact that we can't understand them leaves us with one option, and that is to believe them both and be content with that.

Regarding Isaiah 10:5ff. God says I'm going to judge Assyria, and then He identifies Assyria as the rod of His anger and the staff of His indignation. In other words, Assyria is a weapon in the hands of God. Assyria... God is picking up Assyria like a weapon, to use Assyria to unleash His wrath against Israel. And that's what He did. Assyria was God's tool. Then you come to verse 7, most interesting. I'm going to use Assyria to do this and this is not Assyria's plan. This is not what Assyria is choosing, this is what I am choosing for Assyria to do. This is not Assyria's intent. This is not its plan. Assyria has its plan, but I have My plan, and I without their planning it, or intending to do it, I'm going to pick them up and use them as My weapon.

Well, this is amazing. Assyria has no intention of doing this. God literally, sovereignly picks them up, drives them at Israel to accomplish His will, and then He says in verse 5, "Woe to Assyria." Woe to Assyria, a nation to be destroyed for doing something they didn't choose to do, doing something they didn't plan to do, doing something that was not their intention to do. Assyria had its own plans. God had different plans. But Assyria will be destroyed. This is an amazing juxtaposing. God punishes a nation for doing what God picked them up and made them do. There's no explanation. There's no way to harmonize those things. Full responsibility for pride fell on the king of Assyria. Full responsibility for evil intention and massacre fell on Assyria. Even though they were acting by divine decree, they bore full responsibility for what they did. This again is an illustration of those parallel realities: human responsibility and divine sovereignty. And they will always run parallel, and they will always have to be understood that way. Sinners bear the full weight of responsibility for their acts of defiance against God, even when God is using them to accomplish His purposes. And yet all things are decreed and determined by God as to their final end.

Let me take you into the New Testament, for a moment. Turn to Matthew chapter 11, and this may be a little more on point. Matthew chapter 11, verse 27, this is a verse on divine sovereignty. "All things have been handed over to Me by My Father." Now listen, "And no one knows the Son except the Father, nor does anyone know the Father except the Son and anyone to whom the Son wills to reveal Him." Did you see that? The only one who knows the Son is the one to whom the Son wills to reveal Him. You can't know Christ if He doesn't will for you to believe in Him. If He doesn't will you to know Him. Well, that's verse 27, strong on divine, sovereign, determined purpose. You can't know the Son unless the Son wills you to know Him.

And then verse 28, what does it say? "Come to Me all who are weary and heavy laden and I will give you rest." How can that be? He just said that no one can come unless the Son reveals Him Himself. How can you say that? But that's all over the Bible. They're those two parallel realities, those twin truths again. On the one hand, the sovereign purpose of God; on the other hand, an open offer: "Come to Me all who are weary, heavy-laden, and I will give you rest. Take My yoke upon you, learn from Me. I'm gentle and humble in heart. You'll have rest for your souls for My yoke is easy, My burden is light." You have this firm statement about no one being able to know Christ unless it is revealed to him from above. And then you have an immediate plea from the heart of Christ for anyone and everyone to come.

Turn to John 6, one of the really great chapters in Scripture. But in John 6 we can pick it up at verse 35, Jesus says, feed the multitude; then He taught about the Bread of Life, about Himself being the Bread of Life. In verse 35 He said, "I Am the Bread of Life, he who comes to Me will not hunger. He who believes in Me will never thirst." So if you have spiritual hunger and spiritual thirst, that can be remedied and answered by coming to Christ. What does that mean? It means believing. Verse 35 is one of those "whoever"—"He who believes in Me, whoever believes in Me will never thirst. I said to you, 'You have seen Me and yet do not believe.'" You don't believe. Your problem is, you've seen Me, you've heard Me. I just created food to feed 20 to 25 thousand of you. I've been teaching you. I've said all this. Your problem—you don't believe; you don't believe.

And then He says in verse 37, look at this: "All that the Father gives Me will come to Me."

And He goes from the failure to believe to divine
sovereignty. You won't believe, you won't come.
And then He immediately says, "All that the
Father gives Me will come to Me." And, by the
way, in verse 40 He says, "This is the will of God,
My Father, that everyone who beholds the Son
and believes in Him will have eternal life." It goes
back and forth from divine sovereignty to human
responsibility. It goes from new birth, regeneration as a work of God, the Father chooses, the
Father draws, the Father gives to the Son, the Son
receives, the Son keeps and loses none. That's the
divine side. And it just moves easily without an
explanation to the reality that anyone, whoever
believes, may have eternal life. Down in verse 44,
"No man can come to Me unless the Father Who
sent Me draws him." Well, you can't come unless
the Father draws you, and yet verse 45, "Everyone
who has heard and learned from the Father comes
to Me." That seems to support the idea that this is
a divine work of God. In fact, verse 46, "Not that
anyone has seen the Father except the One Who is
from the Father, He has seen the Father." And this
is talking about the divine side. "You can't know
the Son, you can't know the Father, you can't know
eternal life in Them unless God draws you, unless
God calls you, and yet, verse 47, "Truly, truly I
say to you, he who believes has eternal life." It's
a matter of believing. Verse 57, "As the living
Father sent Me and I live because of the Father, so
he who eats Me, he also will live because of Me."
All you have to do is receive Christ, take Christ
in and you'll have eternal life. Down in verse 63,
it is the Spirit Who gives life. That's regeneration.
That's John 3:1 to 10; it's the new birth, the regeneration born from above. It's the Spirit Who gives

life. And yet verse 64, "There are some of you who do not believe." There are some of you who do not believe, that's your problem. And as a result of that, verse 66, "Many of His disciples withdrew and weren't walking with Him anymore, so Jesus said to the Twelve, 'You do not want to go away also, do you? Simon Peter answered Him, 'Lord, to whom shall we go? You have the words of eternal life, we have believed and have come to know that You're the Holy One of God.'"

Back and forth from the sovereign choice of God, the sovereign revelation of the Father and the Son, the sovereign work of the Spirit Who gives life to believing and not believing. Those things are side-by-side in Scripture everywhere. Two parallel truths to be affirmed if not fully comprehended.

In the second chapter of the book of Acts, there is another one of these illustrations where Peter is preaching on the Day of Pentecost, and he indicts the Jews for rejecting Christ and crucifying Christ. He says, "Men of Israel, listen to these words," Acts 2:22, "Jesus the Nazarene, a Man attested to you by God with miracles and wonders and signs which God performed through Him in your midst, just as you yourselves know, this Man delivered over by the predetermined plan and foreknowledge of God, you nailed to a cross and put Him to death."

Yes, by the predetermined plan and foreknowledge of God, and yet full responsibility on the part of those who rejected Him and took His life.

From Hosea, verse 2:23, "I'll call those who were not My people My people." I'll make that call. I'll make that decision. That's a sovereign decision made by God. That is the most strong section of the New Testament (Rom. 9:25) on the sovereignty of God in choosing people for salvation.

You see, faith, verse 17 (Rom. 10), comes from hearing the Word concerning Christ. So what's our responsibility? Climb into an ivory tower and try to find a solution to these two parallel truths? To try to find a way to resolve the apparent paradox? To try to catapult ourselves to the level of the mind of infinite God? No. Our responsibility is to recognize this. We have been given a command and a commission to go into all the world and preach the Gospel to every creature because anyone who believes can be saved. Anyone who believes will be saved. "Anyone who comes to Me," Jesus said in John 6, "I will never turn away." The only way people can come to Him and believe is if they hear. The only way they can hear is if we go and tell them.

In the end, the final word, and it's a magnificent one, comes in Romans at the close of chapter 11. Verse 33, now we know what our mission is, to go to the world and preach the Gospel, to be the preachers who are sent, to tell the truth so people can hear, believe and be saved. But this is where the final resolution comes, verse 33, Romans 11. This is Paul, and Paul understood these two parallel truths, certainly as well as any human being could understand them. And he says this, "O the depth of the riches both of the wisdom and knowledge of God." The first thing to acknowledge is this, what God knows and what God understands is vastly beyond us. It is at a depth we cannot fathom. In fact, he says, how unsearchable are His judgments and unfathomable His ways.

Can you take the instruction from that? You cannot understand these two things and how they harmonize in the mind of God. You never will understand them in this life. They are unsearchable and unfathomable. There are plenty of people who would like to give God a little advice and their idea of harmonizing these. But the problem is in verse 34, "Who knows the mind of the Lord and who became His counselor." Do you think God's waiting for you to give Him some hints on how He can simplify? Who do you think you are? You don't know the mind of the Lord. You can't even come close. You're not going to counsel Him.

Furthermore, in verse 35, He's not obligated to you to give you any more information than you have. "Who has first given to Him that it might be paid back to Him again." Do you think God owes you something? You think He owes you an explanation? No, in the end, "from Him, through Him, to Him are all things," we put them there and we leave them there. To Him be the glory forever, Amen.

I live my life believing both of those things, but the one that puts the responsibility on me is *sola fide*; divine sovereignty puts no responsibility on me. Faith and believing puts all the responsibility on me, to believe, to not be left in unbelief, and to proclaim a message so that others can hear and also believe.[2]

John MacArthur also mentions this paradox in his book, *Saved Without a Doubt*, where he says:

The paradox of the sovereign work of God and the responsibility of believers is common in Scripture. Believers are saved because God chose

126

them before creation (Eph. 1:4), yet they are not saved without exercising faith (Rom. 10:9–10). They are secure because of the covenant faithfulness of God, but they are still responsible to persevere. Eternal security is wrought through the power of the Spirit in energizing the true believer to endure all trials.[3]

Christian theologian and renowned author, J. I. Packard, discusses this topic in his book, *Evangelism and the Sovereignty of God*, and says this:

What is true is that all Christians believe in divine sovereignty, some are not aware they do, and mistakenly insist and demand that they reject it. What causes this odd state of affairs? The root cause is the same as in most cases of error in the church. The intrusion of rationalistic speculation, the passion for systematic consistency, a reluctance to recognize the existence of mystery and let God be wiser than men, and the consequent subjecting of Scripture to the supposed demands of human logic. People see that the Bible teaches man's responsibility for his actions. They do not see how this is consistent with the sovereign Lordship of God over those actions. They are not content to let the two truths live side by side as they do in the Scripture, but they jump to the conclusion that in order to uphold the Biblical truth of human responsibility they are bound to reject the equally Biblical and equally true doctrine of divine sovereignty, and explain away the great number of texts that teach it. The desire to oversimplify the Bible by cutting out the mystery is natural to our perverse minds, it is not surprising that even good men should fall victim to it, hence this persistence and troublesome dispute. The irony of the situation, however, is that whenever we ask how the two sides pray, it seems apparent that those who profess to deny God's sovereignty really believe it just as strongly as those who affirm it.

Oftentimes, people will try to simplify and categorize this issue of election versus free will or God's sovereignty versus man's responsibility into two categories known as Calvinism and Arminianism.

Calvinism and Arminianism are two systems of theology that attempt to explain the relationship between God's sovereignty and man's responsibility in the matter of salvation. Calvinism is named for John Calvin, a French theologian who lived from 1509–1564. Arminianism is named for Jacobus Arminius, a Dutch theologian who lived from 1560–1609.

Both systems can be summarized with five points. Calvinism holds to the total depravity of man while Arminianism holds to partial depravity. Calvinism's doctrine of total depravity states that every aspect of humanity is corrupted by sin; therefore, human beings are unable to come to God on their own accord. Partial depravity states that every aspect of humanity is tainted by sin, but not to the extent that human beings are unable to place faith in God of their own accord. Note: classical Arminianism rejects "partial depravity" and holds a view very close to Calvinistic "total depravity" (although the extent and meaning of that depravity are debated in Arminian circles). In general, Arminians believe there is an "intermediate" state between total depravity and salvation. In this state, made possible by prevenient grace, the sinner is being drawn to Christ and has the God-given ability to choose salvation.

Calvinism includes the belief that election is unconditional, while Arminianism believes in conditional election. Unconditional election is the view that God elects individuals to salvation based entirely on His will, not on anything inherently worthy in the individual. Conditional election states that God elects individuals to salvation based on His foreknowledge of who will believe in Christ unto salvation, thereby on the condition that the individual chooses God.

Calvinism sees the atonement as limited, while Arminianism sees it as unlimited. This is the most controversial of the five points. Limited atonement is the belief that Jesus only died for the elect. Unlimited atonement is the belief that Jesus died for all, but that His death is not effectual until a person receives Him by faith.

Calvinism includes the belief that God's grace is irresistible, while Arminianism says that an individual can resist the grace of God. Irresistible grace argues that when God calls a person to salvation, that person will inevitably come to salvation. Resistible grace states that God calls all to salvation, but that many people resist and reject this call.

Calvinism holds to perseverance of the saints while Arminianism holds to conditional salvation. Perseverance of the saints refers to the concept that a person who is elected by God will persevere in faith and will not permanently deny Christ or turn away from Him. Conditional salvation is the view that a believer in Christ can, of his/her own free will, turn away from Christ and thereby lose salvation. Note—many Arminians deny "conditional salvation" and instead hold to "eternal security."

So, in the Calvinism vs. Arminianism debate, who is correct? It is interesting to note that in the diversity of the body of Christ, there are all sorts of mixtures of Calvinism and Arminianism. There are five-point Calvinists and five-point Arminians, and at the same time three-point Calvinists and two-point Arminians. Many believers arrive at some sort of mixture of the two views. Ultimately, it is our view that both systems fail in that they attempt to explain the unexplainable. Human beings are incapable of fully grasping a concept such as this. Yes, God is absolutely sovereign and knows all. Yes, human beings are called to make a genuine decision to place faith in Christ unto salvation. These two facts seem contradictory to us, but in the mind of God they make perfect sense.[4]

When asked to discuss Calvinism vs. Arminianism at a Q&A session several years ago, John MacArthur was recorded as saying,

Let me do it this way, I'm gonna give you a little test. Do you believe that God is sovereign in salvation? Of course, we went through that today. Do you believe God chooses who will be saved? Of course. Do you believe the Father draws? Yes. Do you believe that the Son keeps? Yes. Do you believe the Son raises? Yes. It's all sovereign, it's all predestined, it's all established, absolutely right. This is what the Bible says. Uhh, do you believe that whosoever will may come? Yes. That's what the Bible says. Do you believe that God finds no pleasure in the death and judgement of the wicked? Yes. Do you believe that Jesus wept because sinners wouldn't repent? Of course. Are you willing to call all sinners to repent, and do you believe they're responsible if they don't come? Yes. Well, how do you harmonize that? I don't know. I don't know how to harmonize that. Well, you're asking too much of me; I'm not God. You want my little peanut, pea, pusillanimous brain to grasp that? Give me a break! It's not my problem. But, the one thing I can't do is deny what Scripture says.

This will comfort you. Who wrote Romans? This is basic Christianity 101 here. Who wrote Romans? Can't answer the question can you? Why? All of Paul. All his vocabulary. All his heart. All his thoughts. All his words. All of God. And yet not mechanical.

Since you did so well on that question, I'll ask you another one. Who lives your Christian life? God? So you wanna hold Him responsible for the condition of your Christian life? Who lives your Christian life? This is pretty basic, right? You're doing it right now. Everyday. Who's living your Christian life? You say, "I am." Really? You say, "God is." I don't know whether you could convince everybody who knows you. You can't even answer that question. Listen to what Paul said, "I am crucified with Christ, nevertheless, I live, yet, not I." He didn't know either.

This is the divine mystery. It's all of me and all of Him, and what's wrong is me and what's right is Him. In every major doctrine of the Bible, in every major doctrine, you have an apparent paradox that you cannot resolve. I know that I'm kept eternally, secured by God, but I also know I'm commanded to persevere in faith. Two sides of the same thing. I know I can't be saved unless I'm chosen and called, and I know I can't be saved unless I'm willing to repent and believe. I don't have to harmonize it. But, nor can I deny those things. And in the end, mark it folks, in the end, God will get all the glory for every righteous thing that is done, because it is all His work.

So, rather than answering the question by removing your confusion I just spread your confusion over a wider area. And you rest in the fact that you don't need to grasp the mysteries that are clear in the mind of eternal God.

American composer, George W. Chadwick, in the hymn entitled "I Sought the Lord," eloquently states it this way, "I sought the Lord and afterward, I knew that He moved my soul to seek Him, seeking me. It was not I that found oh Savior true, I was found by Thee."

It is ultimately God's calling us and electing us by His grace leading us to Him that saves us (John 6:44–45; Acts 13:48). We do have to accept this free gift (John 6:47; Rom. 10:9–10, 13), but our faith in Him in order to accept is also a free gift of His grace (Eph. 2:8–9). Essentially, it is all His doing leading to our salvation (Rom. 8:29–30); therefore, He gets all the credit and glory for any and all acceptance (Eph. 2:8b), yet if we choose to reject Him, that fault rests on our own shoulders (John 3:18b).

These are two truths, both plainly taught throughout Scripture, that run parallel and that will always run parallel and that we as humans with feeble minds will never be able to marry together. To try, you will always end up damaging or destroying one or both of these Biblical doctrines. Our only option is to take God at His Word and believe both as entirely true (Joel 2:32; Matt. 11:27–28; John 6:37, 44–47), knowing that God is omniscient and so far beyond our mental capacity. We do not need to understand how they fit together; we take that in faith, knowing that God is in complete control, and His will is perfect (Rom. 8:28).

A. W. Tozer says of this:

> If all this appears self-contradictory—amen, be it so. The various elements of truth stand in personal antithesis, sometimes requiring us to believe apparent opposites while we wait for the moment when we shall know as we are known. Then truth which now appears to be in conflict with itself will arise in shining unity and it will be seen that the conflict has not been in the truth but in our sin-damaged minds. In the meantime, our inner fulfillment lies in loving obedience to the commandments of Christ and the inspired admonitions of His apostles.[5]

My suggestion would be to take Pastor John MacArthur's advice and live your life wholeheartedly believing both, but live your life intentionally pursuing the one aspect of this paradox that places responsibility on us. We have no influence over God and His sovereign control; it is a gracious gift given to us through His Son but *Sola Fide*, by Faith Alone, places responsibility on us. To place our faith in Christ, to not be found or left in unbelief, and to follow the Great Commission of Christ at the end of Matthew, to go and proclaim the Gospel and the Message of Christ so that others can hear of God's love and Word and Truth and of salvation only through Christ and may also come to Him in belief in order to be saved—in that sense, you become a sovereign vessel of God's grace divinely leading others into saving faith in Him.

6

Man's Responsibility:
Faith/Belief/Acceptance/Surrender

In the last chapter, we dealt with the paradox of God's sovereignty versus man's responsibility. Again, these two concepts are both entirely Biblically true and accurate, yet to us, they run parallel to each other and cannot be married together; and therefore, we are left trusting in God, not being able to fully understand how two seemingly opposite concepts can both be fully true. We have already seen in past chapters that we are entirely fallen and depraved and fall far short of the demands of a perfect and holy God and are incapable of being holy and righteous by ourselves by any form of obedience (only absolute 100 percent perfect obedience would be acceptable) or religious performance and are, therefore, in desperate need of a Savior.

We have also determined that it is ultimately God which has known us from past eternity, predestined us from past eternity, chosen us, and called us and led us to Himself. These are the doctrines of total depravity followed by God's sovereignty and election in our salvation. So where and how does man's responsibility come into play? We may also go back and ask the questions we have previously asked, "How do I receive salvation so that I may be saved and be with God in Heaven? What is my part in all of this?"

God has foreknown me. He has predestined me. He has chosen me. He has called me. He has hung on the cross, bearing every single one of my sins that I have ever committed and ever will commit. He died in my place, taking on and paying the penalty that I deserved. Some of the last words He spoke while on the cross just before His death were, "It is finished" (John 19:30)!

In the original written Greek of the New Testament, the word Jesus spoke here as He willingly (John 10:18) gave up His spirit and succumbed to death was *tetelestai*. In *Strong's Exhaustive Concordance*, it is defined to mean "not merely to terminate a thing, but to carry out a thing to the full."

> Literally translated the word *tetelestai* means, "It is finished." The word occurs in John 19:28 and 19:30 and these are the only two places in the New Testament where it occurs. In 19:28 it is translated, "After this, when Jesus knew that all things *were now completed*, in order that the Scripture might be fulfilled, He said, "I thirst." Two verses later, He utters the word Himself: "Then when He received the sour wine Jesus said, 'It is finished,' and He bowed His head and gave up His spirit."
>
> The word *tetelestai* was also written on business documents or receipts in New Testament times to show indicating that a bill had been paid in full. The *Greek-English Lexicon* by Moulton and Milligan says this: "Receipts are often introduced by the phrase [sic] *tetelestai*, usually written in an abbreviated manner" (p. 630). The connection between receipts and what Christ accomplished would have been quite clear to John's Greek-speaking readership; it would be unmistakable that Jesus Christ had died to pay for their sins.[1]

So we see that every demand of justice has been paid in full. He took every sin and failure to the cross and then to the grave and buried it with Himself. He willingly gave up His life for this purpose. In John 10:18, Jesus Himself tells us, speaking of His Own life, "No one takes it from Me, but I lay it down of My Own accord. I have authority to lay it down, and I have authority to take it up again. This charge I have from My Father." And He also then rose from that same grave, defeating death, resurrecting back to life, and therefore became victorious over temptation, sin, death, hell, satan, all evil, etc., and lives to never be affected by it again. And since He did all of this, Himself being innocent, in place of us, He offers this same gift of victory over sin, death, and hell to each one of us if we acknowledge His substitution in our place. What an amazing gift! There is no greater gift given by anyone in all of history! So how is this gift made ours?

> There is no way to recognize Jesus Christ for Who He is apart from a miracle of God to open spiritually blind eyes. But when Christ opens the eyes of a soul, suddenly truth becomes recognizable. Faith is the necessary compliment to the Sovereignty of God. Though divine initiative is ultimately responsible for redemption—although men and women are elected, predestined, chosen before the foundation of the world—there will still be on our part the submissive response of personal faith in Jesus Christ.[2]

In this chapter, I am going to list many verses that coincide with the doctrine of man's responsibility, but I am going to start off here with what is probably the most well-known and maybe even the most popular verse in all of Scripture. I am talking about John 3:16. These are Jesus's Own words, and He is directly telling us how to get to Heaven. In John 3:16, Jesus states, "For God so loved the world that He gave His one and only Son, that whoever believes in Him will not perish but have eternal life." Martin Luther called this "The Gospel in a nutshell."

The word *gospel* means "good news" and refers to the good news of Jesus Christ and our salvation through Him to eternal life in His Heavenly presence. John Piper, in an interview on the topic of the Gospel, once stated, "The Gospel is the news that Jesus Christ, the Righteous One, died for our sins and rose again, eternally triumphant over all His enemies, so that there is now no condemnation for those who believe, but only eternal joy."

We are all fallen sinners, in need of a Savior, and Jesus Christ played that substitutionary role perfectly as our propitiation and set us free from the bondage of sin and death. John 3:16 sums up beautifully the entire Gospel of Jesus Christ. Stephen Daly, a professor of practical theology, graduate from Dallas Seminary, and a pastor/teacher who preaches at Colonial Baptist Church, a church that he planted in Cary, North Carolina, describes it this way:

> John 3:16 says, "For God so loved the world that He"—what?—"**He gave** His one and only Son that whoever believes in Him will not perish but have everlasting life." That verse tells us several things about the gift-giving pattern of God. First of all, that the gift of God was freely supplied, "for God so loved the world that <u>He gave</u>!"
>
> Like a present under a Christmas tree or beside a birthday cake there are no price tags for the receiver. There's no comment about paying up later. It's a free gift, provided for by the giver. The gift is free. Paul wrote in chapter 6 of Romans verse 23, "The wages of sin is death, but the free gift of God"—is what?—"is eternal life through Jesus Christ our Lord."
>
> I have asked many people over the years as I have explained to them the nature of the Gospel and the definition of salvation, I have illustrated as I held my Bible toward them, and I have said to them, "Suppose that I told you that this Bible was a gift from me to you. I wanna give it to

you. What would you have to do to receive it and make it yours? Why you'd simply have to reach out and take it, right? But what if while you were reaching I pulled it back and said, 'You know, my truck, needs a good wash and a wax, and uh, what do you think?' Well, if you washed and waxed my truck would this be a free gift? No! You'd be my favorite church member but this would not be a free gift. If you paid me a dollar for this Bible it would not be a free gift. If you paid me a penny? No!"

While going to the assembly or church is commanded in Hebrews 10:25, while giving money to the cause of Christ is commanded in 1 Corinthians 16:2, while getting baptized with water is commanded, that is the church to fulfill that command, in Matthew 28:19, while these things are things you do for God because you are commanded to do them if you want to be obedient, salvation is only offered to those who do not fulfill demands but to those who cannot fulfill demands. They are wonderful things you do for God not to get it, but because you have it! Be careful that you don't confuse the evidences of salvation and obedience and the prerequisites to salvation. The gift of God is free of any work on the part of man, because it is based upon the finished work of Christ.

The second thing about the gift-giving of God is that it is personally self-sacrificing. Eternal life to you is free because Jesus Christ paid it all. He did everything. He hung on the cross and He paid the penalty for your lust, your covetousness, your pride, your hypocrisy, your infidelity, your dishonesty. Peter wrote "He bore in His Own body our sins on the tree" (1 Pet. 2:24).

He paid the infinite penalty for an infinite number of sins over an infinite period of time. Being the God-man He could compress all of infinity into a matter of three days and three nights. So He came and when He was born on earth, God in the flesh, it was a statement to mankind that mankind was inadequate. So Joseph heard the angel in a dream when he came to him saying there would be a baby born and He would save His people from all of their sins. In other words, mankind could not save itself from its sins. The birth of that baby was just another way of saying that man was totally unable to save himself. And while it announced that, at the same time it announced that while man was unable God had chosen to intervene on behalf of man. His gifts were personally self-sacrificing.

The third thing about God's gift is that it was eternally significant. Eternally significant. "Whoever believes in Him will not perish but have"—what—"everlasting life." This is the way in which God gives gifts. And for a man who desires to be Godly or God-like in the giving of gifts, his gifts will mirror those kinds of characteristics.[3]

We have already established that by works of the law no one will be saved. We have already seen that God's gift of redemption and salvation is a free gift. Romans 5 and 6 repeat this over and over—free gift, free gift, free gift. We will retouch later on what is unnecessary for salvation, but what is necessary? How do we receive this free gift? Just like the analogy that Stephen Davey just gave us, if I was to offer you a Christmas present or birthday present, a free gift for some special occasion, and upon handing it to you I drew it back and said that you owe me something in order to receive it or that you must do something or perform something in order to receive it, is that gift a "free gift?" Of course not! There is some type of payment, monetary, physical or whatever, necessary in order to receive it. That is not free!

God's gift to us is a "free gift" (Rom. 5:15, 16, 17, 6:23). Imagine it this way: upon handing you the gift you pulled out your wallet and said, "Wow, thank you! Here's $20. Does that cover it?" Or, "Wow, thank you! I'm going to clean your house to deserve this gift." Or, "Wow, thank you! I'm going to go take a shower, clean myself up, and I am going to follow you around and do everything you tell me to do for a while so that I feel like I have earned and deserve this gift, and in order to obtain this gift."

Does any of that make sense to you either? Of course not! A gift is a gift! A free gift is a free gift! It is given to you free of any charge whatsoever. To have God offer you the free gift of salvation through the death and sacrifice of His Son and to then say, "Here, let me pay You back, let me do this for You, let me obey You, let me earn it or deserve it through whatever means, let me perform some ritual, let me feel like I have obtained it through my own actions" nullifies the entire work of Christ on the cross and His resurrection! Just as in receiving the Christmas present I handed you, you simply need to reach out and accept it. You don't need to earn it or even deserve it or obey in order to obtain it. It is given to you completely free of charge.

Now, before someone tries to take this too lightly, let's dig deeper. Unlike the Christmas present analogy, where you simply reach out and grab with your hands, accepting the gift of salvation is a wholehearted surrender to Christ as Lord and Savior. Accepting the gift of salvation is realizing that you are a wretched, sinful, and helpless and spiritually dead sinner (going back to the issue of total depravity) and absolutely hopeless without the deliverance of a Savior, and that you simply cannot by any means of your own enter into Heaven and the perfect holiness and presence of a perfect, just, and righteous God. It is wholeheartedly relying on what Christ did in our place to pay our price, to justify us before God, fulfilling the payment necessary for our penalty, and acknowledging that it is only through His work, and none of our own, that we are permitted entrance into eternity with Him.

As we have already discussed, you cannot do enough or be good enough or perform well enough to be perfect and fulfill the entire law perfectly, which holiness demands—perfect obedience. We are saved entirely by His perfect sacrifice as the propitiation for our sins. Our part in this is complete surrender to this beautiful truth. Throwing aside every desire to achieve it through some means or merit of our own. We certainly don't deserve it. There's no possible way we can earn it. We added nothing to it, we can do nothing to enhance it; we are entirely at the grace and mercy of Christ's perfect substitution.

Again, Christ stated, "It is finished!" He did not say, "It is finished…as long as you do this or that, or achieve a certain status, perform a certain task, clean yourself up, obey Me in a certain area, or pay some price." There are absolutely no payment options! Why? Because it is entirely a "free gift!"

Oswald Chambers speaks of this in one of his devotionals, when he says:

> A pitiful, sickly, and self-centered kind of prayer and a determined effort and selfish desire to be right with God are never found in the New Testament. The fact that I am trying to be right with God is actually a sign that I am rebelling against the atonement by the cross of Christ. I pray, "Lord, I will purify my heart if You will answer my prayer—I will walk rightly before You if You will help me." But I cannot make myself right with God; I cannot make my life perfect. I can only be right with God if I accept the atonement of the Lord Jesus Christ as an absolute gift. Am I humble enough to accept it? I have to surrender all my rights and demands and cease from every self-effort. I must leave myself completely alone in His hands. Jesus is not just beginning to save us—He has already saved us completely. It is an accomplished fact, and it is an insult to Him for us to ask Him to do what He has already done.[4]

Romans 10:9–10 says, "If you confess with your mouth that Jesus is Lord and believe in your heart that God raised Him from the dead, you will be saved. For with the heart one believes and is justified, and with the mouth one confesses and is saved."

It is entirely an issue of the heart. It is entirely an issue of confession and surrender and turning away from sin, which is repentance to the One Who did do everything necessary to justify you in front of God. He performed everything, He earned it, He deserved it, He accomplished all necessities, He fulfilled the law perfectly, He did absolutely everything that needed to be done to gain your entrance into Heaven, He made it possible entirely through His Own work without a single milligram of help from you! He alone is the Messiah, and He needed no help from any of us. His work is complete. "It is finished!"

All you have to "do"—all you can "do"—is to realize that you can't "do" anything. It is to bow at His feet and acknowledge Him as your passport into Heaven. Only through Him. Only by Him. "If you confess with your mouth that Jesus is Lord and believe in your heart that God raised Him from the dead, you will be saved. For with the heart one believes and is justified, and with the mouth one confesses and is saved." R. C. Sproul adds:

> What Paul was speaking of here was a righteousness that God, in His grace, was making available to those who would receive it passively, not those who would achieve it actively; but that would receive it by faith and by which a person could be reconciled to a holy and righteous God.

Let me quickly dispel another possible misunderstanding. It is not just a simple act of believing in Jesus that He was a real person, that He was Who He said He was and performed miracles and stuff and died on the cross. "For even the demons believe—and shudder" (James 2:19)! The demons, the fallen angels, were once with the Triune God in Heaven. They know the truth of the Trinity. They knew and believed Jesus was Who He said He was, but they still hated Him and would not surrender to Him as Lord and Savior, and therefore, they are lost. It is not an issue of "simple" belief but of wholehearted surrender to the Lordship and "Saviorship" of Jesus Christ.

This type of surrender is also taught to us by Jesus's Own words. In Matthew 16:24–25 (and also Mark 8:34–35; Luke 9:23–24), He tells us, "If anyone wishes to come after Me, he must deny himself, and take up his cross daily and follow Me. For whoever wishes to save his life will lose it; but whoever loses his life for My sake and the Gospel's will save it." This speaks of total surrender and commitment to Jesus. Back when Jesus spoke these words, the image of the cross was not an image of salvation and loving gracious sacrifice; it was a brutal and horrific symbol of torture and death, through crucifixion, from which the word *excruciating* was given birth. So for Jesus to say "you must carry your cross" forced the image of commitment even to excruciating death—total abandon and surrender to Christ no matter what! "Whoever loses his life for My sake will save it."

Once again, surrender to Christ at all costs, no matter the outcome. Christ demanded that this be taught as part of the message of the Gospel that was to be proclaimed to others. Jesus also taught in Luke chapter 14 verses 26–27 that, "If anyone comes to Me and does not hate his own father and mother and wife and children and brothers and sisters, yes, even his own life, he cannot be My disciple. Whoever does not bear his own cross and come after Me cannot be My disciple."

And verse 14:33, He says, "Any one of you that does not renounce all that he has cannot be My disciple."

This image of complete surrender could not be any more clear. We must surrender all that we have, including family and even ourselves entirely to God, and carry our cross, even to death if that is where God leads. This is what true saving belief and faith in Jesus Christ consists of. Not "simply" believing He is Lord and Savior but surrendering your entire existence on this fact. "Faith is the confident and continuous confession of total dependence on and trust in Jesus Christ for the necessary requirement to enter God's Kingdom. And that requirement is the righteousness of Christ, which God imputes to every believer."[5]

The Amplified Holy Bible puts it this way in 2 Timothy 1:5, "Faith [the surrendering of your entire self to God in Christ with absolute confident trust in His power, wisdom and goodness]." Also, just for the sake of possible misinterpretation, Jesus is not saying in 14:26–27 that we need to emotionally hate and despise and disconnect from our family, not caring for them at all, but what these statements mean is that our love and dedication to Christ should infinitely outweigh our love and relation to our family that in comparison our love for family almost looks like hatred. It is a far lesser form of love than our love and commitment to Christ.

God loves and created the family structure. He is not here reversing and telling us to discard the family structure but instead that our devotion to family pales in comparison to our complete even-to-death devotion to our Savior. He must be our highest priority. As He teaches in Matthew 10:37, "Whoever loves father and mother more than Me, and whoever loves son and daughter more than Me is not worthy of Me."

"Simply" believing that Jesus Christ existed is not enough. You have to fully surrender to the fact that He died for your sins and took your place. Your absolute trust and faith regarding your entrance into Heaven has to fully rest in the finished work of Christ at the cross. Not anything of yourself or anyone else for that matter. It is not by your obedience or merit or ceremonial partaking but in your acceptance of what Christ did in your place, fully making it possible for you to enter into the presence of a perfect and holy God in the eternal realm of Heaven, and relying on His work alone as your entrance pass because once again, you cannot possibly be good enough by yourself to merit your way in. No amount of obedience or saving actions or performances will equate to you adding to Christ's saving work. "It is finished!"

"Real faith, saving faith, is all of me (mind, emotions and will) embracing all of Him (Savior, Advocate, Provider, Sustainer, Counselor and Lord God). The Gospel demands surrender."[6]

It demands not just passive acceptance of
Christ but active submission to Him as well.

> Those unwilling to surrender to Christ cannot
> recruit Him to be part of a crowded life. He will
> not respond to the beckoning of a heart that
> cherishes sin. He will not enter into partnership
> with one who loves to fulfill the passions of the
> flesh. He will not heed the plea of a rebel who
> simply wants Him to enter and by His presence
> sanctify a life of continued disobedience.[7]

This doctrine of man's responsibility is also built and solidified all throughout the entirety of Scripture, beginning to end. Let's start by looking at the very words spoken by Jesus Himself. Jesus's ministry lasted three and a half years leading to His death and resurrection and ascension. During that time, He fulfilled the entire law of the Old Testament perfectly and verified and taught the way of salvation and entrance into Heaven, backing it up with teachings from the Old Testament (seeing that during the New Testament time period, they would not have had the New Testament writings yet because they were still living through them and haven't written about them yet; the entirety of Scripture to them at this time in history only consisted of the Old Testament writings).

We will start looking at His words by looking at a bit of an obscure teaching. In this Jewish culture, they believed that disease and disability were signs of sinfulness and unrighteousness (John 9:2, "Rabbi, who sinned, this man or his parents, that he was born blind?"). Therefore, to have Jesus at this point saying, "your faith has made you well" (Matt. 9:22; Mark 5:34, 36; Luke 8:48, 50; Mark 10:52; Luke 18:42; Luke 7:36–50; Luke 17:19) or "your sins are forgiven" when He saw their faith (Matt. 9:2; Mark 2:5; Luke 5:20) or similar type expressions, He was, in essence, saying that these people were now no longer unrighteous and, therefore saved, which makes sense when you see that it leads to the Pharisees and scribes accusing Him of blasphemy when He forgave sins and healed people (Matt. 9:3; Mark 2:7; Luke 5:21) and even accused Him of being possessed with demons when He expelled demons from others (Matt. 9:34; Matt. 12:24; Mark 3:22; Luke 11:15, etc.).

We see in Matthew 9:2 (Mark 2:5; Luke 5:20), "When Jesus saw their faith, He said to the paralytic, 'Take heart My son, your sins are forgiven.'"

Matthew 9:22 (Mark 5:34, 36; Luke 8:48, 50) shows us, "Jesus said, 'Take heart daughter, your faith has made you well.'"

Matthew 9:27–30 tells us, "Two blind men crying aloud, 'Have mercy on us, Son of David.' Jesus said to them, 'Do you believe that I Am able to do this?' They said to Him, 'Yes, Lord.' He touched their eyes, saying, 'According to your faith be it done to you.' And their eyes were opened."

Matthew 15:28 states, "Jesus answered her, 'O woman, great is your faith! Be it done for you as you desire.' And her daughter was healed instantly."

Mark 10:52 (Luke 18:42) says, "Jesus said to him, 'Go your way; your faith has made you well.' And immediately he recovered his sight."

Luke 7:36–50 states, "Your faith has saved you; go in peace."

Luke 17:19 reads, "Rise and go your way; your faith has made you well."

We also see this same teaching in Acts 3:16 where it says, "And His name—by faith in His name—has made this man strong whom you see and know, and the faith that is through Jesus has given this man this perfect health in the presence of you all." All of this ties in perfectly with Scripture because by relying on and basing all of your trust in Jesus's spiritually healing you, you are placing saving faith in Jesus Christ which is our sole formula for salvation. Let's look at more of Christ's words and get deeper into this.

We read in Matthew 10:32–33, Jesus says, "Everyone who acknowledges Me before men, I will also acknowledge before My Father Who is in Heaven, but whoever denies Me before men, I will also deny before My Father Who is in Heaven." If you acknowledge Jesus as Lord and Savior, He will in turn acknowledge you to His Father and call you His Own. Like stated earlier, your salvation depends on your acceptance/acknowledgement of Christ's finished work as your propitiation and your redemption, not by any of your own actions. Simply acknowledge Him as Lord and Savior, and He will acknowledge you as His Own. Deny Him as Lord and Savior, and He will deny you.

Both sides of this concept are also taught in Mark 16:16, in which Jesus says, "Whoever believes and is baptized will be saved, but whoever does not believe will be condemned."

As far as baptism goes, we will get much more in depth on that subject later on in chapter 9, but for now, I want to focus on the rest of this passage. This passage again shows both sides of the issue. If you believe in Jesus Christ, you will be saved, and if you do not believe in Him, you will be condemned. And as will always be the case, this speaks of not just a "simple" belief in Christ but a wholehearted trust in Christ as your Lord and Savior-Messiah and full surrender of your life to Him and full reliance upon His finished work being your entrance into eternity and salvation entirely through Him. If you simply do not believe this, then you will be condemned.

In Luke 8:11–12, Jesus is teaching the parable of the sower and the seeds and the different soils. We read His words, "Now the parable is this: The seed is the Word of God. The ones along the path are those who have heard; then the devil comes and takes away the Word from their hearts, so that they may not believe and be saved." Again, we see here that belief in Jesus Christ is directly linked to salvation and that not believing in Him equates to being unsaved. This passage also adds depth in that our saving belief and faith in Christ comes from the Word being in our hearts, which comes from hearing the Word. You could say that these are the building blocks of our saving faith.

The Gospel of John is packed full of Jesus's teachings on this subject. We start with a lesson that Jesus taught when speaking to Nicodemus. Three times in four short verses, He basically repeats Himself, solidifying this doctrine of great depth. We have already touched on one of these verses but we will look at them all here. Starting in John chapter 3, we will focus on verses 15–18. Starting at v. 14:

> And as Moses lifted up the serpent in the
> wilderness, so must the Son of Man be lifted up,

that whoever believes in Him may have eternal life. For God so loved the world, that He gave His one and only Son, that whoever believes in Him shall not perish but have eternal life. For God did not send His Son into the world to condemn the world, but in order that the world might be saved through Him. Whoever believes in Him is not condemned, but whoever does not believe is condemned already, because he has not believed in the name of the only Son of God.

Nowhere in these verses do you see any other formula on our part or necessity for salvation other than believing in Jesus Christ as your Savior. "Whoever believes in Him may have eternal life… whoever believes in Him shall not perish but have eternal life…whoever believes in Him is not condemned." All the other requirements are made entirely by God Himself. "The Son of Man must be lifted up… For God so loved the world, that He gave His one and only Son… For God did not send His Son into the world to condemn the world, but in order that the world might be saved through Him."

Our part is simply accepting His finished work in our place as our substitute. It really is a simple equation, though it must be a complete and entirely surrendered one—ALL His work, and simply our acceptance of His work and surrender to Him! John MacArthur discusses the analogy mentioned in John 3:14–15:

The point of Jesus's analogy is that just "as Moses lifted up the serpent in the wilderness, even so must the Son of Man be lifted up" (crucified; cf. 8:28; 12:32, 34). The term "must" emphasizes that Christ's death was a necessary part of God's plan of salvation. He had to die as a substitute for sinners. The stricken Israelites were cured by obediently looking to the elevated serpent, apart from any works or righteousness of their own, in complete hope and dependence on God's Word. In the same way, whoever looks in faith alone to the crucified Christ (apart from any works or righteousness of their own) will be cured from sin's deadly bite and 'will in Him have eternal life.[8]

Verse 18 also shows us the negative side of this doctrine, "whoever does not believe is condemned already, because he has not believed in the name of the only Son of God." So we see here the other side, just as we saw in Matthew 10:32–33, Mark 16:16, and Luke 8:11–12, if we do not believe in Christ, if we do not accept Him as Lord and Savior, we are condemned and therefore unsaved. And John reiterates both sides of this issue at the end of this chapter in verse 36, "He that believes in the Son has everlasting life; and he that believes not in the Son shall not see life; but the wrath of God abides on him."

Both the positive and negative side of this doctrine are plainly taught here: believe in Jesus Christ and be saved; believe not in Christ and be condemned. There is no other part to the formula on our end. The rest is all up to God. Again, none of this is to say it is a "simple" belief or faith but a completely surrendered commitment to Christ as Lord and Savior.

John continues on through his gospel and we see in chapter 5 more from the teachings of Jesus. In verse 24, He tells us, "Truly, truly, I say to you, whoever hears My Word and believes Him Who sent Me has eternal life. He does not come into judgment, but has passed from death to life." We again see that it is in our belief in Christ that we are given eternal life. And we also again see in verse 38 that not believing in the One Whom God has sent, Jesus Christ, our Savior, equates to Christ being absent in us and which therefore means we are condemned and unsaved. "You do not have His Word abiding in you, for you do not believe the One that He has sent."

In the following verses of chapter 5 of John's gospel, we see an interesting element to this teaching. Verses 39–40 says, "You search the Scriptures because you think that in Them you have eternal life; and it is They that bear witness about Me, yet you refuse to come to Me that you may have life." Jesus again is saying that it is only through Him that we may have eternal life, but He is also making a valid and effectual point that it is not in doctrine or in searching the Scriptures that they will receive life.

> The verb *search* implies diligent scrutiny in investigating Scriptures to find "eternal life." However, Jesus points out that with all their fastidious effort, they miserably failed in their understanding of the true way of eternal life through the Son of God. Christ is the main theme of Scripture.[9]

John also shows some of the crowd's misunderstandings and Jesus's correction in chapter 6 verses 28–29, "'What must we do to be doing the works of God?' Jesus answered them, 'This is the work of God, that you believe in Him Whom He has sent.'"

"They thought Jesus was saying [through the teachings of previous verses] that God required them to do some works to earn everlasting life, which they thought they would be able to do. The only work God desired was faith or trust in Jesus as Messiah and Son of God. The "work" that God requires is to believe in His Son."[10]Again, it is not through any physical works of our own but through belief in Jesus Christ as our Lord and Savior.

We also see from Jesus, in John 6:35, 40, and 47:

> I Am the Bread of Life; whoever comes to Me shall not hunger, and whoever believes in Me shall never thirst... For this is the will of My Father, that everyone who looks on the Son and believes in Him should have eternal life, and I will raise him up on the last day... Truly, truly, I say to you, whoever believes has eternal life.

When we come to Him and place our belief in Him as Savior, He raises us up and gives us eternal life. It is wholly and only upon our belief and faith in Jesus as our Savior. Nothing else is required.

> Verse 40 emphasizes human responsibility in salvation. Although God is sovereign, He works through faith, so that a person must believe in Jesus Christ as the Messiah and Son of God Who alone offers the way of salvation (cf. John 14:6). However, even faith is a gift of God (Rom. 12:3; Eph. 2:8–9). Intellectually harmonizing the sovereignty of God and the responsibility of man is impossible humanly, but perfectly resolved in the mind of God.[11]

Moving on to chapter 7 in John, we read in verses 38–39, "Whoever believes in Me, as the Scripture has said, 'Out of his heart will flow rivers of living water.' Now this He said about the Spirit, Whom those who believed in Him were to receive, for as yet the Spirit had not been given, because Jesus was not yet glorified."

Again, Jesus is teaching the same point, but here He has added another dimension of the transaction. Upon saving belief in Christ, we will receive the Holy Spirit Who will come and dwell in us. We also see a bit of this teaching in 1 Corinthians 6:19–20 where we read, "Do you not know that your body is a temple of the Holy Spirit Who lives within you, Whom you have received from God? You are not your own, for you were bought with a price. So glorify God in your body." The result of the Holy Spirit dwelling in us will be made manifest in that He will flow out of our hearts as that of rivers of living water, i.e., the gifts and fruits and works of the Spirit (1 Cor. 12:7–11; Gal. 5:22–23).

In chapters 8 and 9, we also see more of Jesus's teachings regarding belief in Himself. In 8:24, we read, "I told you that you would die in your sins, for unless you believe that I Am, you will die in your sins." Here again, we have a lesson of the negative; if we do not believe in Christ as our Savior we are dead in our sins. And in 9:35–38, "Jesus said, 'Do you believe in the Son of Man?' He answered,

'Who is He, Sir, that I may believe in Him?' Jesus said to him, 'You have seen Him, and it is He Who is speaking to you.' He said, 'Lord, I believe,' and worshipped Him." Belief is the key to our salvation. That's all Jesus ever asked for. Surrender to Him as Lord and Savior.

In John chapter 11, we find ourselves in the story of Jesus's resurrection of Lazarus from the dead. When Jesus came to Bethany where Lazarus had lived, he had already been dead for four days. When Martha comes to Jesus to console in Him, He asks her a straightforward and deep theological question which we could apply to each and every one of us as a direct question from Christ to us. Verses 25–26, "I Am the resurrection and the life. Whoever believes in Me, though he die, yet shall he live, and everyone who lives and believes in Me shall never die. Do you believe this?"

Do you believe this? Again, not just do you "simply" believe this, but do you rest your entire faith in this truth? Do you rest your entire eternity on the truth of Jesus Christ being your resurrection and life? Do you, through surrender to Him and acceptance of what He has done for you as your Substitute, trust that by believing in His finished work, you will be saved and never die? In verse 40, Jesus follows up with another similar question, "Did I not tell you that if you believed you would see the glory of God?" Surrender yourself to Him and believe in Him as your Savior, and He will bring you into eternal glory and everlasting life.

In John 12, we see further illustration of this in verses 36, 46–48 where Jesus uses a bit of a metaphor, "While you have the Light, believe in the Light, that you may become sons of light... I have come into the world as light, so that whoever believes in Me may not remain in darkness." Jesus is telling us that, Himself being the Light of the world, that if we believe in Him, He will make us sons of the light and that we will not remain in darkness; or in other words, death. In verse 48, we also receive another lesson in the negative, "The one who rejects Me and does not receive My words has a judge; the Word that I have spoken will judge him on the last day." It is not by any act or obedience but by acceptance and surrender and belief in Him that we are saved. And if we reject Him and refuse to live by His Word, we will be judged accordingly, and it will not end well.

In John 14:12, Jesus tells us, "Truly, truly, I say to you, whoever believes in Me will also do the works that I do." Rest assured this is speaking of a salvational effect. You could not perform the works that Jesus does if you are unsaved and wretched. Belief in Him will lead to a salvational relationship with Him which will result in performing His works. He will work through you. John 15:5 pretty much states the same thing as well. "Whoever abides in Me and I in him, he it is that bears much fruit, for apart from Me you can do nothing." We cannot perform His works and bear His fruit until we are saved by Him. We can do nothing for Him if we are apart from Him. We will discuss the topic of works more in depth in a later chapter.

In John 16:8–9, we learn more about the impact of the Holy Spirit's presence, "When the [Helper] comes, He will convict the world concerning sin and righteousness and judgment: concerning sin, because they do not believe in Me."

> The singular use of "sin" here indicates that a specific sin is in view; i.e., that of not believing in Jesus as Messiah and Son of God. This is the only sin, ultimately, that damns people to hell. Though all men are depraved, cursed by their violation of God's law and sinful by nature, what ultimately damns them to hell is their unwillingness to believe in the Lord Jesus Christ as Savior.[12]

In John 16:27, we read, "For the Father Himself loves you, because you have loved Me and have believed that I came from God." By loving and believing in Christ, God's love will shine toward you.

In John chapter 17, we are given what might be the most beautiful words in Scripture. All of chapter 17 consists of a direct prayer from the mouth of Jesus and is directed to His Father. A face-to-face communion of God the Father and God the Son. Also, in the majority of this prayer, Jesus is praying in regards to our relationships with Him and the Father. And you can rest assured that when Jesus prayed to His Father, all of His prayers were answered, seeing as Christ always acted and lived in accordance with the will of the

Father. We will spend a lot more time in chapter 17 in a later chapter, but here I want to focus on verses 19–21 in which Jesus prays:

> For their sake I consecrate Myself, that they also may be sanctified in truth. I do not ask for these only, but also for those who will believe in Me through their word, that they may all be one, just as You, Father, are in Me, and I in You, that they also may be in Us, so that the world may believe that You have sent Me.

Absolutely beautiful and astounding! We will be sanctified by Christ, and those who believe in Him will be unified as one with the Triune God and dwell in Him! Amazing!

After Jesus's resurrection, He appeared several times to His disciples. At the end of chapter 20, we find the story of His appearance to Thomas who was not present during an earlier appearance and subsequently did not believe the other disciples when they told him of the account in which they all witnessed His post-death presence. Jesus appears once again behind closed doors to the disciples, this time with Thomas present. Then starting in verse 27, He tells Thomas to "Put your finger here, and see My hands; and put out your hand, and place it in My side. Do not disbelieve, but believe."

At that point, Thomas answered, "My Lord and my God!"

Jesus then responded back to him, "Have you believed because you have seen Me? Blessed are they who have not seen and yet have believed."

This last statement applies to each and every one of us. We were not there 2,000 years ago when Jesus was still physically walking on this earth after His resurrection and prior to His ascension. Yet, by believing His words and by believing in His resurrection and by trusting in His finished work, we are blessed by Him and, therefore, found saved by Him. It is by our belief, not our works or obedience.

The last words of Jesus on this subject were given to Paul who definitely knew and understood the Gospel of salvation. In Acts 26, we find Paul giving his testimony regarding his conversion to the Christian Way. Paul used to be known as Saul, the Pharisee of pharisees. He had arrested, persecuted, and even murdered many Christians for apostasy and for blasphemy in the preaching of Christ as the Son of God and Messiah. That was until Christ revealed Himself to him and changed him forever.

Paul recounts the words given to him by Jesus on the road to Damascus where Christ revealed Himself to Paul. In verse 18, he reiterates Jesus's words, "The Gentiles—to whom I Am sending you, to open their eyes, so that they may turn from darkness to light and from the power of satan to God, that they may receive forgiveness of sins and a place among those who are sanctified by faith in Me." We are united with God, we are forgiven of our sins, and we are even sanctified entirely through our faith in Him.

A few other phrases Jesus spoke that hinged on this topic can be found in the gospels. In Mark, we read a couple different ones. In Mark 1:15, we read, "Now after John (the baptist) was arrested, Jesus came into Galilee, proclaiming the Gospel of God, and saying, 'The time is fulfilled, and the Kingdom of God is at hand; repent and believe in the Gospel.'" Here, we see Jesus's words and we see the same formula that He always preached for salvation. Repent and believe speaks of the wholehearted surrender to Jesus Christ as Lord and Savior that we have been looking at. These are the two responses that we are responsible for when it comes to receiving God's gracious gift of redemption and salvation: to turn from our old ways and give ourselves entirely to Him, to carry our cross daily and commit to Him fully.

We also see in Mark 9:23, "Jesus said to him, 'If you can! All things are possible for one who believes.'" Jesus said these words in the context of the healing of a demon-possessed boy, but the word for "all things" in the Greek is *pas* or *pan* which literally does mean "all things" or "anything" or "everything;" and just as Jesus said in Matthew 17:20 and Luke 17:6, "If you have faith the size of a mustard seed, you can say to this mountain, 'Move from here to there,' and it will move, and nothing will be impossible for you."

Now, none of these statements are saying that you in your own power can do these things, but because of your faith in Christ, by the power of Christ you can do these things. In Christ, we are made new. We are made children of God and we are one with God. These are not actions or abilities of an unsaved person but a child of God.

We also see in Luke 18:8 the statement, "When the Son of Man comes, will He find faith on earth?" This verse is speaking of the return of Christ for His church and that when He comes the world may be somewhat sparse in those possessing true faith, as was the case in Noah's day. But the point here is that He will come looking for those who do possess that true saving faith in Jesus Christ as Lord and Savior. He will not come to look for those who performed the best or obeyed the best or finished some checklist or acted a certain way. It will solely depend on our faith in Him and what He has done for us.

Jesus's teachings on this subject never shifted. By our belief in Him—that is, by our complete surrender to Him as our Lord and Savior and our acceptance of His finished work for us—we are saved and unified with Him as One and given eternal life. It is not by our works, obedience, or merit that we can obtain any of this. It is all in His finished work. "It is finished."

Not to say that Jesus's Own teachings on this subject aren't sufficient and that more is needed, but let's see what the rest of Scripture has to say about this topic as it is all God's Word.

Starting now all the way back into Genesis, we see that the way of salvation has always been the same. John MacArthur describes this point in his book The Gospel According To Jesus.

> The Old Testament plainly taught the way of salvation (cf. 2 Tim. 3:15). Jesus was not announcing a new way of salvation (John 3:3–15) distinct from Old Testament redemption (cf. Matt. 5:17). This is to say that salvation under the dispensation of grace is no different from salvation under the law. There is perfect unity in God's Word, and the way of salvation revealed in the Old Testament was the same as salvation after Christ's work on the cross. Salvation was never

a reward for human works; it has always been a gift of grace for repentant sinners, made possible by the work of Christ. The experience of conversion—a new birth, involving the washing of regeneration and renewing of the Holy Spirit—has been the plan of God from the beginning. Even in the Old Testament, salvation was not a payoff for those who observed the law; it was a gift to those who humbly and by faith sought redemption from their sin. Yet it always meant a new start (sometimes a new name), a rebirth, a turning from sin to God. The central theme of the Old Testament is redemption by grace. But incredibly, the pharisees entirely missed it. In their rigid emphasis on religious works, they deemphasized the truth of God's grace and forgiveness to sinners, evident throughout the Old Testament. They stressed obedience to law, not conversion to the Lord, as the way to gain eternal life. They were so busy trying to earn righteousness that they neglected the marvelous truth of Habakkuk 2:4, "The just shall live by faith."

They looked to Abraham as their father but overlooked the key lesson of his life: "He believed in the Lord; and the Lord credited it to him as righteousness" (Gen. 15:6). They scoured the Psalms for laws they could add to their list, but they ignored the most sublime truth of them all—that God forgives sins, covers transgressions, and refuses to impute iniquity to sinners who turn to Him (Ps. 32:1–2). They anticipated the coming of their Messiah but closed their eyes to the fact that He would come to die as a sacrifice for sin (Isa. 53:4–9). They were confident that they were guides to the blind, lights to those in darkness, correctors of the foolish, and teachers of the immature (cf. Rom. 2:19–20), but they missed the most basic lesson of God's law: that they themselves were sinners in need of redemption.

People have always stumbled over the simplicity of salvation. That is why there are so many denominations. Each one has a unique slant on the doctrine of salvation—and each one corrupts the simplicity of the Gospel revealed in God's Word (cf. 2 Cor. 11:3) by espousing salvation by human works. Each one claims to have a key that unlocks the secret of salvation, yet they are all alike in propagating self-righteous achievement as the way to God (cf. Eph. 2:8–9; Rom. 3:20, 28).[13]

As these words point out, the way of salvation has always been taught the same way all the way back to the beginning. Genesis 15:6 says that, "Abraham believed the Lord, and the Lord counted it to him as righteousness." Abraham was not found righteous before God by his actions or obedience but by his faith in God to deliver a Messiah that a Savior would come. He did not rely on his own works; he relied on God's promise. The way to salvation did not change when Jesus came; it just manifested the Figure of the promise given, the coming Messiah, the One to Whom we look to for redemption and salvation. The message itself never changed; it only became fulfilled.

We read from the Prophet Jeremiah chapter 17 verse 7, "Blessed [with spiritual security] is the man who believes and trusts in and relies on the Lord, and whose hope and confident expectation is the Lord" (AMP). This speaks of one who is devoted to the Lord and His Word and receives all the spiritual blessings and benefits of God through his devotion.

In Joel chapter 2 verse 32, we read, "And it shall come to pass that everyone that calls on the name of the Lord shall be saved." This phrase we also find repeated a couple times in the New Testament, even after Jesus was crucified and rose from the dead and ascended into Heaven, which proves that God's plan of salvation never changed from beginning to end; before or after Christ, it was the same. It has always remained the same. In the Old Testament, before He ever became incarnate, and in the New Testament after His death, resurrection, and ascension.

It has always been based solely on dependence upon the Messiah and never of any works or obedience of our own. It does not say, "Obey Him and you shall be saved," or "Perform well and you will be saved." It says, "Call upon Him, and you will be saved."

We find Peter quoting this verse in Acts 2:21 during his sermon at Pentecost. Peter spent three and a half years directly at the side of Jesus as His disciple learning from none other than Christ Himself. He knew that our salvation rested in Christ's finished work and that we merely have to come to Him in true faith to be made new in Him. Later in his sermon, there is a verse which is often misinterpreted, but we will touch on that in a later chapter. Paul also repeated this same verse from Joel in Romans 10:13.

The rest of Romans chapter 10 has plenty of other teaching to this, and we will get into that later in this chapter, but again, the point is Paul also understood and taught that the way to salvation is simply by calling upon Christ's finished work and not anything of our own. Throughout the entirety of Scripture, the message has always been the same. It did not change before or after Christ, before or after Pentecost, or at any other point. Anyone who truly turns to Christ as Lord and Savior will be saved.

Habakkuk 2:4 also contains a verse that is reiterated a few times in the New Testament. It simply reads, "The righteous shall live by his faith." Paul quoted this verse in both the epistle to the Romans and the Galatians. In Romans 1:17, he states, "For in the Gospel the righteousness of God is revealed from faith for faith, as it is written, 'The righteous shall live by faith.'"

In Galatians 3:11, he says, "Now it is evident that no one is justified before God by the law, for 'The righteous shall live by faith.'"

The writer to the Hebrews, who many believe to be Paul, also quoted this same verse from Habakkuk, just two verses prior to the beginning of chapter 11 of Hebrews, nicknamed by some as the "Hall of Fame of Faith."

> In contrast to the proud, the righteous will be truly preserved through his faithfulness to God. This is the core of God's message through/ to Habakkuk. Both the aspect of justification by faith, as noted by Paul's usage in Romans 1:17 and Galatians 3:11, as well as the aspect of sanctification by faith, as employed by the writer of Hebrews (Heb. 10:38), reflect the essence of Habakkuk; no conflict exists. The emphasis in both Habakkuk and the New Testament references goes beyond the act of faith to include the continuity of faith. Faith is not a one-time act, but a way of life. The true believer, declared righteous by God, will persevere in faith as the pattern of his life (cf. Col. 1:22–23; Heb. 3:12–14).
>
> Paul intends to prove that it has always been God's way to justify sinners by grace on the basis of faith alone. God established Abraham as a pattern of faith (Rom. 4:22–25; Gal. 3:6–7) and thus calls him the father of all who believe (Rom. 4:11, 16). Elsewhere, Paul uses the same phrase to argue that no one has ever been declared righteous before God except by faith alone (Gal. 3:11) and that true faith will demonstrate itself in action (Phil. 2:12–13).[14]

A couple of other verses found in the Old Testament can be found at Psalm 78:21–22 which says, "the Lord...was full of wrath... His anger rose against Israel, because they did not believe in God and did not trust His saving power." This verse again shows the negative side of the belief issue. If you do not believe in God, His wrath will be upon you.

We also see a bit of teaching in Isaiah 28:16, "Thus says the Lord God, 'Behold, I Am the One Who has laid as a foundation in Zion… 'Whoever believes will not be in haste.'" The word *haste* here in the Hebrew is *chuwsh*, which is an onomatopoetic word which has a feeling of "hurry or fleeing with alarm." This verse is referring to Jesus Christ as the prophesied coming Messiah and that those who believe in Him will not be put to shame or alarm. You are safe in Christ through your faith in Christ.

Moving back into the New Testament, we have already discussed a lot of the teachings in John, those by Jesus Himself, but John also mentions a few words himself. In the very beginning of John, we see the apostle forming the picture of the coming Messiah. He starts in verse 9:

> The true Light, which enlightens everyone, was coming into the world. He was in the world, and the world was made through Him, yet the world did not know Him. He came to His Own, and His Own people did not receive Him. But to all who did receive Him, who believed in His name, He gave the right to become children of God, who were born, not of blood nor of the will of the flesh nor of the will of man, but of God.

John starts out his Gospel with these words, making the point that it is all done by God and that by simply receiving Him and believing in Him, we are made to be His children. It is not by any acts or obedience but simply by receiving and believing that He is our Savior and Messiah. John also closes his Gospel with the same teaching. In chapter 20, verses 30–31, he writes, "Now Jesus did many other signs in the presence of the disciples, which are not written in this book; but these are written so that you may believe that Jesus is the Christ, the Son of God, and that by believing you may have life in His name."

Beginning to end, John taught exactly what Jesus taught us. It is simply and entirely by placing saving faith in Jesus Christ as our

Lord and Savior that we are given eternal life in His name, not by acts of obedience or works or anything else other than by faith in His finished works. When we receive Him through faith and surrender to Him as our Lord and Savior, we receive everything that He did in our place to make us right with God so that we become children of God.

The book of Acts also teaches us a lot about man's responsibility. Starting in chapter 8, we read in verses 35–38 the story of Philip preaching to the Ethiopian eunuch. The eunuch was reading from Isaiah chapter 53 (which foretells of Jesus Christ fulfilling prophecy as the Messiah) when Philip came up to him and asked him if he understood what he was reading. The eunuch said no and asked Philip to interpret it for him.

> Then Philip spoke, starting with this Scripture he told him the good news about Jesus. And as they were going along the road they came to some water, and the eunuch said, "See, here is water! What prevents me from being baptized?" And Philip said, "If you believe with all your heart, you may." And he answered, "I believe that Jesus Christ is the Son of God." And he commanded the chariot to stop, and they both went down into the water, Philip and the eunuch, and he baptized him.

Now, first of all, if you are reading along in your Bible at home, you may notice that there seems to be a difference between what I quoted here and what you find in your Bible at home, depending on what translation you use. Some translations leave out verse 37 or simply include it as a footnote. Some people argue whether or not it should be included as it is not found in some early manuscripts and may contest whether or not it is part of the original text. But without diving into that issue too deeply, whether it should be included or not, we do see that it does mirror the rest of what Scripture teaches on this subject. Anyway, verse 37 is the one that states, "And Philip said, 'If you believe with all your heart, you may.' And he answered, 'I believe that Jesus Christ is the Son of God.'"

Now I know this section mentions baptism; however, baptism here is not being taught as a salvational act. In other words, it is not being taught that salvation is received at the moment of baptism but is instead being shown to be preceded by saving faith in Jesus Christ. Believing in Jesus Christ as the Son of God, faith in Jesus as Savior, is what is necessary for salvation. Baptism is/should be an immediate response to salvation, but it is not an act leading to salvation. As mentioned earlier in this chapter, we will get much deeper into the issue of baptism in chapter 9 of this book.

In Acts chapter 9, we see the narrative of the conversion of Saul the pharisee into the Apostle Paul. Saul was a devout pharisee who was bent on persecuting and destroying the Christian followers. He arrested, imprisoned, and even executed many of them during his reign of terror. That is until Jesus Himself stepped in. Saul was traveling the road to Damascus when he was blinded by the light of God which stopped him in his tracks. Jesus spoke directly to him and asked him why he was persecuting Him. Paul then answers, "Who are You, Lord?"

The Greek word here for Lord is *kyrios*, which is a title given to God the Messiah and shows a sense of surrendering. Jesus then reveals the Gospel to him as we are shown in Galatians 1:11–12 where Paul admits, "The Gospel that was preached by me is not man's gospel. For I did not receive it from any man, nor was I taught it, but I received it through a revelation of Jesus Christ" (also cf. Gal. 1:16). Jesus then directs Saul to go into Damascus and wait there.

Still being blind from the encounter with Jesus, he was led to a private house where he spent three days fasting and praying (Acts 9:9–11). God then sent a man named Ananias to meet him and relieve him from his ailment. We pick up the story in verse 17.

> So Ananias departed and entered the house.
> And laying his hands on him said, "Brother Saul,
> the Lord Jesus Who appeared to you on the road
> by which you came has sent me so that you may

> regain your sight and be filled with the Holy Spirit." And immediately something like scales fell off his eyes, and he regained his sight. Then he arose and was baptized; and taking food he was strengthened.

We see here that Saul's faith in Jesus as Lord along with his understanding of the Gospel which Jesus Himself gave to Saul while still on the road to Damascus was evidenced by the fact that Saul had received the filling of the Holy Spirit when Ananias came and laid his hands over Saul as God told him to, resulting in Saul regaining his sight and something like scales falling from his eyes; which, just like in Acts 8, all preceded Saul's baptism.

In Acts chapter 10, we see another narrative, this time featuring Peter and a Gentile centurion named Cornelius who feared and believed in God and prayed continuously to Him but did not yet know the Gospel of Jesus Christ. An angel of the Lord came to Cornelius and told him to send for a man named Peter. Then Peter was also met by an angel who told him to follow his summons to a man named Cornelius.

Upon meeting each other, Cornelius had called many of his relatives and close friends to listen to the message that Peter was to bring to them. Peter spoke of his eyewitness account of the ministry of Jesus Christ. He spoke of Jesus's teachings and healings and the work of the Holy Spirit through Him. He also spoke of Jesus's arrest, conviction, death, burial, and resurrection, followed by His physical appearances to those whom God chose to be witnesses of His post-resurrection presences. He then stated in verse 42 that "He commanded us to preach to the people and to testify that He is the One appointed by God to be Judge of the living and the dead. To Him all the prophets bear witness that everyone who believes in Him receives forgiveness of sins through His name."

So we see in this part of the narrative that Peter preached to them the Gospel of Jesus Christ and tells them specifically that "everyone who believes in Him receives forgiveness of sins through His name." Peter affirms that it is through saving faith in Jesus Christ and belief in His name that we are saved. Our sins are forgiven, and we are reconciled to God upon our belief in Jesus as Savior. This is the full responsibility of man. We continue in verse 44:

> While Peter was saying these things, the Holy Spirit fell on all who heard the Word. And the believers from among the circumcised who had come with Peter were amazed, because the gift of the Holy Spirit was poured out even on the Gentiles. For they were hearing them speaking in tongues and praising God. Then Peter declared, "Can anyone withhold water for baptizing these people, who have received the Holy Spirit just as we have?" Then he commanded them to be baptized in the name of Jesus Christ.

Once again, we see that these Gentiles possessed saving faith, which is evidenced in the fact that the Holy Spirit was poured out on all those who believed in the Word, and they even started speaking in tongues and praising God, and Peter even references them as "these people who have received the Holy Spirit just as we have." These are all signs and evidences of their already-possessed salvation which, again, they received prior to being baptized. Peter also recounts this story in chapter 11 when upon the hearing by those throughout Judea of the fact that the Gentiles had also received the Word of God, he is summoned to Jerusalem and is there criticized for going and ministering to them.

He tells of the vision he received and recounts the entire interaction with them and declared in verse 15:

> As I began to speak, the Holy Spirit fell on them just as on us at the beginning. And I remembered the Word of the Lord, how He said, "John baptized with water, but you will be baptized with the Holy Spirit." If then God gave the same gift to them as He gave to us when we

believed in the Lord Jesus Christ, who was I that
I could stand in God's way?

Again, here, Peter makes the point that it is upon belief in Jesus Christ that we receive this gift of the Holy Spirit falling on us. Being baptized with the Holy Spirit here is shown in being in contrast with being baptized in water as John did, but we will explore that in much more detail later. The main point is that in these last four chapters, we see evidence of salvation upon the presence of saving faith and all of it being present before the act of baptism in water.

Continuing on in the book of Acts, we read in chapter 13 verses 38–39 and 48:

> Through this Man Jesus, forgiveness of sins
> is proclaimed to you, and by Him everyone who
> believes is freed from everything from which you
> could not be freed by the law of Moses... When
> the Gentiles heard this, they began rejoicing and
> glorifying the Word of the Lord, and as many as
> were appointed to eternal life believed.

In chapter 3, we discussed the law and the inadequacy of it in regards to offering salvation. We are not made holy and righteous by the law or obedience to it (except for perfect obedience to it as in the case of Christ), but it was given merely as a mirror to show us our vast array of faults and failures. Here, in verses 38–39, we are told that everyone who believes in Jesus is set free from those inadequacies and insufficient character of the law and that we are forgiven of all of our sins through Him. Verse 48 continues and links our belief in Christ to our eternal life and also includes a glimpse at the divine election of our souls by God Himself by saying "as many as were *appointed* to eternal life believed." This divine action of God's sovereignty in our election we already discussed in chapter 4 and the paradox between divine sovereignty and man's responsibility we looked at in chapter 5.

In the beginning of chapter 15 of Acts, we find the account of the Jerusalem Council between the church leaders, apostles, and elders discussing the necessity of circumcision in regards to salvation. We will discuss circumcision more in chapter 9 also, but here we find a disagreement regarding its necessity. After much debate, Peter stood up and said in verse 7:

> Brothers, you know that in the early days God made a choice among you, that by my mouth the Gentiles should hear the Word of the Gospel and believe. And God, Who knows the hearts, bore witness to them, by giving them the Holy Spirit just as He did to us, and He made no distinction between us and them, having cleansed their hearts by faith. Now, therefore, why are you putting God to the test by placing a yoke on the neck of the disciples that neither our forefathers nor we have been able to bear?

Again, hinting at the insufficiency of the law to save and the inadequacy of our obedience. "But we believe that we will be saved through the grace of the Lord Jesus, just as they will."

> Throughout its history, the church's leaders have met to settle doctrinal issues. Historians point to seven ecumenical councils in the church's early history, especially the Councils of Nicea (AD 325) and Chalcedon (AD 451). Yet the most important one was the first one—the Jerusalem Council of Acts 15:1–30—because it established the answer to the most vital doctrinal question of all: "What must a person do to be saved?" The apostles and elders defied efforts to impose legalism and ritualism as necessary prerequisites for salvation. They forever affirmed that salvation is totally by grace through faith in Christ alone.[15]

In these passages, we see the implications of what is called legalism.

> Legalism is using any set of rules—bad rules, good rules, even God's laws—in a wrong way. In his book, *The Cross Centered Life*, C. J. Mahaney writes, "Legalism is seeking to achieve forgiveness from God and acceptance by God through my obedience to God." Legalism is trying to add to what Jesus did when He died and rose again. Legalism is seeking to relate to God based on our work, instead of based on the work of our representative and mediator Jesus Christ.[16]

We see here in these verses of Acts that members, even esteemed members of the church at this time, were holding to legalistic standards with regards to salvation and Peter stood up against this. We see Peter first of all link belief to hearing the Word of the Gospel. He also points out that belief and salvation are issues of the heart and that God knows and reads our hearts, bears witness to us, and cleanses our hearts through our faith by pouring the Holy Spirit upon us just as He did the apostles. Peter ended his statements by saying, "'But we believe that we will be saved through the grace of the Lord Jesus, just as they will.' And all the assembly fell silent." Just as we find in the entirety of Scripture, Peter plainly says we are saved by God's grace through our faith and belief in Jesus Christ as our Savior, not by our actions or obedience or some ritual performed.

In Acts chapter 16, we find another great illustration and example of this teaching. Toward the end of chapter 16, we find Paul and Silas locked in prison for expelling a demon from a slave girl and preaching the Gospel of Christ which sat in contrast to the accepted customs and practices of the Romans. While confined in the inner prison, during the night, they were rejoicing and singing songs of praise to the Lord when suddenly, there was a massive earthquake which rocked the prison and busted open the doors of the prison cells and even loosed the bonds on each of the prisoners. The earthquake also awoke the prison guard who rushed to see what had happened, and when he noticed that the entire prison was left wide open, he was about to commit suicide thinking the prisoners had escaped. You see, in this culture, he was responsible for these prisoners. If they had escaped, then he would've been made to serve out the sentences of the prisoners, so instead of enduring that, he was going to kill himself.

> But Paul cried with a loud voice, "Do not harm yourself, for we are all here." And the jailer called for lights and rushed in, and trembling with fear he fell down before Paul and Silas. Then he brought them out and said, "Sirs, what must I do to be saved?"

Isn't that the exact question that we have been trying to get to this entire book so far? We are six chapters into this thing, and we may finally get a direct answer to that question, directly taken out of the Bible, spoken by one of its authors. Before we get there, notice what isn't included. Notice what Paul and Silas do not include in the answer to this question. Notice the simplicity of what they say. We continue in verse 31. "And they said, 'Believe in the Lord Jesus Christ, and you will be saved, you and your household.'"

That's it! That is man's responsibility! That is our part of the equation! Paul and Silas did not run off a list of things to do or laws to obey or rituals to participate in or a certain prayer to pray. This was after Christ's death. This was after the Resurrection and Ascension. This was after Pentecost. Our responsibility is simply to place our trust and belief and faith in Jesus Christ as Lord and Savior! That is it! God takes care of everything else—leading up to, during, and after our surrender to Him! We have already discussed that God knew us even before Creation and predestined us (Eph. 1:4–5), called us (Rom. 8:29–30), sent His Son to take our place (Rom. 5:8), and Christ fully paid the punishment and judgment that was due to us, defeated death and rose again to new life (John 3:16), and our whole part of this equation is simply accepting His free gift (Rom. 6:23).

We do not have to obey the Ten Commandments perfectly or have a perfect attendance at church or pay a certain number of tithes, or be circumcised or be baptized or pray a certain well-worded prayer or hold a certain position or status or devote our lives to feeding the poor or orphans or widows. These things are all great things and may likely manifest themselves at least to some degree upon being saved as fruit of the Spirit within us, but none of them add to the manifestation of our salvation. Our responsibility in receiving salvation rests solely on our faith in Jesus Christ as our Savior and our surrender to Him as Lord of our lives.

If you believe that Jesus Christ died for your sins and took your place and offers you entrance into Heaven through His name, then you are saved. Period! You do not have to wait for a certain moment in time or accomplish any other form of necessity. There is no application to fill out; there is no checklist to complete; there is no obedience to submit to; there is no ritual or ceremony or sacrament needed to be held or partake in in order to finally receive the Spirit. "Believe in the Lord Jesus Christ, and you will be saved!" Beautiful, isn't it? There is nothing that you can offer God to add to your salvation or to appropriate it, other than your surrender to what He has already accomplished for you.

Just like every other aspect and doctrine of grace, the letter to the Romans has much to say about man's responsibility also as Paul understood this message quite well. After his initial greeting to the recipients of this letter, Paul immediately illuminates the thesis of the entire letter, the Gospel of Jesus Christ. He starts in verses 16–17:

> For I am not ashamed of the Gospel, for it is the power of God for salvation to everyone who believes, to the Jew first and also to the Greek. For in it the righteousness of God is revealed from faith to faith, as it is written, "The just shall live by faith."

We have already talked about the end of this passage earlier in this chapter as it was quoted from Habakkuk 2:4 and reiterated in Galatians 3:11 and Hebrews 10:38, "The just shall live by faith." In the beginning of this passage, Paul shows his devotion to the Gospel and first makes the point that salvation is entirely done by the power of God and then continues to say that it is offered to whom? To everyone that believes!

Once again, that is our sole responsibility. He lists no other requirements from us, no other demands on our part; it is entirely based upon our faith in Jesus Christ, and he goes on to make the point that everyone means everyone and that there is no discrimination as it is offered to both Jew and Gentile. Paul makes the point then in verse 17 that the righteousness of God is completely on the basis of faith from beginning to end.

Other translations word this verse in different ways which all help to show the true meaning of this verse. The NIV words it, "For in the Gospel the righteousness of God is revealed—a righteousness that is by faith from first to last."

The NLT puts it like this, "This Good News tells us how God makes us right in His sight. This is accomplished from start to finish by faith." The only responsibility He gives to us from beginning to end is that of our belief and faith in this beautiful Gospel of Jesus Christ.

Skipping ahead to chapter 3, we see Paul continue this great lesson. Starting in verse 21, Paul ends his comprehensive lesson on the overall and hopeless state of the total depravity of man (1:18–3:20) and transitions his way into the theme that he introduced in 1:16–17, that of a righteousness that is graciously provided by God Himself and is based and received entirely and solely upon faith alone. "But now the righteousness of God has been manifested apart from the law." As we have already shown, righteousness does not depend on our obedience (or actually the lack thereof) to the law, "although the Law and the Prophets bear witness to it—the righteousness of God is through faith in Jesus Christ for all who believe," which is exactly what he told us in chapter 1.

"For there is no distinction: for all have sinned and fall short of the glory of God." Again, as he showed us in chapter 1, there is no distinction; it is offered to everyone who believes:

> [A]nd are justified by His grace as a gift,
> through the redemption that is in Christ Jesus,

> Whom God put forward as a propitiation by His blood, to be received by faith. This was to show God's righteousness, because in His divine forbearance He had passed over former sins. It was to show His righteousness at the present time, so that He might be just and the Justifier of the one who has faith in Jesus.

Again, mirroring chapter 1, it is completely by the power of God that all of this is accomplished. It is by His grace through Christ's sacrifice Whom God put forward to show His Own righteousness because He passed over our former sins so that He may be shown to be just, all of this for who? "The one who has faith in Jesus!" It really is that simple! That is our only responsibility in the act of salvation—belief/faith/trust/surrender/acceptance! That is man's responsibility.

It is an issue of a surrendered heart that has turned to Christ and relies on His finished works for his redemption. And to bring it even further along, it has to be this way! It cannot be any other way because if it was, there is a terrible consequence that surfaces—that of pride and boasting. Verse 27, "Then what becomes of our boasting? It is excluded. By what kind of law? By a law of works? No, but by the law of faith!" If we had to obey or perform in order to achieve, then we would have reason to boast. You will have a sense of pride because it was you who accomplished it. That absolutely cannot be so because then God would owe us something. That cannot be. It is all done by God's grace simply through our faith.

"For we hold that one is justified by faith apart from works of the law. Or is God the God of Jews only? Is He not the God of the Gentiles also? Yes, of Gentiles also, since God is One—Who will justify the circumcised by faith and the uncircumcised through faith." God shows no partiality. Anyone who believes is justified entirely on the grounds of faith in Christ alone!

Carrying on into chapter 4, really the entire chapter and the first 11 verses of chapter 5, it is all about the issue of justification by faith. "What then shall we say was gained by Abraham, our forefather according to the flesh? For if Abraham was justified by works, he has something to boast about, but not before God." Again, Paul is saying that it is not by our own works or acts of the flesh that we are saved; if it were, we would have reason to boast, we would have reason to be prideful, as if we had played a part in our own salvation. And as Paul always taught that justification is by faith alone in Christ, and since Judaism had become such a legalistic works-based obedience system, Paul uses Abraham, the forefather of Israel, as a symbol or model to portray that it has always been righteousness by faith alone. "For what does the Scripture say? 'Abraham believed God, and it was counted to him as righteousness.'"

Abraham's righteousness was based entirely and solely on his faith in God, nothing else. Not works of the flesh or obedience or, as we will see later, by circumcision or any other form of act of worship. Abraham believed... God credited him with righteousness! It's that simple! "Verse 3 is a quotation from Gen. 15:6," which we have already touched on a bit earlier in this chapter, "and is one of the clearest statements in all of Scripture about justification. Faith is not a meritorious work. It is never the ground of justification—it is simply the channel through which it is received and it, too, is a gift (cf. Eph. 2:8). It is a one-sided transaction—Abraham did nothing to accumulate it; God simply credited it to him. God took His Own righteousness and credited it to Abraham as if it were actually his. This God did because Abraham believed in Him."[17]

Verse 4 continues, "Now to the one who works, his wages are not counted as a gift but as his due." This is the point Paul was making about boasting. If you work or act your way to righteousness, then your justification is no longer considered a gift but as your due. Righteousness is then owed to you for your performance, and God must pay you your dues; therefore, you would be then entitled to boast about your performance and what is owed to you. You would have the right to expect something in return from God Himself.

However, this cannot be.

> To the one who does not work but believes
> in Him Who justifies the ungodly, his faith is
> counted as righteousness, just as David also

speaks of the blessing of the one to whom God
counts righteousness apart from works: "Blessed
are those whose lawless deeds are forgiven, and
whose sins are covered; blessed is the man against
whom the Lord will not count his sin."

Again, it does not depend on works but upon believing in Him
Who justifies the ungodly. All your lawless deeds and sins are washed
clean and forgotten by simply putting your faith in the One Who
took them from you and paid your price. Verse 9:

Is this blessing then only for the circumcised, or also for the uncircumcised? We say that
faith was counted to Abraham as righteousness.
How then was it counted to him? Was it before
or after he was circumcised? It was not after but
before he was circumcised. He received the sign
of circumcision as a seal of the righteousness that
he had by faith while he was still uncircumcised.

We will touch on these verses again in a later chapter, but if
these verses were written today, you could also include baptism.
Many today believe that baptism, as was thought of with circumcision back then, is a necessary part to receiving salvation, and salvation is not received until circumcised or baptized. But as we saw in
several occasions in Acts, those people were evidenced at receiving
the Holy Spirit and being saved prior to water baptism, just like here,
Paul narrates that Abraham received the sign of circumcision merely
as a seal of the righteousness that he already had by his faith alone
prior to ever being circumcised. And as since Acts and all of today,
we receive the sign of water baptism as a seal of the righteousness that
we already have by our faith in Christ alone prior to being baptized.

"The purpose was to make him the father of all who believe
without being circumcised, so that righteousness would be counted
to them as well, and to make him the father of the circumcised who
are not merely circumcised but who also walk in the footsteps of

the faith that our father Abraham had before he was circumcised."
Whether they were circumcised or not, their righteousness was
counted to "all who believed," simply because of their faith, just as it
was with their father Abraham.

Verse 13, "For the promise to Abraham and his offspring that
he would be heir of the world did not come through the law but
through the righteousness of faith." Again, plainly stated, righteousness comes from faith, not obedience to the law. "For if it is the
adherents of the law who are to be the heirs, faith is null and the
promise is void." If righteousness and justification depended upon
obedience or acts and works of the flesh, then faith would be absolutely unnecessary and pointless. And even more than that, if justification depended on obedience and the law, the promise that is
Christ, would become void also.

Christ said, "It is finished." Everything necessary was accomplished by Christ, so if it were to be accomplished through acts and
works of the law and obedience, then Christ's work would be nul-
lified and made void also (Gal. 2:21), but Christ did not say, "It is
finished…once you complete a task, obey a command, partake in
some ritual, etc."

"For the law brings wrath, but where there is no law there is no
transgression."

As we spent all of chapter 3, talking about the inadequacies of
the law to save us, we have already shown that the law is incapable of
producing righteousness but instead brings wrath and solidifies our
sinfulness. But where there is no law, where the law has been fulfilled
and upheld by Christ in its entirety, "It is finished," there is no transgression. Christ has perfectly fulfilled every part of the law, which we
could never do, and has offered His perfect obedience to us, that we
may be made perfect through Him (2 Cor. 5:21).

> That is why it depends on faith, in order
> that the promise may rest on grace and be guar-
> anteed to all his offspring—not only to the adher-
> ents of the law but also to the one who shares the
> faith of Abraham, who is the father of us all, as it

is written, "I have made you the father of many nations"—in the presence of the God in Whom he believed, Who gives life to the dead and calls into existence the things that do not exist.

It must entirely depend upon faith so that it can entirely rest on and be a product of God's grace and be guaranteed to all; otherwise, it would rest on our fallen and incapable ability to reach it ourselves as we are all completely sinful and dead (Rom. 5:6, 8, 10; Eph. 2:5), apart from God's grace to bring dead men back to life. God is the only one that can call into existence the things that do not exist, that being the life and justification of the spiritually dead.

In hope he believed against hope, that he should become the father of many nations, as he had been told, "So shall your offspring be." He did not weaken in faith when he considered his own body, which was as good as dead (since he was about a hundred years old), or when he considered the barrenness of Sarah's womb. No distrust made him waver concerning the promise of God, but he grew strong in his faith as he gave glory to God, fully convinced that God was able to do what He had promised.

Despite the seemingly complete impossibility, from the human perspective, considering Abraham's age and Sarah's barrenness, Abraham trusted and kept his faith in God with regards to His promise of fathering many nations. Abraham relied on God's divine ability, not man's incapability.

That is why his faith was counted to him as righteousness. But the words "It was counted to him" were not written for his sake alone, but for ours also. It will be counted to us who believe in Him Who raised from the dead Jesus our Lord,

Who was delivered up for our trespasses and
raised for our justification.

Again, it was simply and entirely by Abraham's faith that he was
made righteous, and more so if Abraham was justified on the basis of
faith alone, then so too will all others be justified by the same means,
that of faith alone in Christ alone, not by anything else. It applies to
everyone. He Who raised Christ from the dead and offered Him up
for our transgressions and raised Him for our justification credits His
righteousness to those who believe in Him.

Continuing on into chapter 5, "Therefore, since we have been
justified by faith (how many times does this need to be stated, and
how much more plainly can it be stated, that justification comes
entirely and simply by faith alone) we have peace with God through
our Lord Jesus Christ."

Peace: the Greek word there means binding
together what had been separate. The key here
is how we found that peace. We are justified
through faith. Made righteous. Set right with
God. All that He asks is faith in Jesus. See, it had
to be faith. If it were religion, if it were works and
earning it, there would never be peace, because
how much good is good enough? How many
good deeds do you need to cover your bad? When
you're good you're filled with pride. When you
screw up you have guilt, and they both stink, and
neither of them are peaceful. Religion is like play-
ing a game of spiritual red-light/green-light with
an angry god. "He's not looking. How much can
I get away with? He's turning around! Everybody
stop! Aww, caught! Start over again! Banished
from God!" Christians, there are way too many
of us in the endless cycle in between pride and
guilt, still fighting a battle that should've ended

the day you surrendered to Jesus. It is finished!
Lay down your guns and rest in Jesus.[18]

Continue on into verse 2, "Through Him we have also obtained access by faith into this grace in which we stand, and we rejoice in hope of the glory of God." It is only through His grace, accessed by our faith, that we can stand in total hope of His glory. The Greek word for hope here, unlike the English word for "hope," carries no sense of uncertainty with it. It speaks of something that is absolutely certain, just not yet realized or fulfilled.

Verse 3, "More than that, we rejoice in our sufferings, knowing that suffering produces endurance, and endurance produces character, and character produces hope, and hope does not put us to shame, because God's love has been poured into our hearts through the Holy Spirit Who has been given to us." Our righteousness, which is produced through faith, becomes evident in us by our ability to rejoice in suffering, which produces endurance, character, and hope and the gift of the Holy Spirit in us.

Verses 6–11 are some of the most beautiful passages in all of Scripture, reevaluating our fallenness and absolute depravity and evidencing God's immense love for us.

> For while we were still weak, at the right time Christ died for the ungodly. For one will scarcely die for a righteous person—though perhaps for a good person one would dare even to die—but God shows His love for us in that while we were still sinners, Christ died for us. Since, therefore, we have now been justified by His blood, much more shall we be saved by Him from the wrath of God. For if while we were enemies, we were reconciled to God by the death of His Son, much more, now that we are reconciled, shall we be saved by His life. More than that, we also rejoice in God through our Lord Jesus Christ, through Whom we have now received reconciliation.

It is ALL His work. We were weak, ungodly, wretched sinners, enemies of God, dead in our sins, and God shows His infinite, unconditional, and sacrificial love for us in that while we were still in our worst form and wretchedness He sent His Son to die in our place that we may be reconciled to Him. We are justified by His blood, not any action, works, or obedience of ourselves. A dead sinner and enemy of God cannot exact his righteousness by any means. He is dead. Only God can bring to life that which is dead (Rom. 4:17).

Later on in Romans, Paul continues his teaching on this subject. In chapter 9, he spends most of the chapter talking about God's sovereign choice in choosing and calling His elect and chosen people (which we looked at in detail in chapter 4), and then in the last few verses, he comes back to this topic of man's responsibility. Starting in verse 30, he says:

> What shall we say, then? That Gentiles who did not pursue righteousness have attained it, that is, a righteousness that is by faith; but that Israel who pursued a law that would lead to righteousness did not succeed in reaching the law. Why? Because they did not pursue it by faith, but as if it were based on works.

Paul never deviates from this. Repetition is used all throughout Scripture to reinforce and emphasize the importance of a subject, and this topic is readily restated and reinforced through much repetition. His teachings are consistent throughout his books. Once again, he is saying that it is not by works of the law or obedience that one is found justified but by faith alone.

Back in the days of Jesus, the Jewish leaders were so bent on a strict legalist obedience system to the law that they were completely blind when the real and true Messiah that was prophesied had finally come. He had preached that it was only through Himself that one was justified and therefore they accused Him of blasphemy, arrested Him, tortured Him, and murdered Him. Righteousness only comes by faith in Him, not by works or obedience.

Paul continues by quoting Isaiah 28:16, "They have stumbled over the stumbling stone, as it is written, 'Behold, I Am laying in Zion a stone of stumbling, and a rock of offense; and whoever believes in Him will not be put to shame.'" As we looked at this passage from Isaiah earlier in this chapter, we see Paul emphasizing that God will not shame and destroy those who believe in Christ for salvation. It is simply by our faith and belief in Him that we are protected and saved.

Paul carries this into chapter 10. When Paul originally wrote his letter to the Romans, as with all his other letters, he did not include the separation of chapters and verses. Those were all added many centuries later by numerous Biblical scholars, preachers, and theologians to make referencing and navigation through the Scriptures easier, so when these letters were written, as with all of the Bible, it would've all been written as one big whole. So there would be no separation between chapters; chapter 9 would've seamlessly flowed into chapter 10.

Anyway, in verse 4, we see Paul kind of putting the metaphorical "nail in the coffin" of the righteousness through the law issue by saying, "For Christ is the end of the law for righteousness to everyone who believes." Christ came to this earth as God incarnate to do what we never could: to fulfill the law perfectly. Christ fulfilled every aspect of the law perfectly, took our punishment as our substitution, and therefore offers righteousness through Himself to everyone who believes and places their faith in Him as Lord and Savior. He took what we deserved, and in return, He gave us what we do not deserve and could not possibly earn. We receive it through faith, not obedience.

Paul continues his lesson on justification through faith in verse 6:

> But the righteousness based on faith says, "Do not say in your heart, 'Who will ascend into Heaven?' (that is, to bring Christ down) or 'Who will descend into the abyss?' (that is, to bring Christ up from the dead). But what does

> it say? 'The word is near you, in your mouth and
> in your heart' (that is, the word of faith that we
> proclaim)."

Paul here is quoting Deuteronomy 30:12–14 and "his point is that the righteousness of faith does not require some impossible odyssey through the universe to find Christ. The journey of Romans 10:6–7 is unnecessary because God has clearly revealed the way of salvation: It is by faith. The message of faith is the way to God."[19]

Paul then culminates this with some of the most straightforward and complete passages regarding man's responsibility in all of Scripture. Starting with verse 9, "because if you confess with your mouth that Jesus is Lord and believe that God raised Him from the dead, you will be saved. For with the heart one believes and is justified, and with the mouth one confesses and is saved."

That is our whole contribution to this infinite equation of salvation. The Amplified Holy Bible translation is an English translation which strives to capture and pull out the full meaning behind the original Hebrew and Greek texts because both Hebrew and Greek are far more detailed and substance-packed languages than English is. Oftentimes, some of the depth of a passage is limited due to shallow English translation. The AMP translation, trying to pull out the full depth of the original Greek text, reads like this:

> [B]ecause if you acknowledge and confess
> with your mouth that Jesus is Lord [recognizing
> His power, authority, and majesty as God], and
> believe in your heart that God raised Him from
> the dead, you will be saved. For with the heart a
> person believes [in Christ as Savior] resulting in
> his justification [that is, being made righteous—
> being freed of the guilt of sin and made accept-
> able to God]; and with the mouth he acknowl-
> edges and confesses [his faith openly], resulting
> in and confirming [his] salvation.

Christ has done all of the work. "It is finished," and our entire piece of the formula is confessing in our hearts that we are sinful and in need of His substitutionary work, and placing our faith in Him Who took our place and offers justification through His name. Paul states and restates this twice here in this single passage to emphasize the completeness of this.

Again, this is not a simple belief in Jesus's existence but a confessing and repenting of sins, a full heart surrender to Christ as Savior, and placing your faith in the Only One Who can save you and bring you to Heaven, not in your own works or obedience. This is man's responsibility.

Paul goes on to quote Isaiah 28:16 again, "For the Scripture says, 'Everyone who believes in Him will not be put to shame.'" Once again, reinforcing that it is only through belief in Christ as Savior that we are justified.

Verse 12, "For there is no distinction between Jew and Greek; for the same Lord is Lord over all, bestowing His riches on all who call on Him. For everyone who calls on the name of the Lord will be saved." Here, Paul restates and quotes again from Joel 2:32 that anyone who turns to Christ and calls on Him will be saved. There is no other requirement by man in order to attain salvation. It is offered to anyone and everyone—there is no distinction—who call on Him and come to Him for salvation. You cannot attain it any other way but through faith in Christ alone. That is man's responsibility.

In the beginning of the first letter to the Corinthians, Paul makes a quick mention to this topic also. In verse 21, he starts off by mentioning the foolishness of the world and those that are perishing. "For since, in the wisdom of God, the world did not know God through wisdom."

John MacArthur explains this by saying:

> God wisely established that men could not
> come to know Him by human wisdom. That
> would exalt men, so God designed to save help-
> less sinners through the preaching of a message
> that was so simple the "worldly wise" deemed it

nonsense (cf. Rom. 1:18–23). From the human side, salvation requires and comes only through faith (cf. John 1:12 and Rom. 10:8–17).

Then Paul states, "It pleased God…to save those who believe." As is always the case, we are saved entirely by our belief in Him. The perishing fools of the world see this as folly, but time and time again, we are taught that it is by our faith in Jesus Christ alone that justifies us to God and not by any wisdom, knowledge, work, or obedience of our own.

Paul continues in verse 22, "For Jews demand signs and Greeks seek wisdom, but we preached Christ crucified, a stumbling block to Jews and folly to Gentiles, but to those who are called, both Jews and Greeks, Christ [is] the power of God and the wisdom of God." To everyone that is not initially called and known by God, this simple and straightforward message of salvation will seem like utter nonsense and foolishness. Regardless, the simple message of Christ crucified is the only message that has the power to save. And Paul backs this up in chapter 2, verse 2 of this same letter to the Corinthians by proclaiming of himself, "For I decided to know nothing among you except for Jesus Christ and Him crucified." Though simply possessing the knowledge and wisdom of this message is not enough, it requires complete belief and faith in this message.

Paul carries this teaching right into his letter to the Galatians. In chapter 2, he gives us another section in which he discusses justification by faith. Starting in verse 15, we read:

> We ourselves are Jews by birth and not Gentile sinners; yet we know that a person is not justified by works of the law but through faith in Jesus Christ, so we also have believed in Christ Jesus, in order to be justified by faith in Christ and not by works of the law, because by works of the law no one will be justified.

Paul once again through repetition states this simple and complete concept twice in the same verse. Justification comes through faith in Jesus Christ. Period! That's it! It does not come by our works or any form of obedience to the law! "NO ONE will be justified by works of the law" or through obedience to it. Whether that's the Ten Commandments, sacraments, rituals, works, acts, obedience, etc., it does not count toward righteousness. It is entirely and simply through our faith in Jesus Christ alone. That is it! To add anything else to it destroys the Gospel as Paul shows in verses 20–21.

> I have been crucified with Christ. It is no longer I who live, but Christ Who lives in me. And the life I now live in the flesh I live by faith in the Son of God, Who loved me and gave Himself for me. I do not nullify the grace of God, for if righteousness were through the law, then Christ died for no purpose.

Once we place our faith in Jesus Christ, we are crucified with Him, and His life becomes our life, and our life becomes His life. We are immediately attached to Him by our faith, and then we subsequently live our lives with Him in faith. It all depends on faith. To add any other piece or any other responsibility of our own to it warps and distorts the Gospel and renders void, unnecessary, and pointless the sacrifice of Christ.

By adding any form of obedience or action on our own part nullifies the grace of God and turns it into our dues and something that is owed to us (Rom. 4:4). For God's grace to be upheld and for the sacrifice and completed work of Christ to remain valid, nothing can be added to it. Salvation is received entirely by God's grace, through Christ's completed work, and is accessed only through our faith in Christ alone as our Savior and acceptance of His finished work done in our place. Anyone that insists that they can earn salvation by their own efforts undermines the foundation of Christianity and renders unnecessary the entire work and death and resurrection of Christ.

Chapter 3 of Galatians is packed full of teaching as well. Starting in verse 2, we read:

> Let me ask you only this: Did you receive the Spirit by works of the law or by hearing with faith? Are you so foolish? Having begun by the Spirit, are you now being perfected by the flesh? Did you suffer so many things in vain—if indeed it was in vain? Does He Who supplies the Spirit to you and works miracles among you do so by works of the law, or by hearing with faith—just as Abraham "believed God, and it was counted to him as righteousness?"

Paul is ridiculing them for the foolish notion that they could be saved by works and obedience of the law. He plainly states that it cannot be through any actions of the flesh that they are perfected but only and entirely through faith, and then he requotes Genesis 15:6, "Just as Abraham 'believed God, and it was counted to him as righteousness.'"

Righteousness comes from belief in Christ as Savior, plain and simple. Continuing on in verse 7:

> Know then that it is those of faith who are sons of Abraham. And the Scripture, foreseeing that God would justify the Gentiles by faith, preached the Gospel beforehand to Abraham, saying, "In you all the nations shall be blessed." So then, those who are of faith are blessed along with Abraham, the man of faith.

Anyone and everyone who has faith in Jesus Christ as Savior is seen as a son of Abraham, the man of faith, and is found righteous just as he is righteous entirely on the basis of that faith, not by any other qualification. Faith, again and again, is listed as the only prerequisite on our part for righteousness and justification. Verse 10 once again assaults the reliance to the law:

> For all who rely on works of the law are under a curse; for it is written, "Cursed be everyone who does not abide by all things written in the Book of the Law, and do them." Now it is evident that no one is justified before God by the law, for "the righteous shall live by faith." But the law is not of faith, rather 'the one that does them shall live by them.

We have already discussed Galatians 3:10–11 several times in previous chapters, but Paul here is quoting Deuteronomy 27:26, Habakkuk 2:4, and Leviticus 18:5 and showing that it has always been this way. Righteousness comes through faith alone, and no one will be found righteous and justified before God through the law or obedience. For anyone to live by the law, they have to keep it perfectly in its entirety, which is utterly impossible; therefore, they are cursed if they choose that route for salvation and are bound for condemnation.

But for those who put their faith in Jesus, "Christ redeemed us from the curse of the law by becoming a curse for us—for it is written, 'Cursed is everyone who is hanged on a tree' (Deut. 21:23)—so that in Christ Jesus the blessing of Abraham might come to the Gentiles, so that we might receive the promised Spirit through faith."

Christ became cursed Himself instead by taking our place and being our substitution, bearing all of our sins for us, and since He did fulfill the law perfectly and was therefore innocent, He was able to redeem us from being cursed by the law ourselves. For those who still insist on making it an obedience system to righteousness, then they are still cursed by the law as they have not put their faith in Christ as their Savior and His saving work. They are still relying on their own works to earn their way to righteousness.

This is not what Christ came for. He came to fulfill the law and abolish the complete inability we possess to fulfill it perfectly ourselves. All we need to do is acknowledge His perfect and finished work done in our place and put our faith in that completed work as being our passport into righteousness, none of it being done by us but entirely by the work of Christ. Our part is acceptance, surrender, and faith. And through all of this, we are assured of our salvation by the receiving of the promised Holy Spirit.

In verses 3:15–22:

> Paul refutes an anticipated possible objection to his use of Abraham to prove the doctrine of justification of faith, that the giving of the law at Sinai after Abraham brought about a change and a better method of salvation. The apostle dismissed that argument by showing the superiority of the Abrahamic Covenant (vv. 15–18), and the inferiority of the law (vv. 19–22). Paul emphasized that there is no middle ground between law (works) and promise (grace); the two principles are mutually exclusive ways of salvation (cf. Rom. 4:14). An "inheritance" by definition is something granted, not worked for, as proven in the case of Abraham. Paul's persuasive argument that the promise is superior to the law raises an obvious question: What was the purpose of the law? Paul's answer is that the law reveals man's utter sinfulness, inability to save himself, and desperate need of a Savior—it was never intended to be the way of salvation (cf. Rom. 7:1–13).[20]

Verse 21 shows the absurdity of placing the law above the promise. "Is the law then contrary to the promises of God? Certainly not! For if a law had been given that could give life, then righteousness would indeed be by the law."

> Paul uses the strongest Greek negative here to disdain the idea that the law and the promise

are at opposite purposes. Since God gave them both and does not work against Himself, law and promise work in harmony; the law reveals man's sinfulness and need for the salvation freely offered in the promise. If the law could have provided righteousness and eternal life, there would be no gracious promise.[21]

Verse 22 continues, "But the Scripture imprisoned everything under sin, so that the promise by faith in Jesus Christ might be given to those who believe." As always, it is simply by our faith in Jesus Christ that we receive the promise of righteousness and relief from sin, just as was given to Abraham. In verse 23, Paul explains a little of the history of redemption:

> Now before faith came, we were held captive under the law, imprisoned until the coming faith would be revealed. So then, the law was our guardian until Christ came, in order that we might be justified by faith. But now that faith has come, we are no longer under a guardian, for in Christ Jesus you are all sons of God, through faith.

Prior to the arrival of the coming Messiah, the law was present to show us our sinfulness and need for the Messiah and was meant to help keep our focus looking toward Him. It was not to take the place of Him. Once the Messiah was presented, the source of righteousness was revealed. The law simply acted as a mirror, showing us our sins, and therefore escorted us to Christ. Verse 27 raises some questions and possible objections as some people insist that it teaches baptismal salvation, that baptism is necessary for salvation, and that salvation is not achieved until baptism is met, which goes against everything we've already discussed and shown. We will dive deeply into that issue later on in chapter 9.

What we want to see here at this point, though, is that through everything we have looked at and read in the rest of these verses, we become one with Christ. We are spiritually united with Him, and positionally, we are placed into His death and resurrection and receive righteousness through Him. And once this takes place, we are also united with everyone that is in Christ as "For as many of you were baptized into Christ have put on Christ. There is neither Jew nor Greek, there is neither slave nor free, there is no male and female, for you are all one in Christ Jesus. And if you are Christ's, then you are Abraham's offspring, heirs according to promise."

In chapter 5, Paul gives us a little bit more. He is still discussing the inabilities of the law and compares it to a yoke of slavery and says in verses 4–6, "You are severed from Christ, you who would be justified by the law; you have fallen away from grace. For through the Spirit, by faith, we ourselves eagerly wait for the hope of righteousness. For in Christ Jesus neither circumcision nor uncircumcision counts for anything, but only faith working through love." By trying to reach righteousness through the law, you are severed from Christ and have fallen away from God's amazing grace! He offers everything to you graciously and freely; your part is merely accepting it by faith. It does not depend on obedience or any actions of the flesh or even any type of religious ceremonies, here symbolized by circumcision. It is entirely and only through faith in Christ as Savior.

Paul's letter to the Ephesians has much to teach us as well. In the early part of the first chapter, we found the beautiful truth of God's divine sovereignty in His election of those chosen to be His children and His adoption of us as sons and daughters, but then in verse 13, we see our responsibility in this eternal equation. Starting in verse 11, we read, "In Him we have obtained an inheritance,"—this is a passive past tense verb signifying that we have already passively obtained this inheritance without any active work of our own—"having been predestined according to the purpose of Him Who works all things according to the counsel of His will, so that we who were the first to hope in Christ might be to the praise of His glory."

We have already spent a great deal of time on this verse in the issue of divine sovereignty, but again we see that it is ultimately and initially all God's work in predestination and according to His purpose that we are brought to Him, but we start to see our side in this in verses 12 and 13. As we discussed in the last chapter, to our feeble and simple minds, the issues of divine sovereignty and man's responsibility seem to contradict each other and run parallel, but we must accept them both as truth as they are both Biblically taught in great substance throughout Scripture. God ultimately calls us to Him and elects those who will be His children, but we do need to accept this call. And we see our part of the equation here.

In verse 12, we read that this inheritance is provided to "we who were the first to hope in Christ…to the praise of His glory." As stated earlier, the Greek word for hope here carries a sense of absolute assurance with it. It does not contain a sense of possible uncertainty as is common in the English use of the word. This verse speaks of a wholehearted faith and assurance in Christ as Savior all for the praise of His glory. This is saving faith. Verse 13 continues, "In Him you also, when you heard the Word of Truth, the Gospel of your salvation, and believed in Him, were sealed with the Holy Spirit, Who is the guarantee of our inheritance until we acquire possession of it, to the praise of His glory."

This verse contains the entire formula and outcome of man's responsibility. First, we see the words of Romans 10:17 reiterated here ("faith comes from hearing, and hearing through the Word of Christ") in that we must first hear the Word of Truth, the Gospel of our salvation, and then upon hearing the Word, once we believe in Him, we are immediately sealed with the Holy Spirit. There is no delay in that process. The moment you accept Christ as Savior, you enter into righteousness and are immediately sealed with the Spirit. Just as we saw in many examples during the book of Acts, the moment someone accepted Christ, "the Spirit fell on them, just as He has fallen on us" (Acts 10:44, 11:15).

There is no interim waiting for you to complete some checklist or any other complimentary acts of obedience. We are immediately sealed with the Spirit. He is the immediate assurance of our salvation upon acceptance of Christ as Savior. And He is also the immutable guarantee that we will be held secure until the full completion of our glorification when we will acquire the full possession of this inheritance offered to us by God—all for the glory of God.

We also see this in verse 19ff, which says:

> [W]hat is the immeasurable greatness of His power toward us who believe, according to the working of His great might that He worked in Christ when He raised Him from the dead and seated Him at His right hand in the Heavenly places, far above all rule and authority and power and dominion, and above every name that is named, not only in this age but also in the one to come. And He put all things under His feet and gave Him as head over all things to the church, which is His body, the fullness of Him Who fills all in all.

We see again that it is simply to us who believe in Him that this immeasurable gift is given that we receive all of His greatness simply by faith in Him. There is no other part of the formula on our part. The rest is all done by the workings of His great might. All rule, authority, power, dominion, and all other things are put under the control of Christ. Christ is entirely given control; we simply need to accept that reality.

Ephesians chapter 2 contains a few beautiful verses that touch on man's responsibility also. In verses 8–9, we read, "For by grace you have been saved through faith. And this is not of your own doing; it is the gift of God, not a result of works, so that no one may boast."

There is much more to this passage than just what I am going to pull out of it in this chapter, which we will speak about in the following chapters; but for this chapter, focusing on man's responsibility, we look at "you have been saved through faith...not a result of works, so that no one may boast."

As has been continually shown to us throughout Scripture, our part of the equation is simply and fully based on faith. That is our sole responsibility in the equation leading to salvation. We are saved through faith. And it also shows us once again here, that it is NOT by ANY of our own works, not a single one; that way, no one can be prideful of their salvation as something that they earned or deserved. There is no other action or piece mentioned on our part. We are saved entirely and fully by faith alone in Jesus Christ as Savior and Lord. And this is reiterated in chapter 3, verses 12 and 17, which read, "in Jesus Christ our Lord we have boldness and access with confidence through our faith in Him...so that Christ may dwell in your hearts through faith."

Just like the hope and assurance that was talked about in the verses we looked at in chapter 1 of Ephesians, we are told here that we have boldness and access to the Kingdom of God through our faith and that we can have complete confidence in this truth and that Christ will dwell in our hearts through faith. If Christ is in your heart, rest assured that you are saved and belong to Him. All these things are made beautiful truth and reality upon our faith in Him. That is our only responsibility in all of this.

In his letter to the Philippians, Paul gives us a little bit more to reinforce this topic. In chapter 3, verses 8–9, we read:

> I count everything as loss because of the surpassing worth of knowing Christ Jesus my Lord. For His sake I have suffered the loss of all things and count them as rubbish, in order that I may gain Christ and be found in Him, not having a righteousness of my own that comes from the law, but that which comes through faith in Christ, the righteousness from God that depends on faith.

In verse 8, here we see that Paul considers everything else in his life to be utterly meaningless when in comparison to his relationship with Christ. If this isn't a perfect picture of total surrender to Christ as Savior, then I don't think there is one. This is a mirror image of the words that Christ spoke back in Luke 14:26–27, 33, when He preached about the cost of discipleship:

> If anyone comes to Me and does not hate his own father and mother and wife and children and brothers and sisters, yes, and even his own life, he cannot be My disciple. Whoever does not bear his own cross and come after Me cannot be My disciple. Anyone of you who does not renounce all that he has cannot be My disciple.

Now, before anyone jumps to legalistic conclusions, as I said before, this is not saying that you have to emotionally hate and divorce yourself from your parents and family and never have any loved ones throughout your lives if you are going to follow Christ. This is merely a strict lesson comparison. Jesus is saying, just as Paul is showing in verse 8 of Philippians, that everything else in your life, when considered alongside of Christ, should pale in comparison to your love and devotion for Him. God created the family structure and marriage and blesses those unions. So He is not reversing His teachings of those relationships but simply stating that your love and devotion to Him should be of the highest priority in your life, even far beyond your devotion and love to your earthly relationships. And this is the exact same picture we are seeing here from the mouth of Paul.

Paul is making that same claim when he says that he counts all earthly things as rubbish when compared to knowing Christ and being found in Him. This is the picture of full surrender and faith in Christ that we have been trying to portray leading to salvation. He goes on to say, just as he has preached time and time again, that his righteousness certainly cannot be of his own doing through works of the law. His righteousness strictly comes from God and is facilitated through faith in Christ's completed work. It is not through the law or obedience to such. It "depends on faith."

In Paul's letters to the Thessalonians, we are also given a few more references on man's responsibility. In his first letter, in chapter

4, verse 14, he says, "For since we believe that Jesus died and rose again, even so, through Jesus, God will bring with Him those who have fallen asleep." This verse is in the middle of a section of passages in which Paul is preaching about the rapture of the church, which is a topic for a whole different book, but here we will look at the only condition on being brought to Heaven, whether dead or alive here on earth. That one condition is "since we believe that Jesus died and rose again."

Just as throughout all of Scripture, our entrance into Heaven does not depend on obedience or works of the law but upon our belief in Jesus as Savior. And again, it's not just a simple belief that Christ existed, but it is a wholehearted surrendered belief in Christ as Savior. That is true saving faith, like Paul just described in Philippians. And by it, "God will bring with Him" those who "believe that Jesus died and rose again."

In the first chapter of his second letter, we read in verse 10 "when He comes on that day to be glorified in His saints and to be marveled at among all who have believed." All those who have believed in Jesus Christ as Savior will be together on that day that Jesus comes and will marvel at His glory. Your belief in Jesus Christ as Savior will assure your presence in that moment.

In chapter 2 of the second letter to the Thessalonians, we first see a couple references to the negative side of belief and surrender. In verses 9–10, we read: "The coming of the lawless one is by the activity of satan with all power and false signs and wonders, and with all wicked deception for those who are perishing, because they refuse to love the truth and so be saved."

If you refuse to love and do not believe in the truth of Christ, you will be among those that are perishing alongside of satan. Verse 12 tells us "in order that all may be condemned who did not believe the truth but had pleasure in unrighteousness." Again, we see that those who do not believe the truth, those who lived a life of unrighteousness will all be condemned and will perish. There is no exception. Belief in Jesus Christ is our access to Him, and without it, we will forever be apart from Him and condemned.

This is followed up by verse 13 which reads, "But we ought always to give thanks to God for you, brothers beloved by the Lord, because God chose you as the firstfruits to be saved, through sanctification by the Spirit and belief in the truth." This verse first touches on God's divine election of us, which we have talked about in a previous chapter but also mentions our responsibility which is our "belief in the truth." Our part of the eternal formula of salvation is simply belief and faith, which is surrender in the truth and the Gospel of Jesus Christ.

In Paul's letters to Timothy, we receive a couple more references to man's responsibility. In his first letter, first chapter, we read in verses 15–16:

> The saying is trustworthy and deserving of full acceptance, that Jesus Christ came into the world to save sinners, of whom I am the foremost. But I received mercy for this reason, that in me, as the foremost, Jesus Christ might display His perfect patience as an example to those who were to believe in Him for eternal life.

In these verses, Paul first of all confesses the enormity of his fallenness and admits himself as the worst of all sinners. This is the Apostle Paul speaking, arguably the holiest man that has walked throughout any part of history—next to Jesus Himself, of course (even though the gap between those two is still immensely vast),[22] yet he is calling himself out as the worst of all sinners!

This mirrors his words in Romans 7:24, "O wretched man that I am." Before his conversion Paul, then named Saul, blasphemed the name of God and vehemently persecuted, arrested, tortured, and murdered the Christian church. He arguably was the worst of all sinners, prior to Jesus working in his life. But now, here as the converted and reborn Apostle Paul, he teaches us the enormous beauty of the Gospel and expresses the highest emphasis by pre-labeling this statement by saying "the saying is trustworthy and deserving of full acceptance."

What he is telling us in these verses is that despite being as the worst of sinners and therefore being the most extensive example possible of the never-ending love of God, Christ poured out His mercy upon Paul and also, subsequently, all sinners worldwide throughout history in order to display the infinite and perfect inexhaustible patience of Jesus, even to reach down and save even the deepest and worst of all sinners, and that this great and glorious interaction is formulated on our part simply by our belief in Him, which is all that is necessary to lead us to eternal life! This is the one and only demand Paul gives from the human side as far as our participation or responsibility in salvation.

In Paul's second letter to Timothy, we see another quick point in this matter. In chapter 3 verses 14–15, we read:

> But as for you, continue in what you have learned and have firmly believed, knowing from whom you learned it and how from childhood you have been acquainted with the sacred writings, which are able to make you wise for salvation through faith in Christ Jesus.

Here, Paul is urging Timothy to stay strong and persevere in what he has been taught and is referring to the Gospel and the Scriptures, the sacred writings of God's chosen and inspired authors. This also hints back to what we have learned about faith being produced upon hearing the Word of God in Romans 10:17 and Ephesians 1:13 from the words "the sacred writings, which are able to make you wise for salvation." It is through the Word that our faith is built, and it is through our faith that we have salvation in Jesus Christ as this verse states in closing. And as verses 16 and 17 continue, we are told, "All Scripture is God-breathed and profitable for teaching, for reproof, for correction, and for training in righteousness, that the man of God may be competent, equipped for every good work."

God's Word is not only where our faith is built from, but it is our source of all we need to know for righteousness and to live and act as men and women of God. One more thing from this passage, the use of the "every good work" used here in no way refers to some type of work that is necessary to be righteous but instead refers to good works of the righteous (Eph. 2:10). It is referring to the effect of righteousness, not the cause of righteousness.

In Hebrews chapter 4, we are offered a small glimpse at this also. In the first part of verse 3, we read, "For we who have believed enter that rest." Here, the writer to the Hebrews is writing about a type of rest that is a reference back to the Old Testament.

> The earthly rest that God promised to give was life in the land of Canaan, which Israel would receive as their inheritance (Deut. 12:9– 10; Josh. 21:44; 1 Kings 8:56). Because of rebellion against God, an entire generation of the children of Israel were prohibited from entering into that rest in the Promised Land (cf. Deut. 28:65; Lam. 1:3). The application of this picture is to an individual's spiritual rest in the Lord, which was precedent in the Old Testament (cf. Ps. 116:7; Isa. 28:12). At salvation, every believer enters the true rest, the realm of spiritual promise, never again laboring to achieve through personal effort a righteousness that pleases God.[23]

Here in the New Testament, the writer is not referring to the rest of the Promised Land, but it is a reference to the spiritual rest we receive in Jesus Christ, which is evidenced by verse 1, "Therefore, while the promise of entering His rest still stands," and we enter that rest simply by believing in the source of that rest, Jesus Christ, our Lord and Savior.

In chapter 10:38–39 we read, "'but My righteous one shall live by faith, and if he shrinks back, My soul has no pleasure in him.' But we are not those who shrink back and are destroyed, but of those who have faith and preserve their souls." The first part of verse 38 we have already touched on. It is a quote from Habakkuk 2:4 and is also requoted in Rom. 1:17 and Gal. 3:11, "The righteous shall live by faith." Strictly by your faith alone in Christ alone you are found righteous. In the second part of verse 38, we find a passage that some may mistake as teaching that one can lose his/her salvation. We will save that for later in chapter 8. The end of verse 39 tells us that it is those who have faith that are the ones who are preserved. So we see here that through our faith alone we are made righteous and also preserved unto Christ.

Chapter 11 of Hebrews is a beautiful account of thirteen specifically named saints of the Old Testament and also of many more referred to in a general sense. This chapter has been given many nicknames over the years, such as "The Saints' Hall of Fame," "The Honor Roll of Old Testament Saints," "Heroes of Faith," and the "Hall of Fame of Faith," just to name a few. The entire chapter deals with the topic of faith and focuses on the lives of the saints named as they all testify to the value of living by faith and not by acts or works. The first verse of chapter 11 offers us a definition of what faith is.

"Now faith is the assurance of things hoped for, the conviction of things not seen."

"Faith is the assurance of things hoped for."

This speaks of absolute confidence in these things with not even the slightest sense of doubt. The word used here for assurance, *hypostasis* in the Greek, is the same word that is used elsewhere to mean "exact imprint" or "confidence," and the Greek word that is used for hope here, *elpizo*, as we have mentioned before, carries that same sense of assurance carrying with it zero sense of doubt. The sense of this passage in the Greek displays a sense of a title deed or confirmation that is divinely guaranteed. In the English, the word *hope* usually carries with it some negative sense of uncertainty, but the Greek word used here carries the sense of absolute certainty. Zero doubt. This faith described here in verse 1 "involves the most solid possible conviction, the God-given present assurance of a future reality."[24] It is also a "conviction of things not seen."

This faith is not based on empirical evidence that can be seen and touched but on a divine and absolute assurance which is only a gift that can be given to us by God (cf. Eph. 2:8). This calls to mind the words of Jesus when He said, "Blessed are those who have not seen and yet have believed" (John 20:29). True faith carries with it full surrender to the manifestation of a future truth that has not yet been revealed. It does not instill any sense of uncertainty or doubt. It is full assurance that God will do what He says He will do and accomplish what He promises. It is wholehearted faith that Jesus is Who He said He is, did what He said He did, and will come again to fulfill the prophecy of His completed work in our lives bringing us into the presence of God in Heaven once we leave this earth, and that it is only through His work that any of this can be fulfilled. It is full assurance that Jesus Christ is our Lord and Savior and our One and Only Way to be found righteous, holy, and redeemed before God.

Verse 2 shows us the reward of this faith defined. "For by it the people of old received their commendation." This verse shows us that the post-mentioned saints, all those named, specifically and in general, have received their commendation simply and solely through their faith. It says nothing of receiving due to their acts or works or obedience. The word here for commendation in the Greek, *martyreo*, refers to God's divine approval or affirmation of each of these saints, and it is being granted to them due to their faith alone and for no other reason.

Verse 3, "By faith we understand that the universe was created by the Word of God, so that what is seen was not made out of things that are visible." This testifies and references our infinite and true Creator God Who created and controls all things which we touched on in chapter 1; He Who our faith must rely on.

Verse 4 of Hebrews, chapter 11, starts the Hall of Fame of the Saints and starts with the testimony of Abel. Some may wonder why Adam and Eve were skipped over and not included in this section, but they had seen God. They had communed with Him in the Garden of Eden prior to the fall. They fellowshipped with Him and talked to Him face-to-face; therefore, their children were the first to exhibit faith in the unseen God; God Whom they had not seen directly, personally, like Adam and Eve had. Notice also that in each of the following examples and testimonies of the saints, they are all introduced by the phrase "By faith," signifying that it is only by this kind of true saving faith, an inherent trust and enduring confidence in the power, wisdom, and goodness of God that they were commended, brought to, and found righteous before God.

Verse 4 starts this off, "By faith Abel offered to God a more acceptable sacrifice than Cain, through which he was commended as righteous, God commending him by accepting his gifts. And through his faith, though he died, he still speaks." In the story of Cain and Abel, found in Genesis chapter 4, we see that the offerings provided by Cain were not acceptable to God because they were not according to the instructions of God regarding offerings (though not recorded or laid out in Genesis but throughout the rest of Scripture) that blood must be shed (cf. Gen. 3:21; Heb. 12:24) to atone for sin. Cain gave of his harvest of the ground with crops; Abel gave of the firstborn of his flock and their fat portions which obediently corresponded with the instructions of sacrifice.

Both brothers would have known what God's instructions were, but only Abel responded accordingly. Through Abel's faith, evidenced by his obedience to God's requirements regarding sacrifices, Abel was "commended as righteous" by God.

> Christ Himself referred to the righteousness of Abel (Matt. 23:35). Cain's sacrifice evidenced that he was just going through the motions of ritual in a disobedient manner, not evidencing authentic faith. Without faith no one can receive imputed righteousness (cf. Gen. 15:6). Abel's offering proved something about his faith that was not demonstrated by Cain's offering.[25]

> Righteousness has always been imputed by God to sinful men only on the basis of obedient faith in His Word. Abel's "more acceptable sacrifice" could have been pronounced as such by God only on the basis that Abel believed God and offered the type of sacrifice specified by God—a slain animal, whose blood was shed as an atonement, or "covering," for the sin of the

one offering it as a substitute; whereas Cain, for reasons of pride, did not.[26]

Verse 5 continues:

> By faith Enoch was taken up so that he should not see death, and he was not found, because God had taken him. Now before he was taken he was commended as having pleased God. And without faith it is impossible to please Him, for whoever would draw near to God must believe that He exists and that He rewards those who seek Him.

Enoch was one of only two people mentioned throughout all of Scripture that did not see death, that did not die a physical death, but instead was taken straight to Heaven. The other was Elijah. Some have debated that Melchizedek was a third to not have seen death, but there is also good evidence that Melchizedek was a preincarnate theophany of Jesus Christ to Abraham during a very tumultuous time in history when Abraham needed special comfort and encouragement from God (cf. Gen. 14:18–19 and Heb. 7).

Anyway, we read the account of Enoch in Genesis 5:21–24:

> When Enoch had lived 65 years, he fathered Methuselah. Enoch walked with God after he fathered Methuselah 300 years and had other sons and daughters. Thus all the days of Enoch were 365 years. Enoch walked with God, and he was not, for God took him.

Enoch is also only one of two people in the Bible, the other being Noah, to be listed as having enjoyed the distinct intimacy of a relationship in "walking with God." This is clearly a unique and blessed attribute, whereas Enoch was taken straight to Heaven without dying, and Noah was the single patriarch who was, along with his direct family members, saved from a worldwide catastrophe which destroyed the rest of the (very wicked) earthly population at that time. This intimacy that Enoch had with God, "walking with Him," being "commended as having pleased God," was all attributed to his faith and belief in God alone. These two verses, 5 and 6, also mention straightforwardly that it is impossible to please God without faith, and that in order to draw near to Him, you must believe that He exists and that He rewards those who seek Him. There are no other prerequisites listed for righteousness. Faith and belief in the One True God alone and that He is the only One that is able to do so and will reward men's faith in Him, leading to forgiveness and righteousness just as He has promised, are the only requirements.

Verse 7 lists the testimony of Noah:

> By faith Noah, being warned by God concerning events as yet unseen, in reverent fear constructed an ark for the saving of his household. By this he condemned the world and became an heir of the righteousness that comes by faith.

First of all, this is not advocating obedience leading to righteousness. Noah obeyed out of his faith and reverence to God. Noah's faith in God led to his trusting and respect of God's Word and warning and to his "reverent fear" to the validity of God's warning, so as to obey. Like Enoch before him, Noah "walked with God" (Gen. 6:9), pleasing God, and was commended by his faith. We are specifically told that he "became an heir of the righteousness that comes by faith."

Verse 8 starts the testimony of Abraham and Sarah and is the lengthiest of the personal testimonies presented here. The term "By faith" is used four times throughout their testimony.

> By faith Abraham obeyed when he was called to go out to a place that he was to receive as an inheritance. And he went out, not knowing where he was going. By faith he went to live in

> the land of promise, as in a foreign land, living in tents with Isaac and Jacob, heirs with him of the same promise. For he was looking forward to the city that has foundations, who's Designer and Builder is God.

This first part of this section references the divine call of Abraham to leave the nation of his youth and heritage and to move to the land of promise that God tells him will be his inheritance. We pick up the story in Genesis chapter 12.

> The Lord said to Abraham, "Go from your country and your kindred and your father's house to the land that I will show you, and I will make of you a great nation, and I will bless you and make your name great, so that you will be a blessing. I will bless those who bless you, and him who dishonors you I will curse, and in you all the families of the earth shall be blessed." So Abraham went, as the Lord had told him.

Abraham obeyed God's call and command to uproot his family and move to the Promised Land, but his blessing and his right standing with God was not based on his obedience but by his faith which led to his obedience. "By faith," as we read twice so far in the Hebrews passage, Abraham believed God's promise and accepted His divine call to inherit this new Promised Land and that his name would be made great and that he would become a great nation, and therefore, he obeyed God's call and followed. And all of us who believe in Jesus Christ are beneficiaries of this beautiful blessing as we are all children of Abraham through faith (Rom. 4:16).

Jumping back to Galatians chapter 3, let's look again at what it tells us about Abraham, our forefather. Starting in verse 6,

> Abraham "believed God, and it was counted to him as righteousness." Know then that it is

those of faith who are the sons of Abraham. And the Scripture, foreseeing that God would justify the Gentiles by faith (there's that phrase again), preached the Gospel beforehand to Abraham, saying, "In you shall all the nations be blessed." So then, those who are of faith are blessed along with Abraham, the man of faith.

And in verse 29, "And if you are Christ's, then you are Abraham's offspring, heirs according to promise." So again, we see that Abraham was counted as righteous by his faith and that by his faith, he received the promise, and that by faith, we have all become Abraham's offspring and have received that same blessing.

In verse 11, back in Hebrews, we switch over to the testimony of Sarah, Abraham's wife.

> By faith Sarah herself received power to conceive, even when she was past the age, since she considered Him faithful Who had promised. Therefore from one man, and him as good as dead, were born descendants as many as the stars of Heaven and as many as the innumerable grains of sand by the seashore.

Now Sarah was barren. She could not have children. Yet, we see God's covenant promise in Genesis 15, starting at verse 1:

> The Lord came to Abram in a vision: "Fear not, Abram, I Am your Shield; your reward will be great..." But Abram said, "Behold, You have given me no offspring, and a member of my household will be my heir." And behold the word of the Lord came to him: "This man shall not be your heir, one who comes from your own body will be your heir.' And He brought him outside and said, "Look toward Heaven, and number the stars, if you are

able to number them." Then He said to him, "So
shall your offspring be." And he believed the Lord,
and He counted it to him as righteousness.

Even though Sarah was barren, the Lord promised Abraham
and Sarah that a child of their own blood would be the promised
child that this great nation of Abraham would come from. However,
they had to wait twenty-five years for that promise to be fulfilled.
During this time, they grew impatient and tried to take matters into
their own hands. The custom of this time was that if a wife were
barren, she would give her maidservant as a surrogate mother. So
Abraham slept with Hagar, Sarah's maidservant, and they gave birth
to Ishmael. Yet this was not God's promise.

Regardless, through Ishmael, Abraham did give birth to many
nations as Ishmael is the forefather of the entire Arab nations. The
birth of the Jewish and later the Christian nations were to come from
God's promise of a blood son through Abraham and Sarah, not a
surrogate.

Picking up in Genesis 17:15, we read:

> God said to Abraham, "Your wife... Sarah...
> I will bless her, and moreover, I will give you a
> son by her. I will bless her and she shall become
> nations; kings of peoples shall come from her...
> Sarah your wife shall bear you a son, and you
> shall call his name Isaac. I will establish My cov-
> enant with him as an everlasting covenant for his
> offspring after him... I will establish My cove-
> nant with Isaac, whom Sarah shall bear to you at
> this time next year."

We then read the story of the birth of Isaac in Genesis chapter 21:

> The Lord visited Sarah as He had said, and
> the Lord did to Sarah as He had promised. And
> Sarah conceived and bore Abraham a son in his

old age at the time of which God had spoken to him. Abraham called the name of his son who was born to him, whom Sarah bore him, Isaac.

Despite Abraham being a hundred years old and Sarah being ninety years old and barren, and despite some laughter on their part (Gen. 17:17, 18:11–12), God fulfilled His promise and gave Abraham and Sarah a blood son and rewarded their faith in God's promised covenant.

Continuing on in verse 13, back in Hebrews 11, referring to Abraham, Sarah, and also Isaac:

These all died in faith, not having received the things promised, but having seen them and greeted them from afar, and having acknowledged that they were strangers and exiles on the earth. For people who speak thus make it clear that they are seeking a homeland. If they had been thinking of that land from which they had gone out, they would have had opportunity to return. But as it is, they desire a better country, that is, a Heavenly one. Therefore God is not ashamed to be called their God, for He has prepared for them a city.

These verses are referring to the fact that even though Abraham, Sarah, Isaac, Jacob, and subsequently even Jacob's offspring, for almost 500 years, did not receive the Promised Land of Israel, yet they all, in faith, saw them and greeted them from afar. They knew and believed that God would fulfill that part of His promise and covenant also, even if it was not in their lifetimes. They did so, nonetheless, by pressing on toward their Heavenly Home in faith.

Hebrews gives us one more example of this "man of faith" starting in verse 17.

By faith Abraham, when he was tested, offered up Isaac, and he who had received the promises was in the act of offering up his only son, of whom it was said, "Through Isaac shall your offspring be named." He considered that God was able to raise him from the dead, from which, figuratively speaking, he did receive him back.

We read the story of the sacrifice of Isaac in Genesis chapter 22:

> God tested Abraham and said to him, "Take your son, your only son Isaac, whom you love, and go to the land of Moriah, and offer him there as a burnt offering on one of the mountains of which I shall tell you." So Abraham rose early in the morning...and took his son Isaac...and went to the place of which God had told him. On the third day Abraham lifted up his eyes and saw the place from afar.

God decided to test Abraham's faith in Him and asked him to sacrifice his son Isaac to the Lord. Abraham didn't even hesitate. The very next morning, he went. It was a three-day journey to the mountain that God specified for this sacrifice to take place, and without wavering or turning back with second thoughts, he went on. During this journey, Isaac was as good as dead to Abraham. He knew he was going to sacrifice his son, Isaac, in obedience to the Lord's command.

As we read in Hebrews, he was so confident in the assurance of God's promise that he believed that if Isaac's life was to be taken that God would either raise him back from the dead or would provide a substitute for Isaac. Upon arriving at the specified mountain, Abraham told his servants, "Stay here with the donkey; I and the boy will go over there and worship and we will come again to you." Without any signs of wavering or questioning of God's purposes, Abraham showed absolute confidence in saying to his servants that both he and Isaac would return to them alive after going up upon the mountain to worship. Abraham then went up, prepared the altar, and prepared to offer up his son.

At the last second:

> [A]n Angel of the Lord called to him from
> Heaven and said, "Abraham, Abraham! Do not
> lay your hand on the boy or do anything to him,
> for now I know that you fear God, seeing you
> have not withheld your son, your only son, from
> Me."

God saw that he was ready and prepared to obey His command to sacrifice his son, and God stopped him and then provided a substitute in the form of a ram that was caught in the thickets (Gen. 22:13). For three days, Abraham considered his son dead and trusted in a resurrection from God to fulfill the promise, and so figuratively speaking, Abraham received his son back from the dead. This is also a prophetic picture of God sacrificing His Son Who was dead for three days and was resurrected from the dead. The Lord blessed Abraham for his faith, which had been made evident through his obedience. Verse 16, "By Myself I have sworn, declares the Lord, because you have done this and have not withheld your son, your only son, I will surely bless you, and I will surely multiply your offspring as the stars of heaven and as the sand that is on the seashore."

Moving on in chapter 11 of Hebrews, in verses 20–22, we continue with the testimonies of Isaac, Jacob and Joseph.

> By faith Isaac invoked future blessings on
> Jacob and Esau. By faith Jacob, when dying,
> blessed each of the sons of Joseph, bowing in worship
> over the head of his staff. By faith Joseph, at
> the end of his life, made mention of the exodus
> of the Israelites and gave directions concerning
> his bones.

The three patriarch generations following Abraham all believed until the end of their lives and carried on the legacy of the covenant given to their forefather, Abraham, and the promise given to him by God that he would be a great nation. None of these three men would live to see this period take shape, but they all passed on the blessing to their lineage. Furthermore, even though Joseph would spend his entire adult life in Egypt and would end up dying in Egypt and would never again see his homeland, Joseph even made "mention of the exodus of the Israelites," which would not come for over 400 years, and instructed his heirs to return his bones to the land of promise and bury them there. They all, by faith, believed that God would keep His promise and lived to their dying day envisioning the fulfillment of that promise.

In verse 23, we receive the testimony of Moses' parents, Amram and Jochebed. "By faith Moses, when he was born, was hidden for three months by his parents, because they saw that the child was beautiful, and they were not afraid of the king's edict." Moses was a man who was born beautiful in God's sight (Acts 7:20). He was divinely favored. God had massive plans for him.

In Exodus chapter 2, we read, "Now a man from the house of Levi went and took as his wife a Levite woman. The woman conceived and bore a son, and when she saw that he was a fine child, she hid him three months." Just prior to this, Pharaoh issued a command that all "sons born to the Hebrews" (Ex. 1:22) were to be put to death because the people of Israel were becoming too many and too mighty for the Egyptians. God had prospered "the sons of Israel who came to Egypt with Jacob" (Ex. 1:1) and "the people of Israel were fruitful and increased greatly; they multiplied and grew exceedingly strong, so that the land was filled with them" (Ex. 1:7), and this frightened Pharaoh that they may overpower the Egyptians.

But the parents of Moses placed their faith in God and kept their son alive and hid him from the Egyptian authorities who were commanded to kill all Hebrew boys. After three months, it became too hard for Moses' mother to keep him hidden, so she devised a plot to save him by sending him into the hands of the Pharaoh's daughter who took him in as her own and raised him through his youth, and he was raised in the Egyptian royalty as the adopted son of Pharaoh's daughter and was therefore offered all the extensive amenities, education, and pleasures that came with it.

In verse 24, we transition over to Moses himself, and we see four more "by faith" statements made about him.

> By faith Moses, when he was grown up, refused to be called the son of Pharaoh's daughter, choosing rather to be mistreated with the people of God than to enjoy the fleeting pleasures of sin. He considered the reproach of Christ greater wealth than the treasures of Egypt, for he was looking to the reward. By faith he left Egypt, not being afraid of the anger of the king, for he endured as seeing Him Who is invisible.

As Moses grew toward his adulthood, he saw the plight of his fellow Israelites as they had become mistreated slaves of the Egyptians and gave up the renown that he could have had in Egypt, possibly even to become king, to follow God's command to rescue His chosen people, Moses' kinsmen. By faith, he left and later returned to Egypt unafraid of what Pharaoh's response may be, and followed the clear and certain conviction that "God was giving them salvation by his hand" (Acts 7:25).

Not too surprisingly, Pharaoh did not just let the Israelites exodus when Moses commanded, "Let my people go" (Ex. 7:16, 8:1, 20, 9:1, 13, 10:3), which God instructed him would happen. God answered by bringing about ten plagues to the people and region of Egypt, leading up to the final plague, that of the death of all firstborn. God provided a way to opt out of this plague being affected by what was known as the Passover. For those who had faith in God, He instructed them to take the blood of an unblemished year-old male lamb (another image of our sacrificial Lord and Savior Jesus Christ) and place it upon the door posts and header of the houses in which they ate the lamb on the night that the plague was to take place.

Continuing on in verse 28 of Hebrews, "By faith he kept the Passover and sprinkled the blood, so that the Destroyer of the firstborn might not touch them." By faith, Moses obeyed the command of God, trusting that God would pass over his house and spare his firstborn. This was the final breaking point for Pharaoh, however. Pharaoh's son had died during this final plague, and he finally relented and allowed the Israelites to exodus from the land of Egypt.

So Moses rallied up his people, and they headed out from the slavery in Egypt. However, upon seeing all of his slave force leave, Pharaoh had a change of heart and chased after them to retrieve them. Moses and the Israelites were pinned up against the Red Sea when the Egyptians caught up to them, and when Moses cried out to God, God once again provided a way. He told Moses to stretch out his hand and part the Red Sea, so as to cross it on dry ground.

Verse 29, "By faith the people crossed the Red Sea as on dry land, but the Egyptians, when they attempted to do the same, were drowned." Moses and the Israelites, by faith, followed God's command to cross the Red Sea as the water was held apart from them on both sides, and they safely reached the other side. When the Egyptians followed, however, God instructed Moses to stretch out his hand over the sea once again that the waters may return to their place, and it came down upon the pursuing Egyptians and drowned the whole army.

We then see the testimony of Joshua in verse 30. "By faith the walls of Jericho fell down after they had been encircled for seven days." After the Exodus and the forty years in the wilderness, Joshua led the Israelites into the Promised Land. One of the main and most formidable cities that they came across was that of Jericho.

The Lord told Joshua in Joshua chapter 6:

> See, I have given Jericho into your hand,
> with its king and mighty men of valor. You shall
> march around the city, all the men of war going
> around the city once. Thus shall you do for six
> days. Seven priests shall bear seven trumpets of
> rams' horns before the ark. On the seventh day
> you shall march around the city seven times, and
> the priests shall blow the trumpets. And when
> they made a long blast with the rams' horn, when
> you hear the sound of the trumpet, then all the

people shall shout with a great shout, and the
wall of the city shall fall down flat, and the people
shall go up, everyone straight before him.

Now you might ask, "What kind of military strategy is that?"

It wasn't. They performed nothing militarily but instead followed God's orders in faith that He would deliver Jericho over to
them. Envision this picture. The people inside of Jericho had to think
that the Israelites had lost their minds. It had to have been a somewhat comical sight. Little did they know that after those seven days of
watching them simply march in circles that God would honor their
faith and bring the walls of this fortified city down to the ground and
hand over the people of Jericho to the army of the Israelites.

The last of the specifically mentioned saints of faith is that of
the testimony of Rahab. Rahab was a female gentile prostitute that
lived in Jericho. Before the encirclement and taking of Jericho, Joshua
had sent two men to go and spy it out and gather some intel on the
city. They went and came into the house of Rahab and lodged there
as they thought it would be an inconspicuous place. However, they
were found out, and the king sent soldiers to go capture the two men.

Rahab hid the men, though, and sent their pursuers on a wild
goose chase in order to protect the two men.

> God, in His sovereign providence, wanted
> them there for the salvation of the harlot. She
> would provide an example of His saving by faith
> a woman at the bottom of the social strata, as He
> saved Abraham at the top. Most important, by
> God's grace she was in the Messianic line.[27]

After she misdirected the soldiers, she went and talked to the
men. We read in Joshua chapter 2, starting in verse 9:

> I know that the Lord has given you the land,
> and that the fear of you has fallen upon us, and
> that all the inhabitants of the land melt before

you. For we have heard how the Lord dried up
the water of the Red Sea before you when you
came out of Egypt… And as soon as we heard
it, our hearts melted, and there is no spirit left in
any man because of you, for the Lord your God,
He is God of the heavens above and the earth
beneath.

Then in return for her help, she asked them:

Now then, please swear to me by the Lord
that, as I have dealt kindly with you, you also
will deal kindly with my father's house, and give
me a sure sign that you will save alive my father
and mother, my brothers and sisters, and all who
belong to them, and deliver our lives from death.

The two spies made a vow to her and brought back word to
Joshua, therefore, going back to Hebrews, verse 31, "By faith Rahab
the prostitute did not perish with those who were disobedient,
because she had given a friendly welcome to the spies."

The writer of the book of Hebrews ends the eleventh chapter
with kind of a broad closing statement. Starting in verse 32:

And what more shall I say? For time
would fail me to tell of Gideon, Barak, Samson,
Jephthah, of David and Samuel and the prophets—who through faith conquered kingdoms,
enforced justice, obtained promises, stopped the
mouths of lions, quenched the power of fire,
escaped the edge of the sword, were made strong
out of weakness, became mighty in war, put foreign armies to flight. Women received back their
dead by resurrection. Some were tortured, refusing to accept release, so that they might rise again
to a better life. Others suffered mocking and

flogging, and even chains and imprisonment. They were stoned, they were sawn in two, they were killed with the sword. They went about in skins of sheep and goats, destitute, afflicted, mistreated—of whom the world was not worthy—wandering about in deserts and mountains, and in dens and caves of the earth. And all these, though commended through their faith, did not receive what was promised, since God had provided something better for us, that apart from us they should not be made perfect.

All of the men listed in this verse held a position of power or authority, but none of them is praised for his personal status or abilities. Instead, they are recognized for what each one had accomplished by faith in God. The many accomplishments and sufferings described in these verses apply generally to those faithful saints. Some experienced great success, whereas others suffered great affliction. The point is that they all courageously and uncompromisingly followed God, regardless of the earthly outcome. They placed their trust in Him and His promises. They had faith in the ultimate fulfillment of the eternal promises in the covenant. The faith of OT saints looked forward to the promised salvation, whereas the faith of those after Christ looks back to the fulfillment of the promise. Both groups are characterized by genuine faith and are saved by Christ's atoning work on the cross (cf. Eph. 2:8–9).[28]

It is tempting to assume the people listed here were superhuman, or super-saints, and that you or I could never do the kinds of things they did. But did you know that Abraham was afraid for his safety, so he lied about his wife, Sarah, and said that she was his sister...twice? Consider Jacob, who stole his brother Esau's birthright, tricked his father into blessing him, and then fled in fear of Esau. Or did you know that Moses was a murderer and so scared of speaking up that God had to send his brother, Aaron, to be Moses' mouthpiece? Also, we see Rahab, who was a Gentile and a woman (in that time, a serious disadvantage), not to mention a prostitute! Then there's Samson, who had so many issues I don't know where to begin. And, of course, David, a "man after God's Own heart" (1 Sam. 13:14; Acts 13:22) who was an adulterer and a murderer, whose children were evil and out of control. These people were far from perfect, yet they had faith in a God Who was able to come through in seemingly dire situations.[29]

None of these people were found commended or to be righteous by God because of their works or any of their momentary obedience. They were all found righteous and "received their commendation" (Heb. 11:2) "by faith" (Heb. 11:4, 5, 7, 8, 9, 11, 17, 20, 21, 22, 23, 24, 27, 28, 29, 30, 31).

Let's now move ahead to the book of James. There are some that have misinterpreted parts of chapter 2 to understand salvation and righteousness as a works-necessary kind of system. We will dissect this area of chapter 2 of James in a later chapter of this book, but let me just add one verse to this chapter on man's responsibility. In verse 23, we read, "and the Scripture was fulfilled that says, 'Abraham believed God, and it was counted to him as righteousness'—and he was called a friend of God."

This verse cites Genesis 15:6, which we have already looked at several times as it is an often-recited verse throughout Scripture. As we have mentioned already, repetition is often used throughout

Scripture to hammer a point of deep significance, which this topic certainly is. Hence, this chapter being as long as it is. Abraham is given no other basis for his righteousness than that of his belief; that is, his faith in God. And because of it, he was also called a friend of God. How beautiful of a picture is that relationship! And how beautiful is it that Jesus has called all of us friends as well since He has made known all that He has heard from His Father (John 15:15)!

In the first letter of Peter, we are given a couple lessons on this topic as well. In the first chapter, starting at verse 5, we read:

> You, who by God's power are being guarded through faith for a salvation ready to be revealed in the last time. In this you rejoice, though now for a little while, if necessary, you have been grieved by various trials, so that the tested genuineness of your faith—more precious than gold that perishes though it is tested by fire—may be found to result in praise and glory and honor at the revelation of Jesus Christ. Though you have not seen Him, you love Him. Though you do not now see Him, you believe in Him and rejoice with joy that is inexpressible and filled with glory, obtaining the outcome of your faith, the salvation of your souls.

First of all, we see that we are being guarded by the divine power of God Himself through the avenue of faith, which leads to a salvation that will be revealed to us in the last times; that is, when Christ returns to take us to our Heavenly Home. So through our faith, we are being guarded until Christ takes us Home.

Secondly, we see that we are tested through various trials in order to test the genuineness of our faith and that by our perseverance through these trials, our faith may result in praise, glory, and honor upon the glorious return of Christ. We also see that by believing in Him and rejoicing in Him and loving Him, even though we cannot see Him, we will be rewarded for our faith by receiving the salvation of our souls.

All throughout this passage, we see that we are guarded by God Himself; we persevere through the testing of trials, believing and loving and rejoicing in Jesus, all on the basis of faith, and all of this results in our eternal salvation through Jesus Christ. Peter also adds in chapter 2 of this letter, at verse 6, "For it stands in Scripture: 'Behold I Am laying in Zion a stone, a Cornerstone chosen and precious, and whoever believes in Him will not be put to shame.'"

This verse is quoted from Isaiah 28:16, which has also been recited a couple times throughout the rest of Scripture. Simply by placing your faith in Jesus Christ as your cornerstone, that is your foundation and your dependence; you will avoid shame or destruction.

In verse 7, it continues and once again shows both the negative and positive sides of this issue.

> So the honor is for you who believe, but for those who do not believe, "The stone that the builder's rejected has become the Cornerstone," and "A stone of stumbling, and a rock of offense." They stumble because they disobey the Word, as they were destined to do.

This passage shows that through belief in Christ as the cornerstone of your life, you will receive the honor of God; yet if you do not believe and accept Jesus as your foundation, He will be a stumbling block and an offense to you. Belief, as always, is the key to life with Christ. There is no other ingredient on our part for salvation in Him. If you believe, He will honor you; if you do not believe, He will be a nuisance and a stumbling block to you, and you will find Him offensive and bothersome and that is a picture of an unsaved life.

Now turning to the first letter of John. In chapter 2, verse 23, we read, "No one who denies the Son has the Father. Whoever confesses the Son has the Father also." This verse mirrors Matthew 10:32–33 which we have already touched on. This verse shows both the positive and negative response in man's responsibility also. If you deny Jesus Christ, He will also deny you in front of His Father. If you confess and turn to acknowledge Him, He will in turn acknowledge you in front of His Father and you will be with God, which mirrors Romans 10:9.

Continuing on in verses 24–25, "Let what you heard from the beginning abide in you. If what you heard from the beginning abides in you, then you too will abide in the Son and in the Father. And this is the promise He made to us—eternal life."

These verses are speaking of the unchanging Gospel and are telling us to persevere in our faithful abidance so that we may continue to experience an intimate relationship with God which results in the fulfillment of His promise to us which is our eternal life in the direct presence of Him. If we simply confess and abide in Christ, we will be brought to eternity in Heaven.

In chapter 3, starting at verse 23, we see this extended.

> And this is His commandment, that we believe in the name of His Son Jesus Christ and love one another, just as He commanded us. Whoever keeps His commandments abides in God, and God in him. And by this we know that He abides in us, by the Spirit Whom He has given us.

"These verses repeat the three features of this epistle—believing, loving and obeying—which are the major evidences of true salvation. The third benefit of love is the abiding presence and empowering of the Holy Spirit."[30] God's primary commandment is to believe in His Son, which leads to our individual salvation, and through our salvation will be produced love for others, which is God's secondary commandment to us (Matt. 22:37; Mark 12:30). Also, upon our salvation, we will be indwelt with the Spirit, leading us into obedience, which are both evidences of our salvation.

In chapters 4 and 5, we receive a little bit more. In chapter 4, verses 15–16, we see:

> Whoever confesses that Jesus is the Son of God, God abides in him, and he in God (again mirroring Rom. 10:9). So we have come to know and to believe the love that God has for us. God is love, and whoever abides in love abides in God, and God abides in him.

And then in chapter 5 verse 1 and 4–5:

> Everyone who believes that Jesus is the Christ has been born of God, and everyone who loves the Father loves whoever has been born of Him… For everyone who has been born of God overcomes the world. And this is the victory that has overcome the world—our faith. Who is it that overcomes the world except the one who believes that Jesus is the Son of God?

By our confessing in Jesus, God abides in us and we are found in Him, and His love is poured out upon us as His children.

> The term here, *believes*, conveys the idea of continuing faith, making the point that the mark of genuine believers is that they continue in faith throughout their life. Saving belief is not just intellectual acceptance, but wholehearted dedication to Jesus Christ that is permanent. Whoever places faith in Jesus Christ as the only Savior has been born again and, as a result, is an overcomer. The tense of the Greek verb indicates that ongoing faith is the result of the new birth and, therefore, the evidence of the new birth. The new birth brings us into a permanent faith relationship with God and Christ.[31]

In chapter 5, verses 10–13, we are told:

> Whoever believes in the Son of God has the testimony in himself. Whoever does not believe God has made Him a liar, because he has not believed in the testimony that God has borne concerning His Son. And this is the testimony, that God gave us eternal life, and this life is in His Son. Whoever has the Son has life; whoever does not have the Son of God does not have life. I write these things to you who believe in the name of the Son of God that you may know that you have eternal life.

These verses again summarize Matthew 10:32–33, Romans 10:9–10, and the verses here in 1 John that we have just looked at. It is simply by our wholehearted belief in Christ that we are found in Him and by our disbelief in Him that we are found dead, and it is by the testimony of Jesus Christ and our faith in Him that we have been given eternal life in Christ. If you believe in the name of Jesus Christ and place your faith in Jesus Christ for eternal life, you may know with certainty and rest assured that you do have eternal life in Him.

In Jude, we see a quick little point in this. Jude is a small little epistle that speaks about false teachers and offers a call to disciples and children of God to persevere. In verses 4 and 5, we read, "Jesus, Who saved a people out of the land of Egypt, afterward destroyed those who did not believe."

We see one more point given here in Jude at the negative response in man's responsibility. Simply by not believing in Jesus Christ, you will be destroyed in the end. Belief in Jesus is the one essential component that assures your eternal existence and is the one essential component, if missing, that will ensure your destruction.

And finally, in the last book of the Bible, Revelation, we read in 21:8, "[B]ut as for the cowardly, the faithless, the detestable, as for murderers, the sexually immoral, sorcerers, idolaters, and all liars, their portion will be in the lake that burns with fire and sulfur, which is the second death."

These are pretty strong words. This is speaking of the last days when Jesus comes to judge the world and offers a list of those that will be cast into hell. This list includes murders, idolaters, sexually immoral—all the detestable—and adds alongside these vile and wretched people being sent to hell "the faithless!" Nowhere does it say the non-churchgoer, the non-obedient, the unbaptized, the uncircumcised, the one who doesn't tithe, etc. But it clearly states "the faithless!" Faith is the one and only requirement from us that leads to salvation in Christ and to an eternal life in Heaven, not your works or obedience or rituals or ceremonies or sacraments.

One of the old Church fathers, Clement, who pastored the church of Rome from about AD 90–100, which means he may have been a contemporary of the Apostle John and may be the same person Paul was referring to in Philippians 4:3, was quoted as saying in his letter to the Corinthians, which is one of the earliest documents we have outside of the New Testament, showing that they carried on the same teachings after the Bible proper timeline:

> And we, too, being called by His will in
> Christ Jesus, are not justified by ourselves, nor by
> our own wisdom, or understanding, or godliness,
> or works which we have wrought in holiness of
> heart; but by that faith through which, from the
> beginning, Almighty God has justified all men;
> to Whom be glory forever and ever. Amen.[32]

Another of the early Church fathers, Polycarp of Smyrna, who was a disciple of the Apostle John and was martyred in AD 160 for his preaching of the Gospel, wrote about this topic as well in his Epistle to the Philippians:

> I rejoice that the secure root of your faith,
> proclaimed from ancient times, even now con-
> tinues to abide and bear fruit in our Lord Jesus

Christ. He persevered to the point of death on behalf of our sins; and God raised Him up after losing the labor pains of hades. Even without seeing Him, you believe in Him with an inexpressible and glorious joy that many long to experience. For you know that you have been saved by a gracious gift—not from works but by the will of God through Jesus Christ.[33]

Throughout this chapter, as far as man's responsibility is concerned, we have seen that it is simply and entirely through faith alone in Christ alone that our eternal salvation is established. Upon our acknowledgment of Christ as our Messiah and our one and only Savior, and not by any works or acts of obedience of our own, we are found to be justified in Him and our new birth and eternal life in Him is found. There is no other necessary component on our part. There is nothing else that we need to do or accomplish to be saved, and there is nothing else that we have to wait for.

The very moment we place our true and complete faith in Jesus as Lord and Savior, we are saved (Rom. 10:9–10), and as an evidence and guarantee of this, we are indwelt with the Holy Spirit as evidenced throughout the book of Acts (also cf. Eph. 1:13). The rest has all been done and fulfilled by Christ. Some of His last labored words on the cross were, "It is finished." Every necessary component had been fully and successfully completed by Him, and all we have to do is accept His free gift (Rom. 5 and 6) that has been offered to each one of us through His sacrifice in our place. That, plain and simple, is our responsibility. To put anything more on our own plate in order to receive, earn, or deserve our eternal salvation drastically takes away from God's grace and places merit and worthiness into our sinful, dead, and unworthy hands and places an obligation and liability and indebtedness into God's hands that He owes us the right to be given eternal life. It is forever a gift and not something earned or deserved or achieved through meritorious obedience. As R. C. Sproul states, "The only merit that saves us is the merit of Christ received by faith alone."[34]

Pastor John Piper puts it like this:

> Faith in Christ unites us to Christ so that His death becomes our death and His perfection becomes our perfection. Christ becomes our punishment, which we don't have to bear, and our perfection, which we cannot perform (Rom. 8:1). Faith is not the grounds of our acceptance with God. Christ alone is. Faith unites us to Christ so that His righteousness is counted as ours. We are in Christ by faith, and therefore justified (Gal. 2:16).

To close this chapter on faith and man's responsibility, let us present a list of the articles of faith that are fundamental to all evangelical teaching: [35]

- Christ's death on the cross paid the full penalty for our sins and purchased eternal salvation. His atoning sacrifice enables God to justify sinners freely without compromising the perfection of divine righteousness (Rom. 3:24–26). His resurrection from the dead declares His victory over sin and death (1 Cor. 15:54–57).
- Salvation is by grace through faith in the Lord Jesus Christ alone—plus or minus nothing (Eph. 2:8–9).
- Sinners cannot earn salvation or favor with God (Rom. 8:8).
- God requires of those who are saved no preparatory works or prerequisite self-improvement (Rom. 10:13; 1 Tim. 1:15).
- Eternal life is a gift from God (Rom. 6:23).
- Believers are saved and fully justified before their faith ever produces a single righteous work (Eph. 2:10).
- Christians can and do sin (1 John 1:8, 10). Even the strongest Christians wage a constant and intense struggle against sin in the flesh (Rom. 7:15–24). Genuine believers sometimes commit heinous sins as David did in 2 Samuel 11.

Scripture also teaches:

- The Gospel calls sinners to faith joined in oneness with repentance (Acts 2:38, 17:30, 20:21; 2 Pet. 3:9). Repentance is turning away from sin (Acts 3:19; Luke 24:47). It is not a work but a divinely bestowed grace (Acts 11:18; 2 Tim. 2:25). Repentance is a change of heart, but genuine repentance will effect a change of behavior as well (Luke 3:8; Acts 26:18–20).

- Salvation is all God's work. Those who believe are saved utterly apart from any effort on their own (Titus 3:5). Even faith is a gift of God, not a work of man (Eph. 2:1–5, 8). Real faith, therefore, cannot be defective or short-lived but endures forever (Phil. 1:6; cf. Heb. 11).

- The object of faith is Christ Himself, not only a creed or a promise (John 3:16). Faith, therefore, involves personal commitment to Christ (2 Cor. 5:15). In other words, all true believers follow Jesus (John 10:27–28).

- Real faith inevitably produces a changed life (2 Cor. 5:17). Salvation includes a transformation of the inner person (Gal. 2:20). The nature of the Christian is different, new (Rom. 6:6). The unbroken pattern of sin and enmity with God will not continue when a person is born again (1 John 3:9–10).

- The "gift of God," eternal life (Rom. 6:23), includes all that pertains to life and godliness (2 Pet. 1:3; Rom. 8:32), not just a ticket to Heaven.

- Jesus is Lord of all, and the faith He demands involves unconditional surrender (Rom. 6:17–18, 10:9–10). He does not bestow eternal life on those whose hearts remain set against Him (Jas. 4:6).

- Those who truly believe will love Christ (1 Pet. 1:8–9; Rom. 8:28–30; 1 Cor. 16:22). They will therefore long to obey Him (John 14:15, 23).

- Behavior is an important test of faith. Obedience is evidence that one's faith is real (1 John 2:3). On the other

hand, the person that remains utterly unwilling to obey
Christ does not evidence true faith (1 John 2:4).

• Genuine believers may stumble and fall, but they will persevere in the faith (1 Cor. 1:8). Those who later turn completely away from the Lord show that they were never truly
born again (1 John 2:19).

Faith is the necessary complement to the
sovereignty of God. Though divine initiative is
ultimately responsible for redemption—although
men and women are elected, predestined, chosen
before the foundation of the world—there will
still be on our part the submissive response of
personal faith in Jesus Christ.[36]

7

God's Grace

So through chapters 4, 5, and 6, we have seen the necessary components to our salvation—that is, our justification—through Jesus Christ for eternal life. Our justification and therefore our salvation is initially and entirely God's work. It was all accomplished and finished by the work of Christ. He foreknew us, predestined us, called us, and then justified us (Rom. 8:29–30): "It is finished." Our part is simply acknowledging our fallenness and wretched nature of sinfulness and acknowledging our complete inability to save ourselves or reach God through any good works or effort or any merit of our own, and therefore, our absolute necessity of a Savior and acknowledging and accepting Jesus Christ's substitution for us in the form of a free gift offered to anyone who is willing to surrender to Christ as Lord and Savior.

It is not exactly our faith that saves, but it is our faith that links us to Christ Who saves. We also looked at the paradox (to us) of God's sovereign election of those chosen to be His children and our necessary decision made through our free will of acceptance through faith in Christ. "Is it His doing or is it mine?"

As much as these two issues refuse to intersect, they are both completely Biblically true. It is entirely God's election that leads us to even be able to make our decision to follow and surrender to Him. As we read in James 1:17, "Every good and perfect gift is from above, coming down from the Father of lights." That would certainly include our redemption, salvation, and new life in Christ.

To maybe even make the paradox more challenging, you may put it this way: "If we are saved, all thanks and praise and glory goes to God. If we are condemned, it is entirely our own fault." These two doctrines run parallel, will never intersect, but they are both entirely Biblically true and taught without apology.

In this chapter, we are going to go deeper still and look at God's all-encompassing grace and overall sovereign control of all aspects of our salvation. A. W. Tozer gives us a great definition of grace explained.

> As mercy is God's goodness confronting human misery and guilt, so grace is His goodness directed toward human debt and demerit. It is by His grace that God imputes merit where none previously existed and declares no debt where one had been before. Grace is the good pleasure of God that inclines Him to bestow benefits upon the undeserving. And wherever grace found any man it was always by Jesus Christ. Grace indeed came by Jesus Christ. In olden times men looked forward to Christ's redeeming work; in later times they gaze back upon it, but always they came and they came by grace, through faith. We must keep in mind also that the grace of God is infinite and eternal. As it has no beginning, so it can have no end, and being an attribute of God, it is as boundless as infinitude.[1]

Now let's look at the term *salvation*. Grace is the means; salvation is the product. Salvation is more of an overall and all-encompassing term that comprises three different attributes or stages of our saved nature. The initial action in salvation is called justification, which is an instantaneous action performed only once by God at the exact moment that one acknowledges his or her faith in Jesus Christ as Lord and Savior, and we are then at that moment indwelt with the Holy Spirit, God Himself. It is a matter of the heart and not of any outward physical attributes.

As we have seen in past chapters, this isn't just a simple faith or just simple knowledge of Christ's existence but a full surrender in confession and repentance of sin to Jesus Christ as our substitutionary sacrifice Who paid our debt in full. It can be remembered like this: justified means "Just if I'd" never sinned.

> Justification may be defined as an act of God whereby He imputes to a believing sinner the full and perfect righteousness of Christ, forgiving the sinner of all unrighteousness, declaring him or her perfectly righteous in God's sight, thus delivering the believer from all condemnation. Justification is an instantaneous change of one's standing before God, not a gradual transformation that takes place within the one who is justified.[2]

The second stage is called sanctification, and this involves the ongoing transformation done within us by the Holy Spirit to conform us ever more into the image of Christ and to set us apart as God's children. This is a lifelong process from the time we are justified until the time we leave this flesh and enter our Heavenly Home. A phrase that goes along with this is "I'm not yet who I should be, but at least I'm better than who I was."

"Sanctification means that the Christians have been judged already, and that they are being preserved until the coming of Christ and are ever advancing toward it."[3]

The third and final stage of salvation is called glorification, which will happen also as an immediate and one-time occurrence the very moment we enter into God's Kingdom. We will be instantly transformed into our glorified bodies, and we will then fully be removed from sin's influence over us. "We shall be like Him, because we shall see Him as He is" (1 John 3:2).

Justification removes us from the *penalty* of sin as Christ cleanses us and redeems us by paying our debt and suffering our penalty. We are deemed and judicially declared holy and righteous by Christ's payment of our penalty. Justice has been served, and God sees us every bit as holy as He sees Christ Himself. Sanctification removes us from the *power* of sin as we now have the power of the Holy Spirit dwelling inside of us, guiding us and empowering us and granting us the ability to fight and resist sin and obey God's Word and commandments. It is a lifelong maturing into the image of looking more and more like Christ. And glorification finally removes us fully from even the *presence* of sin. We will dwell in Heaven in the holy presence of God where sin and temptation will never be able to reach us again.

When looking at the facets of time in the three aspects of salvation, you might gain some perspective if you view it as a race. A race has a starting line, the entire course of that race, however long it may be, and then a finish line. Justification is an immediate and one-time occurrence at the beginning of the race. You start once, and then you are off and into the race. The race is different distances for different people, but sanctification lasts the entire stretch of that race. It is an ever-progressing growth toward the finish line. And then glorification comes right at the finish line, also an immediate and one-time occurrence, immediately as you cross from this life to the next.

These are the three aspects that make up the all-encompassing term *salvation*. And we will see that each one of these is under the divine control of God. We will mainly focus on His initiatory grace in justification and His ongoing grace in sanctification in this chapter, and then we will finish it off in the next chapter with His finalizing grace in bringing us all the way to our glorification.

Since justification and sanctification are so closely linked and therefore in many ways similar and in other ways very different, I want to spend a little more time distinguishing between the two to best understand both the similarities and the differences.

> Justification is distinct from sanctification because in justification God does not *make* the sinner righteous; He *declares* that person righteous

(Rom. 3:38; Gal. 2:16). Justification *imputes* Christ's righteousness to the sinner's account (Rom. 4:11b); sanctification *imparts* righteousness to the sinner personally and practically (Rom. 6:1–7, 8:11–14). Justification takes place outside sinners and changes their standing (Rom. 5:1–2); sanctification is internal and changes the believer's state (Rom. 6:19). Justification is an event, sanctification is a process. The two must be distinguished but can never be separated. God does not justify whom He does not sanctify, and He does not sanctify whom He does not justify. Both are essential elements of salvation.[4]

John Calvin agrees with this,

> Christ justifies no man without also sanctifying him. These blessings are conjoined by a perpetual and inseparable tie. Those whom He enlightens by His wisdom He redeems; whom He redeems He justifies; whom He justifies He sanctifies. Though we distinguish between them they are both inseparably comprehended in Christ. Would ye then contain justification in Christ? You must previously possess Christ. But you cannot possess Him without being made a partaker of His sanctification: for Christ cannot be divided. Since the Lord, therefore, does not grant us the enjoyment of these blessings without bestowing Himself, He bestows both at once, but never one without the other. We are justified not without, and yet not by works, since in the participation of Christ, by which we are justified, is contained not less sanctification than justification.[5]

Another picture analogy that might help portray this is that of conception and life. Justification would represent the conception of a life, the very first spark of life, the very beginning. It is a one-time immediate occurrence setting into motion all of the following. Sanctification, for this analogy, would then represent the gestation, the birth, the growth, the maturing of that new life, all the way through that life which is all inevitable upon justification. It is not the cause of justification; it is the inevitable result and response of justification/conception in the new life. You cannot have one without the other, conception without gestation and growth, though the latter comes as a result of the first taking place. You cannot have a reborn life without the presence of and the working-in of the Holy Spirit affecting the new life. And if the gestation/growth is nonexistent or unseen, the justification/conception should be called into question and examination. Anyone that is affected by the one is affected by both.

Bishop J. C. Ryle was an English Puritan churchman who lived in the nineteenth century. He also saw justification and sanctification as distinct but inseparable and gives us a beautifully orchestrated comparison of the two.

In what, then, are justification and sanctification alike?

a. Both proceed originally from the free grace of God. It is of His gift alone that believers are justified and sanctified at all.

b. Both are part of the great work of salvation which Christ, in the eternal covenant, has undertaken on behalf of His people. Christ is the fountain of life, from which pardon and holiness both flow. The root of each is Christ.

c. Both are to be found in the same persons. Those who are justified are always sanctified, and those who are sanctified are always justified. God has joined them together, and they cannot be put asunder.

d. Both begin at the same time. The moment a person begins to be a justified person, he also begins to be a sanctified person. He may not feel it, but it is a fact.

e. Both are alike necessary to salvation. No one ever reached Heaven without a renewed heart as well as forgiveness, without the Spirit's grace as well as the blood of Christ, without the meetness for eternal glory as well as a title. The one is just as necessary as the other.

Such are the points on which justification and sanctification agree. Let us now reverse the picture, and see wherein they differ.

a. Justification is the reckoning and counting of a man to be righteous for the sake of another, even Jesus Christ the Lord. Sanctification is the actual making a man inwardly righteous, though it may be in a very feeble degree.

b. The righteousness we have by our justification is not our own, but the everlasting perfect righteousness of our great Mediator Christ, imputed to us, and made our own by faith. The righteousness we have by sanctification is our own righteousness, imparted, inherent and wrought in us by the Holy Spirit, but mingled with much infirmity and imperfection.

c. In justification our own works have no place at all and simple faith in Christ is the one thing needful. In sanctification our own works are of vast importance, and God bids us fight and watch and pray and strive and take pains and labour.

d. Justification is a finished and complete work, and a man is perfectly justified the moment he believes. Sanctification is an imperfect work, comparatively, and will never be perfect until we reach Heaven.

e. Justification admits of no growth or increase: a man is as much justified the hour he first comes to Christ by faith as he will be to all eternity. Sanctification is eminently a progressive work, and admits of continual growth and enlargement so long as a man lives.

f. Justification has special reference to our persons, our standing in God's sight, and our deliverance from guilt. Sanctification has special reference to our natures, and the moral renewal of our hearts.

g. Justification gives us our title to Heaven, and boldness to enter in. Sanctification gives us our meetness for Heaven, and prepares us to enjoy it when we dwell there.

h. Justification is the act of God about us, and is not easily discerned by others. Sanctification is the work of God

> within us, and cannot be hid in its out-
> ward manifestation from the eyes of me.
>
> It can never be too strongly impressed on
> our minds that they are two separate things. No
> doubt they cannot be divided, and every one that
> is a partaker of either is a partaker of both.[6]

So we see that they are very much distinct but also infinitely linked together as coworkers. If God affects you with the one, you are immediately affected by both. To separate the two completely, to distance the two in the form of a timeline, or to marry the two together wholly as one severely corrupts the two.

> Catholic theology confuses the concepts of
> justification and sanctification and substitutes the
> righteousness of the believer for the righteousness
> of Christ. The corruption of the doctrine of justi-
> fication results in several other grievous theological
> errors. If sanctification is included in justification
> then justification is a process, not an event. That
> makes justification progressive, not complete. One's
> standing before God is then based on subjective
> experience, not secured by an objective declara-
> tion. Justification can therefore be experienced and
> then lost. Assurance of salvation in this life becomes
> practically impossible because security can't be guar-
> anteed. The ground of justification ultimately is the
> sinner's own continuing present virtue, not Christ's
> perfect righteousness and His atoning work.[7]

So we have to be studious to keep them distinct, though divinely at work together.

Let's start digging into the Scriptural meat of this chapter with a devotional from John Piper that focuses on God's grace from the very beginning and through to the end.

The Final Ground of Assurance

"God chose you from the beginning to be saved through sanctification by the Spirit" (2 Thess. 2:13).

Dozens of passages in the Bible speak of our final salvation (though not our election) as conditional upon a changed heart and life. The question arises then, how can I have the assurance I will persevere in faith and in the holiness necessary for inheriting eternal life?

The answer is that assurance is rooted in our election (2 Pet. 1:10). Divine election is the guarantee that God will undertake to complete by sanctifying grace what His electing grace has begun.

This is the meaning of the new covenant: God does not merely command obedience, He gives it. "The LORD your God will circumcise your heart and the heart of your offspring, so that you will love the LORD your God with all your heart and with all your soul, that you may live" (Deuteronomy 30:6). "I will put My Spirit within you and cause you to walk in My statutes" (Ezek. 11:19–20, 36:27; see also Heb. 13:20; Phil. 2:13).

Election is the final ground of assurance because, since it is God's commitment to save, it is also God's commitment to enable all that is necessary for salvation.

Election secures that "those who are justified will be glorified" (Rom. 8:30), so that all the conditions laid down for glorification will be met by the power of God's grace. "God chose you from the beginning to be saved through sanctification by the Spirit" (2 Thess. 2:13).

God's grace is the amazingly beautiful, all-encompassing, "come full-circle," doctrinal truth that brings everything we've discussed so far back around to put all of our focus and attention on the One Who deserves it all!

> Grace is a single word definition of the Gospel, the good news of God's offering salvation to sinful and unworthy mankind. God is the God of grace because He is a God Who freely gives; His giving has nothing to do with anything we have done, but is unmerited, unearned and undeserved.[8]

Grace is the unmerited favor that God has lavished upon His children, for no other reason than out of His infinite love for us and to glorify Himself. "Blessing and glory and wisdom and thanksgiving and honor and power and strength belong to our God forever and ever! Amen" (Rev. 7:12; also cf. Rev. 4:11, 5:12–13; Jude 25).

"For by Him and through Him and to Him are all things. To Him be glory forever. Amen" (Rom. 11:36)!

> Grace could be defined as "the free and benevolent influence of a holy God operating sovereignly in the lives of undeserving sinners." Grace is God presently at work in our lives. By grace, "we are His workmanship, created in Christ Jesus for good works, which God prepared beforehand that we should walk in them" (Eph. 2:10). By grace, He "gave Himself for us, that He might redeem us from every lawless deed and purify for Himself His Own people, zealous for good works" (Ti. 2:14). That ongoing work of grace in the Christian's life is as much a certainty as justification, glorification, or any other aspect of God's redeeming work. "I am confident in this very thing, that He Who began a good work in

you will perfect it until the day of Christ Jesus" (Phil. 1:6). Salvation is wholly God's work, and He finishes what He starts. His grace is sufficient. And potent. It cannot be defective in any regard.[9]

There are two verses I want to start off with that kind of piggy-back on each other. The first one was just referenced in the excerpt I just quoted, Philippians 1:6, "For I am confident in this very thing, that He Who began a good work in you will bring it to completion at the day of Christ Jesus."

The second verse I want to start with is Hebrews 12:2, which reads, "Looking unto Jesus, the Author and Finisher of our faith."

Both of these verses show us that from the very beginning until the very end, it is and always has been and always will be Jesus Christ Who has accomplished everything in us. From the very beginning, He was the very Author of the very faith that we have in Him, and it was He that began everything good in us. And He has continued and will continue His work in us until He finishes and brings to completion His work in us when He comes back to this earth to bring us Home. He started it and He will finish it. Isn't that so amazingly beautiful?! Again, all thanksgiving and praise and honor and glory go to God!

I will now jump back into the Old Testament, and we will dive deeper into this beautiful truth. Obviously, starting at Genesis 1:1, God created the universe and everything in it. He created it perfectly and created us with the gift of free will so that our love for Him would be true and genuine instead of robotic and forced. It wasn't until we brought sin into this world that death and decay and pain and disease entered into it because "the wages of sin is death" (Rom. 6:23).

This brought about a major dilemma that we have already discussed, that being the fact that a holy, perfect, and righteous God cannot dwell with wretched unholiness in the form of us sinners. He still infinitely loved us but could not deny His sovereign and just nature in order to commune with us. Justice was demanded for the wrong that was committed. Since we have all inherited the sinful flesh nature through our forefather Adam, God had to fulfill justice and condemnation of us all was the just penalty for that. Adam and Eve messed up big-time and condemned the entirety of the human race—and all of creation, for that matter—for all of history and provided no possible way of fixing it. Zero! Tying fig leaves around themselves was in no way efficient to redemption. And since they were, in essence, our historical spokespeople, we were all without any plans for reconciliation.

However, there was one and only one perfect remedy to this painful dilemma, which God Himself brought about and promised immediately to Adam and Eve after they had sinned. In Genesis chapter 3, starting in verse 15, we see that it is God that promises a Messiah to come and atone for sins in order to produce reconciliation for us. We also see that it is God that makes the first blood-sacrifice of an (innocent) animal to provide garments of skin to clothe them with, which was a prophecy of the coming Messiah Who would shed His Own (holy, perfect, innocent) blood in order to redeem mankind. Just as we saw in Philippians 1:6 and Hebrews 12:2, it is always God that initiates our reconciliation.

In Genesis chapter 15, we see the account of God making His covenant with Abraham. Though this passage does not directly speak of our salvation, it offers a great look at God's covenant-giving toward His chosen people. God promised Abraham that his descendants would number the stars of the sky, even though at the time, he had no heir. Abraham believed God, and God made a covenant with him that He would bring about his offspring and also cause them to inhabit the land of Israel. "The sign of ancient covenants often involved the cutting in half of animals, so that the pledging parties could walk between them, affirming that the same should happen to them if they broke the covenant (see Jer. 34:18–19)."[10]

So God told Abraham to bring Him a heifer, a female goat, a ram, a turtledove, and a pigeon and told him to cut them in half and separate the halves across from each other. Then God caused a deep sleep to pass over Abraham, and God Himself alone passed through the center of the animals, declaring that it was He alone that would bring all of this to pass. God alone, not man, had absolute sovereign control in securing the chosen land of Israel and the chosen ancestry of the Jews, and later, the Christians.

> God makes a covenant with His people and separates them from the world as His Own possession, and vouches Himself for this covenant. "Ye shall be holy: for I the Lord your God Am holy" (Lev. 19:2), and again, "I the Lord, which sanctify you, Am holy" (Lev. 21:8). This is the foundation on which the covenant is based. Like God Himself, the Holy One, the people of His sanctuary are also separated from all things profane and from sin. For God has made them the people of His covenant, choosing them for Himself, making atonement for them and purifying them in His sanctuary.[11]

In Exodus chapter 31, verse 13, we are plainly and matter-of-factly told that it is God alone that sanctifies us as His Own. "That you may know that I, the Lord, sanctify you." The Amplified Holy Bible puts it this way, "That you may know [without any doubt] and acknowledge that I Am the Lord Who sanctifies you and sets you apart [for Myself]."

The Interlinear Hebrew/English Bible says, "I Am Jehovah, your Sanctifier." The word used here in the original Hebrew for sanctify/sanctifies/sanctifier is *qadash* and means "to cause, make, pronounce or observe as clean. Sanctify, prepare, dedicate, consecrate, appoint, purify. This word is used in some form or another to represent being set apart for the work of God. To be holy."[12] God Himself and God Himself alone sanctifies us, cleanses us, and sets us apart as His Own.

In Deuteronomy 30, verse 6, we are told by Moses, "And the Lord your God will circumcise your heart and the heart of your offspring, so that you will love the Lord your God with all your heart and with all your soul, that you may live." It is God that creates in us a love for Himself. It is not something that we just magically decide to create in ourselves under some compulsion of our own, while we are dead sinners (Rom. 5:6, 8, 10; Eph. 2:5). He is the One that initiates our love for Him, and this love is what leads to our desire to know Him, be with Him, and surrender ourselves to Him in faith that we may be born again to new life through His Son. It is His work on our innermost being to turn a wretched and vile dead sinner, spiritually insensitive, into an obedient follower of Christ.

Salvation always results because God first pursues sinners, not because sinners first seek God. Christ is always portrayed as the seeking Savior. His divine initiative made redemption possible, and it is through His initiative that individuals are sought out and saved. No one seeks God unless God has first sought that person (cf. Rom. 3:11). Salvation is first of all a work of God and in no sense the result of human enterprise or individual longing. A blind man has no capacity to give himself sight. Spiritual sight depends on God's initiative and God's power, offered in divine and sovereign grace. The only thing that can change spiritual blindness is a divine miracle. There is no way to recognize Jesus Christ for Who He is apart from a miracle of God to open spiritually blind eyes. But when Christ opens the eyes of a soul, suddenly truth becomes recognizable. Spiritual sight is a gift from God that makes one willing and able to believe.[13]

The story of Job is sometimes a challenging one for some people who want to accuse God of being cruel and allowing all those things to happen to Job, but without getting into that argument, we look at the responses of Job himself. After satan destroys and takes away Job's entire property and his children, Job mourned but responded, "The Lord gave, and the Lord has taken away; blessed be the name of the Lord" (Job 1:21). Despite losing almost everything that he owned,

Job knew that ultimately it is God that provides everything, and if He allows it to be taken away…so be it.

This is followed up by satan then attacking Job's health and striking him with agonizing sores. What follows is thirty-some chapters of Job's laboring responses, even to the point of wishing he was never born, yet never cursing God's name; and also three of Job's friends interrogating him about his situation. Then, finally, in chapters 38–41, God speaks to Job and answers him with a barrage of questions essentially declaring God's ultimate sovereignty over all things. Job is put in his place, and once God is done speaking, "Job answered the Lord, 'I know that You can do all things, and that no purpose of Yours can be thwarted'" (Job 42:1–2). Job acknowledged that God is above all and is in control of all and can do all, and that whatever God wills is guaranteed to be fulfilled.

Moving into the Psalms, we find a few valuable lessons in God's overall sovereignty and grace. In Psalm 3, verse 8, King David tells us that "Salvation belongs to the Lord; Your blessing be on Your people." We also see in Psalm 37, verse 39, that "the salvation of the righteous is from the Lord; He is their stronghold in the time of trouble." Both of these verses clearly teach us that the source of our salvation is the Lord. In Psalm 103, verse 12, we are told that "as far as the east is from the west, so far does He remove our transgressions from us."

We play no part in this glorious truth. Jesus Christ Himself said, "It is finished" and paid the debt for every single sin committed throughout history and infinitely removed them from our existence. God's forgiving grace is absolutely limitless! In Psalms 115:3 and 135:6, we see a pairing of the same truth. "Our God is in the heavens; He does all that He pleases." And "Whatever the Lord pleases, He does, in Heaven and on earth, in the seas and all deep places."

In both these passages, we see the same thing stated. God does whatever He pleases. And since God always and only does things perfectly and righteously, nothing He ever does is evil or wrong (cf. Job 34:12; Jas. 1:13). If God wants to create the universe, He will create the universe perfectly (cf. Gen. 1). If He wants to send His Son to take upon your sins to die and pay your penalty, He will fulfill it perfectly (cf. John 3:16). If He wants to lead you into a relationship with Himself, He will create in you a desire to seek Him and will lead you to Him (cf. Deut. 30:6; Jer. 29:13) to live a new life in Him through Jesus Christ (2 Cor. 5:21).

We find quite a bit more when we head into the major prophets of the Old Testament. Starting with Isaiah in chapter 14, we read starting in verse 24:

> The Lord of hosts has sworn: "As I have planned, so shall it be, and as I have purposed, so shall it stand... This is the purpose that is purposed concerning the whole earth, and this is the hand that is stretched out over all the nations. For the Lord of hosts has purposed, and who will annul it? His hand is stretched out, and who will turn it back?"

First of all, in verse 25, which I did not include in the previous quoting, the passage mentions Assyria as the immediate recipient of this Oracle directly from God, but as is stated in verse 24, which is listed here, this Oracle, this declaration of God's purpose is extended to "the whole earth" and "all nations." This passage speaks of the ultimate and final judgment or fulfillment of God's wrath toward the ungodly. Now this doesn't exactly portray the positive life-giving side of God's grace, but at the very beginning and end of this group of verses, we see that whatever God purposes is exactly what will take place.

No matter what God wills to do or to have done, who is there that can possibly dispute Him or alter His sovereignty?

And as we continue further into Isaiah, we read in Isaiah 38:17, "In love You [Lord] have delivered my life from the pit of destruction, for You have cast all my sins behind Your back."

Isaiah 43:25, "I, I Am He Who wipes out your transgressions for My Own sake, and I will not remember your sins."

In these two verses, we see the glorious grace of God's providential will to erase our sins, saving us from death, and promising to never again remember them. He will never change His mind and say,

"You know what, I've... I've reconsidered. I'm going to rehash those old sins of yours, and I'm now going to decide to be cruel and deal harshly with you from here on out."

That would be absurd. He promises to remember them no more! And He does this all for His Own sake! He does this for His Own desire and delight! He knew exactly how bad we would be and how many times we would utterly fail and sin against Him, but He chose to erase our sins nonetheless. And if God desires to do this, who can cancel it? Now this doesn't mean that we have a free pass to sin how much and whenever we want, but it does mean that when God forgives, it is forever gone. If we truly repent of a sin, it will never be remembered!

We continue reading in Isaiah 42:1, "Behold My servant, whom I [God] uphold; My elect, in whom My soul delights, I have put My Spirit upon him."

Isaiah 42:6, "I Am the Lord, I have called you in righteousness, I will take you by the hand and keep you, I will give you as a covenant for the people, a light for the nations."

These two verses show us that it is entirely God's will and sovereign action in which all of this is accomplished. If you focus on the verbs of the last four verses we have looked at, every single one has God as its subject. God is the One Who wipes away our sins. It is God Who delivers us from destruction. It is God Who upholds us. It is God Who delights in us. It is God Who places His Own Holy Spirit inside of us. It is God Who has called us to righteousness. It is God Who leads us by the hand and Who keeps us secure in Himself. It is God Who gives us, His children, as a covenant to the world. It is all done by Him according to His loving grace toward us, His elect, and chosen.

Isaiah continues in 46:9–10 with the same verity that we first looked at in Isaiah, "For I Am God, and there is no other; I Am God, and there is none like Me, declaring the end from the beginning and from ancient times things not yet done, saying, 'My counsel shall stand, and I will accomplish all My purpose.'"

God is above all, and therefore, whatever He wills and purposes, He will accomplish. Going back to the previous four verses we just looked at, if God desires to do all of those things for us, who or what is there to stop Him? He is the only One Who is in control.

To hear more from Isaiah, we go to 49:1–2, which is a section of prophetic referencing to Jesus Christ. "The Lord called Me from the womb, from the body of My mother He named My name." It was God Who called Jesus to enter into His creation, to be born of a woman, in order to redeem mankind. God named Jesus Christ the Messiah Who as we see in Isaiah 53:12, "He bore the sins of many and makes intercession for the transgressors." God was the One Who called Christ to be our Messiah, and Jesus was the One Who bore our sins and also became our High Priest Who intercedes for us in front of God the Father.

The last thing we see here from Isaiah is in 54:13, "All your children shall be taught by the Lord." Although the specific promise in this context is given to Israel, this principle is eternal to all God's chosen. Ultimately, God is our Teacher. Our parents, teachers, pastors, etc. are all vessels of God for His purpose to teach us, but God is ultimately our great Teacher.

Moving into Jeremiah, we receive a little bit more. In 1:5, we see the same divine calling from God of His servant similar to the one we just read in Isaiah. "Before I formed you in the womb I knew you, and before you were born, I consecrated you; I appointed you a prophet to the nations." This verse is speaking of God's prophet, Jeremiah, and speaks of God's divine call of Jeremiah, even before he was of the womb. Later on, in Jeremiah, we read in chapters 31 and 32:

> I will make a new covenant with the house of Israel and the house of Judah…this is the covenant that I will make with the house of Israel… I will put My law within them, and I will write it on their hearts. And I will be their God, and they shall be My people…for they shall all know Me, from the least to the greatest, declares the Lord. For I will forgive their iniquity, and I will remember their sin no more" (31:31, 33–34; also quoted in Heb. 8:10–12).

And:

> I will gather them from all the countries to which I drove them in My anger and wrath and in great indignation. I will bring them back to this place, and I will make them dwell in safety. And they shall be My people, and I will be their God. I will give them one heart and one way, that they may fear Me forever, for their own good and the good of their children after them. I will make with them an everlasting covenant, that I will not turn away from doing good to them. And I will put the fear of Me in their hearts, that they may not turn from Me. I will rejoice in doing them good, and I will plant them in this land in faithfulness, with all My heart and all My soul. For thus says the Lord, "Just as I have brought all this great disaster upon this people, so I will bring upon them all the good that I promise them... I will restore their fortunes," declares the Lord (32:37–44).

In contrast to the Mosaic covenant under which Israel failed, God promised a New Covenant with a spiritual, divine dynamic by which those who know Him would participate in the blessings of salvation. The fulfillment was to individuals, yet also to Israel as a nation. In principle, this covenant, also announced by Jesus Christ, begins to be exercised with spiritual aspects realized for Jewish and Gentile believers in the church era. It has already begun to take effect with a "remnant chosen by grace" (Rom. 11:5). It will be also realized by the people of Israel in the last days, including the regathering to their ancient land, Palestine.[14]

We see that in God's wrath and also in His blessing, He is sovereign in His control. Because of rebellious Israel, they did incur anger and wrath from God, but He still kept and sustained His promise and covenant with them and brought them back to Himself. We even read in these passages that He personally wrote His law on their hearts that they may fear Him and know Him in order that they would not turn from Him. Despite their constant rebellious nature and history God rejoices in "doing them good" and bringing upon them all the good that He promised them, all because of His love and desire, not because of anything on their part. This is all God's gracious fulfillment.

We see this exact same providence taught by the Prophet Ezekiel. In 11:19–20, we read, "And I will give them one heart, and a new Spirit I will put in them. I will remove the heart of stone from their flesh and give them a heart of flesh, that they may walk in My statutes and keep My rules and obey them."

Once again, we see that it is God Who directly impacts the heart and places His Spirit in them for His Own purpose. In 34:11–16, we are told:

> For thus says the Lord God: "Behold, I, I Myself will search for My sheep and will seek them out. As a shepherd seeks out his own flock when he is among his sheep that have been scattered, so will I seek out My sheep, and I will rescue them from all places where they have been scattered on a day of clouds and thick darkness. And I will bring them out from the peoples and gather them from the countries, and will bring them into their own land. And I will feed them on the mountains of Israel, by the ravines, and in all the inhabited places of the country. I will feed them with good pasture, and on the mountain heights of Israel shall be their grazing land. There they shall lie down in good grazing land, and on rich pasture they shall feed on the moun-

tains of Israel. I Myself will be the Shepherd of My sheep, and I Myself will make them lie down, declares the Lord God. I will seek the lost, and I will bring back the strayed, and I will bind up the injured, and I will strengthen the weak, and the fat and the strong I will destroy. I will feed them in justice."

And then in 36:22–29 and 32–33:

It is not for your sake, O house of Israel, that I Am about to act, but for the sake of My holy name, which you have profaned among the nations to which you came. And I will vindicate the holiness of My great name, which has been profaned among the nations, and which you have profaned among them. And the nations will know that I Am the Lord, declares the Lord God, when through you I vindicate My holiness before their eyes. I will take you from the nations and gather you from all the countries and bring you into your own land. I will sprinkle clean water on you, and you shall be clean from all your uncleanness, and from all your idols I will cleanse you. And I will give you a new heart, and a new spirit I will put within you. And I will remove the heart of stone from your flesh and give you a heart of flesh. And I will put My Spirit within you, and cause you to walk in My statutes and be careful to obey My rules. You shall dwell in the land I gave your fathers, and you shall be My people, and I will be your God. And I will deliver you from all your uncleanness. And I will summon the grain and make it abundant and lay no famine upon you... It is not for your sake that I will act, declares the Lord God; let that be known

> to you... Thus says the Lord God: "On the day
> that I cleanse you from all your iniquities."

Again, we see that it is plain and simply all done by God according to His purpose, all for the sake of His name, even including causing their own obedience to His rules.

The story of Jonah is another narration that we may receive some teaching from on this topic of God's complete grace also corresponding with His sovereign control of all things. Taking from the book of Jonah in the Old Testament, and also expounding on it using a bit of history and background of the culture of the people and circumstances involved in the story, we will examine this narration.

Jonah was one of God's chosen prophets. The Lord desired and instructed Jonah to go to a very evil and idolatrous city of the time known as Nineveh, which was a very large city, possibly the largest city in the world at that time. It was a very great city both in size and power and therefore had significant influence over the Middle East during this time period. It was also a center of worship for the pagan gods known as Assur and Ishtar, also Nanshe and Dagon.

This is the first and only case in the Bible of a prophet being called and sent to a foreign nation in order to preach God's message of repentance against them. Jonah wanted nothing to do with this calling and tried to comically run away "from the presence of the Lord" (Jon. 1:3). This is also the only recorded instance of a prophet refusing to comply with God's commission (cf. Jer. 20:7–9). So Jonah fled and hopped on a boat heading to Tarshish, which scholars believe to have been a city in the south of Spain, which was directly and distantly the wrong way from the city of Nineveh.

While they were traveling across the Mediterranean Sea, "the Lord hurled a great wind upon the sea, and there was a mighty tempest on the sea, so that the ship threatened to break up" (1:4). Fearful of the ship breaking apart and all of them perishing in the sea, the crew started throwing the cargo of the ship overboard to lighten the load and hopefully prevent more damage to the ship from being tossed around. It didn't work. They began to question Jonah and figured out that it was he who had caused this dilemma by trying to flee from the God of Israel. Jonah actually offered himself to be thrown overboard to remedy this dark situation "for I know that it is because of me that this great tempest has come upon you" (1:12).

Fearing God's judgment toward them for taking a man's life and being accountable for innocent blood, they refrained from doing so at first, but as the tempest only grew, they finally threw Jonah overboard, and the water immediately grew calm. "And the Lord appointed a great fish to swallow up Jonah. And Jonah was in the belly of the fish three days and three nights" (1:17). Jonah spent at least part of those three days in the belly of a fish in prayer with the Lord (Jon. 2:2–9). Then "the Lord spoke to the fish, and it vomited Jonah out upon the dry land. Then the word of the Lord came to Jonah a second time, saying, 'Arise, go to Nineveh, that great city, and call out against it the message that I tell you'" (2:10–3:2).

So this time, Jonah finally honored God and went to Nineveh. When he arrived and went deep into the city:

> [H]e called out, "Forty days remain, and Nineveh shall be overthrown!" And the people of Nineveh believed God. They called for a fast and put on sackcloth, from the greatest of them to the least of them. The word reached the king of Nineveh, and he arose from his throne, removed his robe, covered himself with sackcloth, and sat in ashes. And he issued a proclamation and published through Nineveh, "By the decree of the king and his nobles: Let neither man nor beast, herd nor flock, taste anything. Let them not feed or drink water, but let man and beast be covered with sackcloth, and let them call out mightily to God. Let everyone turn from his evil way and from the violence that is in his hands. Who knows? God may turn and relent and turn from His fierce anger, so that we may not perish." When God saw what they did, how they turned from their evil way, God relented of the disaster

that He said He would do to them, and He did not do it. (Jon. 3:4–10)

Now this is a pretty remarkable story, even on the surface, but it shows God's grace and also His mercy offered to a very evil pagan and foreign country by sending an Israelite prophet to come preach to them the message of God, and God sovereignly sending a fish to swallow Jonah, keeping him alive, and then returning him back to dry land in order to redirect Jonah's attempt at fleeing from this commission and sending him finally to Nineveh. Now, you may read this account and wonder how and why a truly corrupt and pagan and idolatrous nation would instantly invite in this foreigner preaching destruction against the entire city with such immediate response and repentance against their evil ways, including the very king of this nation, declaring that all men and beasts fast and repent of all their evil ways as well.

The obvious and truthful answer is, of course, by God's will as we have seen. It is God Who changes hearts and brings the dead to life, but we will also look further. For a glimpse at this, we look into the history books of this city to find that some of the pagan gods that they worshipped were named Nanshe, who was a fish goddess, the daughter Ea, who was the goddess of fresh water, and Dagon, the fish god who was represented as half man and half fish. If Jonah would've immediately heeded God's commission to go and to preach repentance to an evil and pagan foreign nation and just walked straight into the city in that way, he most likely would've been greatly ridiculed, persecuted, and probably killed for his attempts at preaching a foreign doctrine.

Jonah, through his own free will and unwillingness to go, fled from God's initial command and headed far away on a ship. After a large storm and being thrown overboard, he was then swallowed by a fish, divinely appointed by God Himself to preserve Jonah and return him to dry land and commission him once again to go to Nineveh, who worshipped false, pagan fish gods. Reports of this miraculous fish encounter of Jonah's may have preceded his arrival to Nineveh. Also, it is generally believed that the acid from the stomach of the fish would have bleached Jonah's appearance, offering validity to the account of this miraculous fish experience endured by this foreigner who was now preaching destruction and repentance to the entire city.

All of this most likely had a great effect on his immediate audience and would account for the swift and widespread receptivity of his message, all the way up to the king, leading to the full repentance of the entire city from their evil ways. So a lingering question may be, was it Jonah's free will to flee from God's command? Or was it God's divine and sovereign control over the entire situation, including Jonah's free will, leading to His grace being given?

Moving on into the New Testament, we will really dig in and get to see the full scope of God's sovereign grace when it comes to His overall control of all things, including righteousness, our salvation, and even our faith. A quote from evangelical Christian apologist and author, Ravi Zacharias, helps start this off.

> Jesus Christ didn't come into this world to make bad people good. He came into this world to make dead people live. He came so that those who are dead to God can come alive to God... The Christian concept is no matter how well we live, we cannot live up to the standard and the character of God. The word *sin* means missing the mark. And if that is a correct definition, then the grace of God becomes the most important truth. Apart from Him, we cannot even believe what is right, let alone live the right way. The pattern in Exodus is threefold: God brought the people out of Egypt, He gave them the moral law, and then He gave them the tabernacle. In other words, redemption, righteousness, worship. You can never violate that sequence. Unless you are redeemed, you cannot be righteous. Unless you are redeemed and righteous, you cannot worship, "for who shall ascend unto the hill of the Lord," says the Bible (Ps. 24:3–4), "but he who has clean hands and a pure heart."[15]

To reiterate Ravi's words, the grace of God is the most important truth because without it, we can't even know or believe what is right. Also, God grants us redemption leading to our righteousness, through His grace, culminating in our ability to worship Him.

In the sixteenth chapter of the Gospel of Matthew, we see a few of Jesus's Own words on this subject. Starting in verse 13, Jesus asks His disciples, "Who do people say that the Son of Man is?" referring to Himself. They respond by saying that some people believe that He is John the Baptist; some say that He is the Old Testament prophet, Elijah, and others claimed that He was the Old Testament prophet, Jeremiah, or one of the other prophets who had come back to life. He then asks them, "But Who do you say that I Am?"

To this Peter, responded by saying, "You are the Christ, the Son of the Living God."

We then receive this beautiful response from Jesus, "Blessed are you, Simon Bar-Jonah! For flesh and blood has not revealed this to you, but My Father Who is in Heaven."

Jesus was pointing out that Peter did not come to the realization that Jesus Christ was the divine Son of God the Father, sent to be the Messiah, by any means other than God Himself alone revealing this to him. Peter was given this marvelous and wonderful knowledge directly from God Himself. It wasn't learned or taught to him by man or through study done of his own but divinely revealed to Him by the grace of God. "God had opened Peter's heart to this deeper knowledge of Christ by faith. Peter was not merely expressing an academic opinion about the identity of Christ; this was a confession of Peter's personal faith, made possible by a divinely regenerated heart."[16]

In Mark's Gospel, we are given another lesson of another attribute of God's grace. In chapter 13, Peter, James, John, and Andrew asked Jesus to reveal signs of the ushering in of His Kingdom. Jesus proceeded to tell them that there would be much destruction through war and also natural disaster throughout the world and that there would also be great persecution brought about for proclaiming His Gospel, though He then promised them in verse 11, "When they bring you to trial and deliver you over, do not be anxious beforehand what you are to say, but say whatever is given you in that hour, for it is not you who speak, but the Holy Spirit." We need not fear in times of persecution, for the Spirit dwells in us and will give us His words to speak in defense of our faith in Jesus Christ our Savior. It is not a defense that we give but He offers us through Himself.

In Luke's Gospel, chapter 23, we are given a compassionate view of Christ's love and a beautiful story of salvation promised directly from our Savior's mouth. As He hung on the cross, His purpose and character were in raw display. As His executioners were carrying out the unwarranted and torturous penalty of crucifixion upon Christ, Jesus pleaded to His Father in verse 34, "Father, forgive them for they know not what they do." Jesus pleaded for His Father to have compassion for these men who were fulfilling the sentence of execution against Him. He prayed for the forgiveness of those who were securing Him to His source of extreme and torturous execution.

This is such a beautiful expression of the limitless love and compassion that Jesus had for all men through His divine grace. Now we are not told the outcome of this request from Son to Father, but we could speculate that possibly some of the executioners could have been part of the 3,000 that were saved on the day of Pentecost.

We also see more of Jesus's words while hanging from the cross. There were two other criminals executed next to Jesus. They both actually deserved their punishment, unlike Jesus. While the three of them hung there, one of them was ridiculing Jesus for not saving Himself if He truly was the Christ. The other criminal, having a regenerated spirit within him, spoke up in defense of Jesus and then pleaded of Jesus in verse 42, "Jesus, remember me when You come into Your Kingdom."

> The penitent thief's prayer reflected his belief that the soul lives on after death; that Christ had the right to rule over a Kingdom of the souls of men; and that He would soon enter that Kingdom despite His impending death. His request to be remembered was a plea for mercy, which also reveals that the thief understood that

he had no hope but divine grace, and that the dispensing of that grace lay in Jesus's power. All of this demonstrates true faith on the part of the dying thief, and Christ graciously affirmed the man's salvation, when He says in verse 43, "Truly I say to you, today you will be with Me in Paradise."[17]

There were zero conditions or commands to be obeyed offered, for this man seemingly had just now repented and surrendered to Christ and would now be dead in only a few hours. Christian preacher/teacher/theologian/author H. A. Ironside offers some words on this glorious story as well.

> Consider the repentant thief on the cross. Surely, he had been guilty of wronging many of his fellows! Yet the moment he turned in faith to Jesus he was saved. His hands and feet were nailed to the cross. It was not possible for him to do one thing to repair the many wrongs he had done. But through the merits of the Holy Sufferer on that central cross, he was fully and freely pardoned and fitted for Paradise. He was saved altogether apart from anything that he could or could not do; and that on the ground of propitiatory work of the Lord Jesus Christ. You may be saved in the very same way. Then as a new man in Christ, you can prove your love to Him by striving to live unselfishly and devotedly to His glory. You cannot help God to save you! It is Christ's work alone that counts![18]

The Gospel of John is heavy in theology, even more so than the other Gospels, and in Who Jesus was as the Son of God and as that of His divine nature, so there is quite a bit to learn from John's Gospel. From the very beginning of the book, we are given a deep theological prologue describing Christ's eternality and divinity and Oneness with God. We are shown that it was indeed Christ Himself Who was the hand of Creation in the very beginning. Then in verse 12, we are offered a reference to God's grace and sovereignty. "To all who did receive Him, who believed in His name, He gave the right to become children of God, who were born not of blood nor of the will of the flesh nor of the will of man, but of God."

The first part of this passage shows man's responsibility which we studied back in chapter 6, that by believing in His name, you will receive identity with Him, but the deeper subject of this passage is that "the right to become children of God" He "**gave**" to us, and that by becoming His children, we are not born of any fleshly means but directly of God. And this verb, *gave*, emphasizes God's divine grace in the gift of salvation.

John the Baptist kind of backs this up in chapter 3 verse 27 when he says, "A person cannot receive even one thing unless it is **given** him from Heaven." In context, John was responding to one of his disciples expressing worry that so many people were flocking now to see Jesus and to be baptized by His disciples instead of coming to John as was previously the case and was initially referring to his ministry potential, but the use of his words far outreach just that and that all things are "given" by God.

In chapter 5, we are given a few more words from Jesus. Jesus was preaching on His Own authority and of His being One with the Father in front of His disciples and also many Jews who became infuriated over what they considered blasphemy as Jesus was claiming to be equal with God. In verse 21, we read, "For as the Father raises the dead and gives them life, so also the Son gives life to whom He will." He was here claiming equality with God, but He was also stating that it is His and His Father's will, as they are equally One, that grants life; and not only physical life, but He is actually here referring to spiritual life.

In John chapter 6, we find Jesus preaching to a very large crowd shortly after the feeding of the 5,000. In the beginning of this chapter, we find Jesus miraculously feeding 5,000 men, not including women and children, so actually upward of maybe 15,000 to 20,000 by multiplying five barley loaves and two fish, and then having twelve baskets full of leftovers, even after everyone ate to their fill. That same evening was also when Jesus had walked on water to meet the disciples who were crossing the Sea of Galilee in a boat, leaving the crowd behind them.

The following morning, the crowd of people that Jesus fed the evening before were looking for Jesus, and realizing He wasn't there, they went to the other side of the lake to find Him. Once they did, they began to question about His departure. He then gave the "I Am the Bread of Life" sermon to all of those listening. Jesus described Himself as the Bread from Heaven that gives life to the world and that all that came to Him would never hunger or thirst. Then starting in verse 37, He says:

> All that the Father gives to Me will come to Me, and whoever comes to Me I will never cast out. For I have come down from Heaven, not to do My Own will but the will of Him Who sent Me. And this is the will of Him Who sent Me, that I should lose nothing of all that He has given Me, but raise it up on the last day. For this is the will of My Father, that everyone who looks on the Son and believes in Him should have eternal life, and I will raise Him up on the last day.

This is one of the passages that we looked at earlier, showing the paradox between God's divine sovereignty and man's responsibility, but inside the text, we see the sovereignty of God's grace in both selecting and securing every one of whom He chooses for eternal life. We will dive deeper into the latter part of this verse in the following chapter. But here, the Jews, in response to hearing this, grumble at His claims about coming down from Heaven, saying, "Is this not Jesus, Whose father and mother we know?"

Jesus continues with His sermon in verse 43:

> No one can come to Me unless the Father Who sent Me draws him. And I will raise him

up on the last day. It is written in the prophets, 'And they will all be taught by God (Isa 54:13).' Everyone who has heard and learned from the Father comes to Me—not that anyone has seen the Father except He Who is from God; He has seen the Father. Truly, truly, I say to you, whoever believes has eternal life. I Am the Bread of Life.

The combination of v. 37a and v. 44 indicate that the divine drawing activity that Jesus referred to cannot be reduced to what theologians call "prevenient grace," i.e., that somehow the power to come to Christ is allegedly dispensed to all of mankind, thus enabling everyone to accept or reject the Gospel according to their own will alone. Scripture indicates that no "free will" exists in man's nature, for man is enslaved to sin (total depravity) and unable to believe apart from God's empowerment (Rom. 3:1–19; Eph. 2:1–3; 2 Cor. 4:4; 2 Tim. 1:9). While "whosoever will" may come to the Father, only those whom the Father gives the ability to will toward Him will actually come to Him.

The drawing here is selective and efficacious (producing the desired effect) upon those whom God has sovereignly chosen for salvation, i.e., those whom God has chosen will believe because God has sovereignly determined that result from eternity past. If someone comes to faith and repentance to God, it is because they have been "taught," and hence drawn by God. The "drawing" and "learning" are just different aspects of God's sovereign direction in the person's life. Those taught by God to grasp the truth are also drawn by God the Father to embrace the Son.[19]

Every single aspect of our salvation is rooted in God's sovereign and efficacious grace. He initiates and He finishes, just like we saw in Philippians 1:6 and Hebrews 12:2. At the end of Jesus's sermon, He had a few closing statements to His followers concerning this topic. In verse 63 and 65, "It is the Spirit that gives life; the flesh is no help at all… This is why I told you that no one can come to Me unless it is granted to him by the Father."

Jesus was reaffirming God's sovereignty in the selection of those for salvation and included that the flesh has no ability to do any of this, but it is all entirely of the work of God, the Spirit being the officiator. In verse 66, we read:

> After this many of His disciples (*not the original Twelve, but other followers who at this point had been claiming to be disciples*) turned back and no longer walked with Him. So Jesus said to the Twelve, "Do you want to go away as well?" Simon Peter answered Him, "Lord, to whom shall we go? You have the words of eternal life, and we have believed, and have come to know, that You are the Holy One of God." Jesus answered them, "Did I not choose you, the Twelve? And yet one of you is a devil."

Even after the departure of some of the followers present that could not handle the depth of Jesus's preaching, and Peter boldly declaring his allegiance and faith to Christ for eternal life in response to Jesus's question if any of the Twelve were going to leave also, Jesus still spoke up and reminded them that He was the One that chose them. They did not come to believe in Him by any merit or motive of their own. He chose them to come and to believe in Him. Jesus also even acknowledges that He even chose the one who would ultimately betray Him and have Him arrested. He also reiterated these same words in John 15:16, "You did not choose Me but I chose you and appointed you."

A little bit later in the book of John, we see a few more teachings on this. In chapter 14, verse 26, we see Jesus promising the issuance and provision of the Holy Spirit, which was to come. "But the Helper, the Holy Spirit, Whom the Father will send in My name, He will teach you all things and bring to your remembrance all that I have said to you."

Jesus also says in John 15:15, "I have called you friends, for all that I have heard from My Father I have made known to you."

Upon Jesus's resurrection and ascension to Heaven, the Holy Spirit came to indwell those who belonged to Christ at the time of Pentecost in Acts 2, and from that moment on, whenever someone came to a saving knowledge and relationship with Christ, they were instantly indwelt with the Spirit (cf. Acts 9 and 10). Up until that moment, the disciples and apostles struggled to fully understand and grasp much of what was taught to them by Jesus. But once the Holy Spirit came and took up residence in their hearts, they were fully taught and fully grasped an inerrant and truly accurate understanding of His teachings and recorded it in the Gospels and the rest of the New Testament Scriptures.

This is also reiterated in John 16:13 when Jesus proclaims, "When the Spirit of Truth comes, He will guide you into all the Truth, for He will not speak on His Own authority, but whatever He hears He will speak, and He will declare to you the things that are to come." So as we have seen by going through John, it was the Father that drew them and caused them to come to Christ, it was Christ Who chose them and told them everything that He had heard from His Father. The Father sent the Spirit to them in the name of Christ, and it was the Spirit Who taught them to fully understand His teachings. And this is all solidified in Jesus's words found in John 15, in Jesus's teaching of "The True Vine."

Starting in verse 3, we read:

> Already you are clean because of the Word
> that I have spoken to you. Abide in Me, and I
> in you. As the branch cannot bear fruit by itself,
> unless it abides in the vine, neither can you,

> unless you abide in Me. I Am the vine; you are
> the branches. Whoever abides in Me and I in
> him, he it is that bears much fruit, for apart from
> Me you can do nothing.

Apart from the will and purpose of God and Christ and the Holy Spirit, we cannot come to Him, believe in Him, or be saved by Him; it is all His work in us. We can do nothing apart from Him.

We are given a few lessons in the book of Acts as well. In chapter 2, verse 47, we read of the account of Pentecost when the Spirit came to indwell those who are with Christ. We are told that over 3,000 people came to believe in Christ as their Messiah that day and that "The Lord added to their number day by day those who were being saved."

We plainly see in this verse that it is the Lord that adds the saved and brings them to Himself through a constant ongoing process. We do not come to Him on our own. We are brought to Him by Himself. We see a couple things that back this up in 3:26, 11:18, and 13:48 also.

In chapter 3, when Peter was speaking to the Jews at the temple, he speaks of "God, having raised up His Servant (Christ), sent Him to you first, to bless you by turning every one of you from your wickedness." So we are told that it is Christ Who blesses us and is the One Who turns us away from our wickedness. It is not our work; it is His.

In chapter 11, when Peter reports to the Church what had just taken place with the family of Cornelius receiving the Holy Spirit, "they glorified God, saying, 'Then to the Gentiles also God has granted repentance that leads to life.'" And in chapter 13, when Paul and Barnabas were preaching in Antioch and teaching them of God's command to go and to preach to the Gentiles, "when the Gentiles heard this, they began rejoicing and glorifying the Word of the Lord, and as many as were appointed to eternal life believed."

In these last two verses, we see that it is those who are appointed to eternal life that are the ones who come to believe in Christ, and God is the One Who grants them the repentance necessary that leads to eternal life. The Greek word used here for "appointed" is *tetag-*

menoi, which means "to be ordained, arranged, designated, placed in order, or appointed." It is God's action placing into an eternal relationship with Him, those whom He chooses which leads them to believe in Him. It is because of His ordination of them that turns them from their wickedness that they would come to have belief in Him. The Greek word used here for "granted" is *edoken* which means "gave, put, or to place." So just like the word used for appointed, we see God's divine action in this. God is the One Who gives the repentance necessary for eternal life and places us into an eternal relationship with Himself.

Let's look at repentance really quick. Reverend D. Martyn Lloyd-Jones, describes it like this:

> Repentance means that you realize that you are a guilty, vile sinner in the presence of God, that you deserve the wrath and punishment of God, that you are hell-bound. It means that you begin to realize that this thing called sin is in you, that you long to get rid of it, and that you turn your back on it in every shape and form. You renounce the world whatever the cost, the world in its mind and outlook as well as its practice, and you deny yourself, and take up the cross and go after Christ. Your nearest and dearest, and the whole world, may call you a fool, or say you have religious mania. You may have to suffer financially, but it makes no difference. That is repentance.[20]

> Repentance always speaks of a change of purpose, and specifically a turning from sin. Repentance calls for a repudiation of the old life and a turning to God for salvation. The three elements of repentance are a turning to God, a turning from evil, and the intent to serve God (1 Thess. 1:9). No change of mind can be called

true repentance if it does not include all three elements. A true change of mind will necessarily result in a change of behavior. Repentance is not merely shame or sorrow for sin, although genuine repentance always involves an element of remorse. It is a redirection of the human will, a purposeful decision to forsake all unrighteousness and pursue righteousness instead. Nor is repentance merely a human work. It is, like every element of redemption, a sovereignly bestowed gift of God (Acts 11:18; cf. 5:31; 2 Tim. 2:25). If God is the One Who grants repentance, it cannot be viewed as a human work. Above all, repentance is not a pre-salvation attempt to set one's life in order. The call to repentance is not a command to make sin right before turning to Christ in faith. Rather, it is a command to recognize one's lawlessness and hate it, to turn one's back on it and flee to Christ, embracing Him with whole hearted devotion.

As J. I. Packer has written, "The repentance that Christ requires of His people consists in a settled refusal to set any limits to the claims which He may make on their lives" (J. I. Packer, *Evangelism and the Sovereignty of God*, p. 72). Repentance is not simply a mental activity; genuine repentance involves the intellect, emotions, and will. *Intellectually*, repentance begins with a recognition of sin—the understanding that we are sinners, that our sin is an affront to a holy God, and more precisely, that we are personally responsible for our own guilt. The repentance that leads to salvation must also include a recognition of Who Christ is along with some understanding of His right to govern people's lives. *Emotionally*, genuine repentance often accompanies an overwhelming sense of sorrow. It is difficult to imagine a true repentance that does not include at least an element of contrition; a sense of anguish at having sinned against God. *Volitionally*, repentance involves a change of direction, a transformation of the will. It constitutes a willingness—more accurately, a determination—to abandon stubborn disobedience and surrender the will to Christ. Genuine repentance will inevitably result in a change of behavior. The behavior change is not itself repentance, but it is the fruit repentance will certainly bear. Where there is no observable difference in conduct, there can be no confidence that repentance has taken place (Matt. 3:8; cf. 1 John 2:3–6, 3:17). Real repentance alters the character of the whole man.[21]

So we see that repentance is a full turning away from unrighteousness toward righteousness, and looking back at Acts 11, this change of behavior is granted to us by God Himself.

Also, a little bit later in Acts 18:27, we read of Apollos preaching to those in Achaia. "When he arrived he greatly helped those who through grace had believed." Here we are told that it is all through the grace of God that they had believed. Straightforward, they did not believe in God on their own but came to believe in Him only by and through His grace.

In good ol' Paul fashion, we have much to learn from Romans on this beautiful topic of grace.

Romans 1:1–3:20 speaks of God's *righteousness defied* by a sinful world. Romans 3:21–5:21 shows God's *righteousness supplied* for believing sinners. Chapters 6 through 8 focus on God's *righteousness applied* in the lives of the saints. Justification is the means through which God's righteousness is *supplied* on behalf of believing sinners.[22]

The first thing we shall dig into comes from chapter 2. As we have already dug into the first few chapters of Romans looking at Paul's very in-depth diagnosis of sin and his tirade against all men in regards to the sinful nature that permeates all of mankind and the uselessness of the law to make us pure and holy and righteous before God, we see in verse 4 that it is "God's kindness (which) is meant to lead you to repentance," not our own efforts or will but "the riches of His kindness and forbearance and patience." We then come to the end of chapter 3 where he transitions from condemning all men due to sin and into the acquisition of this redemption and salvation. We will pick this up in verse 21.

> But now the righteousness of God has been manifested apart from the law, although the Law and the prophets bear witness to it—the righteousness of God through faith in Jesus Christ for all who believe. For there is no distinction: for all have sinned and fall short of the glory of God, and are justified by His grace as a gift, through the redemption that is in Christ Jesus, Whom God put forward as a propitiation by His blood, to be received by faith. This was to show God's righteousness, because in His divine forbearance He had passed over former sins. It was to show His righteousness at the present time, so that He might be just and the Justifier of the one who has faith in Jesus.

This set of verses are also some of those that show the duality in the paradox that we discussed in chapter 5, God's divine sovereignty versus man's responsibility. We have already touched on these verses a bit extensively in the previous chapter, but we will focus on a different aspect of this multidimensional verse here in this chapter.

In the last chapter, we focused on man's responsibility in accepting God's free gift of redemption fulfilled and made available through the sacrifice of His Son Jesus Christ and all that is necessary from us is complete surrender and faith in Christ as our Savior and to the fact that it is only through His propitiatory work done in our place and that we can do nothing to help, gain, or even solidify our union with Him. But to go deeper, we see the divine side of the paradox and see that though we do have a responsibility to accept Christ's gift to us, we also paradoxically but also truthfully see that it is all ultimately God's action done within us.

In verse 24, we see that it is God Who justifies us "BY HIS GRACE, AS A GIFT!" Emphasis is added by me because that is such an amazing and beautiful truth! He justifies us, He redeems us, He washes us clean of all sin, He erases our debt, all through His Own glorious grace, entirely as a free gift to us! He acknowledges that the punishment necessary for all of our sin against Him has been paid in full through the substitutionary work of His Son, Jesus Christ, our Savior, and imputes Christ's righteousness onto us all because of His sweet grace shown unto us and all to proclaim His great righteousness.

Paul backs this up in chapter 4, in verse 16, when he says, "That is why it depends on faith, in order that the promise may rest on grace and be guaranteed to all His offspring." From our side, it does depend on our faith and trust in Jesus, but the entire promise ultimately rests on God's grace. If it rested on anything we actually did, then we would have grounds to boast about our own salvational acts, and God would then owe us something, which we discussed in earlier chapters. "Justification is through faith alone, but the power of justification is God's great grace, not man's faith."[23]

We read in the very next verse of chapter 4, in verse 17, "God... Who gives life to the dead and calls into existence the things that do not exist."

> Faith is only reckoned by righteousness. Justification is wholly a work of God's grace. God "calls into being that which does not exist." That is a fascinating statement about God. If you or I were to declare "things that are not as though they were," we would be lying. God can do it because

He is God, and His decrees carry the full weight of divine sovereignty. God spoke, and the worlds were created (Heb. 11:3). He spoke things that were not, and behold! They were. He can call people, places, and events into existence solely by His divinely sovereign decrees. He can declare believing sinners righteous even though they are not. That is justification. But justification never occurs alone in God's plan. It is always accompanied by sanctification. God does not declare sinners righteous legally without making them righteous practically. Justification is not just a legal fiction. When God declares someone righteous, He will inevitably bring it to pass (Rom. 8:30; Phil. 1:6; Heb. 12:2). When justification occurs, the process of sanctification begins. Grace always encompasses both.[24]

God is the only One that possesses the power to bring things into being that do not exist. This includes our lives, both physically and spiritually, and even more so our redemption, justification, and righteousness in front of Him, which as we have looked at earlier in this chapter will always result also in our sanctification and growth in Him.

This is all a free gift given to us by God entirely through His grace toward us, and we see this reiterated over and over again in chapters 5 and 6 of Romans. In 5:12–21, we see Paul explaining this in the context of comparing that through one man, Adam, sin came into the world and that death spread to all men through sin because of his trespass, and contrasting that with, through the One Man, Jesus, the grace of God abounded and brought justification to the many. Five times in chapter 5, and one more time in chapter 6, Paul repeats the phrase "free gift" to emphasize this beautiful point.

Starting in verse 15 of chapter 5, "But the *free gift* is not like the trespass. For if many died through one man's trespass, ***much more*** have the grace of God and the *free gift* by the grace of that One Man Jesus Christ abounded for many."

Also, as we read these verses, notice that Paul uses the phrase "much more" or "all the more" a few different times to really emphasize the infinite difference between Adam's one trespass that brought about condemnation and Christ's immeasurably greater one act of redemption that brings justification.

Continuing in verse 16:

> And the *free gift* is not like the result of that one man's sin. For the judgment following one trespass brought condemnation, but the *free gift* following many trespasses brought justification. For if, because of the one man's trespass, death reigned through that one man, ***much more*** will those who receive the abundance of grace and the *free gift* of righteousness reign in life through the One Man Jesus Christ. Therefore, as one trespass led to condemnation for all men, so one act of righteousness leads to justification and life for all men. For as by the one man's disobedience the many were made sinners, so by the One Man's obedience the many will be made righteous. Now the law came in to increase the trespass, but where sin increased, grace abounded ***all the more***, so that, as sin reigned in death, grace also might reign through righteousness leading to eternal life through Jesus Christ our Lord.

And in 6:23, "For the wages of sin is death, but the *free gift* of God is eternal life in Christ Jesus our Lord."

The Complete Jewish Bible states 6:23 like this, "What one earns from sin is death; but eternal life is what one receives as a *free gift* from God, in union with the Messiah Yeshua, our Lord."

It is entirely a free gift! It is all unearned! It is all done by His much greater and glorious work done for us and gifted to us through

His grace! We are all condemned because of our forefather Adam, and we are "made righteous" because of Christ's perfect life of obedience and sacrificial substitution made in our place, which is gifted to us, free of charge, free of payments necessary, and free of anything that our dead and sinful flesh could offer. You didn't earn the sin Adam gave you. You didn't earn the righteousness Jesus gave you. With regard to the flesh, as we see in this passage and the entirety of Scripture, all that the flesh has accomplished or earned is death and condemnation; it is entirely the grace of God that has accomplished life and redemption, reconciliation and salvation.

Just a few verses earlier in chapter 5, we read just how desolate and dismal our situation was. In verses 6–11, we read:

> For while we were still weak, at the right time Christ died for the ungodly. For one will scarcely die for a righteous person—though perhaps for a good person one would dare even to die—but God shows His love for us in that while we were yet still sinners, Christ died for us. Since, therefore, we have now been justified by His blood, *much more* (there's that phrase again) shall we be saved by Him from the wrath of God. For if while we were enemies, we were reconciled to God by the death of His Son, *much more*, now that we are reconciled, shall we be saved by His life. *More than that*, we also rejoice in God through Our Lord Jesus Christ, through Whom we have now received reconciliation.

Our situation was dire! We were hopeless! We were weak sinners and full-blown enemies of God, and Christ came and died for us, the ungodly, and reconciled us to God and justified us and saved us by His Own shed blood entirely out of His love for us, not because of anything that we did! The Greek word used in verse 6 for "weak" is *asthenes* which means "strengthless, weak, sick, diseased, powerless." We were absolutely powerless and without any strength of our own, and Jesus died for us to reconcile us as redeemed and justified to our holy and righteous God. We were helpless! We owe everything to Jesus, for it is only He "Who gives life to the dead and calls into existence the things that do not exist" (Rom. 4:17).

Besides being weak, powerless enemies of God, we were dead! We were dead in our sins (Eph. 2:5), and it was Christ that breathed life into our dead souls. It is only God that can call into existence the things that do not exist; that is, only "God can declare believing sinners to be righteous even though they are not, by imputing His righteousness to them, just as God made or declared Jesus 'sin' and punished Him, though He was not a sinner."[25]

Christian author, Ken Willig, offers his thoughts regarding his own personal testimony:

> I truly believed that the only way to Heaven was to earn it and I believed that God was keeping score of my good and bad deeds. At one point, when I looked at the scoreboard of my life, I believed losing was inevitable. Although I believed that Jesus's sacrifice on the cross was available to everyone, it was my good deeds that merited the grace I needed in order to get into Heaven. To use a metaphor, I needed to do enough good deeds to fill my bathtub of grace to the brim…when I committed a serious sin, God would pull the plug and all the grace I had earned would drain… I was taught that when I confessed my sins, God would put the plug in my tub and start filling it again. Filling would continue until I committed another serious sin. When I did, the plug would be pulled and it would empty again. This fill, drain, fill, drain cycle would repeat over and over through the years. Finally, wrought with guilt, I could no longer fool myself into thinking that I was on my way to salvation. I felt… it was a losing effort. I had to face my dilemma:

my tub would never be filled, and I would never have peace with God. I was encouraged to pray and to look to God's Word for the solution to my dilemma. The Bible says that if I would place my faith and trust in Jesus as my Savior, then God would fill my empty tub to the brim and overflowing, with the plug out, by submerging it into His ocean of grace created by Jesus Christ's atoning sacrifice for my sins on the cross—the way of salvation. He filled my tub, not me. He earned my salvation, not me. He paid the penalty for all my sins, for all of my life. Jesus did it all. Nothing I did contributed to the filling—not good deeds, good works, prayers, or charitable giving. Nothing! God filled it freely while I was a sinner" (cf. Rom. 5:8, 10:9–11; Eph. 2:4–5, 8–9; Ti. 3:5; 1 Pet. 1:18–19).[26]

What a beautiful picture of God infinitely immersing us in His awesome and overwhelming grace. Speaking on Romans 5:8, John MacArthur says:

God's immense love is supremely demonstrated by Christ's dying for the ungodly—for totally unrighteous, undeserving, and unlovable humanity. Not many people would willingly sacrifice their own lives to save someone of high character. Fewer still would give their lives to save a person they know to be a wicked scoundrel. But God was so inclined, and in that fact is our security and assurance. Saved, we can never be as wretched as we were before our conversion—and He loved us totally then.[27]

Isn't that a beautiful truth to look at? We were so wretched and sinful and vile that Christ, out of His infinite love for us, even as we were in such a wretched and disgusting state, stepped in and died for us and secured us. Even in our absolute worst possible state, God still loved us enough to sacrifice Himself for us. This shows the security that we have in His finished work. You can never do anything to make Him lose His love for you because already having been in your worst, He already died for you and gave you His best. We will dive deeper into that in the next chapter.

We also see in 5:5 that this beautiful and amazing love of God "has been poured into our hearts through the Holy Spirit Who has been given to us." He pours His love into us, all administered to us through the Holy Spirit which He has also given to us. And since His love takes residence in our hearts, all "thanks be to God, that you who were once slaves of sin have become obedient from the heart to the standard of teaching to which you were committed, and having been set free from sin, have become slaves of righteousness" (Rom. 6:17–18).

"For sin will have no dominion over you, since you are not under law but under grace" (Rom. 6:14).

We owe all of this beautiful truth to the glorious grace of God toward us. There is nothing of ourselves that has brought this about. And we have now been "released from the law, having died to that which held us captive, so that we serve in the new way of the Spirit and not in the old way of the written code" (Rom. 7:6).

Moving into chapter 8 of Romans, we read in the first few verses:

> There is therefore now no condemnation for those who are in Christ Jesus. For the law of the Spirit of life has set you free in Christ Jesus from the law of sin and death. For God has done what the law, weakened by the flesh, could not do. By sending His Own Son in the likeness of sinful flesh and for sin, He condemned sin in the flesh, in order that the righteous requirement of the law might be fulfilled in us, who walk not according to the flesh but according to the Spirit.

Once again, we find that it is all God's work in us. The Law, which we went over in chapter 3, is incapable of fulfilling righteousness as it is weakened by the flesh, so God took it upon Himself to send His Own perfect and holy Son to perfectly fulfill the Law and satisfy its righteous requirement and deliver us from our death to sin. He did what the Law could not do. He fulfilled it for us and took our place. He lived perfectly the way that we should've and then died in our place as we should've. We are now set free from sin and death and live by the law of the Spirit Who indwells us and, as we saw before, has been given to us by God.

Verse 11 adds to this, "If the Spirit of Him Who raised Jesus from the dead dwells in you, He Who raised Jesus Christ from the dead will also give life to your mortal bodies through His Spirit Who dwells in you."

It is God the Father that makes all this possible. He raised Christ from the dead giving life to our dead bodies through the Spirit that He gave us. In verse 13, we follow this up with, "if by the Spirit you put to death the deeds of the body, you will live. For all who are led by the Spirit of God are sons of God."

Some people may try to read this and say, "If I put to death the deeds of the body or if I do this or that… If I…" but look at how you are able to do it. It is only by the Spirit! And if you are led by the Spirit, it says that you are sons of God, which means you are already saved and indwelt with the Spirit. We aren't made sons of God by our obedience; our obedience, on the other hand, proves to us and offers us assurance that we have been adopted into God's family and are sons of God.

Obedience is never a prerequisite but instead an effect of a salvational and saved life of the child of God. We will get deeper into that in a later chapter also. Continuing on from verse 14, we see that assurance being solidified.

> For all who are led by the Spirit of God are
> sons of God. For you did not receive the spirit of
> slavery to fall back into fear, but you have received
> the Spirit of adoption as sons, by Whom we cry,
> "Abba! Father!" The Spirit Himself bears witness

> with our spirit that we are children of God, and if children, then heirs—heirs of God and fellow heirs with Christ, provided we suffer with Him in order that we may also be glorified with Him.

It is the Spirit Himself that assures us that we have been adopted by God as His children, and we become not only His heirs, but we become fellow heirs or co-heirs or equal heirs of Christ Himself! That is truly amazing! That means that everything that Christ receives we will receive as fellow heirs with Him! You're not a servant or employee who can be fired or released. You're a child who is secured as part of the Family, an heir to the inheritance. And the presence of the Spirit within us is what verifies our adoption as God's children.

We also see further work of the Spirit in us in verses 25–27.

> Likewise the Spirit helps us in our weakness. For we do not know what to pray for as we ought, but the Spirit Himself intercedes for us with groanings too deep for words. And He Who searches hearts knows what is the mind of the Spirit, because the Spirit intercedes for the saints according to the will of God.

The Spirit helps us and prays for us when we have no idea what to even pray for, and since the Father and the Spirit are One, They agree perfectly in will, and the Spirit intercedes for us accordingly. Verse 28 follows this by saying, "And we know that all things work for the good of those who love Him, who are called according to His purpose." He intercedes for us and brings about everything for our good, and it is all done to those of us who are His elected and chosen, all for His Own great purpose.

The verses that follow that are some of the most beautiful and full verses on this topic. Verses 29 and 30 read:

> For those whom He foreknew He also predestined to be conformed to the image of His

> Son, in order that He might be the firstborn among many brothers. And those whom He predestined He also called, and those whom He called He also justified, and those whom He justified He also glorified.

This says it all. From the very beginning, pre-Genesis, all the way until we are brought to perfect glory in Heaven, it is all His work! Just as we saw in Philippians 1:6 and Hebrews 12:2. Before He created any of this, He foreknew us and predestined us. He called us to Himself, and He is the One that justified us, and He is the One that brings us to Heaven where we will be glorified perfectly into the image of Christ.

> God's part in salvation begins with election and ends in glory. In between, every aspect of the redemptive process is God's work, not the sinner's. God will neither terminate the process nor omit any aspect of it. Titus 3:5 is clear: Salvation—all of it—is "not on the basis of deeds which we have done." It is God's work done "according to His mercy." It is not merely a declaratory transaction, legally securing a place in Heaven but leaving the sinner captive to his sin. It involves a transformation of the disposition, the very nature, through, "the washing of regeneration and renewing by the Holy Spirit' as well."[28]

Praise God!

Heading into chapter 9, starting in verse 10, we see another aspect of this.

> When Rebekah had conceived children by one man, our forefather Isaac, though they were not yet born and had done nothing either good or bad—in order that God's purpose of elec-

tion might continue, not because of works but because of Him Who calls—she was told, "The older will serve the younger." As it is written, "Jacob I loved, but Esau I hated." What shall we say then? Is there injustice on God's part? By no means! For He says to Moses, "I will have mercy on whom I have mercy, and I will have compassion on whom I have compassion." So then it depends not on human will or exertion, but on God, Who has mercy. For the Scripture says to Pharaoh, "For this very purpose I have raised you up, that I might show My power in you, and that My name might be proclaimed in all the earth." So then He has mercy on whomever He wills, and He hardens whomever He wills.

We see in the beginning of this passage that it was God Who chose Jacob over Esau, the younger over the older, before they were even born, all for His Own purpose. God Himself will determine who He chooses and has compassion on as it is His sovereign gift to offer and whom to harden, based upon His Own will. It is not any of us that decides this.

This same concept is also shown just a little bit later in Romans chapter 11. This time, in speaking about the remnant of Israel and rhetorically asking his reader if God has rejected and abandoned His people, he says in verse 4:

But what is God's reply to him? "I have kept for Myself seven thousand men who have not bowed the knee to Baal" (referring back to 1 Kings 19:18). So too at the present time there is a remnant, chosen by grace. But if it is by grace, it is no longer on the basis of works; otherwise grace would no longer be grace. What then? Israel failed to obtain what it was seeking. The elect obtained it, but the rest were hardened.

God chooses and elects those who will be a part of His chosen people all on the simple basis of His grace and also those whom He will harden, all according to His will. If this is altered in any way, to be apart from His overall divine choosing, then it is no longer done by grace, and it would then fall into the category of being dependent on the basis of works. A little bit later in Romans 11, Paul speaks of the coming salvation for this remnant of Israel. Starting in verse 25:

> Lest you be wise in your own sight, I want you to understand this mystery, brothers: a partial hardening has come upon Israel, until the fullness of the Gentiles has come in. And in this way all Israel will be saved, as it is written, "The Deliverer will come from Zion, He will banish ungodliness from Jacob; and this will be My covenant with them when I take away their sins."

Paul is saying once again here that God will choose whom He will harden, but here he also says that God will restore them to a saving relationship with Himself and remove their sins once the fullness of the Gentiles comes in. The Greek word here used for "fullness" is *pleroma*, which means "completion, replenishing, to fill or fulfill." What this means is that there is a specific preordained number of elect Gentiles that will come to salvation, and when that number is reached and the "pleroma" of the Gentiles is finished, that is when God will bring back the hearts of the elect Jews to Himself.

Chapter 11 ends with a few passages that tie into this topic as well. In verse 32, we read, "For God has consigned all to disobedience that He may have mercy on all." And verse 36, "For from Him and through Him and to Him are all things. To Him be glory forever. Amen."

"Though not the author of sin (Ps. 5:4; Hab. 1:13; Jas. 1:13), God allowed man to pursue his sinful inclinations so that He could receive glory by demonstrating His grace and mercy to disobedient sinners. God is the source, the sustainer, and the rightful end of everything that exists."[29]

In chapter 12, we see Paul give us a little more still. In verse 3, he says, "For by the grace given to me," which even that right there is amazing! Paul, formerly known as Saul, a Pharisee of pharisees who was known for savagely arresting and persecuting the Jews and having them put to death, was divinely lavished upon by God's divine and undeserved grace and favor, turning Paul's heart toward Christ, becoming the greatest apostle that ever lived and the man who ended up writing about half of the entire New Testament. That was not Paul's choice. He was on his way to Damascus to arrest and persecute even more followers of the Way (Christians as they were known at that time) when He was ambushed on the road, blinded and spoken to directly by Christ Himself Who questioned him and taught him, and Paul immediately surrendered to Him in faith, being a very witness to Jesus's post-resurrection presence (cf. Acts 9, 22, 26; Gal. 1:12, 15–16).

Getting back to verse 3:

> For by the grace given to me I say to everyone among you not to think of himself more highly than he ought to think, but to think with sober judgment, each according to the measure of faith that God has assigned. For as in one body we have many members, and the members do not all have the same function, so we, though many, are one body in Christ, and individually members one of another. Having gifts that differ according to the grace given to us, let us use them.

The word *faith* here is not referring to saving faith but instead "faithful stewardship." Here, Paul is comparing each individual believer to a certain part of the body of Christ and expressing that the measure of each member's "faithful stewardship" is divinely appointed to him by God, all sovereignly chosen completely apart from any personal merit, obedience, or fulfillment but instead solely by God's grace.

In the beginning of chapter 14, Paul is cautioning to be gentle and sensitive to those who may be weaker in the faith and not quarreling over opinion, when it comes to certain things like what you may or may not eat. In verse 4, we read, "Who are you to pass judgment on the servant of another? It is before his own master that he stands or falls. And he will be upheld, for the Lord is able to make him stand." Even those who are weak, the Lord Himself will uphold and make him to stand.

In chapter 15, verse 15, we see Paul speaking of his ministry unto the Gentiles and speaking of his instruction and preaching to them. "But on some points, I have written to you very boldly by way of reminder, because of the grace given to me by God to be minister of Christ Jesus to the Gentiles in the priestly service of the Gospel of God, so that the offering of the Gentiles may be acceptable, sanctified by the Holy Spirit." We see Paul giving all of the credit for his knowledge and bold instruction in ministry to God Himself and the grace that God has given to him. He takes no credit of his own. We also see him give credit for their sanctification to the Holy Spirit.

Moving on into Paul's letters to the Corinthians, we see Paul give us a little bit more on God's grace and sovereignty over all things. In the beginning of his first letter, we see him opening up with a greeting and then a bit of thanksgiving to the church in Corinth, and then he quickly warns against divisions in the church. In verse 18, he says, "For the word of the cross is folly to those who are perishing, but to us who are being saved it is the power of God."

Very quickly here, we see the phrase "are being saved." This is a passive action on our part. It is done unto us by God. There is no conditionality here on our part. It is all God's work. And in verses 27–31, we read further:

> God chose what is foolish in the world to shame the wise; God chose what is weak in the world to shame the strong; God chose what is low and despised in the world, even things that are not, to bring to nothing things that are, so that no human being might boast in the presence of God. And because of Him you are in Christ Jesus, Who became to us wisdom from God,

righteousness and sanctification and redemption, so that, as it is written, "Let the one who boasts, boast in the Lord" (Jer. 9:24).

Besides the verb tense that is used for "being saved" in verse 18, this is why it is and must be a passive action on our part and that it depends all on God so that none of us can boast in ourselves, but we instead entirely boast in what God has done for us. "God chose... God chose... God chose...what is foolish...what is weak...what is low...to shame the wise and the strong" so that no human being has any right at all to boast in himself. God will even bring things that do not exist into existence (cf. Rom. 4:17) to prove His sovereignty over all things. "Because of Him [we] are in Christ Jesus."

He is the entire reason that we have a relationship with Christ, not because of any of our actions or obedience. Because of Him, He became wisdom to us. Because of Him, He became our righteousness, our sanctification, and our redemption, all of this done to us, from His Own actions, not ours.

Biblical redemption is the act by which God Himself pays the ransom price to satisfy His Own holy justice and to buy back fallen men and women and set them free from their sin. Jesus is our Redeemer from sin. He paid the price for our release from iniquity and death. Because we now belong to Christ and by faith are made one with Him, we are now acceptable to God."[30]

The great miracle of redemption is not that we accept Christ, but that He accepts us. In fact, we would never love Him on our own (1 John 4:19). Salvation occurs when God changes the heart and the unbeliever turns from sin to Christ. God delivers the sinner from the domain of darkness into the Kingdom of light (Col. 1:13). In the process Christ enters the heart by faith to dwell there (cf. Eph. 3:17). Thus conversion is not simply a sinner's decision for Christ, it is first the sovereign work of God in transforming the individual."[31]

We have absolutely no right to boast in ourselves because we have done nothing to gain it or access it. It is ultimately all His divine and free gift (cf. Rom. 5 and 6) to us.

In chapter 2, we see Paul talking about his ministry among the Corinthians, and placing all credit to the One Who deserves it. Verses 4 and 5 tell us, "My speech and my message were not in plausible words of wisdom, but in demonstration of the Spirit and of power, that your faith might not rest in the wisdom of men but in the power of God."

Once again, Paul is warning the Gentile believers of the sin of pride in boasting of their own merit (cf. 4:7) in understanding and accepting the Gospel message, saying that even their faith must not rest in the wisdom of man but fully in the power of God. God Himself even provides us with our faith to believe (cf. Eph. 2:8). He follows up on this throughout chapter 2 and into chapter 3. Verses 9–10, "No eye has seen, nor ear heard, nor the heart of man imagined, what God has prepared for those who love Him (quoted from Isa. 64:4)—these things God has revealed to us through the Spirit. For the Spirit searches everything, even the depths of God."

These verses are again speaking of the wisdom of God in regards to the message of the saving truth of the Gospel that cannot be achieved by any of our own means but is instead granted and given to us through the indwelling of the Holy Spirit, for:

> No one comprehends the thoughts of God except the Spirit of God. Now we have received not the spirit of the world, but the Spirit Who is from God, that we might understand the things freely given to us by God. And we impart this in words not taught by human wisdom but taught by the Spirit, interpreting spiritual truths to those who are spiritual. (11–13).

We are taught all these things directly from the Spirit Himself, and we see in chapter 3, verses 6–7, that it is "only God Who gives (us) the growth" in this wisdom and understanding of the Gospel.

In chapter 6, we see Paul give quite a rebuking to some of the Corinthians. Starting in verse 9, he says:

> Do you not know that the unrighteous will not inherit the Kingdom of God? Do not be deceived: neither the sexually immoral, nor idolators, nor adulterers, nor men who practice homosexuality, not thieves, nor the greedy, nor drunkards, nor revilers, nor swindlers will inherit the Kingdom of God. And such were some of you. But you were washed, you were sanctified, you were justified in the name of the Lord Jesus Christ and by the Spirit of our God.

Paul makes reference to their past sinfulness but then onto their redeemed life being washed, sanctified, and justified by Christ. In the Greek, these three verbs are again in the passive form, referring to God's divine work done within us and to us, not by us.

Chapter 12, verse 3, offers us a great insight into God's grace when we pair it with our responsibility, and we again see the paradox of man's responsibility and God's divine sovereignty. Verse 3 says, "Therefore I want you to understand that no one speaking in the Spirit of God ever says, 'Jesus is accursed!' and no one can say 'Jesus is Lord' except by the Holy Spirit."

First of all, if the Spirit dwells in us and speaks through us, we simply cannot speak and say that Jesus is accursed since that would mean that God would be cursing Himself. So He keeps us from speaking such absurdities. But then, to take the second part of this verse and pair it with Romans 10:9, which we looked at earlier, "If you confess with your mouth that Jesus is Lord" (Rom. 10:9a); which "No one can say 'Jesus is Lord' except by the Holy Spirit" (1 Cor. 12:3); "[A]nd you believe in your heart that God raised Him from the dead, you will be saved" (Rom. 10:9b).

So looking at this pair, we see that we cannot be saved unless we confess that Jesus is Lord, but we cannot even do so except by the Holy Spirit! We are simply unable and hopeless to do any of this without God's amazing grace working within us. Then, it is immediately followed in verse 6, "And there are [distinctive] ways of working [to accomplish things], but it is the same God Who produces all things in all believers [inspiring, energizing, and empowering them]" (AMP). So we see that every good thing in us is from the Lord Himself.

Toward the end of Paul's first letter, in chapter 15, verse 10, he speaks again of his ministry giving credit where credit is due, "But by the grace of God I am what I am, and His grace toward me was not in vain. On the contrary, I worked harder than any of them, though it was not I, but the grace of God that is with me." He gratefully admits that everything that he is and everything that he has done even in works was all done entirely through the grace of God in him. He takes no credit of his own. Again, giving thanks in verse 57, he says, "The sting of death is sin, and the power of sin is the law. But thanks be to God, Who gives us the victory through our Lord Jesus Christ."

In Paul's second letter to the Corinthians, we find a bit more teaching on our sanctification. In chapter 3, verses 4–6, he reviews a little with us:

> Such is the confidence that we have through Christ toward God. Not that we are sufficient in ourselves to claim anything as coming from us, but our sufficiency is from God, Who made us sufficient to be ministers of a new covenant, not of the letter but of the Spirit. For the letter kills, but the Spirit gives life.

We see again that Paul is giving all credit to God, not only for himself but also in honor of us as well. We are entirely insufficient apart from God. Our entire sufficiency comes only from Him! In everything! We are entirely unable to claim anything of ourselves. He alone made us sufficient through the sacrifice of His Son. He also reiterates that the law or the letter, the written word, is also insufficient and that it is only the Spirit that brings us to life. We have no part in making this happen. We are merely passive recipients of a free gift.

Continuing on in chapter 3, verse 18, we see, "And we all, with unveiled face, beholding the glory of the Lord, are being transformed into the same image from one degree of glory to another. For this comes from the Lord Who is the Spirit."

This is speaking of an ongoing and progressive transformation within us performed by the Spirit.

> As they gaze at the glory of the Lord, believers are continually being transformed into Christlikeness. The ultimate goal of the believer is to be like Christ (cf. Rom. 8:29; Phil. 3:12–14; 1 John 3:2) and by continually focusing on Him the Spirit transforms the believer more and more into His image. From one level of glory to another level of glory—from one level of manifesting Christ to another. This verse describes progressive sanctification. The more believers grow in their knowledge of Christ, the more He is revealed in their lives (Phil. 3:12–14).[32]

In chapter 5, we are given a very beautiful passage speaking of God's all-encompassing grace and unmerited favor toward us. Starting in verse 17, we read, "Therefore, if anyone is in Christ, he is a new creation." This speaks of complete regeneration and rebirth. We, by and of ourselves, are absolutely powerless to create this in ourselves. This is all a divine working of God within us.

> The old has passed away; behold the new has come. All this is from God, Who through Christ reconciled us to Himself and gave us the ministry of reconciliation; that is, in Christ God was reconciling the world to Himself, not count-

ing their trespasses against them, and entrusting to us the message of reconciliation. Therefore, we are ambassadors for Christ, God making His appeal through us. We implore you on behalf of Christ, be reconciled to God. For our sake He made Him to be sin Who knew no sin, so that in Him we might become the righteousness of God.

What an amazing part of Scripture! That we might become the righteousness of God through Jesus Christ! WOW! As we look back through this entire passage, we again see that it is all God's divine work for and in us that brings this to fulfillment. We play no part in it, other than being the joyful, thankful, and incredibly blessed recipients of it. God creates us as new. Through Christ, He reconciled us to Himself. He gave us the ministry of reconciliation. Through Christ, God reconciled the world to Himself. He forgave our trespasses. He makes us His ambassadors, and makes His appeal to others through us. And for our sake, He sacrificed His Own Son to take our place in death that we would be given the righteousness that belongs to Christ. "All this is from God" (v. 18).

All praise, honor, and glory be to God!

God alone is righteous. When we are brought to faith in the death of Christ, we receive the righteousness of God triumphant on the cross in the very place where we receive our own condemnation as sinners. We can then receive justification because we willingly renounce every attempt to establish our own righteousness and allow God alone to be righteous. Thus, the only way we can be righteous in the sight of God is by recognizing that He only is righteous, and we ourselves sinners in the totality of our being. The only ground for our justification is the justification of God. All that can happen has happened already, not only on the cross, but also in us.

We have been separated from sin, we are dead, we are justified. With that the work of God is complete.[33]

Because Christians are justified by faith alone, their standing before God is not in any way related to personal merit. God receives as righteous those who believe, not because of any good things He sees in them—not even because of His Own sanctifying work in their lives—but solely on the basis of Christ's righteousness, which is reckoned to their account. In Biblical terms, justification is a divine verdict of "not guilty—fully righteous." It is the reversal of God's attitude toward the sinner. Whereas He formerly condemned, He now vindicates. Although the sinner once lived under God's wrath, as a believer he or she is now under God's blessing. Justification is more than simple pardon; pardon alone would still leave the sinner without merit before God. So when God justifies He imputes divine righteousness to the sinner (Rom. 4:22–25). Christ's Own infinite merit thus becomes the ground on which the believer stands before God (Rom. 5:19; 1 Cor. 1:30; Phil. 3:9). So justification elevates the believer to a realm of full acceptance and divine privilege in Jesus Christ. Therefore because of justification believers not only are perfectly free from any charge of guilt (Rom. 8:33) but also have the full merit of Christ reckoned to their personal account (Rom. 5:17). At justification, we are adopted as sons and daughters (Rom. 8:15); we become fellow heirs with Christ (v. 17); we are united with Christ so that we become one with Him (1 Cor. 6:17); and we are henceforth "in Christ" (Gal. 3:27) and He in us (Col. 1:27).[34]

Paul also starts off his letter to the Galatians, acknowledging God's grace in himself. Starting in verse 11, he tells the Galatians, "For I would have you know, brothers, that the Gospel that was preached by me is not man's gospel. For I did not receive it from any man, nor was I taught it, but I received it through a revelation of Jesus Christ."

He is referring here to his encounter with Jesus and his conversion to Jesus while on the road to Damascus. Jesus Himself revealed to and taught Paul all that he knew. Jesus alone was Paul's teacher of the entire Gospel message. He received none of it from any other man but every single piece of it from Christ Himself. Verse 15:

> When He Who had set me apart before I was born (acknowledging predestination and election), and Who called me by His grace, was pleased to reveal His Son to me, in order that I might preach Him among the Gentiles, I did not immediately consult with anyone.

Paul again is acknowledging that it was only through the grace of God that God chose him, even before he was born, to go and to preach His Word; and here again, he makes it known that he did not receive any of his knowledge and wisdom of the Gospel from consulting with others but from Christ alone.

Paul gives us a whole lot more in his letter to the Ephesians. In the first part of chapter 1, we see Paul describing the beautiful and gracious spiritual standing that we have in God through Christ. Starting in verse 3, we read:

> Blessed be the God and Father of our Lord Jesus Christ, Who has blessed us in Christ with every spiritual blessing in the Heavenly places, even as He chose us in Him before the foundation of the world, that we should be holy and blameless before Him.

We see that it is God alone that has poured upon us His divine grace and blessed us with EVERY spiritual blessing of His Heavenly realm. In the Greek, the word for "every" is *pase*, which means "all, the whole, or every kind of." Every spiritual blessing that God could give us, which includes, but is not limited to, foreknowledge, pre-destination, election, divine calling, justification, reconciliation, redemption, new life, forgiveness, sanctification, holiness, righteousness, salvation, glorification, etc.; every single spiritual blessing that God could give us, He "has blessed us in Christ with."

In the Greek, this phrase could be better translated as "having blessed" and is an aorist "simple past" tense verb. It denotes a simple past occurrence without regard for the amount of time taken to accomplish the action. God lavished ALL of His gracious and glorious spiritual gifts and blessings to us, back whenever it was He decided to do so, pre-Creation, pre-Genesis 1:1, pre-eternity, out of His gracious love for us. We had no part in making this happen since "He chose us in Him before the foundation of the world (vs 4)." He deemed us holy and righteous and blameless before Himself (vs 4), before He even created us, because, as He is an infinite and eternal Being, and is not bound by time, which was a limiting and dimensional part of His Creation, He sees the end from the beginning, and even though we weren't yet created, He saw all the way to the cross and our redemption through His Son. To us, it is all past tense, but to Him, it is all now and perfect and completed tense.

Carrying on into verse 5, "In love He predestined us for adoption as sons through Jesus Christ, according to the purpose of His will, to the praise of His glorious grace, with which He has blessed us in the Beloved." Again, before He even created this world, God chose us to be His adopted children.

> The primary action is that of God the Father Who chose unto Himself a people out of the whole of mankind before the foundation of the world, and then presented, gave these people whom He had chosen to the Son, in order that the Son might redeem them and do everything

that was necessary for their reconciliation with Himself.[35]

> In Roman law, adoption was required, even of a legitimate son, to inherit. This ceremony, legally held in the forum, was called the "Adoption." All born in his family were children, but only those adopted were recognized as sons. After adoption, they could never be disowned.[36]

God chose us to be His, never to be lost or disowned. When He made us His children, He secured us forever. This topic, we will get into deeper in the following chapter, but this was all done "according to the purpose of His will, and to the praise of His glorious grace." And it is by His glorious grace that He blessed us in the Beloved (i.e., Christ; cf. Matt. 3:17; Col. 1:13).

Continuing on into verse 7:

> In Him we have redemption through His blood, the forgiveness of our trespasses, according to the riches of His grace, which He lavished upon us, in all wisdom and insight making known to us the mystery of His will, according to His purpose, which He set forth in Christ as a plan for the fullness of time, to unite all things in Him, things in Heaven and things on earth.

Again, we see that this is all His work, done according to His purpose and His will, lavished upon us all according to the amazing riches of His grace toward us. He redeems us and forgives us because He chose to out of His love for us, before the foundations of the world. Verse 11:

> In Him we have obtained (once again, aorist "simple past" tense verb) an inheritance, having been predestined (aorist tense; both of

these verbs are also in the passive voice) according to the purpose of Him Who works all things according to the counsel of His will, so that we who were the first to hope in Christ might be to the praise of His glory.

It is all done according to His purpose and His will. He didn't need our help. You did not nor could you help Him fulfill any of this. You are His because He made a choice.

The reason the Lord chose the body before the foundation of the world, the reason He pre-ordained it, the reason He laid it all out, the reason He did it all Himself, with no human will and no help, is that the glory might all be His! If salvation was half God and half man, then God would get half the glory and man would get the other half. If salvation was 95 percent God and 5 percent man, then God would get 95 percent of the glory and man would get 5 percent of the glory, but salvation is 100 percent God so He gets all the glory, and just to make sure nobody ever got confused He laid it all out (Eph. 1:4) before any human being was ever born. So there's no question about it.[37]

In chapter 2 of Paul's letter, we see more amazing Scripture teaching on this. Paul starts this off, similar to the way he started off the letter to the Romans, by showing us first the complete and desolate natural state we were in.

And you were dead in the trespasses and sins in which you once walked (cf. Luke 15:24), following the prince of the power of the air, the spirit that is now at work in the sons of disobedience—among whom we all once lived in the pas-

sions of our flesh, carrying out the desires of the
body and the mind, and were by nature children
of wrath, like the rest of mankind.

This references back to the issue of the total depravity of man
that we looked at in chapter 2. All men were dead and sons of disobedience, sons of wrath, and following satan. What a horrible and
helpless state we were all in! The beautiful verse 4 offers us hope, "But
God." What a beautiful and glorious phrase! "But God being rich in
mercy"—which means overloaded, abounding, wealthy—"because of
the great love with which He loved us" (cf. John 3:16). In the Greek,
His love for us is known as *agape* or *agapao* which means the divine
love of God in which He chooses and makes His unchanging preference toward us, "even when we were dead in our trespasses (cf. Rom.
5:6, 8, 10), made us alive together with (this is all one word/verb in
the Greek, 'made us alive together with') Christ—by grace you have
been saved (passive voice)—and raised us up with Him and seated
us (both *raised* and *seated* are active third-person verbs which means
the action is being done unto us, not by us) with Him (cf. Phil. 3:20)
in the Heavenly places in Christ Jesus, so that in the coming ages He
might show the immeasurable riches of His grace in kindness toward
us in Christ Jesus."

WOW! Do you feel like your head is about to explode? Those
are some deep and beautiful verses! Every part of this is God's action
toward us. We play no part in this. Because of His immense love
for us and overflowing in mercy, while we were completely dead
to sin, through nothing other than His grace alone, His unmerited
and undeserved favor toward us, He made us alive, He raised us, He
seated us in Heaven (past tense) with Christ (in His eyes it's as good
as completed), all so that He may be forever glorified for bestowing upon us His infinite, immeasurable and eternal grace, mercy,
love, and kindness. If we were to take any credit in bringing this to
completion, we would also be the ones deserving of being eternally

glorified for our part in this, which is absurd! John Piper offers a great devotional on these first few verses of chapter 2:

> The Freeness of Grace
>
> But God, being rich in mercy, because of the great love with which He loved us, even when we were dead in our trespasses, made us alive together with Christ—by grace you have been saved—and raised us up with Him and seated us with Him in the Heavenly places in Christ Jesus. (Ephesians 2:4–6)
>
> The decisive act of God in conversion is that He "made us alive together with Christ" even when "we were dead in our trespasses." In other words, we were dead to God. We were unresponsive; we had no true spiritual interest; we had no taste for the beauties of Christ; we were simply dead to all that mattered. Then God acted—unconditionally—before we could do anything to be fit vessels of grace. He made us alive. He sovereignly awakened us to see the glory of Christ (2 Corinthians 4:4). The spiritual senses that were dead miraculously came to life.
>
> Verse 4 says that this was an act of "mercy." That is, God saw us in our deadness and pitied us. God saw the terrible wages of sin leading to eternal death and misery. And the riches of His mercy overflowed to us in our need. But what is so remarkable about this text is that Paul breaks the flow of his own sentence in order to insert, "by grace you have been saved." "God...made us alive together with Christ—by grace you have been saved—and raised us up with Him."
>
> Paul is going to say this again in verse 8. So why does he break the flow in order to add it here? What's more, the focus is on God's mercy

responding to our miserable plight of deadness; so why does Paul go out of his way to say that it is also by grace that we are saved?

I think the answer is that Paul recognizes here a perfect opportunity to emphasize the freeness of grace. As he describes our dead condition before conversion, he realizes that dead people can't meet conditions. If they are to live, there must be a totally unconditional and utterly free act of God to save them. This freedom is the very heart of grace.

What act could be more one-sidedly free and non-negotiated than one person raising another from the dead! This is the meaning of grace.[38]

Amen! Such beautiful truth! If we were dead in our sins, how is it that we could do anything to bring ourselves or even help contribute to ourselves being raised again from the dead? We can't! Dead men cannot bring themselves or even aid in bringing themselves back from the dead. Only a divine Being Who is on the other side can do so, all without any assistance from the one that is dead!

This is reiterated as we go into the next couple verses, my favorite individual verses in the entirety of God's Word. "For by grace you have been saved through faith. And this is not your own doing; it is the gift of God, not a result of works, so that no one may boast."

What gloriously amazing verses! The Amplified Holy Bible translation, trying to pull out the full depth of the original Greek text, reads like this:

> For it is by grace [God's remarkable compassion and favor drawing you to Christ] that you have been saved [actually delivered from judgment and given eternal life] through faith. And this [salvation] is not of yourselves [not through your own effort], but it is the [undeserved, gra-

cious] gift of God; not as a result of [your] works [nor your attempts to keep the Law], so that no one will [be able to] boast or take credit in any way [for his salvation].

How humbling and praise-inducing are these two verses? No matter what translation you prefer to use, the message found here in these verses is that it is simply by God's grace alone that you are saved, yes, through faith, but even that faith that we possess, which is our part in this, is also a gift from God! None of this is any of our own doing! It is all, beginning to end, God's gift to us because we were entirely dead in our sins (v. 5) so that not one single person has any possible ability whatsoever to boast about anything in his or her own salvation.

> Repentance is granted by God; it is not a human work (Acts 11:18; 2 Tim. 2:25). Likewise, faith is a supernatural gift of God (Eph. 2:5, 8–9). Spiritually dead, we were helpless until God intervened to quicken us. Faith is an integral part of the "gift" His grace bestowed upon us. Consistently, the Scriptures teach that faith is not conjured up by the human will but is a sovereignly granted gift of God (John 6:44, 65; Acts 3:16; Phil. 1:29; 2 Pet. 1:11).
>
> How do we know that faith is God's gift? Left to ourselves, no one would ever believe (Rom. 3:11; 9:16). God draws the sinner to Christ and gives the ability to believe. Without that divinely generated faith, one cannot understand and approach the Savior (1 Cor. 2:14; cf. Matt. 16:17). Faith is graciously given to believers by God Himself. As a divine gift, faith is neither transient nor impotent. It has an abiding quality that guarantees it will endure to the end. It is a living, enduring trust in God (Hab. 2:4; 1 Cor.

1:8; Col. 1:22–23; Heb. 3:14). The faith God graciously supplies produces both the volition and the ability to comply with His will (cf. Phil. 2:13). Thus faith is inseparable from obedience.[39]

Even our faith, even our ability to believe in God, to acknowledge Christ as our Savior, to understand even our need for a Savior, even our ability and the distinct divine privilege that has been granted to us to seek Him and come to Him, it has all been given to us as a free gift from God, distributed to us entirely through His grace alone through Christ alone.

Not only the grace but also the faith, is not of our own doing. Although men are required to believe for salvation, even that faith is part of the gift of God, which saves and cannot be exercised by one's own power. God's grace is preeminent in every aspect of salvation.[40]

Verse 10 continues, "For we are His workmanship, created in Christ Jesus for good works, which God prepared beforehand, that we should walk in them." In verse 4, we see that this is all out of God's immense love for us. In verse 7, we see that all of this is to show and therefore eternally glorify God in lavishing us with His grace and kindness. And here in verse 10, we see that He created us all so that we may produce good fruits through Jesus Christ. Notice the entire progression here. Our works do not and cannot produce salvation. They are instead produced by our salvation. They are a resultant effect of our salvation and also act as evidence of our salvation. And just like our salvation itself, God prepared all of this beforehand.

In chapter 3, we see Paul again offering credit to the One Who brought him into his ministry starting in verse 7.

Of this Gospel, I was made a minister according to the gift of God's grace which was given me by the working of His power. To me,

> though I am the very least of all the saints, this grace was given, to preach to the Gentiles the unsearchable riches of Christ and to bring to light for everyone what is the plan of the mystery hidden for ages in God Who created all things, so that through the church the manifold wisdom of God might now be made known to the rulers and authorities in the Heavenly places.

Paul never took credit for any of this. He always gave the credit to God. He always referred to himself as unworthy, wretched, the least, the worst, etc. (cf. Rom. 7:24, 1 Cor. 15:9, 1 Tim. 1:15). A few verses later, he praises God for his spiritual strength. Verse 14:

> For this reason I bow my knees before the Father, from Whom every family in Heaven and on earth is named, that according to the riches of His glory He may grant you to be strengthened with power through His Spirit in your inner being, so that Christ may dwell in your hearts through faith—that you being rooted and grounded in love, may have strength to comprehend with all the saints what is the breadth and length and height and depth, and to know the love of Christ that surpasses knowledge, that you may be filled with all the fullness of God. Now to Him Who is able to do far more abundantly than all that we ask or think, according to the power at work within us, to Him be glory in the church and in Christ Jesus throughout all generations, forever and ever. Amen.

Paul again gives all the credit to God, for it is entirely through His glory that all are named, strengthened by the Holy Spirit so that Christ can dwell in us through the faith which we just saw is also a gift from God, and so that we may be able to miraculously comprehend the immense love that is far beyond any form of knowledge that we could possess apart from Him.

In chapter 4, verse 7, we see Paul mentioning the spiritual gifts that have been given to each of those in the body of Christ. "But grace was given to each one of us according to the measure of Christ's gift."

> Each believer has a unique spiritual gift that God individually portions out according to His sovereign will and design. The Greek term for "gift" focuses not on the Spirit as the source like the term used in 1 Corinthians 12:1 nor on the grace that prompted it in Romans 12:6, but on the freeness of the gift (cf. Rom. 12:6–8, 1 Cor. 12:4–10, 1 Pet. 4:10).[41]

In chapter 5:25–27, we read:

> Husbands, love your wives, as Christ loved the Church, and gave Himself up for her, that He might sanctify her, having cleansed her by the washing of water by the Word, so that He might present the Church to Himself in splendor, without spot or wrinkle or any such thing, that she might be holy and without blemish.

We see here that it is all Christ's work sanctifying, cleansing, and presenting us holy and blameless to Himself as His holy and righteous bride. All of this is passive on our part.

We also see a bit more of this in Paul's letter to the Philippians. In chapter 1, verses 28 and 29, we see Paul encouraging and commending those in Philippi to live a life worthy of the Gospel and to stand firm in one spirit when up against opposition and to be "not frightened in anything by your opponents. This is a clear sign to them of their destruction, but of your salvation, and that from God.

For it has been granted to you that for the sake of Christ you should not only believe in Him but also suffer for His sake."

We see that we are told that our salvation is directly from God Himself. We also see that it is given to us as a privilege to believe in Christ and also to suffer all for His sake. The Greek word here used for "granted" is *echaristhe,* which has its root in the noun for grace. The believer's suffering in Christ is actually a gift of grace which brings about power and eternal reward (2 Cor. 7:9–10; Jas. 1:2–3; 1 Pet. 4:13, 5:10).

In chapter 2 of his letter, we see side by side passages which seem contradictory and can sometimes lead people astray. In verses 12 and 13, we see Paul express to the Philippians to "work out your own salvation with fear and trembling for it is God Who works in you, both to will and to work for His good pleasure." Advocates for salvation by works, those who believe that they have to perform a certain way in order to be justified and found righteous, use this first statement in verse 12 to justify their viewpoint by saying you must "work out your own salvation with fear and trembling." And, yes, that is the exact words of the text, but for one, the very next verse says, "for it is God Who works in you, both to will and to work for His good pleasure."

So even on the shallow surface, we find a contradiction. So we must look deeper. First of all, as we mentioned earlier, there are three different aspects or stages to the whole of salvation. To assume that salvation here means justification, and our being saved from death is unwarranted. Salvation here is referring to the ongoing process of eradicating our old nature and transforming ourselves ever more into the image of Christ.

> The Greek verb rendered "work out" is *katergazesthe* and means "to continually work to bring something to fulfillment and completion." It cannot refer to salvation by works (cf. Rom. 3:21–24; Eph. 2:8–9), but it does refer to the believer's responsibility for active pursuit of obedience in the process of sanctification. Christians

are to pursue their sanctification with attitudes of fear and trembling as it involves a healthy fear of offending God and a righteous awe and respect for Him (cf. Prov. 1:7, 9:10; Isa. 66:1–2). Although the believer is responsible to work, the Lord actually produces the good works and spiritual fruit in the lives of believers (John 15:5; 1 Cor. 12:6). This is accomplished because He works through us by His indwelling Spirit (Acts 1:8; 1 Cor. 3:16, 6:19; Gal. 3:3). God energizes both the believer's desires and his actions. The Greek word for "will" indicates that He is not focusing on mere desires or whimsical emotions but on the studied intent to fulfill a planned purpose. God's power makes His Church willing to live godly lives (cf. Ps. 110:3). God wants Christians to do what satisfies Him (cf. Eph. 1:5, 9; 2 Thess. 1:11).[42]

In chapter 3, in verses 12–14, we see Paul again talking about this struggle of sanctification.

Not that I have already obtained this or am already perfect, but I press on to make it my own because Christ Jesus has made me His Own. Brothers, I do not consider that I have made it my own. But one thing I do: forgetting what lies behind and straining forward to what lies ahead, I press on toward the goal for the prize of the upward call of God in Christ Jesus.

Then in verses 20–21:

But our citizenship is in Heaven, and from it we await a Savior, the Lord Jesus Christ, Who will transform our lowly body to be like His glorious body, by the power that enables Him even to subject all things to Himself.

Paul is incorporating the image of a runner running a race and striving with all of his might to reach the finish line, straining and giving it all he has to win. Paul pursued his sanctification with everything that he had in him, but he also acknowledges that it was Christ Who made him His and called him to Himself and acknowledges that it is only Christ Who can transform our lowly bodies to be like His glorified body. Pastor John Piper has this to say on Philippians 3:12 and sanctification:

> All my reaching and yearning and striving is not to belong to Christ (which has already happened), but to complete what is lacking in my likeness to Him. One of the greatest sources of joy and endurance for the Christian is knowing that in the imperfection of our progress we have already been perfected—and that this is owing to the suffering and death of Christ. (cf. Heb. 10:14)—Being sanctified means that we are imperfect and in process. We are becoming holy—but are not yet fully holy (glorified). And it is precisely these—and only these—who are already perfected. The joyful encouragement here is that the evidence of our perfection before God is not our experienced perfection, but our experienced progress. The good news is that being on our way is proof that we have arrived. The suffering of Christ secures our perfection so firmly that it is already now a reality. Therefore, we fight against our sin not simply to become perfect, but because we are perfect. The death of Jesus is the key to battling our imperfections on the firm foundation of our perfection.[43]

WOW! Our experienced progress is the visual positive proof of our arrival! This perfectly ties in with Hebrews 10:(9)–10 and 14, so we will quickly jump ahead to there. "'Behold, I [Jesus] have come to do Your [the Father's] will.' And by that will we have been sanctified through the offering of the body of Jesus Christ once for all."

And, "For by a single offering [namely Himself] He has perfected for all time those who are being sanctified."

We see that the power of Christ, through His perfect sacrifice and offering, is what initially justified and made us perfect permanently, but it is also that same perfect power by which we are being sanctified toward perfection.

> "Sanctify" means "to make holy" and to be set apart from sin for God (cf. 1 Thess. 4:3). When Christ fulfilled the will of God, He provided for the believer a continuing and permanent condition of holiness (Eph. 4:24; 1 Thess. 3:13). This is the believer's positional sanctification as opposed to the progressive sanctification that results from daily walking by the will of God (cf. Rom. 12:1–2; 2 Cor. 7:1).[44]

> Justification secured our entrance into fellowship and communion with Christ through the unique and final event of His death, and sanctification keeps us in that fellowship in Christ. We also see these two parts referenced in 1 John 2:8. "The darkness is passing away (*sanctification*) and the true light is already shining (*justification*)."[45]

Moving on into Paul's letter to the Colossians, we are given a little more. In the intro to this letter, as he often would do, we see him giving thanksgiving and even commendations to the recipients. Starting in verse 11, we read:

> May you be strengthened with all power, according to His glorious might, for all endurance and patience with joy, giving thanks to the Father, Who has qualified you to share in the inheritance of the saints in light. He has delivered us from the domain of darkness and transferred us to the Kingdom of His Beloved Son, in Whom we have redemption, the forgiveness of sins.

As always, we see here that it is God alone that strengthens us with power, endurance, patience, and joy, all by His Own will. In the Greek, "having qualified" is *hikanosanti,* which means "I make sufficient, render fit, qualify, empower, authorize." It is God alone that qualifies us and delivers us and makes us fit to move from darkness to life and into His holy Kingdom. We have no power or ability to make ourselves or prepare ourselves to be worthy for the holy Kingdom of Heaven. God does all this only according to the finished work of Jesus Christ our Savior. Apart from God's amazing grace through His Son, we would only be deservingly qualified to receive nothing but His wrath.

As R. C. Sproul Jr. has been quoted as saying, "Why do bad things happen to good people? That only happened once, and He volunteered!" None of us have ever done or could ever do anything worthy enough to receive perfect redemption, holiness and reconciliation to God. And absolutely no form of obedience, short of absolute perfection which we are born incapable of, makes us worthy enough either. It is all His gracious appointment and production done for us and in us out of His love for us to bring all praise and glory to His name.

Paul then begins to talk about the preeminence and greatness of Christ Himself. Starting in verse 19, we read, "For in Him all the fullness of God was pleased to dwell, and through Him to reconcile to Himself all things, whether on earth or in Heaven, making peace by the blood of His cross." Jesus, being fully God, came as fully Man to sacrifice Himself for all of us, and through this sacrifice of His Son God reconciled us to Himself, completely apart from anything that we could or would contribute.

Continuing in verse 21:

> And you, who once were alienated and hostile in mind, doing evil deeds, He has now reconciled in His body of flesh by His death, in order to present you holy and blameless and above reproach before Him, if indeed you continue in the faith, stable and steadfast, not shifting from the hope of the Gospel that you heard, which has been proclaimed in all creation under Heaven, and of which I, Paul, became a minister.

We see confirmation of the statements in the previous verses here in these verses and the desperateness of the dilemma that we were in. We were utterly hopeless and destitute in our own evil and wretched states. We were completely alienated to Him and had nothing in and of ourselves to be able to bring ourselves to Him. It was all His doing, according to His purpose, that perfectly reconciled us and made us holy and perfect and righteous before Him so that we could be brought to Him by Himself. All credit, praise, and glory belong to God. The last part of this passage, starting in verse 23, tends to lead some astray when it comes to perseverance and eternal security, which we will dive into in the next chapter. So we will come back to verse 23 at that time.

In chapter 2, starting in verse 13, we see almost the same exact sequence of statements:

> And you, who were dead in your trespasses and the uncircumcision of your flesh, God made alive together with Him, having forgiven us all our trespasses, by canceling the record of debt that stood against us with its legal documents.

> This He set aside, nailing it to the cross. He dis-
> armed the rulers and authorities and put them to
> open shame, by triumphing over them in Him.

Almost verbatim, Paul describes the wretched and destitute state that we were all found to be in and then acknowledges God's entire gracious will in reconciling us back to Himself, entirely by Himself, and without any form of credit or merit or obedience of our own. He redeemed us entirely without our help or participation.

In Paul's first letter to the Thessalonians, we see him commending them by saying in verse 4, "For we know, brothers loved by God, that He has chosen you, because our Gospel came to you not only in word, but also in power and in the Holy Spirit and with full conviction."

> In salvation, the initiating will is God's, not
> man's (cf. John 1:13; Acts 13:48; Rom. 9:15–16;
> 1 Cor. 1:30; Eph. 1:4–5; Col. 1:13; 2 Thess. 2:13;
> 1 Pet. 1:1–2). Man's will participates in response
> to God's promptings as Paul makes clear when
> he says the Thessalonians received the Word (1
> Thess. 1:6) and then turned to God from idols
> (v. 9). These two responses describe faith and
> repentance, which God repeatedly calls sinners
> to throughout the Scriptures (e.g., Acts 20:21).[46]

When Paul, Silvanus, and Timothy (v. 1) came and preached to the Thessalonians, they eagerly received the Word with full conviction only through the power and presence of the Holy Spirit (cf. 1 Cor. 2:4–5; 2 Pet. 1:21).

Paul also tells us in verses 12–13 of chapter 3:

> May the Lord make you increase and
> abound in love for one another and for all, as
> we do for you, so that He may establish your
> hearts blameless in holiness before our God and

Father, at the coming of our Lord Jesus with all
His saints.

Christ alone is the One Who creates in us holy and perfect
blamelessness and presents us before His Father as pure and righteous
as well as making us increase in love for one another.

In Paul's second letter to the Thessalonians, we find these words
of praise offered to them. Verse 11:

> To this end we always pray for you, that our
> God may make you worthy of His calling and
> may fulfill every resolve for good and every work
> of faith by His power, so that the name of our
> Lord Jesus may be glorified in you, and you in
> Him, according to the grace of our God and the
> Lord Jesus Christ.

All too often, people give themselves the credit for coming to God and doing good to earn His favor. That just isn't true.
Throughout Scripture, we have seen that we were evil and wretched
and lost and dead in our sins, and therefore, we were helpless and
hopeless to do any of this ourselves. In Ephesians and several other
places, we also saw that even our faith in Christ itself is a gift of God's
grace. And here in this passage, we see that it is God Himself Who
makes us even worthy of His calling. He fulfills in us everything that
pleases Himself, and we see here, again, that our faith is a product of
His doing, not ours. All of this is absolutely necessary. It cannot be
any other way. It all has to rely on grace alone so that all of the glory
goes to God.

In chapter 2 of 2 Thessalonians, Paul says to them, starting in
verse 13:

> But we ought always to give thanks to God
> for you, brothers beloved by the Lord, because
> God chose you from the beginning to be saved,
> through sanctification by the Spirit and belief

in the truth. To this He called you through our
Gospel, so that you may obtain the glory of our
Lord Jesus Christ.

Just as we have seen all along, it is God Who predestined and
chose us from the very beginning, calls us to Himself, justifies us, and
even once we are justified, He also performs the work of sanctification within us through the work of the Spirit and also through our
belief, which He has implanted within us (cf. Job 32:8; Prov. 2:6; Isa.
11:2; Matt. 16:16–17; John 17:26; Phil. 1:29; Col. 1:27, 2:2–3; 2
Pet. 1:20–21).

"Knowing this first of all, that no prophecy of Scripture comes
from someone's own interpretation. For no prophecy was ever produced by the will of man, but men spoke from God as they were
carried along by the Holy Spirit" (2 Pet. 1:20–21).

As we also see in Matthew 16:16–17, Peter acknowledges Jesus
as "'the Christ, the Son of the living God.' And Jesus answered him,
'Blessed are you, Simon Bar-Jonah! For flesh and blood has not
revealed this to you, but My Father Who is in Heaven.'"

Our knowledge of Who God is, our belief in Jesus as the Christ
and as the Messiah, and our faith in Him as our Savior are all gifts
of God's grace. We cannot come to a knowledge of Him leading to a
faith in Him without God granting it to us. "I told you that no one
can come to Me [Jesus] unless it is granted him by the Father" (John
6:65).

"May the Lord direct your hearts to the love of God, and to the
steadfastness of Christ" (2 Thess. 3:5).

Just a couple more passages to close off Paul's second letter to
the Thessalonians, in 2:16–17, we read, "Now may our Lord Jesus
Christ Himself, and God our Father, Who loved us and gave us eternal comfort and good hope through grace, comfort our hearts and
establish them in every good work and word."

And in 3:3, "The Lord is faithful. He will establish you and
guard you against the evil one."

It is only God that can create in us the ability to stand against
the enemy. He does this by establishing us in everything good, which

in turn brings us not just temporary comfort or relief but eternal comfort and a lasting hope all through His grace. And again, Biblical hope is an absolute assurance that it will come to pass because it rests on Christ Who never fails.

> God is faithful in regard to creation (Ps. 119:90), His promises (Deut. 7:9; 2 Cor. 1:18; Heb. 10:23), salvation (1 Thess. 5:24), temptation (1 Cor. 10:13), suffering (1 Pet. 4:19), and here faithful to strengthen and protect from satan (cf. John 17:15; Eph. 6:16; 1 Thess. 3:5).[47]

In Paul's first letter to his pupil and protégé Timothy, we see probably the greatest personal witness and testimony that has ever been, which shows the infinite scope of God's reach and grace extended. Starting in verse 12, Paul says, "I thank Him Who has given me strength, Christ Jesus our Lord, because He judged me faithful, appointing me to His service, though formerly I was a blasphemer, persecutor, and insolent opponent."

Paul also calls himself the "foremost" or the "worst" of all sinners in verse 15 and 16. But what is Christ's response to this—the worst of all sinners, and a blasphemer and persecutor of the Church, His insolent opponent?

Continuing on in verse 13:

> But I received mercy because I had acted ignorantly in unbelief, and the grace of our Lord overflowed for me with the faith and love that are in Christ Jesus. The saying is trustworthy and deserving of full acceptance, that Christ Jesus came into the world to save sinners, of whom I am the foremost. But I received mercy for this reason, that in me, as the foremost, Jesus Christ might display His perfect patience as an example to those who were to believe in Him for eternal life.

Paul is saying that he was completely unworthy of receiving any of God's blessings as he was the worst of all sinners (cf. Rom. 7:14–24). It was Christ Who gave Paul the Gospel (Gal. 1:12), and as he says here, it was Christ Who gave him his strength, appointed him to his service in Christ, and granted him mercy, grace, faith and love in Jesus Christ. None of this was found in Paul until Jesus entered into Paul's life and took over. All of this was to show God's infinite reach, and that He could save any sinner, no matter how far gone, lost, and evil he was, and in order to display the scope of God's amazing and far-reaching grace and mercy to even the foremost of sinners.

In his second letter to Timothy, Paul speaks of God as He "Who saved us and called us to a holy calling, not because of our works, but because of His Own purpose and grace, which He gave us in Christ Jesus before the ages began" (1:9). As we continue to see time and time again, it is God Himself Who saves us, calls us, and gives us life in Christ, all because of His amazing grace and sovereign purpose and that nothing we do can add to it, appropriate it, or merit it.

Toward the end of chapter 2 in his second letter, Paul is speaking of how we should have patience and gentleness among any who present opposition to the Gospel, and he offers this in verse 25, "God may perhaps grant them repentance leading to a knowledge of the truth." Again, this, in context, Paul is referring to the attitudes we must have toward any who oppose the Gospel message and may rebuke us and try to quarrel against us, but we are to be kind to all our neighbors, endure any evil with patience, and be able to teach and correct showing love and gentleness so that God Himself may bring their hearts into repentance, which would then lead to an understanding and knowledge of the truth.

So as we have been seeing up until this point, the knowledge that we have of the Gospel is given to us by God Himself and not of ourselves or of the doctrines of man, so our knowledge of God and truth is a gift from God, but we also see here that our ability to come to Him in repentance is a gift from God Himself also! Going back over all that we have been looking at, a wretched and dead sinner can't know anything; he can't understand truth, for he is dead. A dead sinner cannot bring himself to life; he cannot even bring himself to repentance or be in a repentant state of mind because he is dead. A dead man can only do any of this when he has been brought to life by the sacrifice of Christ which is entirely done apart from anything we have to offer. It is all one sovereign, gracious, and loving act done to us and in us by God's infinite loving grace and mercy "while we were yet still sinners" (Rom. 5:6, 8, 10) and dead (Eph. 2:5). Our ability to believe in Him and our faith in Him is a gift of His grace (Eph. 2:8–9), and our repentance to Him is granted or gifted to us as well (2 Tim. 2:25); therefore, ALL of the glory goes to God. I do not nor can I give myself any of the credit when it comes to my salvation. It is all thanks to God.

In Paul's letter to his other pupil and protégé, Titus, we are given a little more education on this subject. In chapter 2, starting at verse 11, we see Paul kind of giving some godly guidelines to live by for those who are called in order to be proper witnesses to God's plan.

> For the grace of God has appeared, bringing salvation for all people, training us to renounce ungodliness and worldly passions, and to live self-controlled, upright, and godly lives in the present age, waiting for our blessed hope, the appearing of the glory of our great God and Savior Jesus Christ, Who gave Himself for us to redeem us from all lawlessness and to purify for Himself a people for His Own possession who are zealous for good works.

One thing that's so beautiful about this passage is that it perfectly lays out God's plan of salvation according to each of the three phases of salvation that we mentioned earlier in the chapter. Justification is the one-time initial act of God, perfectly redeeming us, paying the penalty of our sin through the blood of Christ which is perfectly summed up in verse 11; sanctification, which is the ongoing work of the Spirit to mature us in the flesh to look more and more like Christ and strengthen us against the power of sin and temptation, which is beautifully explained in verse 12; and then glorification which is arriving at the final product once we reach Heaven and receive our glorified bodies and live in the full presence of God, and the full absence of the presence of sin, which is described in verse 13. All of this is laid out from beginning to end by God's grace which saves us, trains us, strengthens us, helps us to persevere, and purifies us all for Himself. It does say here that we are zealous for good works, but as we will examine later, good works never lead to salvation; instead, they are products and evidence of salvation.

In chapter 3 of this letter to Titus, we see a bit more in the final chapter. We begin in verse 4:

> But when the goodness and loving kindness of God our Savior appeared, He saved us, not because of works done by us in righteousness, but according to His Own mercy, by the washing of regeneration and renewal of the Holy Spirit, Whom He poured out on us richly through Jesus Christ our Savior, so that being justified by His grace we might become heirs according to the hope of eternal life.

As we continue to see throughout the Scriptures, salvation is never achieved through acts of obedience or works or any deeds of our own. Here we again see all the work being done unto us is by God Himself. He sent Christ to die in our place, redeeming us against the cost of sin, and washed us clean by renewing and regenerating us by generously filling us with the Holy Spirit, and therefore adopted us as His Own children, all of which is administered to us through His great and amazing mercy and grace. We mercifully did not get what we deserved, and we graciously did receive what we did not deserve. And all of this was accomplished apart from any works or deeds or acts of obedience on our part. It is specifically stated here, as with everywhere else, that we are justified by His grace.

In the letter to the Hebrews, we are given more insight into the fullness of this doctrine. In chapter 2, starting at verse 9, we read:

> But we see Him Who for a little while was made lower than the angels, namely Jesus, crowned with glory and honor because of the suffering of death, so that by the grace of God He might taste death for everyone. For it was fitting that He, for Whom and by Whom all things exist, in bringing many sons to glory, should make the Founder of their salvation perfect through suffering. For He Who sanctifies and those who are sanctified all have one source.

We aren't told, and therefore, we are not exactly sure who the author of this letter to the Hebrews was. Many believe it was also Paul, but either way, we see that it is entirely in-sync with everything else that we have looked at. Just like we later see in Hebrews 12:2, Jesus is called the Founder of our salvation, which also corresponds to what we saw in Ephesians 2:8. Even our saving faith is a gift from God and Christ is labeled as the Founder of that salvation. It is not something we just formulate on our own, but it is granted to us through grace.

The Greek word used here for "founder" is *archegon*, which means "originator, author, founder, leader." Jesus originates and is the Author of our faith leading to salvation. It is He Who left the holy and perfect realm of Heaven, came down to dwell among His creation as one of them, suffered and tasted death for us, implanted our faith in Him as Savior within us, and brought us to glory—all through the grace of God. We also see supported here that it is Christ Who sanctifies us as we have seen earlier (cf. 1 Cor. 1:30, 6:11; Eph. 5:26; 2 Thess. 2:13; Ti. 2:12), which is facilitated by the Holy Spirit dwelling within us.

In the final chapter of Hebrews, we are given a little bit more concerning the post-justified works of God in us. Once He redeems us and saves us from death, verse 21, God "equip[s] you with everything good that you may do His will, working in us that which is pleasing in His sight, through Jesus Christ, to Whom be glory forever and ever. Amen." So we see that even when we are redeemed and become His children, He still is the One at work bestowing within us the ability to please Him and do what He desires, only through Christ. And this was also shown to us back in Ephesians 2:10.

> Since salvation is truly a work of God, it cannot be deficient. It cannot fail to impact an individual's behavior. It cannot leave his desires unchanged or his conduct unaltered. It cannot result in a fruitless life. It is the work of God and will continue steadfastly from its inception to ultimate perfection (Phil. 1:6, Heb. 12:2).[48]

In the beginning of Peter's first letter, we see Peter, who was a directly side-by-side disciple of Christ's, support all of Paul's teachings. "Peter, an apostle of Jesus Christ, to those who are elect exiles of the dispersion…according to the foreknowledge of God the Father, in the sanctification of the Spirit, for the obedience to Jesus Christ and for sprinkling with His blood: May grace and peace be multiplied to you."

The Greek word for "elect" is *eklektos*, which means "called-out, picked, selected" and indicates those sovereignly chosen by God to believe in and to belong to Him and chosen by God for salvation.

> Foreknowledge means a predetermined relationship in the knowledge of the Lord. God brought the salvation relationship into existence by decreeing it into existence ahead of time. Christians are foreknown for salvation in the same way Christ was foreordained before the foundation of the world to be a sacrifice for sins (cf. Acts 2:23). Foreknowledge means that God planned before, not that He observed before. Thus, God pre-thought and pre-determined or

predestined each Christian's salvation (cf. Rom. 8:29; Eph. 1:4). To sanctify means "to consecrate, to set apart." The objective of election is salvation, which comes to the elect through the sanctifying work of the Spirit. The Holy Spirit thus makes God's chosen holy, by savingly setting them apart from sin and unbelief unto faith and righteousness (cf. 1 Thess. 1:4; 2 Thess. 2:13). Sanctification thus begins with justification (declaring the sinner just before God by graciously imputing Christ's righteousness to him (cf. Phil. 3:9), and continues as a process of purification that goes on until glorification, when the Christian sees Jesus face-to-face. Believers are also set apart from sin to God in order that they might obey Jesus Christ. True salvation produces obedience to Christ (cf. Eph. 2:10; 1 Thess. 1:4–10).[49]

A little bit later in the first chapter, in verses 20–21, Peter is speaking of Jesus when he says, "He was foreknown before the foundation of the world but was made manifest in the last times for the sake of you who through Him are believers in God, Who raised Him from the dead and gave Him glory, so that your faith and hope are in God." God not only predestined Christ to be our Savior but for us to put our faith and hope in Him. It is only "through Him [we] are believers."

In chapter 2, verse 24, we read a beautiful account of Christ's work done for us. "He Himself bore our sins in His body on the tree, that we might die to sin and live to righteousness. By His wounds you have been healed." And in the third chapter, verse 18, we read a bit more of His wondrous work. "For Christ also suffered once for sins, the righteous for the unrighteous, that He might bring us to God, being put to death in the flesh but made alive in the Spirit."

Just as Jesus said, "It is finished" as He was about to depart from the cross, all of the redeeming actions necessary to reconcile us to the Father were made and completed in full. Christ bore every single one of our sins, though He Himself was innocent and righteous and suffered for our sins, suffering as if unrighteous and was put to death. He did all this so that we may be declared dead to sin and alive to righteousness because of His substitution for us. Through Him, we are fully reconciled to God and made alive in the Spirit.

In the final chapter of Peter's first letter, verses 6–7 and 10 tell us:

> Humble yourselves, therefore, under the mighty hand of God so that at the proper time He may exalt you, casting all your anxieties on Him, because He cares for you... And after you have suffered a little while, the God of all grace, Who has called you to His eternal glory in Christ, will Himself restore, confirm, strengthen, and establish you.

These verses are speaking of already believing Christians and shows that in His divine timing, He will also exalt, restore, confirm, strengthen, and establish us all out of His grace and love for us. We will have to endure trials and persecution in this life; even Jesus promised us persecution will come (cf. Matt. 10), but God will help us and strengthen us to endure.

In Peter's second letter, we see more verification from Peter on this subject. Right away, in his greeting of the letter we see him address, "to those who have obtained a faith of equal standing with ours by the righteousness of our God and Savior Jesus Christ."

> The word *obtained* can mean "attaining by divine will." Here, Peter was emphasizing that salvation was not attained by personal effort, skill, or worthiness, but came purely from God's grace. Peter is speaking of a subjective faith, i.e., the Christian's power to believe for his salvation. Faith is the capacity to believe (Eph. 2:8–9). Even though faith and belief express the human

side of salvation, God still must grant that faith. God initiates that faith when the Holy Spirit awakens the dead soul in response to hearing the Word of God (cf. Matt. 16:16–17, Eph. 2:8; 2 Pet. 1:20–21).[50]

Continuing on into verses 3 and 4, he tells us:

> His divine power has granted us all things that pertain to life and godliness, through the knowledge of Him Who called us to His Own glory and excellence, by which He has granted to us His precious and very great promises, so that through them you may become partakers of the divine nature.

> The genuine Christian is eternally secure in his salvation and will persevere and grow because he has received everything necessary to sustain eternal life through Christ's power. To live in godliness is to live reverently, loyally and obediently toward God. Peter means that the genuine believer ought not to ask God for something more (as if something necessary to sustain his growth, strength and perseverance were missing) to become godly, because he already has every spiritual resource to manifest and sustain perfect godly living. The knowledge of Christ emphasized here is not a superficial knowledge, or a mere surface awareness of the facts about Christ, but a genuine, personal sharing of life with Christ, based on repentance from sin and personal faith in Him (cf. Matt. 7:21).[51]

All knowledge and every gift necessary for the genuine Christian believer is supplied to us by God and the indwelling Holy Spirit, made possible by the work of Christ. These are not things that come from ourselves but instead all from God's grace to make us His Own.

In John's first letter, in chapter 4, we see this all being tied to God's love for us. Verse 10, "In this is love, not that we have loved God but that He [first] loved us, and sent His Son to be the propitiation for our sins." And verse 19, "We love because He first loved us."

Just like we saw when we looked at Romans 5:6, 8, 10, we were enemies of God and evil and wicked sinners when Jesus came and died for us. We came to love Him because He first loved us and sacrificed Himself for us and redeemed us and reconciled us to His Father through Himself because we were completely incapable of doing anything ourselves as we were dead in sin (Eph. 2:5). All of this is the gracious fruit of His love for us.

To kind of sum all of this up, you cannot help God to save you through obedience, good works, even through the performance of a sacrament! It ALL rests in Christ's work for us. Nothing you do, besides coming to Him broken and completely realizing that you are entirely incapable of doing anything by yourself to get yourself to Heaven, can bring salvation to your soul, except for Christ's propitiatory work done at the cross. Yet, even our knowledge of Him, even our faith in Him and our repentance in Him is part of His gracious and saving gift to us because we were dead and helpless as we have seen throughout this chapter.

When He said, "It is finished," He meant it. The work was done. He paid our price in full! He took our penalty and our punishment and gave us new life! We did nothing and can do nothing to earn it or deserve it or even appropriate it to our account.

> Conversion then, lies in the thorough change both of the heart and life... If ever you would be savingly converted, you must despair of doing it in your own strength. It is a resurrection from the dead (Eph. 2:1), a new creation (Gal. 6:15; Eph. 2:10), a work of absolute omnipotence (Eph. 1:19). Are not these out of the reach of human power? If you have no more than you

had by your first birth, a good nature, a meek
and chaste temper, etc., you are a stranger to true
conversion. This is a supernatural work![52]

It is infinitely and eternally a free gift made by Him before the
foundations of the world and given to us by His substitutionary act
for our vile and wretched lives without Him. He did it all! We did
nothing! We can do nothing! Accept what He did for you, allow Him
to take your place, receive His payment in full for your life! That's it!
Only God can bring dead men to life!

Let's look at it this way: What brings the most glory to God
possible? Would it be: If you yourself are able to do something to
earn, merit, or deserve your salvation as a prize or reward or due?
Or even if God "graces" you to be able to have the desire, ability,
and strength to obey Him, even in the form of performing some
sacrament such as baptism or through obedience in order to receive
or obtain salvation? Or would it bring God greater glory if knowing
you, predestining you, electing, choosing and calling you, granting
you salvation the moment you accept Christ as your Lord and Savior
through the knowledge in Him and faith in Him that He has instilled
in your heart, realizing that you are entirely dead, lost and helpless
without Him and surrendering your life entirely over to Him, He
then cleanses you entirely by immersing you into Jesus Christ, and
fills you with the Holy Spirit? Which in turn creates in you a new
heart and mind for the things of Christ, and out of this new life in
Christ, you are given a desire to serve Him and obey Him through
the indwelling of His Holy Spirit within you, and you follow this
up by your willful acceptance of giving your life over completely to
Him, and then publicly declare your new life through baptism, obedience, good works, etc.?

Even in the belief that God grants you the grace to obey Him
and perform some physical act in order to receive salvation, it still
remains contingent on your personal actions and, therefore, becomes
something that you can boast about, "I did it!" NO! It is ALL HIM!
All the glory and praise and honor goes to God for saving us from
what we entirely deserve.[53]

Pastor, teacher, Christian author, David Platt puts it this way:

> Christ is the basis of our justification. In order for you and I to be righteous before God, we need somebody else's righteousness because we're not righteous! So if I asked you, "How do you know if you're right before God?" If the first words out of your mouth are "Because I..." then you've missed the point. How are you right before God? "Because I did... Because I..." No, no, no, no! How do you know you're right before God? "Because Jesus! Lived a life I couldn't live. He died the death I deserved to die. And He conquered the enemy that I couldn't conquer: sin and death." It's all because of Jesus! He is the basis of our justification. He's everything. Romans 5 says that while we were still sinners, Christ died for us. Very rarely will anyone die for a righteous man, but for a good man, someone might possibly dare to die now and then, but God demonstrates His love for us in this, Christ died for us as sinners. We were dead, we were wretched, and we have now been justified by His blood, saved from His wrath.[54]

> If it were possible to get to Heaven—to gain salvation and to be justified before God—by following rules and traditions, or through a religious do-it-yourself system of do's and don'ts to merit salvation, then Christ died for nothing!" (cf. Gal. 2:21; also Gal. 5:4, 6b)[55]

In Revelation, John kind of sums it up and gives all the credit to Whom it belongs. Chapter 4, verse 11, "Worthy are You, our Lord and God, to receive glory, honor and power, for You created all things, and by Your will they existed and were created." It is God the Creator Who set out from pre-eternity to foreknow, predestine, elect, choose, call, justify, sanctify, and make us His very Own (Rom. 8:29–30, 38–39; Eph. 1:4–5), when we were dead in our sins and absolutely helpless and hopeless (Rom. 5:6, 8, 10; Eph. 2:1–3, 5), all out of His grace and love for us (John 3:16; Eph. 2:8–9; 1 John 4:19).

There's one more aspect of God's amazing grace that I want to point out before we end this chapter.

The Grace of God Cannot Be Extinguished

"And the grace of our Lord was exceedingly abundant with faith and love which is in Christ Jesus" (1 Timothy 1:14).

Brethren, we should be keenly aware that the living God can no more hide His grace than the sun can hide its brightness.

We must keep in mind also that the grace of God is infinite and eternal. Being an attribute of God, it is as boundless as infinitude!

The Old Testament is indeed a book of law, but not of law only. Before the great flood Noah, "found grace in the eyes of the Lord" (Gen. 6:8), and after the law was given God said to Moses, "Thou hast found grace in My sight" (Ex. 33:17).

There never was a time when the law did not represent the will of God for mankind nor a time when the violation of it did not bring its own penalty, though God was patient and sometimes "winked" at wrongdoing because of the ignorance of the people.

The great source and spring of Christian morality is the love of Christ Himself, not the law of Moses; nevertheless, there has been no abrogation of the principles of morality contained in the law. The grace of God made sainthood possible in Old Testament days just as it does today! God has promised that He will always be Himself. Men may flee from the sunlight to dark and musty caves of the earth, but they cannot put out the sun. So men may in any dispensation despise the grace of God, but they cannot extinguish it.[56]

"God's Grace is amazingly uncontrollable, you can't turn it off. God unstoppingly pursues us. Even when we resist, it doesn't slow Him down. He doesn't care about your past, He just wants a relationship with you."[57]

There is an analogy that fits quite well here. Imagine a good-ole southern homestyle diner. And when served your meal you notice in the center of the plate a pile of white stuff.[58] You ask the waitress, "What is this?"

To which she replies, "That's grits."

"Well, I didn't order grits," you might say.

To which she would then reply, "That's okay, honey, around here, you don't order grits. You just gets 'em."

Well, we don't order grace, we just "gets it." It is because of God's great love for us that He made us alive together with Christ. God's grace is incomparable; it is a gift. It is unearned, unmerited, undeserved, unstoppable, unending, unceasing, and unlimited. It is like a water faucet that is stuck open. It just keeps flowing, and you can't shut it off. You can't make it go away. You can't turn it off.

If it was not for God's infinite grace, mercy, and love, there is no possible way that we could reach Him. If God was any bit less than Who He is, we would be absolutely hopeless. Do not try to do this on your own. Do not try to be saved by any of your own actions, merits, obedience...you will always fail. You can't do it!

8

Eternal Security/Perseverance of the Saints/Once Saved, Always Saved

In the last chapter, we started to look at God's grace throughout the entire process of our salvation, redeeming us and reconciling us to Himself, and also in the ongoing process of sanctification, maturing us into more and more of the image of Christ through the work of the Spirit and erasing our old habits of sin and producing godly spiritual fruit to work for Him and to please Him. This chapter we will take that further to see that God finishes what He started and secures us and holds us all the way to the end. I will reiterate the two passages I started the last chapter with.

Philippians 1:6, "I am sure of this, that He Who began a good work in you will bring it to completion at the day of Jesus Christ."

And Hebrews 12:2, "Looking to Jesus, the Founder and Perfecter of our faith."

Both of these verses show us that He started it and He will finish it. He is the Founder or the Author of our salvation and our faith, and He is the One Who began this good work in us, and He will perfect it in us and bring us all the way to its final glorification when He comes again to take us Home. We owe Him everything because He did it all for us! He owes us nothing because we served no part in any of this. We simply accepted in faith, which was also a gift of His grace. We have no place to rightfully demand anything from Him.

We were dead and helpless (Rom. 5:6, 8, 10; Eph. 2:1–3, 5) when He came to set us free, entirely out of His mercy and grace and His love for us (John 3:16; Eph. 2:4, 8–9; 1 John 4:19), and He secures us, leads us, and holds us safe until we are safely brought all the way Home to His Heavenly Kingdom where we will forever rest in His presence, worship Him, and dwell with Him. This is when the third aspect of our salvation will occur, that of glorification.

At the moment of our faith in Jesus and our surrender to Christ as our Lord and Savior, we are redeemed by His blood sacrifice for us, and we are justified and made holy, righteous, and pure in the eyes of God. When He looks at us, He sees Christ's perfect work and substitution for us. Then, receiving the Holy Spirit Who then dwells in us, we are fitted with all the strength of Christ on the cross, and the Spirit will guide us and lead us through our sanctification until we are brought Home by Christ, and we will then receive our glorified bodies and we will look like Christ fully, never to be even tempted by sin again, completely and eternally removed from its very presence. Oh, how I long for that day! Imagine never, ever feeling, even the slightest and most remote inkling or influence of temptation EVER again! Not even a hint of evil trying to get at you or wear you down! Oh, what a glorious day that will be!

To start this chapter off, I'm going to start with a sermon excerpt from John MacArthur that perfectly introduces the aspect of salvation that we will be discussing in this chapter.

> In the epistle of Jude, we come to that marvelous statement with which Jude closes his letter, "Now to Him Who is able to keep you from falling and to make you stand in the presence of His glory, blameless with great joy, to the only God our Savior through Jesus Christ our Lord, be glory, majesty, dominion and authority before all time now and forever. Amen." And Jude closed out his epistle with that great statement that we are 'kept from falling.' We are kept by God, and therefore God deserves all the glory.

And that introduces us to a doctrine known as The Perseverance of the Saints. True believers will persevere in faith to the end. Often that doctrine is called the doctrine of Eternal Security. Sometimes it's stated as "Once Saved, Always Saved," and of course all of those things are true.

I want you to understand that this is a historic doctrine. It's the most important component of salvation, because if salvation were not permanent then the doctrine of election would be called into question, the doctrine of justification would be called into question, the doctrine of sanctification would be called into question, and the doctrine of glorification would be called into question, the calling of God would be called into question, and therefore the work of the Father, Son and Holy Spirit would all be called into question as well.

And so, what makes the whole of the doctrines of salvation come together and stay together is the eternality of salvation… The Perseverance of the Saints. And this has been the historic doctrine of the true church.

In 1649, after 5 years, well-known Puritans like Thomas Goodwin, James Usher, Jay Lightfoot, Samuel Rutherford, Jeremiah Burroughs, and the chairman of this group, a man named Twisse, labored for these five years to produce what has become the most important Christian creed called "The Westminster Confession of Faith."

In that creed, among other things, is a statement about the security of salvation, about the fact that salvation is eternal. This, they were convinced, was what the Bible taught. They didn't call it the "security of salvation," they actually called it "perseverance," and they named it correctly. In The Westminster Confession of Faith there is a brief and unambiguous declaration, and I quote. "They, whom God hath accepted in His beloved Son effectually called and sanctified by His Spirit can neither totally nor finally fall away from the state of grace, but shall certainly persevere therein to the end, and be eternally saved."

That is the Biblically accurate and well-summarized statement of the perseverance of the saints and that statement needs no amending. It is Biblically accurate. This is supported by many, many scriptures (He then cfs. John 3:16 and 18, 4:14, 5:24, 6:37, 10:27–29; 1 Cor. 1:8–9; 1 Thess. 5:23–24; 1 John 2:19). The Westminster Confession accurately affirms that saving faith cannot fail. And at this point, I think it's crucial for us to understand what the perseverance of the saints does not mean, to help us understand what it does mean.

First of all, it does not mean that Christians don't ever fail. It does not mean that Christians don't fail seriously and severely in their Christian lives. We do. What it does mean is what the Confession says it means, they do not completely nor finally fail. Fail, yes. Fail severely, yes. Fail repeatedly, yes. Fail completely, no. Fail finally, no.

The Westminster Confession went on to say this, and I quote again, "'Nevertheless, believers may, through the temptations of satan and of the world, through the prevalency of corruption remaining in them, through the neglect of their means of preservation, fall into grievous sins and for a time continue therein, whereby they incur God's displeasure and grieve His Holy Spirit, come to be deprived of some measure of their graces and comforts, have their hearts hardened and their consciences wounded, hurt and scandalize others, and bring temporal judgements upon themselves."

And the writers of the Westminster Confession understood that this is not to say we are perfect. To say we persevere is not to say we are perfect. That is not what we're saying. In fact, there is no perfection to be had here at all. And so this, in a sense, describes all of us to one degree or another. So when we say that believer's persevere, we're not talking about perfection. We're not talking about reaching a state of sinlessness. We're talking about persevering in faith, not unaccompanied by failure.

Secondly, it is important to understand that not only does perseverance not mean perfection, but it does not mean that anyone and everyone who "accepts" Christ can therefore live any way they like without any fear of hell. It is not enough to have a superficial faith in Christ. It is not enough to have a superficial commitment to Christ, a superficial interest in Christ. It is not enough to have some good feelings about Jesus and make some momentary commitment to Him. That is not what the Westminster Confession was saying.

And that is why—this is important—the correct way to describe this doctrine is the "Perseverance of the Saints" rather than "Eternal Security." It is not just that we are eternally secure, it is that we are eternally secure because our faith perseveres. In John 8:31–32, Jesus said, "You're My true disciples if you continue in My

Word." True disciples continue in faith and they don't live like nonbelievers.

A person who's "accepted" Jesus, made a decision for Jesus, prayed a prayer, and goes on to live in a sinful pattern of life with no fear of hell because they think they're eternally secure is deluded. That's why we have to be careful when we talk about the doctrine of eternal security as if the one prayer makes you forever secure.

So to speak of the security of the believer is not in itself wrong. We are secure. But the other expression is more careful and it's more accurate. It is not true that someone is secure no matter how much they live in sin, no matter how much they turn against Christ and even flatly deny Him, as many have said. Security is simply a reality because of perseverance. A believer may sin, as I said, may sin seriously, may sin repeatedly, but he will not abandon himself to sin. He will not come again under the utter domination of sin. He will not lose faith in Christ, and he will not deny his Lord and the Gospel. No true believer will shun holiness and embrace sin all together.

The doctrine of perseverance is this, at salvation you are given a supernatural faith from God to believe the Gospel, to believe the testimony of the Holy Spirit concerning Christ and therefore to believe in Christ and having come to Christ you have come to know the true and living God. This faith is a supernatural gift from God. It is a gift of grace and it is a gift of mercy.

Again, Ephesians 2:8 and 9, "For by grace you have been saved through faith and that is not of yourselves, it is the gift of God." The grace is from God and so is the faith. And what kind of faith does He give you, a temporary faith? If saving faith is a gift from God, then what kind of gift would God give you? He would not give you a temporary gift of faith. And if your salvation depends upon a human faith, I will promise you that it will die. If we could lose our salvation, we would lose it. That is why Jesus said, "He that endures to the end, the same will be saved" (Matt. 24:13). You can tell who the saved are. You can tell who those are that are going to enter into the full salvation in the next life. They are those whose faith endured to the end because it is an enduring faith. That's the kind of faith God gives. Very different than human faith, very different.

When it comes to putting your faith in Jesus Christ, you literally have to deny yourself, completely abandon yourself to Someone you've never seen and never experienced, and can't know or experience until you come to that complete abandonment. That requires a faith that is beyond the normal human faith. It requires a faith that is a gift from God, a supernatural faith. And the only kind of faith that God gives is a faith that endures.

You could not muster up your own faith to be saved, nor could you muster up enough of your own faith to stay saved. And were you to depend upon your own faith, it would fail you when God didn't do what you thought He should do, when He didn't take care of your life in the way you thought He should, and when you had your many disappointments and tragedies and sorrows, etc., etc. Your own human faith would constantly be weaker and weaker and you would begin to call all kinds of things into question because your experience would not be sustaining—at least visibly for you—what you expected from God, particularly if somebody told you, "Come to Jesus and everything will be great."

It is the gift of faith, supernatural faith given by God, that endures so that you believe even when everything does not go the way you think it should. This enduring faith is inexplicable humanly. It has taken martyrs all the way to the stake, all the way to the guillotine, all the way to the loss of everything. It's not explicable humanly. Security in Christ, then, is tied to a persevering faith that endures to the end.

And any idea of salvation that leaves out security is a distortion of the truth and any idea of security that leaves out perseverance is a distortion of the truth. You cannot have salvation without security. You can't have eternal life that's not eternal, and you can't have a secure salvation without a persevering faith.

If your salvation was up to you, you'd never be saved. If keeping your salvation was up to you, you'd never be saved. Your human faith can't save you. Your human faith can't keep you. Therefore, you need a faith that is not human, a faith that is supernatural, that has to come from God. The faith to believe the Gospel in the beginning came from God and it is an enduring faith that always believes.

Listen to Jeremiah 32:40. This is the statement about the New Covenant, the Covenant that saves us. "I will make an everlasting covenant with them that I will not turn away from them; and I will put the fear of Me in their hearts"—listen—"so that they will not turn away from Me."

What a statement. It is the nature of this everlasting salvation covenant that God will never turn away from us and He will put in us, in our hearts, a fear of Him that is supernatural so that we will not turn away from Him. It is an everlasting covenant of an everlasting salvation based upon an enduring faith. This faith never fails. There are no true Christians who are dropouts.[1]

Wow! I kind of feel like we don't even need to continue after that! As Pastor John so eloquently defines for us, any true believer in Christ is given a supernatural faith that we do not muster on our own, one that is secure until the very end. It is a gift from God that surpasses all human ability that will stay secure no matter what is presented to us in this life here. If our salvation and our security were left up to us, we would all at some point buckle under the pressure, and we would all fail to make it securely to the end. But through the supernatural faith given to us by God, He secures us eternally because it is a faith that perseveres supernaturally.

We may stumble and fail and even do so repeatedly and severely, but we will not do so completely or finally because our security does not depend on us. It does not give us free license to sin and live in whatever way we please, but even though we may fail horribly, we will persevere because the supernatural faith we have been given will persevere.

The mark of a true disciple is not that he never sins, but rather that when he does sin he inevitably returns to the Lord to receive cleansing and forgiveness. Unlike a false disciple, the true disciple will never turn away completely. He may occasionally turn back to his fishing nets, but ultimately, he is drawn again to the Master. When Christ confronts him, he will return to a life of service for the Savior. A real disciple, may fail Christ but will never turn against Him. A true Christian might temporarily fear to stand up for the Lord but would never willingly sell

> Him out. Inevitably, true disciples will falter, but
> when they fall into sin, they will seek cleansing.
> They won't wallow in the mire (cf. 2 Pet. 2:22).
> Their faith is neither fragile nor temporary; it is
> a dynamic and ever-growing commitment to the
> Savior.[2]

Even though Pastor John has given us such a great description of it, let us look through the Scriptures and see what is taught on this doctrine known as "Eternal Security" or that is best labeled "The Perseverance of the Saints."

Starting all the way back in the beginning, when sin first entered into the picture in Genesis 3, we already touched on this narrative, but here we will look at God's prophecy of His grace. In verse 15, in the middle of Him cursing satan and Adam and Eve, God proclaims the prophecy of His Son coming as the Messiah to redeem mankind and defeating the enemy. Despite Adam and Eve's complete inability to save themselves from the corruption they had cast themselves into, God promised the way to salvation, redemption, and reconciliation provided only by His Son. He also symbolized this prophecy by clothing them with "garments of skin" to cover their nakedness, which was a foreshadowing of the death and sacrifice of the Messiah Who would shed His innocent blood to reconcile humankind back to God. We sent Him to the cross, and He brought us back from it.

A little bit later in Genesis, throughout the history of Abraham, Isaac, and Jacob (Israel), we see that God constantly provides, protects, and secures the generations of His chosen one, Abraham, to whom He promised that his offspring would be as numerous as the stars in the sky and the grains of sand in the sea throughout many centuries leading up to the fulfillment of that promise when the Israelites finally entered and possessed the Promised Land.

This promise endured through at least three barren wombs (Sarah, Rebekah, and Rachel) and at least as many "rights of the firstborn" being transferred to younger sons. It also endured through Jacob's most beloved son, Joseph, being sold into slavery (expected by his brothers never to be seen again and considered as dead to his father), and then Joseph being lifted up into prosperity as being second only to Pharaoh in command of Egypt after a few years spent in prison, and then residing in that position for several more years as Egypt itself prospered through Joseph's revelation of a dream held by Pharaoh that God interpreted through Joseph regarding seven years of bounty in harvest, followed by seven years of absolute famine.

During this famine, every surrounding country and territory came to buy grain, eventually selling off all land, cattle, and even selves unto Egypt to escape starvation, all leading up to Joseph's own family coming to buy grain and being reunited with his family and father, and then being blessed by Pharaoh and bringing Joseph's entire family to Egypt and offering them the choicest of land and prosperity. At one point, Joseph's brothers feared payback from Joseph for selling him into slavery, and Joseph responded in 50:19–21 of Genesis:

> Do not fear, for am I in the place of God? As for you, you meant evil against me, but God meant it for good (cf. Rom. 8:28), to bring it about that many people should be kept alive, as they are today. So do not fear; I will provide for you and your little ones.

During this time of dwelling in Egypt, Israel prospered greatly and multiplied in great number over 400 years, even when a latter Pharaoh became afraid of their prosperity and started to abuse them and persecute them through slave labor. Eventually, into the book of Exodus, God sent His chosen servant Moses who survived an infantile genocide commanded by Pharaoh, only to be raised among Pharaoh's own family to come and save His people from slavery at the hand of Pharaoh; and through the issuance of ten divine plagues, Pharaoh finally agreed to let God's people free. The last of these ten plagues was the death of every firstborn in the region. However, God provided a substitution for the people of Israel to save them from this most terrible plague. If they would offer up a sacrificial lamb and spread its blood across the doorframe of the house that they stayed in, the Lord would pass over them and keep them alive.

This also is a major prophecy of the coming Messiah Who would give up His Own life and shed His innocent blood to save His chosen people. Through this blessing, God provided a way to secure His people and save them from destruction until the end.

Now they did have to follow God's command, but picture this:

> Imagine a Jewish youth on that night in Egypt reasoning thus: "I am the firstborn of this family and in thousands of homes tonight the firstborn must die. I wish I could be sure that I was safe and secure, but when I think of my many shortcomings, I am in deep distress and perplexity. I do not feel that I am by any means good enough to be saved when others must die. I have been very willful, very disobedient, very undependable, and now I feel so troubled and anxious. I question very much if I shall see the morning light." Would his anxiety and self-condemnation leave him exposed to judgment? Surely not! His father might well say to him, "Son, what you say as to yourself is all true. Not one of us has ever been all that we should be. We all deserve to die. But the death of the lamb was for you—the lamb died in your stead. The blood of the lamb outside the house comes between you and the destroyer." When the destroying angel passed through that night, He would not be permitted to enter any blood-sprinkled door, for God had said, "When I see the blood, I will pass over you (Ex. 12:23; paraphrased)." Inside the house, some might have been trembling and some rejoicing, but all were safe. Their security depended, not on their frames of mind, or feelings, but on the fact that the eye of God beheld the blood of the lamb and they were sheltered behind it. The moment a repentant sinner puts

his trust in Christ, he is viewed by God as shel-
tered behind the blood-sprinkled doorpost.[3]

In the same way, just as our faith in Christ is not exactly the
direct substance that saves us—it is not the object of our salvation—
it is instead what connects us to the object of our salvation and that
of Christ. And as we saw in the last chapter, even that faith in Him is
a gift of His grace birthed within us, and as we will see in this chapter,
it is a persevering faith that will not fail.

Following the exodus of the Israelites from Egypt, God continued to protect and keep secure His chosen people. Only a couple
days, after they left Egypt, they were surrounded by the Egyptians
and up against the shores of the Red Sea, so God parted the waters
of the Red Sea and made them stand up to the sides so that the
people could pass through on dry ground. And when the Egyptians
tried to follow, God let the waters return to their place, and all of
the Egyptians perished with every one of the Israelites safely on the
opposite shore on dry ground. Then throughout forty years of wandering in the desert wilderness, God provided enough water to drink
and enough food to eat for all of the people, which from the point
of the exodus from Egypt was upward of a million people in population, maybe even more, and sustained their needs, clothing that
never faded, protection from enemies, and despite their constant
grumbling, finally brought them into the chosen Promised Land.

Once they got to the Promised Land, it wasn't necessarily a walk
in the park, but God was still with them and protected and provided
all they needed. See, the land was largely populated by pagan enemies
who weren't about to just give up all their land to these foreigners.
The Israelites had to go in and defeat all of these people groups,
many of which were of much greater stature in size and strength. But
once again, luckily, this task did not rest on the Israelites' abilities
but instead, it rested on God's power, grace, provision, and strength.

Numerous times throughout the Old Testament, we see many
statements regarding God's protection and enduring security when
it comes to His chosen people of Israel throughout this time. Going
back to Exodus 14:13, which was immediately prior to God spread-

ing the Red Sea so the Israelites could cross to flee the prevailing Egyptians, we see in Moses' words:

> Fear not, stand firm, and see the salvation
> of the Lord, which He will work for you today.
> For the Egyptians whom you see today, you shall
> never see again. The Lord will fight for you, and
> you have only to be silent.

Staring into the face of imminent doom, that of the massive battle-ready army of the Egyptians, God alone provided deliverance and rescue for His people. As the Egyptians followed them through the Red Sea, they began to get bogged down in the mud with their chariots and screamed out in verse 25, "Let us flee from before Israel, for the Lord fights for them against the Egyptians."

In chapter 19, verse 4, the Lord tells Moses to tell the people of Israel: "You yourselves have seen what I did to the Egyptians, and how I bore you on eagles' wings and brought you to Myself."

Into Deuteronomy, when the Israelites start to go in and take possession of the Promised Land, we see several of these same statements being reiterated. We will go through and mention several of them, though I doubt we will exhaust this list. Right away in chapter 1, verses 30–31, we read:

> The Lord your God Who goes before you
> will Himself fight for you, just as He did for you
> in Egypt before your eyes, and in the wilderness,
> where you have seen how the Lord your God car-
> ried you, as a man carries his son, all the way that
> you went until you came to this place.

In chapter 3, verses 21–22, we see a very similar statement: "Your eyes have seen all that the Lord your God has done to these two kings. So will the Lord do to all the kingdoms into which you are crossing. You shall not fear them, for it is the Lord your God Who fights for you."

In chapter 7, we see a very beautiful section discussing God's divine selection of the people of Israel as His Own. Starting in verse 6:

> For you are a people holy to the Lord your God. The Lord your God has chosen you to be a people for His treasured possession, out of all the peoples who are on the face of the earth. It was not because you were more in number than any other people that the Lord set His love on you and chose you, for you were the fewest of all peoples, but it is because the Lord loves you and is keeping the oath that He swore to your fathers, that the Lord has brought you out with a mighty hand and redeemed you from the house of slavery, from the hand of Pharaoh king of Egypt.

It was not because of anything they did or their size or obedience (or should I say lack thereof along with constant grumbling and rebellion throughout the forty years of wandering in the wilderness) but entirely and simply because God chose them to be His Own and secured them until the end and upheld them and redeemed them and set His love on them and kept the promise He made to Abraham.

A bit later in Deuteronomy, in chapter 20, verses 3–4, we read, "Let not your heart faint. Do not fear or panic or be in dread of them, for the Lord your God is He Who goes with you to fight for you against your enemies, to give you the victory."

In Deuteronomy chapter 31, verses 6, 8, and 23, we read:

> Be strong and courageous. Do not fear or be in dread of them, for it is the Lord your God Who goes with you. He will never leave you nor forsake you... It is the Lord Who goes before you. He will be with you; He will not leave you or forsake you. Do not fear or be dismayed... Be strong and courageous, for you shall bring the

people of Israel into the land that I swore to give
them. I will be with you.

We also find quite a few times in Deuteronomy a very similar
phrase in several spots. "The Lord our God gave them over to us" or
"The Lord our God gave all into our hands," etc. in 2:33 and 36 and
also in 3:2–3 and 18. This also is probably not an exhaustive list.

Moving into the book of Joshua, when Moses died Joshua was
commissioned by God to take over as the leader of the Israelites, we
continue to read many of the same statements of God's provision and
security of His people. In the first chapter, verse 5, "No man should
be able to stand before you all the days of your life. Just as I was with
Moses, so I will be with you. I will never leave you or forsake you."
And in verse 9, "Have I not commanded you? Be strong and courageous. Do not be frightened, and do not be dismayed, for the Lord
your God is with you wherever you go."

Now we do see here, in the middle of this and throughout some
of the passages being listed, phrases like "Be strong and courageous,
being careful to do according to all the law that Moses My servant
commanded you... For then you will make your way prosperous,
and then you will have good success."

First of all, this is God speaking to the people of Israel, God's
already chosen people, through Joshua. This is not a salvational
passage. This is promising blessings upon obedience, not salvation
upon obedience. God is the Father of this chosen nation. He created
them, made them, and established them (Deut. 32:6) and is promising them prosperity and success as they cross over into the chosen
land if they follow Him, rely on Him, and obey His commands.
Furthermore, on both sides of this passage, God is promising them
that He will not leave them or forsake them and that He will remain
with them wherever they go; that no matter what comes, they will be
sustained by Him, so He commands them to be strong and courageous because their victories rest on Him, not themselves.

So to speak then, this is a directional passage, but be careful
not to reverse the direction of it. What I mean is their victory is fully
secure in God's covenant promise; therefore, "be strong and coura-

geous," do not worry, do as I command you, and I will make you become prosperous. It should not be interpreted in this way: as long as you are obedient, strong and courageous, then I will reward you with the fulfillment of My covenant promise, and you will become successful and prosperous. It is not situational upon their obedience; instead, it is guaranteed upon God's covenant promise. Therefore, be rest assured and proceed in full absolute confidence.

Throughout the rest of Joshua and parts of the Old Testament, we see several reiterations of these same statements. Such can be found in Joshua 8:1, 10:25, 23:3, 10; 2 Chronicles 20:15, 29; Nehemiah 4:20; and there's probably several more that are not listed here. It also says in 1 Samuel 12:22, "The Lord will not abandon His people for His great name's sake, because the Lord has been pleased to make you a people for Himself." If you belong to God, He will never abandon you, simply because it pleases Him that we belong to Him.

Moving into the Psalms, we see many more beautiful and poetic teachings of this beautiful doctrine. In Psalm 16, we read in verse 10, "For You will not abandon my soul to sheol, or let Your Holy One see corruption." Here, King David is acknowledging his confidence that the Lord will not abandon him and will not allow him to ever be destroyed. He offers no sense of "If I do this or that" but places all the assurance of security upon God. This passage is also reiterated in Acts 2:27 by Peter and in Acts 13:35 by Paul, but in both of those instances, it was used to apply Messianically to the resurrection of Christ instead of David and just as Christ was raised from the dead, never to return to corruption; so have we been raised from the dead, never to return to corruption.

When we look at Psalm 31:23, we see part of the same message that we received from Pastor John earlier in this chapter, "Love the Lord, all you His saints! The Lord preserves the faithful." We are the ones that remain faithful, but it is God Who preserves us as the faithful. The faith that we possess in Him is a supernatural enduring faith given to us by God that will preserve us until the end.

In Psalm 37, we see this in verses 23–24, "The steps of a man are established by the Lord, when He delights in his ways; though he fall, he shall not be cast headlong, for the Lord upholds his hand."

And in verse 28, "For the Lord loves justice; He will not forsake His saints. They are preserved forever, but the children of the wicked shall be cut off." And verses 39–40, "The salvation of the righteous is from the Lord; He is their stronghold in the time of trouble. The Lord helps them and delivers them; He delivers them from the wicked and saves them, because they take refuge in Him."

In these few verses of this Psalm 37, we see that God guides us and upholds us, and also just as we saw from Pastor John, we may at times fall, but we will not fail completely nor finally. He will not forsake us. He will uphold us and preserve us forever. He provides our righteousness and salvation, and He is the One that delivers us from evil and saves us until the end. We simply embrace this glorious fact of infinite love and grace and rest in His safety and security. We see the same thing in verse 10 of Psalm 97, "O you who love the Lord, hate evil! He preserves the lives of His saints; He delivers them from the hand of the wicked."

It is God that preserves us and delivers us. And also, again in Psalm 121, verses 7–8, "The Lord will keep you from evil; He will keep your soul. The Lord will keep your going out and your coming in from this time forth and forevermore."

The Lord Himself is the One that sustains us and protects us and keeps us secure all the way until the end. Forevermore! And we continue to see the same message all the way toward the end of the Psalms. In 145, verse 14, we read, "The Lord upholds all who are falling and raises up all who are bowed down." And verse 20, "The Lord preserves all who love Him."

In Proverbs chapter 24, we see Solomon make a statement concerning the continuing perseverance of the righteous. Verse 16, "For the righteous falls seven times and rises again." We also see Job declare this same basic statement back in Job 5:19, "He will deliver you from six troubles; in seven no evil will touch you." Now, neither wise King Solomon or wise Job are saying that a righteous person will only get knocked down a final total of seven times before he will stay down, give up, and be defeated forever. They are both meaning to say that they will often and many times fall and experience trouble but will continue to rise again and persevere through the grace of God's deliverance.

Moving into Isaiah, we see quite a bit more. In 32:17, we read that "the effect of righteousness," which we have seen in past chapters has been made possible by and given to us by God Himself, "will be peace, and the result of righteousness, quietness and confident trust forever" (AMP). If God has made us righteous, we are made righteous forever, and we can rest in that assurance and confidence in absolute trust of God's grace.

In Isaiah chapter 41, we see some beautifully descriptive words of God's love and intimacy with His chosen people of Israel. Starting in verse 8:

> But you, Israel, My servant, Jacob, whom I have chosen, the offspring of Abraham, My friend; you whom I took from the ends of the earth, and called from its farthest corners, saying to you, "You are My servant, I have chosen you and not cast you off;' fear not, for I Am with you; be not dismayed, for I Am your God; I will strengthen you, I will help you, I will uphold you with My righteous right hand."

And then into verses 13 and 14:

> For I, the Lord your God, hold your right hand; it is I Who say to you, "Fear not, I Am the One Who helps you." Fear not, Jacob, you men of Israel! I Am the One Who helps you, declares the Lord; your Redeemer is the Holy One of Israel.

Wow! Notice the intimacy that God uses when He speaks of His chosen people of Israel! It's beautiful! And just as we saw quite often in the earlier portions of the Old Testament that we have looked at, we see a lot of the same similar statements here. God chose His people, and He promises to hold them secure to never be cast aside, never lost. It is God Who will strengthen them and Who will uphold them until the end. They need not fear anything! He is their Redeemer, which here is referring to a kinsman-redeemer, which was a Hebrew practice where a close relative could buy back or redeem a family member from slavery. This is meant to symbolize God being the Redeemer, not just of Israel from the earthly slavery they escaped from in Egypt, but moreover, being the Redeemer of Israel and all mankind spiritually from slavery to sin.

In Isaiah 42, we read in verse 1, "Behold My servant, whom I uphold, My chosen, in whom My soul delights; I have put My Spirit upon him; He will bring forth justice to the nations." And in verse 6, "I Am the Lord; I have called you in righteousness; I will take you by the hand and keep you, I will give you as a covenant for the people, a light for the nations."

Again, we see several of the same phrases we saw earlier. God chooses and calls whom He pleases, He takes, upholds, and keeps, and He implants His Spirit in order to ensure security.

In the following chapter of Isaiah, chapter 43, we are given this absolutely incredible and overwhelmingly beautiful statement in verse 25, "I, I Am He, that blots out your transgressions for My Own sake, and I will not remember your sins."

WOW! How beautiful is that? Rest assured that when Christ said, "It is finished," it was finished for good, forever. If God promises that He has completely removed ALL of your sins and will NEVER REMEMBER THEM AGAIN, who are we to say that we are not safely secure? On top of it, He says He has done this for HIS OWN SAKE! He didn't do it for us. He did it for Himself, which has a massively important meaning to it! He didn't do it for us…_so it doesn't depend on us!_ He did it for His Own reasons, for His Own sake because of His Own desire! If you do not believe in eternal security, if you do not believe that God holds you secure until the end, get off your self-righteous and prideful high horse and get over yourself because it does not depend on you! He chose to do it for His Own sake and flat out promises us that He will never again remember our sins, and if none of our sins are ever to be remembered, then there is absolutely no reason at all that we would have to be worried about our end destination. If you belong to God, then you are absolutely forever secure! "This verse is probably the high point of grace in the Old Testament. In spite of Israel's utter unworthiness, the Lord in His grace has devised a way that He can forgive their sins and grant righteousness, without compromising His holiness."[4]

This verse also mirrors what we have seen back in Psalm 103:12, "As far as the east is from the west, so far does He remove our transgressions from us." They will never be remembered! And that phrase was written thousands of years before any of us were born or committed any of our sins.

In chapter 46, we see a few more verses of assurance. Starting in verse 3:

> Listen to Me, O house of Jacob, all the remnant of the house of Israel, who have been borne by Me from before your birth, carried from the womb; even to your old age I Am He, and to gray hairs I will carry you. I have made, and I will bear; I will carry and will save.

Reminiscent of Philippians 1:6 and Hebrews 12:2, we see here that God covers us from before we were even born and saves us all the way until the end. If we are His, He will never let go. We can never be separated. And He further promises this in 54:6–10:

> "For the Lord has called you...with great compassion I will gather you...with everlasting love I will have compassion on you... I have sworn that I will not be angry with you, and will not rebuke you... My steadfast love shall not depart from you, and My covenant of peace will not be removed," says the Lord, Who has compassion on you.

In chapter 56 of Isaiah, in verse 5, we read, "I will give them an everlasting name that shall not be cut off." If God calls us His Own, if He gives us a new name as His children, we will forever belong to Him, absolutely secure in Him, never to be cut off or lost again.

We see further continuance of this into chapter 63, in verse 9. "In all their affliction He was afflicted, and the Angel of His presence saved them; in His love and in His pity He redeemed them; He lifted them up and carried them all the days of old." This verse is, of course, referring to Jesus Who endured the affliction that was due to us and redeemed and saved us from what we deserved, and He will be the One Who lifts us up and carries us the rest of the way also.

We receive a couple very enlightening passages from the prophet of Jeremiah in his book. First, in chapter 31 verses 33–34, we read God's Own words:

> But this is the covenant I will make with the house of Israel after those days declares the Lord: I will put My law within them, and write it on their hearts. And I will be their God, and they shall be My people. And no longer shall each one teach his neighbor and each one his brother, saying, "Know the Lord," for they shall all know Me, from the least of them to the greatest, declares the Lord. For I will forgive their iniquity, and I will remember their sin no more.

Here we see that God Himself is the One Who writes His Own law on our hearts, therefore allowing us the ability and privilege to even be able to obey Him. And He also promises us that He will forgive us for our sins and to never remember them ever again! Just like we saw in Isaiah 43:25. And then in chapter 32, verses 39–40, we read God's Own words again:

> I will give them one heart and one way, that they may fear Me forever, for their own good and the good of their children after them. I will make an everlasting covenant with them, that I will not turn away from them. And I will put the fear of

Me in their hearts, so that they will not turn away
from Me.

These words are directly quoted in Hebrews 8:10, and are also
incredibly similar to a few of the passages we've looked at in Ezekiel
chapter 11, which also reiterates that it is God Who puts a new heart
in us "that [we] may walk in [His] statutes and keep [His] rules and
obey them." And in Ezekiel 36:26–27, it is God Who puts His Spirit
in us "and causes [us] to walk in [His] statutes and be careful to obey
[His] rules."

These words are specifically, in context, being spoken to and
about the people of Israel, yet they just as much apply to us today
as well. It is God Who works in us and makes us a people for His
Own possession, and He makes us people who are zealous for His
good works (Phil. 2:13; Ti. 2:14). Renowned Biblical commentator,
Matthew Henry, has this to say about this passage:

> God promised to renew His covenant with
> them, a covenant of grace, the blessings of which
> are spiritual, and such as will work good things
> in them, to qualify them for the great things God
> intended to do for them. It is called an everlast-
> ing covenant, not only because God will be for-
> ever faithful to it, but because the consequences
> of it will be everlasting. For, doubtless, here the
> promises look further than to Israel according to
> the flesh, and are sure to all believers, to every
> Israelite indeed. Good Christians may apply
> them to themselves and plead them with God,
> may claim the benefit of them and take comfort
> of them. God will own them for His, and make
> over Himself to them to be theirs: "They shall
> be My people" (v. 38). He will make them His
> by working in them all the characters and dispo-
> sitions of His people, and then He will protect,
> and guide, and govern them as His people. "And,

to make them truly, completely, and eternally happy, I will be their God." They shall serve and worship God as theirs and cleave to Him only, and He will approve Himself theirs. All He is, all He has, shall be engaged and employed for their good. God will give them a heart to fear Him (vs 39). That which He requires of those whom He takes into covenant with Him as His people is that they fear Him, that they reverence His majesty, dread His wrath, stand in awe of His authority, pay homage to Him, and give Him the glory due unto His name. Now what God requires of them He here promises to work in them, pursuant to His choice of them as His people.

Note, as it is God's prerogative to fashion men's hearts, so it is His promise to His people to fashion theirs aright; and a heart to fear God is indeed a good heart, and well fashioned. It is repeated in vs 40, "I will put My fear in their hearts," that is, work in them gracious principles and dispositions, that shall influence and govern their whole conversation. Teachers may put good things into our heads, but it is God only that can put them in our hearts, that can work in us both to will and to do. Also, He will effectually provide for their perseverance in grace and the perpetuating of the covenant between Himself and them. First, God will never leave nor forsake them: I will not turn away from them to do them good. Earthly princes are fickle, but God's mercy endures forever. Whom He loves He loves to the end. God may seem to turn from His people (Isa. 54:8), but even then, He does not turn from doing and designing them good. Secondly, they shall never leave nor forsake Him; that is the thing we are in danger of. We have no reason to distrust God's fidelity and constancy, but our own; and therefore, it is here promised that God will give them a heart to fear Him forever, all days, to be in His fear every day and all the day long (Prov. 23:17), and to continue so to the end of their days. He will put such a principle into their hearts that they shall not depart from Him. Even those who have given up their names to God, if they be left to themselves, will depart from Him; but the fear of God ruling in the heart, will prevent their departure. That, and nothing else, will do it. If we continue close and faithful to God, it is owing purely to His almighty grace and not to any strength or resolution of our own.[5]

Pastor John Piper has this to add, "When Christ died, He secured for His people not only new hearts but new security. He will not let them turn from Him. He will keep them. They will persevere. The blood of the covenant guarantees it."[6] We do not have the power to change ourselves, especially when we are dead (Rom. 5:6, 8, 10; Eph. 2:5); it is God Who does this for us, and in so doing, He gives us a new heart in which He instills the fear of Himself, so as to prevent us from turning away from Him. And He also promises to never turn away from us. So we may all rest assured that we are secured. He will not leave us, and we will not leave Him.

In Joel, we are given a small glimpse at this as well. In verse 27 of chapter 2, we read, "You shall know that I Am in the midst of Israel and that I Am the Lord your God and there is none else. And My people shall never again be put to shame." Know that if you are God's child, you will never again be put to shame or be lost again because He promises to hold you secure.

From the Prophet Micah, we are given a few more in chapter 7. First of all, looking at verses 7–9:

But as for me, I will look to the Lord; I will wait for the God of my salvation; my God will hear me. Rejoice not over me, O my enemy; when I fall, I shall rise; when I sit in darkness, the Lord will be a light to me. I will bear the indignation of the Lord because I have sinned against Him, until He pleads my cause and executes judgment for me. He will bring me out to the light; I shall look upon His vindication.

We must depend upon God to work deliverance for us, and put a good issue to our troubles in due time; we must not only look to Him, but look for Him: 'I will wait for the God of my salvation, and for His gracious returns to me.' In our greatest distresses we shall see no reason to despair of salvation if by faith we eye God as the God of our salvation, Who is able to save the weakest upon their humble petition, and willing to save the worst upon their true repentance. And, if we depend on God as the God of our salvation, we must wait for Him, and for His salvation, in His Own way and His Own time.[7]

All who are in Christ will persevere because it is God Himself Who pleads our case and executes His judgment in our favor, brings us from darkness to light, and He is the One Who also vindicates us, which is such a beautiful word. It means He will fully clear us of any and all blame and every suspicion; He will show us to be righteous, reasonable and justified. We also see in verses 18–19:

Who is a God like You, Who pardons iniquity and passes over the transgressions of the remnant of His inheritance? He does not retain His anger forever, because He delights in steadfast love. He will again have compassion on us; He will tread our iniquities underfoot. You [He] will cast all our sins into the depths of the sea.

Hallelujah! There is no God like our God! He forgives our absolute wickedness and passes over all of our rebellious acts because we are His. The Hebrew word used here for "inheritance" is *nahalatow*, which means "possession, property, inheritance, heritage." When we belong to Him, He will never stay angry at us because He finds greater pleasure in showering us with His love. He promises us that He will erase every single one of our gross and negligent sins.

God's forgiveness of our sins is absolute. He promises to eradicate them forever. Throughout the Old Testament, we are given several lessons on this. Here we see two of them: He will tread our sins underfoot, and He will cast every single one of them into the depths of the sea. Going back to Psalm 103, we are told that God removes our sins as far as the east is from the west. That's infinite. In Isaiah chapter 1, we are told that He will completely cleanse us from the stain of our sins, and in chapter 38, we are told that He throws our sins behind His back. And then in Jeremiah 31, we are told that He will remember our sins NO MORE! How beautiful is that? And, remember, God looks at the eternal. When He removes your sins and promises never to remember them ever again, that includes all of your future (as we see it) sins as well. He has removed the sins that we (confined to time) have not even committed yet. Nothing you do in the future will make Him change His mind and say, "You know what? Nope! I can't do this anymore. That was too much. You messed up to a degree that I can no longer forgive and forget. You crossed the line, and now it's too much. I'm reversing my stance with you and you are therefore now lost again and doomed for eternity."

If you are truly repentant, once He has forgiven you, YOU ARE FORGIVEN! Amen! You are secure in Him! You will persevere because you belong to Him. To ignore perseverance and eternal security:

> The extent of God's forgiveness would be at stake. When Christ died, which of your sins did He die for? Which sins were you forgiven of when you trusted Him as Savior? If the sins you commit after becoming a Christian can annul your

relationship with the Savior, clearly those sins were not covered at Calvary. Forgiven is forgiven. To differentiate between forgiven and unforgiven sins is to make a distinction foreign to Scripture. The timing of your sins is irrelevant since they were all in the future from the perspective of the cross. To disregard eternal security is to take away from what happened at Calvary.[8]

A statement from an anonymous believer says this:

> If anyone is ever to be kept out of Heaven for my sins, it will have to be Jesus, for He took them all upon Himself and made Himself responsible for them. But He is in Heaven already, never to be turned out, so now that I know that, I am secure![9]

Jumping back just a little bit to Psalm 103 because it perfectly parallels what we just looked at in Micah, we see a few passages that are quite amazing and beautiful. Starting in verse 6:

> The Lord works righteousness and justice for all who are oppressed. He made known His ways to Moses, His acts to the people of Israel. The Lord is merciful and gracious, slow to anger and abounding in steadfast love. He will not always chide, nor will He keep His anger forever. He does not deal with us according to our sins, nor repay us according to our iniquities. For as high as the heavens are above the earth, so great is His steadfast love toward those who fear Him; as far as the east is from the west, so far does He remove our transgressions from us.

Again, we see that it is God Himself Who works in us and makes His ways and laws known to us. He will not remain angry at us but will shower us with His gracious and merciful love because of His infinite love for us. And He will remove every single one of our sins (past, present, future), as far as infinitely possible, never to be remembered again. His love for us is infinite, and the security He provides us is infinite.

Moving into the New Testament, we continue the lesson given to us about our security and perseverance. We are given this direct statement on our perseverance, reiterated twice throughout Matthew, and one additional time in Mark. In chapter 10 of Matthew, we read Jesus's words. In context, Jesus is sending out His apostles to spread His word of the coming Kingdom of God and warns them that they will be sent out as sheep among wolves and warns them that they will be hated, persecuted, arrested, even beaten or killed in order that they may be placed in front of governors and kings for Christ's sake so that they may bear witness in front of them. He does provide them with this bit of relief in verses 19–20:

> When they deliver you over, do not be anxious how you are to speak or what you are to say, for what you are to say will be given to you in that hour. For it is not you who speak, but the Spirit of your Father speaking through you.

And then He also offers them these words in verse 22, "The one who endures to the end will be saved." We see the parallel narration of this commission of Jesus's to His disciples in 13:13 of Mark's gospel with the same words being offered, "The one who endures to the end will be saved." Returning to Matthew, in chapter 24, verse 13, we read these same exact words again, "The one who endures to the end will be saved." In context here, Jesus is speaking to His disciples about the coming end of the age, the end-times, and explaining that the world will be in absolute chaos, with wars, deceptions, famines and disasters, and even persecutions against and killings of Christians.

In verses 10–12 He says, "Then many will fall away and betray one another and hate one another. And many false prophets will arise and lead many astray. And because lawlessness will be increased, the love of many will grow cold." But then He promises in verse 13 that those who endure will be saved.

The ones that persevere are the same ones who are saved—not the ones whose love grows cold. This does not suggest that our perseverance secures our salvation. Scripture everywhere teaches precisely the opposite: God, as part of His saving work, secures our perseverance. True believers "are being guarded through faith for a salvation" (1 Pet. 1:5).

The guarantee of our perseverance is built in to the New Covenant promise. God says: "I will put the fear of Me in their hearts, that they may not turn from Me" (Jer. 32:40). Those who do fall away from Christ give conclusive proof that they were never truly believers to begin with (1 John 2:19). To say that God secures our perseverance is not to say that we are passive in the process, however. He keeps us "through faith" (1 Pet. 1:5)—our faith. Scripture sometimes calls us to hold fast to our faith (Heb. 10:23; Rev. 3:11) or warns us against falling away (Heb. 10:26–29). Such admonitions do not negate the many promises that true believers will persevere (John 10:28–29; Rom. 8:38–39; 1 Cor. 1:8–9; Phil. 1:6).

Rather, the warnings and pleas are among the means God uses to secure our perseverance in the faith. Notice that the warnings and promises often appear side by side. For example, when Jude urges believers, "Keep yourselves in the love of God" (Jude 21), he immediately points them to God, "Who is able to keep you from stum-

bling" (Jude 24). This endurance does not produce salvation; it is Spirit-empowered perseverance and proof of the reality of salvation in the
one who endures.[10]

Those who are truly saved will endure and persevere to the end
because they are truly saved and belong to God.

At the end of Matthew's gospel, we see the Great Commission
of Christ to His disciples:

> Go therefore and make disciples of all
> nations, baptizing them in the name of the Father
> and of the Son and of the Holy Spirit, teaching
> them to observe all that I have commanded you.
> And behold, I Am with you always, to the end of
> the age.

He is saying these words to His disciples, but they are also spoken to all of us, His children and followers of Christ, and He says
that He is with us and will always be with us until the end. These
words are spoken in regards to unbelievers, but they are not spoken to
unbelievers. They are spoken to those who belong to God. Everyone
that is a child of God is promised that Christ will always be with
them. Once a person belongs to God, Christ will never leave them.

In the gospel of Luke, we receive a very intimate look at this
topic. In chapter 22, we see Jesus speaking to His apostles just prior
to the crucifixion. Jesus offers these warm and protective words to
Peter in verse 31–32, "Simon, Simon, behold, satan demanded to
have you, that he might sift you like wheat, but I have prayed for
you that your faith may not fail. And when you have turned again,
strengthen your brothers."

What a beautiful testimony to Christ's protection of us and His
intercessory prayer for us. In context, Jesus is specifically praying for
Peter individually, but as we will see in John 17, He prays the same
prayer for all of His apostles and all believers of the church. If you
do not think that you would be included in this same prayer that

Christ offered in Peter's defense, you are deceptively misled. satan would love to destroy every single one of us, but Jesus prays directly to His Father that our faith may not fail. Jesus Himself prays for our perseverance, and any prayer that Jesus prays to His Father you can guarantee to be answered as They are in and of each other (John 10:30, 14:11). He was in this context assuring Peter personally of his ultimate victory made possible by Christ's Own prayers, but He assures all of us, His true followers, just the same.

And then, almost in Christ's very next breath, He foretells of Peter's outright denial of Christ three times later that same night. Just moments later, Peter would commit the very serious sin of denying his association with Christ three times in a row in the courtyard outside of the high priest's house while Jesus was being interrogated by the council. Jesus assures Peter that He is praying for his security, a mere breath or two before He tells Peter that he will outright deny his association with Christ! Peter's security clearly didn't depend on his perfect submission or compliance to Jesus, nor does ours. Christ's assurance predates our failures!

Moving into the Gospel of John, we will see a lot taught on this, so buckle up! First, in chapter 3, we see Jesus talking to the pharisee, Nicodemus, and explaining the way of salvation. In verse 15, He says these straightforward words, "Whoever believes in Him may have eternal life." Then in chapter 4, we see Jesus talking to the Samaritan woman at the well. After an intimate conversation with the woman where Jesus convicted her of her unlawful and un-marital behavior, He spoke of Himself as the "living water" and offered these words in verse 14, "Whoever drinks of the water that I will give him will never be thirsty again. The water that I will give him will become in him a spring of water welling up to eternal life."

Then in John 5:21 and 24, we see Jesus speaking of His authority and oneness with God the Father and says these words:

> For as the Father raises the dead and gives
> them life, so also the Son gives life to whom He
> will… Truly, truly, I say to you, whoever hears
> My Word and believes in Him Who sent Me has

> eternal life. He does not come into judgment,
> but has passed from death to life.

In these few passages, we see Jesus speaking about believers having eternal life; in 5:24, the verb being used is a present tense verb *has*. We know that anyone who confesses with their mouth that Jesus is Lord and believes in their heart that God raised Him from the dead is saved (Rom. 10:9–10), and as we see here in 5:24, if they believe in God, they are given eternal life. They have it; the Greek verb used is a present tense verb. They do not wait to receive it; they have it.

This is also verified in 1 John 5:11–13:

> And this is the testimony, that God gave us
> eternal life, and this life is in His Son. Whoever
> has the Son has life; whoever does not have the
> Son does not have life. I write these things to you
> who believe in the name of the Son of God that
> you may know that you have eternal life.

If you believe in Christ as God and Savior, you have eternal life. You don't wait to get it; you have it. Present tense verb.

> If you believe in Jesus Christ today and have
> eternal life, but lose it tomorrow, then it was
> never "eternal" at all. Therefore, if you lose your
> salvation, the promises of eternal life in the Bible
> would be in error. So for a believer to lose his sal-
> vation, or become unsaved, he would have to be
> "un-regenerated" or "un-indwelt" with the Holy
> Spirit and detached from the Body of Christ.[11]

Again, verse 24 says, we do "not come into judgment, but have passed out of death into life." There is no returning to the (salvational) judgment seat. God has declared us not guilty and we are eternally secure. We do not have to worry about returning to a guilty verdict ever again.

It, therefore, becomes more of an issue or question of "Was he really saved to begin with?" instead of "He had it but then lost it." Plus, God wants us to be able to have and dwell in the total joy of full assurance (1 John 5:13–14).

> If our salvation hinges on anything but the finished work of Christ on the cross, we are in trouble. If you and I have a part in maintaining our salvation, it will be difficult to live in much assurance. Hope, yes; assurance, no. Yet John wrote an entire epistle to assure a group of people, people he was not even around to observe, that they were in fact saved (1 John 5:13). Where there is no assurance of God's acceptance, there is no joy. Where there is no joy, there is a limitation of one's ability to love unconditionally. Why? Because a person with no assurance is by definition partially motivated by fear. Fear and love do not mingle well. One will always dilute the other. Furthermore, fear spills over into worry. Let's be realistic for a moment. If my salvation is not a settled issue, how can I be anxious for nothing (see Phil. 4:6)?[12]

In John chapter 6, we see Jesus giving His "I Am the Bread of Life" teaching. In verses 37–40, we read these words:

> All the Father gives to Me will come to Me, and whoever comes to Me I will never cast out. For I have come down from Heaven, not to do My Own will but the will of Him Who sent Me. And this is the will of Him Who sent Me, that I should lose nothing of all that He has given Me, but raise it up on the last day. For this is the will of My Father, that everyone who looks on the

Son and believes in Him should have eternal life, and I will raise him up on the last day.

This verse emphasizes the sovereign will of God in the selection of those who come to Him for salvation. The Father has predestined those who would be saved. The absolute sovereignty of God is the basis of Jesus's confidence in the success of His mission. The security of salvation rests in the sovereignty of God, for God is the guarantee that "all" He has chosen will come to Him for salvation. The idea of "gives Me" is that every person chosen by God and drawn by God must be seen as a gift of the Father's love to the Son. The Son receives each "love gift," holds on to each, and will raise each to eternal glory. No one chosen will be lost. This saving purpose is the Father's will, which the Son will not fail to do perfectly."[13]

R. C. Sproul adds, "The only reason why I'm a Christian is because I'm a gift of the Father to the Son, not because of anything I've ever done."

Jesus assures us that He will never cast us out and that He will never lose a single one of us for any reason whatsoever. Every single person that God has predestined to come to Him has come to Jesus, and not a single soul will ever be lost from the hands of the Savior. Jesus reiterates the last few words of verse 40 in verse 54, "Whoever feeds on My flesh and drinks My blood has eternal life and I will raise him up on the last day." The eating of His flesh and drinking of His blood metaphorically symbolized the need of accepting Jesus's finished work of the cross, being united with His body and blood, and by so relying on Christ's promise to secure us until the end and raise us up on the last day. He reiterates this again in verse 58. "Whoever feeds on this bread will live forever." Again, Jesus is speaking of His

Own flesh symbolically and promising eternal life from relying on Him.

We also see a parallel teaching by Christ of His sovereign handling of those who are His in chapter 10. Starting in verse 28, we read:

> I give them eternal life, and they will never perish, and no one will snatch them out of My hand. My Father, Who has given them to Me, is greater than all, and no one is able to snatch them out of the Father's hand. I and the Father are One.

As we just saw a little bit ago, eternal life is a present possession for the believer, and Christ here promises that they will never perish. That only makes sense; if you are eternally alive, you will not perish. Jesus assures that no one, not even the devil, has the power to steal anyone from His grasp. And even though Jesus Himself is omnipotent and One with the Father, He says that His Father is greater than all, the infinite of omnipotent, and no one can snatch the believer from His hands.

There are only two sets of hands involved here, Jesus's and God the Father's. No one can take us out of Their hands—not even us. Picture this: the infinite and eternal hand of God the Creator, Who created everything in the universe, is holding you secure. Who or what part of the created universe could possibly rip open the hand of God to pluck you from His grasp? What part of the created universe could overpower the Creator of the universe to rip you away from the omnipotent Creator of everything? That's ludicrous to even consider.

Now, there are some people that try to say that you can lose your salvation because of free will. Not that it can be taken away from you or that you can be snatched out of God's hand, but that you, because of free will, could decide to leave because if God holds on to you in a way where you are not able to leave, then you no longer have free will, and God forces you to stay. That seems like a legit argument, but it is simply not true. Though you may still have that choice due to free will, if you have truly surrendered to Christ as your Savior and are saved, you would never desire to leave because you know truly Who God is and that He is the only way.

And as we saw back in Jeremiah 32:40, we saw that God made an everlasting covenant to never turn away from us, and He also put a [healthy] fear of Himself into our own hearts so that we will never turn away from Him. And if you still wanted to try to hang on to that same excuse for the possibility of losing salvation, let me offer it this way: If I still have free will (which is not in debate here) and therefore perseverance and eternal security are not true and I can walk away if I choose to, then wouldn't it be true that once I reach Heaven, I would still be able to walk away? Could I get to Heaven and say, "You know what? This isn't for me. I'm going to exercise my free will and I'm going to leave Heaven because You can't force me to stay."

Careful how you answer! If you say no, it doesn't apply like that, then are you saying that you are forced to stay in Heaven? Are you no longer free to practice free will in Heaven? Are you at that point trapped and forced to comply? Are you in that sense a slave? If you want to say that simply because of free will that you can lose your salvation if you simply choose to walk away, but then when you get to Heaven, you lose your free will and are forced to stay against your will if you chose to leave, then you have a whole new problem. Anyone who walks away never truly gave themselves to God (1 John 2:19) and never truly knew exactly Who God is and what He has done and what He has given us and that He truly is All in All.

Anyone who is saved by God knows exactly Who God is and would never ever leave Him, no matter what, and Christ secures that with a security unparalleled. Not an action of force or of disallowing prevention, but of divine confidence and perseverance, even if to the point of martyrdom. To believe that you could simply walk away from true faith means you clearly don't understand a true salvational faith relationship with your Savior and His sustaining perseverance within us, which isn't necessarily condemning or sinful but is injurious due to your lack of confidence in Christ's loving security and is wholly damaging to your assurance.

In chapter 14, we see Jesus speaking again to His disciples and promising them a place with Him in Heaven. In verse 3 we read, "If I go to prepare a place for you, I will come again and will take you to Myself, that where I Am you may be also." As we just saw in chapter 10, anyone who belongs to Christ will never be lost, and so we see here that all who belong to Christ, He will come back and take to Heaven where He has built our eternal Home where we will dwell with Him forever.

Toward the end of chapter 15, Jesus is warning His disciples about the hatred and persecution that they will receive from the rest of the world as they go out and minister the Gospel message to the unbelieving world. And then in the first verse of chapter 16, Jesus says, "I have said all these things to you to keep you from falling away." We see Jesus being the active and intentional source of fortifying our security. Now, as we just looked at, a true believer would never fall away or be turned away or be snatched away, and that is because Christ is constantly providing the necessary elements for our security. He will forever and always intercede for us (Rom. 8:34), provide for, and protect us.

Moving into John chapter 17, we come into what may be one of the most beautiful chapters in the entire Bible. This entire chapter is a prayer, spoken by Jesus, directed to the Father.

> Although Matthew 6:9–13 and Luke 11:2–4 have become known popularly as the "Lord's Prayer," that prayer was actually a prayer taught to the disciples by Jesus simply as a pattern for their prayers. That prayer is a prayer that Jesus did not and could not ever pray, because it speaks of needing forgiveness of sins. The prayer recorded in John 17 is truly the Lord's Prayer, exhibiting the face-to-face communion the Son had with the Father, so this prayer reveals some of the precious content of the Son's communion and intercession with Him.[14]

Jesus first prays for Himself and to glorify God the Father and asks the Father to glorify Him. Jesus then prays for His apostles, and then He prays for all New Testament believers who will make up the Church. This whole prayer shows the entire and complete sovereignty of God's grace and security. If you read this chapter and still believe that your security is not entirely secure in the hands of God or that you play some part in it, I respectfully suggest that you reread this chapter until you truly understand what Jesus did for you!

Let's begin first by looking at the first five verses in which Jesus prays for Himself and to glorify the Father. "Father, the hour has come; glorify Your Son that the Son may glorify You, since You have given Him authority over all flesh, to give eternal life to all whom You have given Him." First of all, we see that the reason Jesus sought His Own glory was in order to glorify His Father.

> The very event that would glorify the Son was His death. By it, He has received the adoration, worship and love of millions whose sins He bore. He accepted this path to glory, knowing that by it He would be exalted to the Father. The goal is that the Father may be glorified for His redemptive plan in the Son.[15]

We also see the sovereign and complete control Christ has over all flesh and the objective that He was given concerning every single person that God Himself gave to Christ. This is also the first of seven times in chapter 17 and once more in chapter 18 that we see the phrase (or similar) "all whom You have given Me." This goes back to the issue of God's sovereign election of every single saved believer. Every single person whom God chose before the foundations of the world (Eph. 1:4; Rev. 13:8) are given to Christ, and He then gives eternal life to every single one of them without exception, which by definition, as we just looked at a few paragraphs ago, will not be taken away at any point. It cannot be eternal life if there is possibility of its loss.

Continuing on in verse 3, "And this is eternal life, that they know You the only true God, and Jesus Christ Whom You have sent." It was Jesus's commission to make known to all of God's elect the name and glory of God and of Himself that we may know Him and be with Him, which is the essence of eternal life, to be in relationship with Him. Into verses 4 and 5, "I glorified You on earth, having accomplished the work that You gave Me to do. And now, Father, glorify Me in Your Own presence with the glory that I had with You before the world existed." Again, Jesus shows that the essence of His mission was to bring glory to the Father, and He did so by perfectly and fully accomplishing the duty that He was sent to do, and that of giving eternal life to every single person that God chose and gave to Him, which would be ultimately finalized when He painfully mouthed the victorious words "It is finished" (John 19:30). "Having completed His work (vs 4), Jesus looked past the cross and asked to be returned to the glory that He shared with the Father before the world began (John 1:1–2)."[16]

Moving into verse 6 of chapter 17, Jesus transitions His prayer toward praying for His apostles and all New Testament believers.

> I have manifested Your name to the people whom You gave Me out of the world. Yours they were, and You gave them to Me, and they have kept Your Word. Now they know that everything that You have given Me is from You. For I have given them the words that You gave Me, and they have received them and have come to know in truth that I came from You; and they have believed that You sent Me.

First of all, we see the phrase "whom You gave Me" twice more here. Also, Christ again proclaims that He has fulfilled His duty and made known the name and Word of God to them and that every single one has come to believe in Christ as the Messiah and Son of God and that they have persevered and have received and come to know the truth and have kept His Word. There is also a phrase in these verses that is really quite telling and pivotal. John MacArthur has some great words on this phrase.

> Go back to verse 6 and look at this phrase: "They were Yours. They were Yours." Who? "The men You gave Me. The men to whom I've manifested Your name; they were the ones You gave Me out of the world; they were Yours." Let me talk about that. Before they were ever converted, before they were ever called, before they ever knew anything, before they ever believed, they were Yours—past tense—they were Yours. It's really a stunning statement. "They were in the world, and You gave them to Me out of the world, but they were Yours even when they were in the world." What is the world? The world is the evil, anti-God, anti-Christ, satanically ruled system of evil and sin, composed of demons and all the unredeemed human beings who oppose God, who belong to satan, and who live in the kingdom of darkness. Within the realm of darkness, there are some sinners who belong to God. 'They were Yours—'Were, not are, but were'—even when they were in the world, they were Yours, and You gave them to Me out of the world."
>
> Back in chapter 15 and verse 18, our Lord said earlier that night, "If the world hates you, you know that it has hated Me before it hated you. If you were of the world, the world would love its own; but because you're not of the world, but I chose you out of the world, because of this the world hates you."
>
> "You were in the world. I chose you out of the world. God delivered you out of the world. When you were still in the world lost in sin, and

darkness, and death, and ignorance, you were still God's, you were God's." Powerful reality.

In the 13th chapter of Acts, there's an illustration of this as Paul is ministering—Paul along with his companion Barnabas—and in the 13th chapter, they're on their early missionary journey. It says in verse 48, "When the Gentiles heard this—'they heard from Isaiah that the Messiah was a light to the nations, the Gentiles; bring salvation to the ends of the earth.' When the Gentiles heard this, they began rejoicing and glorifying the Word of the Lord—'listen to this'—and as many as had been appointed to eternal life believed." Did you get that? "As many as had been appointed to eternal life believed."

They had been appointed to eternal life, that's why they believed. They had been appointed to eternal life before they believed. Look at the 18th chapter of the book of Acts, and again, the ministry of Paul. The Lord comes to Paul in Corinth, down in verse 9, "And the Lord said to Paul in the night by a vision, 'Do not be afraid. Go on speaking; do not be silent,'" no matter what the threats were. There were some serious threats earlier in the chapter. "Go on; for I Am with you, and no man will attack you in order to harm you, for I have many people in this city." There were people in the city of Corinth who belonged to Christ, who belonged to God. They were still in the world, in the darkness, in the ignorance of sin, but they belonged to God. How did they become God's? Ephesians 1:4 says, "He chose us before the foundation of the world, that we would be holy and blameless before Him."

Colossians 3:12 says, "We are those who have been chosen of God, holy and beloved." Back to Ephesians 1:5–6, "He predestined us to adoption as sons through Jesus Christ to Himself, according to the kind intention of His will, to the praise of the glory of His grace, which He freely bestowed on us in the Beloved." Verse 11, "Predestined according to His purpose Who works all things after the counsel of His Own will, to the praise of His Own glory."

So God, for His Own glory, made an uninfluenced choice. He chose some people and they are His, even though they are not yet saved. They were predestined for justification, they were predestined for adoption, they were predestined for Heaven because they were chosen by God.

In 2 Thessalonians 2, verse 13, Paul says, "We should always give thanks to God for you, brethren beloved, because God has chosen you from the beginning for salvation." Those who believe in the Son of God, those who accepted the ministry of Jesus and believe in Him, did so because they are God's. They've always been God's. They were God's before there was a Creation.

Revelation 13:8, 17:8, "Their names were written in the Book of Life before the foundation of the world." Did you get that? "Their names were written in the Book of Life before the foundation of the world." God chose them before He ever created them. God wrote their names down. And Revelation 20:15 says, "If anyone's name was not found written in the Book of Life, he's thrown in the lake of fire."

"They were Yours; You gave them to Me, You gave them to Me." This is not new to us in the Gospel of John. Go back to chapter 6. Much earlier in our Lord's ministry, He made it clear to the disciples that anyone who came to salvation was a gift from the Father. Listen to John 6:37, "All that the Father gives Me will come to Me, and the one who comes to Me I will certainly not cast out, or reject." Verse 39, "This is the will of Him Who sent Me, that of all that He has given Me I lose none, but raise it up on the last day." Verse 40, "This is the will of My Father, that everyone who beholds the Son and believes in Him will have eternal life, and I Myself will raise him up on the last day." In verse 44, "No one can come to Me unless the Father Who sent Me draws him; and I will raise Him up on the last day." And we've learned this through the years, the Father chooses, the Father writes names down before Creation. There are people throughout all of human history who are born sinners in the world, engulfed in sin, spiritually dead and blind and ignorant, but they are God's; and in God's time, He plucks them out of the world, then they become love gifts to His Son. The Father chooses, the Father gives; the Son receives, the Son keeps, and the Son raises, and no one is lost. It's as if the Father gives a gift and it's up to the Son to protect the gift and bring that one to glory, that's John 6. "All that the Father gives to Me come to Me. My job is to receive and not reject. My job is to guard and keep and raise them all in the end to glory." That then is the much more work of Christ, the work of getting all of us through all the vicissitudes and issues of life, and all the battles with sin and doubts and fears, to get us all to glory. That's His intercessory, mediatorial ministry. "You gave them to Me, and I'm going to get them to glory."[17]

Continuing on into verses 9 and 10, "I Am praying for them. I Am not praying for the world but for those whom You have given Me, for they are Yours. All Mine are Yours, and Yours are Mine, and I Am glorified in them." Amen! Praise God! Is there anyone that you would rather have praying for you than Jesus? The Messiah and Redeemer and Savior, the Son of God, the Hand of Creation is praying for us, and He is indeed constantly interceding for us (Isa. 53:12; Rom. 8:34; Heb. 7:25; 1 John 2:1). And again, we see the phrase "Those whom You have given Me." Every single person that God has given to Christ belongs to Christ and belongs to God, and Christ is praying for the security of every single one of them and is also glorified in them.

> Even though they are weak, even though they stumble, even though their faith is shaken, even though they will abandon Him in just a few hours, He prays for their eternal glory. Why? Because it says in John 13:1, "Having loved His Own who were in the world, He loved them, *eis telos*, He loved them to the limits of divine love." In other words, He loved them with an infinite, divine love, He loved them as much as God can love, and it is that love that brings them to glory."[18]

In verses 11–12, we read these amazing words:

> And I Am no longer in the world, but they are in the world, and I Am coming to You. Holy Father, keep them in Your name, whom You have given Me, that they may be one, even as We are one. While I was with them, I kept them in Your name, whom You have given Me. I have guarded

> them, and not one of them has been lost except
> the son of destruction, that the Scripture might
> be fulfilled.

WOW! Since Jesus was about to be executed in just a few short hours from this point, He was praying for the protection and security of His disciples. He says that while He was here with them, He was the One that kept them and guarded them and that not one of them has been lost (cf. John 6:37–40, 44, 10:28–29), that is except for Judas who was to betray Jesus and aid in His arrest, and this was to fulfill Scripture. Don't misunderstand this, though. Judas' defection was not in any way a failure on Christ's part, but it was foreseen and foreordained in Scripture (Ps. 41:9, 109:8; cf. John 13:18).[19] And since Jesus is about to depart through death, and they would no longer be in His direct physical presence, Jesus prays that the Father would now take over and protect all those whom God had given Him and that He would keep them eternally secure in His name.

So just as none were lost in the hands of Christ, none will be lost in the hands of the Father. There was never a time when they or we were unsecure. All of those whom have been given to Christ have been held secure by Christ and by the Father (cf. John 6:37–40, 44; 10:28–29; 17:2, 6, 9, 11–12, 15, 24, 26; 18:9). And if that's not amazing enough, He prays that just as the Trinity experiences eternal unity, all believers may share in that same quality of unity as with the Trinity (cf. Rom. 8:17)!

Continuing on into verse 13–14:

> But now I Am coming to You, and these
> things I speak in the world, that they may have
> My joy fulfilled in themselves. I have given
> them Your Word, and the world has hated them
> because they are not of the world, just as I Am
> not of the world.

Through Jesus's ministry here, He has provided the ability to have joy in a world that hates us because we are not of the world. He has given us His Word to live by, and our joy is through His Word and His finished work. Verse 15, "I do not ask that You take them out of the world, but that You keep them from the evil one." Amen! Thank You, Lord!

Jesus asks the Father to keep us safely away from the evil grasps of all the forces of evil. And who is there that can overpower the omnipotent Creator God? Now we may trip and stumble sometimes against temptation, and we will still sin here in this fleshly body, but as we stated earlier, we will not completely or finally fail because we are kept secure by God Himself. We see this portrayed in 1 Corinthians 10:13, "No temptation has overtaken you that is not common to man. God is faithful, and He will not let you be tempted beyond your ability, but with the temptation He will also provide the way of escape, that you may be able to endure it."

> Though Jesus's sacrifice on the cross was the defeat of satan, he is still loose and orchestrating his evil system against believers. he seeks to destroy believers (1 Peter 5:8), as with Job and Peter (Luke 22:31–32), and in general (Eph. 6:12), but God is their protector (Ps. 27:1–3; Jude 24–25; cf. John 12:31, 16:11).[20]

Back to verses 16–19 of John chapter 17:

> They are not of the world, just as I Am not of the world. Sanctify them in the truth; Your Word is Truth. As You sent Me into the world, so I have sent them into the world. And for their sake I consecrate Myself, that they may also be sanctified in truth.

Because we belong to Christ, we do not belong to this world. We are aliens or exiles (1 Pet. 1:1) here as our Home is in Heaven (Eph. 2:19; Phil. 3:20; Heb. 13:14). We also see that Jesus prays twice here, that the Father would sanctify us in the truth of the

Word. As we looked at in the last chapter, and as we see here, it is God Who controls and secures our sanctification also. As we saw, we have no ability in ourselves to reform ourselves into more of an image of Christ; it is only through the work of the Spirit in us, though we must do our part and intentionally fight to resist the evil temptations and desires of the flesh and the world; though again, we can only do so by relying on His strength provided within us.

Continuing on into verses 20–21, Jesus is now specifically praying for all New Testament believers:

> I do not ask for these only, but also for those who will believe in Me through their word, that they may all be one, just as You, Father, are in Me, and I in You, that they also may be in Us, so that the world may believe that You have sent Me.

Jesus is praying to His Father for the lasting security of every single believer, all those whom the Father gave to Him from the time of His ministry here on earth until the time of His return when we will all safely be with Him in Heaven, where we will share holy and perfect unity with the Trinity, just like we saw back in verse 11. How amazing and beautiful is that? As the Triune God is One, we will also be One with Them! And as we have mentioned before, you can rest assured that anything that Jesus prayed to His Father will perfectly be fulfilled, and none will be lost (John 6:37–40, 10:28–29, 17:2, 11–12, 15, 24, 26).

> The basis of this unity centers in adherence to the revelation the Father mediated to His first disciples through His Son. Believers are also to be unified in the common belief of the truth that was received in the Word of God (Phil. 2:2). This is not still a wish, but it became a reality when the Spirit came (cf. Acts 2:4; 1 Cor. 12:13). It is not experiential unity, but the unity of common

eternal life shared by all who believe the truth, and it results in the one body of Christ all sharing His life.[21]

We see some similar words in verses 22 and 23:

> The glory that You have given Me I have given to them, that they may be one even as We are One, I in them and You in Me, that they may be perfectly one, so that the world may know that You sent Me and loved them even as You loved Me.

Jesus says some of the same words here in that we may be One with the Triune God, in perfect eternal unity with Him, but Jesus also adds here that He has given the same glory to us that He received from the Father and that the Father loves us, even to the same infinite extent that He loves His holy, righteous, and perfect Son! How incredibly elating is that? I personally do not feel worthy for that type of honor, but thankfully, it doesn't depend on me. God has chosen us, redeemed us, called us, justified us, and holds us secure all out of His immense and infinite love for us, even though we are all absolute failures in the flesh. The same love and glory that Christ receives from the Father Whom He has dwelt with throughout eternity past and future, Whom He created the universe with, Whom He shares an intimacy with that we can't even begin to ponder, we have also been given—I repeat, "given"—as a gift this same love and glory! We do not deserve it, and we certainly are not able to be "good enough" to earn it. It is given to us out of God's infinite eternal agape love for us.

To finish off this incredibly beautiful chapter of John's Gospel, let's look at the final verses.

> Father I desire that they also, whom You have given Me, may be with Me where I Am, to see My glory that You have given Me because You loved Me before the foundation of the world. O

> righteous Father, even though the world does not
> know You, I know You, and these know that You
> have sent Me. I made known to them Your name,
> and I will continue to make It known, that the
> love with which You have loved Me may be in
> them, and I in them.

First of all, we see again this phrase "whom You have given Me," and again, we see some of the same similar words from the last few verses, but here we see Jesus take it even further. He specifically asks that the Father secures us and leads us all the way to the end so that we may be with Christ where He is which of course is in His Heavenly Kingdom. He is there now preparing a place for us (John 14:2–3), and we will be held secure until He returns to bring us to our eternal Heavenly Home.

As we stated earlier, any prayer that Jesus prayed to His Father is sure to be answered as They are One, so when Christ asks His Father for all whom have been given to Him to be with Him where He is, we can entirely be assured that we will make it there, not by our tough-willed endurance but by the security of God Himself through the perseverance of the enduring faith that has been instilled in us by the presence of the Holy Spirit. Jesus backs this up by stating that He has made His Father's name known to us, and He will also be the One to continue making Him known to us. He will hold us securely in the knowledge of the name of God the Father, constantly interceding for us (John 17; Rom. 8:26–27, 34; Heb. 7:25; 1 John 2:1), never to slip away (John 6:37–40, 44, 10:28–29, 17:2, 6, 9, 11–12, 15, 24, 26, 18:9) again so that we may be One in perfect unity with Him and that we may receive the same infinite love that the Son has received.

This entire chapter, this entire prayer, shows us so solidly that Christ intercedes for us and prays to the Father for our security, and all that the Son asks the Father will be granted as They are of one will and heart. Christ never desired or asked for a single thing that the Father did not concur with. They never disagreed, they never "butted heads," they never contradicted each other; they were and always will be of the same mind, will, desire, purpose, inclination, disposition, and propensity. If Christ asked and prayed directly to His Father that every single person that the Father ever gave to Him would be kept from the evil one, sanctified in the truth, given eternal life, made to understand, and to know the name of God and to be kept in that same name, guarded as to not be lost, filled with the joy of Christ Himself, in perfect unity and oneness with the Trinity, given the same glory and love that the Father gave to the Son, and are made to continue in the knowledge of His name, ALL those whom the Father gave to the Son can rest in absolute assurance of their security and perseverance!

> Jesus is saying this, "Father, I want You to show them the glory. I want You to bring them into eternal glory. I want You to protect them. I want You to hold on to them. I want You to keep them. I want You to make sure their faith never fails so that We are all together as One in eternal glory as was planned and intended at the foundation of the world when You set this redemptive plan in motion. Keep them from the evil one, sanctify them by Your Word. Bring them to eternal glory that they may share with Us in that glory and not just these"—verse 20 says—"but everybody who will believe in Me through their words."[22]

> To say you can lose your salvation is to say that Christ lost you. That's absurd. If I can lose it, then He's blown it. If I can lose it, then God's lost something much bigger, He's lost His integrity (cf. Luke 22:32, John 6:37–40, John 10:28–29, John 17).[23]

John also includes the phrase "Of those whom You gave Me I have lost not one" once more in verse 9 of chapter 18.

As we move into the epistles, we come to Paul's letter to the Romans. We will start in a similarly amazing and beautiful chapter, chapter 8. In the very beginning verses, we read some very uplifting and glorious words. "There is therefore now no condemnation for those who are in Christ Jesus. For the law of the Spirit of life has set you free in Christ Jesus from the law of sin and death." The word used here for "condemnation" in the Greek is *katakrima* which means "punishment following condemnation, penal servitude, penalty, or the exact sentence of condemnation handed down after due process (establishing guilt)."

> It refers to a verdict of guilty and the penalty that verdict demands. No sin a believer can commit—past, present or future—can be held against him, since the entire penalty was paid by Christ and righteousness was imputed to the believer. And no sin will ever reverse this divine legal decision.[24]

It was all accomplished and done by Christ; He said, "It is finished." There is not, nor will there ever be any other judicial demand for justice in regards to any sin ever performed again; it has all been taken care of perfectly by Christ. Do we still need to repent and confess and ask for forgiveness? Absolutely! Though this does not offer us a free pass to "sin away" as we please intentionally without conscience, thinking, *Well, this one's covered too, what happens in Vegas stays in Vegas. I'm gonna do whatever I want.*

No! The term *confess* means to think the same thing about sin that God does; to acknowledge His perspective about sin. True confession of a true saved believer will bear a heart that desires to obey God and please Him out of sheer thankfulness and devotion to their Savior. Will we still stumble in the flesh and sin? Yes. Will we stumble and fail repeatedly and maybe even horribly? Yes. Will we be condemned for it? No. Should we strive to sin less? Absolutely! And with the Spirit dwelling inside of us we will feel the conviction for what we use to possibly never consider even being a bad behavior or action. Once we belong to Christ, if we accept His judicial payment for our sins and absolute failures, we will never have to worry about being condemned for any of it—past, present, future—ever again. He didn't pay the price of all of your sins, except for that one that will be committed on such and such a night a couple years from now, when you just couldn't take it anymore or resist some temptation, and you finally give in and indulge in whatever it is.

When Jesus finished His work and perfectly fulfilled His mission, every single person reading this book was a couple millennia away from even being born, so none of our sins had ever been committed yet. Christ's work was eternal from the fall of Adam in Genesis 3 to the time of Revelation 22. When we belong to Christ, we are secure forever! Also:

> [T]he Spirit, Who was mentioned only once in chapters 1–7 of Romans, is referred to nearly twenty times in chapter 8. He frees us from sin and death (8:2–3); enables us to fulfill God's law (v. 4); changes our nature and grants us strength for victory over our unredeemed flesh (vv. 5–13); confirms our adoption as God's children (vv. 14–16); and guarantees our ultimate glory (vv. 17–30). For the Spirit has replaced the law that produced only sin and death (7:5, 13) with a new, simple law that produces life: the law of faith (3:27), or the message of the Gospel.[25]

Christ's work justified us and redeemed us and placed us cleansed anew in front of the Father, and with that beautiful truth, the Spirit was also placed within us, and it is the Spirit that preserves us and matures us through sanctification during the rest of our time here in this flesh. We are seen as pure and holy and righteous in front of God because when He looks at us, He sees Christ, our Substitute, and the Spirit acts as our Guide on how to live in a godly fashion and also confirms our new life and eternal relationship with God. "Perseverance is that continuous operation of the Holy Spirit in the believer, by which the work of divine grace that is begun in the heart, is continued and brought to completion."[26]

We see further security through the Spirit in verse 11, which tells us, "If the Spirit of Him Who raised Jesus from the dead dwells in you, He Who raised Christ Jesus from the dead will also give life to your mortal bodies through His Spirit Who dwells in you." And also in verses 14–17:

> For all who are led by the Spirit of God are sons of God. For you did not receive the spirit of slavery to fall back into fear, but you have received the Spirit of adoption as sons, by Whom we cry, "Abba! Father!" The Spirit Himself bears witness with our spirit that we are children of God, and if children, then heirs—heirs of God and fellow-heirs with Christ, provided we suffer with Him in order that we may also be glorified with Him.

We looked at these same verses in the last chapter, but this is so key I think it justifies repeating. As children of God, His Spirit dwells in us and assures us of our adoption as children of God and that as His children, we become heirs of God and co-heirs with Christ! That is overwhelmingly mind blowing! Just as Ephesians 1:3 says, your inheritance consists of "every spiritual blessing" in Heaven. Everything that Christ has inherited for His perfect life and sacrifice as Son of God and Savior, we will also receive!

> God has appointed His Son to be Heir of all things (Heb. 1:2). Every adopted child will receive by divine grace the full inheritance Christ receives by divine right (cf. John 17:22; 2 Cor. 8:9). We cannot even begin to imagine what vs. 17 fully means. "What no eye has seen, nor ear heard, nor the heart of man imagined, what God has prepared for those who love Him" (1 Cor. 2:9).[27]

Moving into verse 26, until the end of the chapter, we come across one of the most phenomenal stretches of Scripture, much like chapter 17 of John on this topic. You could maybe say that John 17 is Christ's verification of our security, perseverance, or preservation, and Romans 8 would be the Holy Spirit's verification of our security, perseverance, or preservation. "Likewise, the Spirit helps us in our weakness. For we do not know what to pray for as we ought, but the Spirit Himself intercedes for us with groanings too deep for words. And He Who searches hearts knows what is the mind of the Spirit, because the Spirit intercedes for the saints according to the will of God."

When we become children of God, we are indwelt with the Holy Spirit. We become His temple (1 Cor. 6:19). Positionally, we are made perfect in Christ by His finished work, and we are perfected in our practice through the indwelling work of the Holy Spirit Who resides in us. This is the ongoing lifelong process of the sanctification of our flesh that will reach its final complete perfection when Christ comes and brings us to Heaven, and we will then be glorified, evacuated from this sinful fallen body and deposited into our new glorified body. But once we have been justified and redeemed in our spirit and made holy and perfect positionally in Christ, then it is the Spirit's work being done in our flesh.

He guides us and matures us and strengthens us to grow and live in a more Christlike image. He helps us with all of our weaknesses, intercedes for us, and even prays for us when we don't even know what to pray for or how to pray. The Spirit, just as like Christ, is of one mind with the Father, and, therefore, They communicate in perfect and holy unity and share the same will for His children. Just as Christ prayed for us in John 17, the Spirit would similarly pray for us in our moments of weakness, failure, ignorance, incompetence, negligence, imperfection, and inability. They both pray for and intercede for the eternal welfare of all of God's children (27, 34).

One other thing on this verse, there are some that believe that "groanings too deep for words" means speaking in tongues. This is plainly not true as it specifically says, "Too deep for words." This is not speaking in tongues; it is spiritual conversation between the Spirit and the Father. John MacArthur adds this in talking about speaking in tongues (but this statement is true for other issues as well). "Many charismatics have been taught to think of speaking in tongues as verification of their salvation. It's an assurance-giving experience that validates the reality of their conversion. As I've said before, that's not faith: that's doubt looking for proof. The foundation of a Christian's assurance of salvation is objective (faith in the Gospel of Christ), not subjective (faith in experience)."

Verse 28 is a beautiful verse of provision and security. "For we know that all things work for the good of those who love Him, who are called according to His purpose." First of all, we see that this makes mention back to the issue of God's sovereign election in that all who are called. The Greek word used here is the same word we have looked at in earlier chapters, *kletos*, which means "divinely selected and appointed." This is speaking of God's effectual call to all of His elect, leading to salvation. Just as in John 6, we saw that all of those whom the Father gives to the Son will come to Him and that He will cast none of them away, and in John 17, all of those whom the Father gave to the Son were given eternal life, were guarded and kept secure, and that not one of them was lost, except Judas to fulfill prophecy; we see here that every single one of those that God has called to Himself, has and can rest in the assurance of the fact that God is orchestrating every single thing in his or her life, which does necessarily include even temptation, persecution, suffering, and sin for his or her own eternal welfare. And this would of course include our security to the end and our accession into His Heavenly Kingdom.

Also, the word used here for "purpose" in the Greek is *prothesin*, which means "a setting forth, the showbread, predetermination, purpose."

"One puts forth his purpose first, then acts. God put forth the shewbread daily to demonstrate His purpose; He would provide daily bread."[28]

It symbolizes God's providence and protective care. In any sense, you can rest assured that God's complete and holy purpose will be perfectly fulfilled. And for that, may I refer you back to John 17:24 where Jesus prayed, "Father, I desire that they also, whom You have given Me, may be with Me where I Am, to see My glory that You have given Me because You loved Me before the foundation of the world." So when we pair these two passages together, we see Jesus's desire that all of those whom the Father has given to Him would be brought to Him to eternally dwell with Him in His majestic glory, and that God Himself is the One Who works all things in order to bring about His purpose and good desires for all of those who are called and chosen to be His!

The next two verses, we have kind of already looked at in the last chapter, but we will look at deeper here as they are two of the most full and complete passages on God's overall sovereign grace and our perseverance and security in Him.

> For those whom He foreknew He also pre-
> destined to be conformed to the image of His
> Son, in order that He may be the firstborn among
> many brothers. And those whom He predestined
> He also called, and those whom He called He
> also justified, and those whom He justified He
> also glorified.

First of all, this passage starts in pre-eternity. God's foreknowledge of us predates Genesis 1:1. It predates the foundations of the earth (Eph. 1:4–5; 1 Pet. 1:2). Predestination also predates "In the beginning." The combination of these two terms, foreknowledge and predestination, means that before God created any part of the physical universe, He sovereignly predetermined to place His love upon His elected in order to initiate an intimate relationship with them. He didn't just simply predict the future and look ahead to see who would say yes, He lovingly determined beforehand those whom He chose.

We also see that God not only predestined us, but He did so in order for us to be conformed into the holy and perfect image of His righteous and glorious Son. He didn't elect us so that we might barely squeak by and be someone who passes their salvation test with a D minus. If it depended on us, we would all fail miserably with a flat 0 percent, neither would we receive any merit for extra credit. If you break even one law, you've broken them all (Jas. 2:10). So it doesn't depend on us, and God never does shoddy work. His predetermined purpose for us was to make us into the image of His Son. A solid 100 percent.

Obviously, we all have a long ways to go, but Christ will sanctify us through the work of the Holy Spirit (1 Cor. 3:6–7, 6:11; Phil. 1:6, 3:20–21; 1 Thess. 5:23–24; 2 Thess. 2:13–14; Heb. 12:2), and in Him, we will become the righteousness of God (2 Cor. 5:21); and once He comes to bring us Home, we will see Him as He is in all of His righteous glory, for we shall be like Him (1 John 3:2); we will become perfectly glorified as He is (Rom. 8:30). We will become co-heirs with Jesus and receive the full inheritance that He has received (Rom. 8:17; Eph. 1:3).

We then also see that whomever God foreknows and predestines, He will also call unto Himself to become His. This again speaks of an effectual call leading to salvation. And all that are called God Himself will justify and make righteous and holy through the sacrifice of His Son (cf. John 6:37–40, 17:6, 11–12; Rom. 8:1; 2 Cor. 5:21). And because God never does anything imperfect or incompletely, all those whom He has justified and made perfect through the substitution of Christ will also be glorified by God Himself. No one is lost along this process.

From all the way back to pre-eternity, before the foundations of the earth, before Genesis 1:1, before "Let there be light," all the way to final glory in the image of Christ when we enter the Kingdom of Heaven, our eternal Home, God perfectly orchestrates and perfectly executes the salvation of His elect through His perfect grace and redemptive plan. We do not nor can we offer Him any assistance in this. It is all the work of God. Christ victoriously pained the words, "It is finished." He perfectly and completely fulfilled the necessary demands of the law for us and reconciled us to God while we were still dead sinners and enemies of God (Rom. 5:6, 8, 10; Eph. 2:5).

And I want to address one more major point here. Look at the very last word of verse 30—*glorified*. "Those whom He justified He also **glorified**." That is a past tense verb. Even when Paul was writing in the Greek, he purposefully used a past tense verb. To be specific, he used the aorist tense of the verb, which is *edoxasen*. The significance of this diction with the aorist tense verb is that it refers to a simple occurrence in the past with no emphasis on the action's progress, and it stresses that the future event of a believer's glorification is so certain and guaranteed that Paul references it as if it is a past and already-having-occurred and has-been-completed event. It symbolizes that a believer's security is so certain, eternally secure, and can never be lost. All that belong to God, none will be lost (John 6, 10, 17).

The next verse is an interesting one too when you dig into the original Greek. Verse 31 in the English reads like this in the ESV, "What then shall we say to these things? If God is for us, who can be against us?" We will get into the answer to that question in just a second, but here I want to look again at the very specific and telling diction Paul used in the original Greek. We will be focusing on the second question asked in this verse. In the first half of it, "If God is for us," is a conditional statement that obviously as we see in context, Paul saw as a valid and factual truth, not a question of "whether or not." The word *if* in the Greek is *ei* which is a conjunction which means just that—"if." The word used for "for" in the Greek is *huper* and means "on behalf of, for the sake of."

Though Paul's diction in this passage may lead some to misunderstand and question whether or not God is for us because of the English connotation of the word, Paul is not using this word, *if*, as if he was offering that there was a possibility that God is not for or with or considerate of those who belong to Him. Paul just got done speaking of all those whom God foreknew from pre-eternity, justified and glorified, so Paul is speaking about those who are saved in Christ, and as the rest of the context shows, Paul is absolutely confident that God is "for" all of those who belong to Him.

Even though some Greek scholars will tell you not to use the Greek word, *ei*, in this way: others disagree and say it would be better understood and translated in this context as saying "*since* God is for us." Just don't make a habit out of turning all your "ifs" into "sinces" in your Bible because there are many occasions where it certainly would cause turmoil in the meanings. But here, because it is backed by the context, you could cautiously do so to assist in the under-standing of the statement and alleviate an incorrect understanding that "maybe God is not with us (believers)," seeing as the English "if" kind of leaves that possibility open.

Enough of that. Now, taking a look at this whole question, "If God is for us, who can be against us?" and looking at it in the Greek, we see something peculiar in the phrasing. In the original text—and if you don't speak fluent Greek, you can check this out in any good Interlinear Bible—Paul did not use verbs in this question. "Is" and "can be" are imposed into the English text to make it more under-standable and flow better. All that we are left with are nouns and pronouns, conjunctions and prepositions. There was no verbiage used. The significance to this is that verbs distinguish time. With no verbiage, there is no time distinction. So in the original Greek, it is worded, "If God for us, who against us?"

When we become God's, He is always for us—past, present, future—we are secure in Him eternally with no time distinguish-ment, and no one can ever separate us from Him (John 10:28–29; Rom. 8:38–39). To get a deeper and fuller understanding of this verse, you could then state it like this: "Since God is eternally for us, who could possibly ever come against us?"

Paul answers that question by continuing this line of rhetorical questioning in verse 32ff.

> He Who did not spare His Own Son but gave Him up for us all, how will He not also with Him graciously give us all things? Who shall bring any charge against God's elect? It is God Who justifies. Who is to condemn? Christ Jesus is the One Who died—more than that, Who was raised—Who is at the right hand of God, Who indeed is interceding for us.

First of all, the Greek adds the word, *ge*, which means "truly, indeed, assuredly," to the first word in the first of these questions, so it should read, "He Who *truly* did not spare His Own Son." Also, the phrase "graciously give," in the Greek is *charisetai*, which means "freely and graciously give favor to grant forgiveness or pardon." Anyways, starting with the last question posed in verse 31 and the questions and phrases in these verses, Paul is making the point that if God went as far as to sacrifice the life of His Own perfect and innocent, holy, and righteous Son which is the ultimate demonstration of love (John 15:13), in order to make atonement for sin for all of His elect, how would He not also give us all lesser blessings with it. Through the sacrifice of Christ and God's gracious gift to His children, we have been given new life and everything that comes with it.

As we have recently looked at, God desires to give us "every spiritual blessing" (Eph. 1:3), and has given us all things in Christ through His amazing grace as a gift (Rom. 5:15–17, 6:23). He then makes the point that there is no one who could bring a single charge against us, for it is God Who justified us (Rom. 3:24, 8:30), and whatever God does, He does perfectly. So if He has made us perfectly holy and righteous, through Christ, and He no longer sees a single flaw in us but that of the perfect image of His Son, then what is there that anyone else could possibly bring up against us? And besides that, even if they were to bring up some flaw or sin, they are not the ones that condemn or enforce justice.

God alone is the Judge, and it is Christ Who suffered and defeated death through resurrection, condemning sin and death, reconciling us to God, and Who is sitting now at the throne of God, at His right hand, and Whose role now is to be our Intercessor before God (Heb. 7:25; 1 John 2:1), assuring us and guaranteeing us of full acquittal of anything that might be brought against us. He graciously paid the entire price for it all, so there is nothing that can be brought against His elect forevermore!

The next group of verses, 35–39, are some of the most identifying of this aspect of grace of our security:

> Who shall separate us from the love of Christ? Shall tribulation, or distress, or persecution, or famine, or nakedness, or danger, or sword? As it is written, "For your sake we are

being killed all the day long; we are regarded as
sheep to be slaughtered." No, in all these things
we are more than conquerors through Him Who
loved us. For I am sure that neither death nor
life, nor angels nor rulers, nor things present
nor things to come, nor powers, nor height nor
depth, nor anything else in all creation, will be
able to separate us from the love of God in Christ
Jesus our Lord.

Kind of mirroring several of the questions he has already asked,
Paul, in closing, is essentially asking who or what is there that could
possibly separate us eternally from the love of Christ and is posing
the absurdity of such a possibility (cf. John 10:28–30). Jesus Christ
died for the sins of the whole world out of His love for all mankind.
However, that does not mean that all of mankind will be saved. This
is not universalism thinking. God loves all mankind, but only those
whom He has called and elected, those whom He has given to the
Son, will come to Him and be saved. All whom God has chosen will
come to Him, all those whom come to Him will be saved, all that
the Father gives to the Son will be saved, but no one can come to
Him unless the Father draws them to Him (John 6:35–40, 44–48,
10:28–30, 15:5, 16, all of 17).

These are again both sides of the paradox we discussed in chapter 5. "God loves the world, including sinners (John 3:16, Matt.
5:44–45) with compassion and common grace, but He loves His
Own with perfect, saving, eternal love (John 13:1)."[29]

But here in Romans 8:35, 37, and 39, Paul is referring to His
"love for us (John 13:1), specifically here as He demonstrated it in
salvation (1 John 4:9–10)."[30]Once again, here in this context, Paul is
talking about all of those who are without condemnation in Christ
Jesus (8:1), who are indwelt with the Spirit (11, 14–15), who are
adopted as sons of God and are co-heirs with Christ (15–17), who are
called according to God's purpose (28), whom God has foreknown,
predestined, called, justified, and glorified (29–30), who have been
given all things (32), who are His elect (33), who are held secure by

the intercessory work of the Holy Spirit and of Christ (26–27, 34), and who are more than conquerors (the Greek means "over-conquer or to conquer completely") in Christ Who loves us (37).

Paul then lists seventeen different scenarios or possible sources that may cause separation from God; all the way from bodily necessities, harm, danger and persecution, even leading to death, even demonic activity, and climaxes with the comprehensive statement of "anything else in all of creation." I think that pretty much covers it! The Greek word for "all" is *pas*, which means "all, every, the whole," and includes absolutely everything. "Nothing in life's path, from beginning to end (29–30), can separate us (His elect [v. 33] and adopted sons [v. 15]) from Christ's love (35, 38–39). All of creation covers everything but the Creator Himself,"[31] and as we saw several times back in the Gospel of John, Jesus will not lose a single one of them! All of creation also includes yourself. Yes, we have free will, but no one who is truly saved and devoted to Christ will ever walk away from Him. Refer back to the section of this chapter covering Jeremiah 32:40 and John 10.

Just a few verses later, into chapter 9, we read in verse 3, "For I could wish that I myself were accursed and cut off from Christ for the sake of my brothers." First of all, this is such a beautiful picture of the love that Paul had for the church. The Greek word for "accursed" is *anathema* which means "to devote to destruction in eternal hell." That is an agape, sacrificial godly type of love, to be willing to give one's own salvation for the sake of others, and that is what Paul is referring to here. And even though "Paul understood the exchange he was suggesting was impossible (Rom. 8:38–39; John 10:28), it was still the sincere expression of his deep love for his fellow Jews" (cf. Exo 32:32).[32] To really get the full intent of this verse, we again will look deeper into the Greek diction. The verb used for "could wish" is *euchomen* and the significance of this verb is that it is in the imperfect tense and is in what's called the optative mood, which is rarely used in the New Testament.[33]

The optative mood of a verb is expressive of a wish that implies a contrary-to-the-fact subjunctive, something you wish but know is impossible. The grammar implies it is an absolute impossibility. It is thus another absolute testimony and reference to eternal security!

Paul was under no illusions that *he* could be that redemptive sacrifice. *IF* such had been possible, he was *willing*. But, it was *not* possible. Dr. Kenneth Wuest, in his *Word Studies from the Greek NT*, states, "Paul uses the optative mood in the imperfect tense" when he says, "for **I could wish** that I myself were anathema" (Rom. 9:3).

The *optative* mood is the standard Greek mood employed for expressing a *wish* or *desire*. Wuest then goes on to quote the great Greek scholar, Dr. Alford, who says, "The imperfect is not historical, but quasi-optative, as in 'I was wishing *had it been possible*.' This sense of the imperfect in such expressions is the proper and strict one" (Wuest, *Romans in the Greek NT*, p. 152).

Wuest also quotes the Greek scholar Dr. Vincent who says:

The imperfect here has a tentative force, implying the wish begun, but stopped at the outset by some antecedent consideration which renders it impossible, so that, practically, it was not entertained at all (*Ibid*). The phrase "I could wish" faithfully brings out the idiomatic construction used here for stating an impossible wish. Paul could not actually become anathema (Greek word meaning "to devote to destruction in eternal hell") from Christ (Romans 8 proclaims the impossibility of that). Yet, if it *were* possible, he would gladly make the sacrifice" (*The Expositor's Bible Commentary*, vol. 10, p. 102).

"Imperfects of this kind imply a wish to do a thing *if it were possible or allowable*" (William

Shedd, *A Critical and Doctrinal Commentary on
the Epistle of St. Paul to the Romans*, p. 273)."[34]

Paul is acknowledging that it is impossible for himself to even
willingly give up or walk away from his salvation if he chose to. He
spent all of chapter 8 of Romans hammering away at the fact that
one cannot lose their salvation, and here he is, acknowledging that he
couldn't willfully give it up himself either. This is yet another point
to those who think that one can lose their salvation by walking away
from it with regard to free will. Paul was expressing his will to give his
up for the sake of the church but knew that it was an impossibility,
not just that it could not be transferred to someone else's account but
that he himself could not lose his or willfully give it up either.

Moving into chapter 11, we see another key aspect of this topic.
Starting in verse 28, we read, "As regards the Gospel, they are enemies of God for your sake. But as regards election, they are beloved
for the sake of their forefathers. For the gifts and the calling of God
are irrevocable."

> God's sovereign election of Israel, like
> that of individual believers, is unconditional
> and unchangeable, because it is rooted in His
> immutable nature and expressed in the unilateral
> and eternal Abrahamic Covenant, in which God
> promised to accomplish something based on
> His Own character and not on the response or
> actions of the promised beneficiary.[35]

Even when God made His covenant with Abraham, He made it
alone, by Himself (cf. Gen. 22:17–18; Heb. 6:13). Making an oath
back in the time of Genesis incorporated kind of a strange ritual or
practice. As we saw, the two involved parties would split an animal in
half and separate the two pieces on the ground, then they would each
pass through the middle of them in order to signify the promise of
the oath or covenant being made. When God made this Abrahamic
Covenant with Abraham, however (Gen. 15), He put Abraham into

a deep sleep and passed through the two pieces by Himself, signifying that it did not depend on Abraham's or any of his future generations, involvement, but it depended only on the involvement of God Himself. It was an unconditional covenant sworn by God alone (cf. Heb. 6:13).

Our election and security is irrevocable because it does not depend on us whatsoever, and God Himself is unchanging (Num. 23:19; Ps. 33:11, 102:25–27; Isa. 46:10; Mal. 3:6; Heb. 6:17, 13:8; Jas. 1:17). Your justification cannot be revoked once it is claimed. When you are made new in Christ, you become One with Him, and you are seen as holy and righteous as He is in the eyes of God, and therefore, as long as Christ never changes (Heb. 13:8), neither will you. You become a part of Him, and He becomes a part of you. You have been clothed with Christ (Gal. 3:27), you have been born again with "imperishable seed" (1 Pet. 1:23), and the Holy Spirit lives within you (2 Tim. 1:14), so if you were to "lose" your salvation, in full essence, God would be "losing" a part of Himself! Doesn't that show how ludicrous that teaching is?

Continuing into verse 32ff, we read:

> For God has consigned all to disobedience, that He may have mercy on all. Oh, the depth of the riches and wisdom and knowledge of God! How unsearchable are His judgements and how inscrutable His ways! "For who has known the mind of the Lord, or who has been His counselor?"
>
> "Or who has given a gift to Him that he might be repaid?' For from Him and through Him and to Him are all things. To Him be glory forever. Amen."

Now some that are weak in their faith or are without faith and relationship in Christ may see the first part of this as rather evil and sinister, "For God has consigned all to disobedience," but this does not mean that God is the author of that sin and disobedience (Ps.

5:4; Hab. 1:13; Jas. 1:13), but that "God allowed man to pursue his sinful inclinations so that He could receive glory by demonstrating His grace and mercy to disobedient sinners."[36]

God created us with free will, and sadly, that free will led to sin through pride and rebellion, and God allowed us to continue in our free will of our now sinful nature so that we do not become mindless robots forced to comply and so that He could demonstrate His grace and mercy in sending us a Savior in His Son, our only hope, so that He alone would be able to receive all the glory. And besides, who are we to question God's ways (Rom. 9:20–21) as His mind, wisdom, judgments, and ways are so far beyond our feeble ability at comprehension of the Almighty Creator of the universe? "For from Him and through Him and to Him are all things."

"God is the source, the sustainer, and the rightful end of everything that exists."[37]

In the beginning of Paul's first letter to the Corinthians, we see him opening up with a greeting and then a bit of thanksgiving to the church in Corinth, starting in verse 4:

> I give thanks to my God always for you because of the grace of God that was given to you in Christ Jesus, that in every way you were enriched in Him in all speech and all knowledge—even as the testimony about Christ was confirmed among you—so that you are not lacking in any spiritual gift, as you wait for the revealing of our Lord Jesus Christ, Who will sustain you to the end, guiltless in the day of our Lord Jesus Christ. God is faithful, by Whom you were called into the fellowship of His Son, Jesus Christ our Lord.

First of all, we see that it is because of the grace of God that they were given every spiritual gift, including the testimony and knowledge of Christ (cf. Matt. 16:17). We also then see—and hear this intently; it is a gorgeous truth—that it is Jesus Christ Himself that sustains us and securely holds us guiltless, holy, righteous, true, and fully justified all the way until the very end! Does this not mirror John chapters 6, 10, and 17? Jesus will sustain us! Jesus will hold us secure! Jesus prays for us! He paid our price and made us brand-new and perfect in His image! Jesus will bring us flawless and guiltless and innocent to the end! Jesus guards us and protects us and will not ever lose a single one! Not one! Not ever!

"I will never cast them out!"

"No one can snatch them out of My hand!"

"No one can snatch them out of My Father's hand!"

"I have lost not one!"

"I have guarded them!"

"Father, I ask that You keep them from the evil one!"

"I desire that they will be One with Us, and that they may be with Me where I Am!"

If you truly become a child of God, if you belong to Christ, then you are never getting away from Him! And don't misunderstand this, that is a beautiful thing! That is not a negative of some form of inability to invoke free will. To say that you can freely leave the presence and salvation of God by the means of free will is to not understand the depth of relationship we have with Him. Anyone who is truly saved is given knowledge of Who God is.

We read in Ephesians 1:17–21:

> The God of our Lord Jesus Christ, the Father of Glory, may give you a Spirit of wisdom and of revelation in the knowledge of Him, having the eyes of your hearts enlightened, that you may know what is the hope to which He has called you, what are the riches of His glorious inheritance in the saints, and what is the immeasurable greatness of His power toward us who believe, according to the working of His great might that He worked in Christ when He raised Him from the dead and seated Him at His right hand in the Heavenly places, far above all rule and authority and power and dominion, and above

every name that is named, not only in this age but
also in the one to come.

You still possess the potential of free will, but a truly saved person understands Who God is and the relationship possessed and will never leave. They will persevere. If anyone were to seemingly "walk away," it is not that they lost or gave up their salvation, it is most likely that they were never truly saved to begin with (1 John 2:19) or that possibly they are saved but backsliding, and God will draw him or her back in His divine timeline.

Moving into chapter 3 of Paul's first letter, we receive a very revealing teaching from him with this topic and in regards to works. Starting in verse 11:

> For no one can lay a foundation other than
> that which is laid, which is Jesus Christ. Now if
> anyone builds on the foundation with gold, silver, precious stones, wood, hay, straw—each one's
> work will become manifest, for the Day will disclose it, because it will be revealed by fire, and the
> fire will test what sort of work each one has done.
> If the work that anyone has built on the foundation survives, he will receive a reward. If anyone's
> work is burned up, he will suffer loss, though he
> himself, will be saved, but only as through fire.

As we have already seen, and as we will dig much deeper into during the next two chapters, works are not a prerequisite causing salvation but will inevitably be produced as a product of salvation (Eph. 2:10), and this passage is so telling regarding the relationship between the two, and more importantly, of our security in salvation.

> Two kinds of Christians are portrayed here.
> The first man who steps up to be evaluated represents those who have made real contributions
> to God's Kingdom during their earthly lives. His

works are described as "gold, silver, [and] precious stones." They are of such quality that they
survive the intense examination of the Savior.
Consequently, this man is rewarded for his faithfulness. Then the second man steps up. He represents believers who have no time for the things
of Christ, who live their lives for themselves. One
by one his deeds are evaluated, and one by one
they burn. His works are described as "wood, hay,
[and] straw." His works have no real substance, no
eternal value. When the smoke clears, he is faced
with the reality that in God's estimation, nothing he has lived for has counted. He has spent his
entire life pursuing things. His earthly success has
focused on those things that are perishable, temporary. Paul says this man will suffer loss. That is,
he will have nothing to show for his life; he will
have lost everything. But Paul concludes "but he
himself will be saved!" This passage is so powerful
because we are presented with a Christian who at
no point in his life bore any eternal fruit. And yet
his salvation is never jeopardized. There is never
a question about where he will spend eternity.[38]

Upon salvation, every believer is reborn with a new heart of flesh
(Ezek. 11:19, 36:26) and a desire to obey God (cf. Jer. 31:33, 32:40)
and the ability to produce good fruit/works for God (John 15:5, 8; Eph.
2:10). All of this is impossible (Isa. 64:6; cf. Phil. 3:5–8) until brought
to life in Christ and being filled with the Holy Spirit. Every believer will
inevitably undergo change because the Holy Spirit now lives in them!
Paradoxically, we still do possess free will, and we do have to make
the right choices in life as the Spirit leads us, grows us, and teaches us,
and as a result, our works could have lasting eternal effects or could be
essentially or even completely worthless for the eternal Kingdom.

This passage shows us the extreme outlook that even if absolutely every single one of a person's works, if everything that person

had accomplished over the course of his or her life was found to be burned up in the fire, and they were left with a big fat zero to show for their servitude to God and the Kingdom, their entrance into the Kingdom is still secure, though they may receive nothing else in reward. That is, only if the person has truly believed in and surrendered their heart to Jesus Christ as Lord and Savior.

Toward the beginning of his second letter to the Corinthians, in verses 21–22, we read, "And it is God Who establishes us with you in Christ, and has anointed us, and Who has also put His seal on us and given us His Spirit in our hearts as a guarantee."

> "Anointed" means the Holy Spirit sets apart believers and empowers them for the service of Gospel proclamation and ministry. "Put His seal on us" refers to the ancient practice of placing soft wax on a document and imprinting the wax with a stamp that indicated authorship or ownership, authenticity, and protection. The Holy Spirit attaches all these meanings to His act of spiritually sealing believers. "Guarantee" means a pledge or down payment. The Spirit is the down payment on the believer's eternal inheritance.[39]

The Greek word for "guarantee" is *arrabon*. It refers to "a large part of the payment, given in advance as a security or a pledge that the whole will be paid afterward."[40] We are set aside to minister and proclaim the Gospel of Christ and are sealed, secured, and protected with the Holy Spirit Who is our proof and guarantee that we belong to God and will be brought fully into glory.

A little bit later in chapter 5, verse 17, we are told, "Therefore, if anyone is in Christ, he is a new creation. The old has passed away; behold, the new has come."

> The two words, "In Christ," comprise a brief but profound statement of inexhaustible significance of the believer's redemption, which

includes: (1) the believer's security in Christ, Who bore in His body God's judgment against sin; (2) the believer's acceptance in Him with Whom God alone is well pleased; (3) the believer's future assurance in Him Who is the resurrection to eternal life and the sole Guarantor of the believer's inheritance in Heaven; and (4) the believer's participation in the divine nature of Christ, the everlasting Word.

"New creation" describes something that is created at a qualitatively new level of excellence. It refers to regeneration or the new birth (cf. John 3:3; Eph. 2:1–3; Ti. 3:5; 1 Pet. 1:23; 1 John 2:29, 3:9, 5:4). This expression encompasses the Christian's forgiveness of sins paid for in Christ's substitutionary death (cf. 2 Cor. 5:21; Eph. 4:24). After a person is regenerate, old value systems, priorities, beliefs, loves, and plans are gone. Evil and sin are still present, but the believer sees them in a new perspective, and they no longer control him. The Greek grammar indicates that this newness is a continuing condition of fact. The believer's new spiritual perception of everything is a constant reality for him, and he now lives for eternity, not temporal things. James identifies this transformation as the faith that produces works (cf. Eph. 2:10; Jas. 2:14–25).[41]

Moving into Paul's epistle to the Ephesians, we have already touched on several topics and aspects of God's grace within the first several verses, but here we will look at this aspect of security, starting in verse 11:

In Him, we have obtained an inheritance, having been predestined according to the purpose of Him Who works all things according to

the council of His will, so that we who were the
first to hope in Christ might be to the praise of
His glory.

We again see that God has predestined us from before the foundations of the world to be His children, simply because of His Own
will to do so, but we also see here that because of our relationship
with Him, that we have already obtained an inheritance as His children all for the praise of His glory! The emphasis here is that we
"have obtained" an inheritance. The verb is again an aorist tense verb
which is a simple past tense verb. Our inheritance is so certain and
secure because it rests in Christ that it is referred to here as already
having been received! It is guaranteed! You can bet your life on it!
Literally!

Our Heavenly and eternal and infinite inheritance is waiting
for us, and we will receive it, and there will be none left unspoken
for because someone lost their salvation. Every single person that the
Father gives to the Son will come to Him, and every single one of
them that come to Him will never be cast out (John 6:37), and He
will not lose one of them (John 17:12) because no one can snatch
them out of His hands (John 10:28). Our inheritance and security
are infinitely secure because it rests on Christ. And it is all done
according to the council of His will for His purpose. He decided and
He acted and He completed it.

Continuing on into verse 13:

In Him you also, when you heard the
Word of Truth, the Gospel of your salvation,
and believed in Him, were sealed with the Holy
Spirit, Who is the guarantee of our inheritance
until we acquire possession of it, to the praise of
His glory.

Our salvation and our inheritance are secure and guaranteed in
Christ as the Spirit becomes our guarantee and acts as the evidence
of this beautiful fact. And again, this is all done for the praise of His

glory. Every single aspect of this, from beginning to end, from His foreknowledge, predestination, His election and calling of us, His grace in the gift of our faith, our perseverance and security until the end and our final glorification is all done by Him, for Him, and through Him so that He alone may be praised and receive ALL the glory! We do need to believe in Him and accept His free gift and surrender to Him, but even our faith in Him is a free gift from Him (Eph. 2:8–9); that again is the paradox we discussed in chapter 5, but all is done "to the praise of His glory!"

> God's Own Spirit comes to indwell the believer and secures and seals and preserves the believers eternal salvation. Four primary truths are signified by the seal: (1) security (cf. Dan. 6:17; Matt. 27:62–66); (2) authenticity (cf. 1 Kings 21:6–16); (3) ownership (cf. Jer. 32:10); and (4) authority (cf. Est. 8:8–12). The Holy Spirit is given by God as His pledge of the believer's future inheritance in glory (cf. 2 Cor. 1:21–22).[42]

We also see this mentioned in chapter 4 verse 30. "And do not grieve the Holy Spirit of God, by Whom you were sealed for the day of redemption."

In Paul's letter to the Colossians, we see an extension of this also. Starting in verse 11:

> May you be strengthened with all power, according to His glorious might, for all endurance and patience with joy, giving thanks to the Father Who has qualified you to share in the inheritance of the saints in light. He has delivered us from the domain of darkness and transferred us to the Kingdom of His beloved Son, in Whom we have redemption, the forgiveness of sins.

It is God Himself and God alone that has qualified us as worthy to receive our share of the eternal and infinite and imperishable inheritance (1 Pet. 1:4), the same one Christ has received (Rom. 8:17) that is guaranteed to us and so certain that it is referred to as having already been obtained (Eph. 1:11, 14). It is also God Himself and God alone that has delivered us from darkness, delivered us from sin, delivered us from death, delivered us from this world, and adopted us as His sons (Rom. 8:15) and transferred us to the Heavenly Kingdom of His Son, Jesus, Whose perfect finished work has redeemed us and made us new, perfect, holy, and righteous in Him and given us the entirety of endurance and patience in order that we will persevere until the end in full joy. We are in Christ, and He is in us, so there is no way that we would or could ever, even by our own will, be lost once we have been redeemed, forgiven, and made His and transferred to His Kingdom.

Just a few verses later, in the first chapter of Paul's same letter, we find a verse that some have misunderstood, which has distracted them from the truth. Starting in verse 21, we read:

> And you, who once were alienated and hostile in mind, doing evil deeds, He has now reconciled in His body of flesh by His death, in order to present you holy and blameless and above reproach before Him, if indeed you continue in faith, stable and steadfast, not shifting from the hope of the Gospel that you heard, which has been claimed in all creation under Heaven, and of which I, Paul, became a minister.

The phrase that has caused some to question this issue of security and perseverance is "if indeed you continue in faith." There are also similar phrases found in Acts 11:23 and 14:22. On the surface, it may seem like security may be lost if perseverance is not upheld, and that would actually be entirely true if things were left up to us, but:

> [T]hose who have been reconciled will persevere in faith and obedience because, in addi-

tion to being declared righteous, they are actually made new creatures (2 Cor. 5:17) with a new disposition that loves God, hates sin, desires obedience, and is energized by the indwelling Holy Spirit (cf. John 8:30–32; 1 John 2:19). Rather than defect from the Gospel they heard, true believers will remain solid on Christ, Who is the only foundation (1 Cor. 3:11), and faithful by the enabling grace of God (Phil. 1:6, 2:11–13). The ones that persevere are the same ones who are saved. This does not suggest that our perseverance secures our salvation. Scripture everywhere teaches precisely the opposite: God, as part of His saving work, secures our perseverance. True believers "are being guarded through faith for a salvation" (1 Pet. 1:5).

The guarantee of our perseverance is built in to the New Covenant promise. God says: "I will put the fear of Me in their hearts, that they may not turn from Me" (Jer. 32:40). Those who do fall away from Christ give conclusive proof that they were never truly believers to begin with (1 John 2:19). To say that God secures our perseverance is not to say that we are passive in the process, however. He keeps us "through faith" (1 Pet. 1:5)—our faith.

Scripture sometimes calls us to hold fast to our faith (Heb. 10:23; Rev. 3:11) or warns us against falling away (Heb. 10:26–29). Such admonitions do not negate the many promises that true believers will persevere (John 10:28–29; Rom. 8:38–39; 1 Cor. 1:8–9; Phil. 1:6). Rather, the warnings and pleas are among the means God uses to secure our perseverance in the faith. Notice that the warnings and promises often appear side by side. For example, when Jude urges believers "keep yourselves in the love of God" (Jude 21), he immediately points them to God "Who is able to keep you from stumbling" (Jude 24). This endurance does not produce salvation; it is Spirit-empowered perseverance and proof of the reality of salvation in the One Who endures.[43]

Those who are truly saved will endure and persevere to the end because they are truly saved and belong to God.

Moving into Paul's first letter to the Thessalonians, we come across a very straightforward passage in verses 23–24 of chapter 5.

> Now may the God of peace Himself sanctify you completely, and may your whole spirit and soul and body be preserved complete without blame at the coming of our Lord Jesus Christ. He Who calls you is faithful; He will surely do it.

We looked at the aspect of sanctification quite a bit in the last chapter, and here in this verse, it plainly shows us that it is God Himself and God alone that sanctifies us, and He does so completely! We are also wholly and completely preserved until the coming of Christ without blame, righteous and spotless. It is God Himself that does this and secures this through Christ our perfectly holy and righteous Savior, and "He will surely do it!" It is only God alone that can separate us blamelessly from sin and sanctify us completely and secure us until the end in holiness, and He will surely do it!

The Amplified Translation translates verse 24 from the Greek like this, "Faithful and absolutely trustworthy is He Who is calling you [to Himself for your salvation], and He will do it [He will fulfill His calling by making you holy, guarding you, watching over you, and protecting you as His Own]." We, in and of ourselves, are completely powerless to perform this or even to help in this process (Rom. 5:8, 10; Eph. 2:5; Phil. 1:6; Heb. 12:2).

We see Paul follow this up in his second letter to the Thessalonians in verse 3 of chapter 3. "But the Lord is faithful. He will establish you and guard you against the evil one." This verse mirrors some other very strong passages in regards to God's protection of us against the forces and powers of evil. In John 17:15, we already saw that Jesus prayed to His Father, "I do not ask that You keep them out of the world, but that You keep them from the evil one."

We also read in 1 Corinthians 10:13:

> No temptation has overtaken you that is not common to man. God is faithful, and He will not let you be tempted beyond your ability, but with the temptation He will provide the way of escape, that you may be able to endure it.

God will not let His children fall and fail completely or finally. We will be tempted and we will stumble now and then in the flesh, but God will protect us from the evil one and protect us against a final and condemning end. He is faithful and will keep us and guard us against evil and provide us with the way of escape. He will not allow His Own children to be lost (John 17:12). He provides us with the way to persevere to the end.

This same topic of God guarding His Own is also made in Paul's second letter to his protégé, Timothy, in chapter 1, verse 12. "I know Whom I have believed, and I am convinced that He is able to guard until that Day what has been entrusted to me." And also in chapter 4, verse 18. "The Lord will rescue me from every evil deed, and will bring me safely to His Heavenly Kingdom." Paul was entirely convinced that God would protect him and guard him and rescue him from all evil and bring him safely to His Heavenly Kingdom, and he suffered greatly during his ministry (2 Cor. 11:23–33).[44] so we can all rest assured with that same full confidence in God's protection and security as did Paul. There is zero threat of being lost (John 17:12).

Stepping back for just a second, once again, Paul showed his responsibility in the duality of this back in Philippians 3:12–14 when he said speaking of gaining Christlikeness:

> Not that I have already obtained this or am already perfect, but I press on to make it my own, because Christ Jesus has made me His Own. Brothers, I do not consider that I have made it my own. But one thing I do: forgetting what lies behind and straining forward to what lies ahead, I press on toward the goal for the prize of the upward call of God in Christ Jesus.

He shows himself straining and striving to reach the end of the race, toward the goal of God's upward call, but he is only able to do so because Christ made him His Own, and Paul had this absolute confidence that we talked about here in these verses in 2 Timothy that Christ would guard him and sustain him and safely deliver him to that victorious end-goal.

Stepping back into chapter 2 of Paul's second letter to Timothy we read in verse 19, "But God's firm foundation stands, bearing this seal: 'The Lord knows those who are His,' and 'Let everyone who names the name of the Lord depart from iniquity.'" The word used for "seal" in the Greek is *sphragida* and means "seal, signet, proof." It means "a symbol of ownership and authenticity. Paul gives two characteristics of those with the divine seal of authenticity. God has known His Own ever since He chose them before time began. The second mark of God's ownership of believers, is their pursuit of holiness (cf. 1 Cor. 6:19–20)."[45] Once again, God seals us, and we are made His, and through Him, we will depart from our old and dead ways.

In Paul's letter to his other protégé, Titus, we read in the initial greeting:

> For the sake of the faith of God's elect and their knowledge of the truth, which accords with

godliness, in hope of eternal life, which God, Who never lies, promised before the ages began and at the proper time manifested in His Word through the preaching with which I have been entrusted by the command of God our Savior.

God's elect refers to:

> [T]hose who have been graciously chosen for salvation "before the foundation of the world" (Eph. 1:4) but who must exercise personal faith which is prompted and empowered by the Holy Spirit. God's choice of believers always precedes and enables their choice of Him (cf. John 15:16; Acts 13:48; Rom. 9:15–21; 2 Thess. 2:13; 2 Tim. 1:8–9). This "hope of eternal life" is divinely promised and divinely guaranteed to all believers, providing endurance and patience (cf. John 6:37–40; Rom. 8:18–23; 1 Cor. 15:51–58; Eph. 1:13–14; Phil. 3:8–11, 20–21; 1 Thess. 4:13–18; 1 John 3:2–3). God's plan of salvation for sinful mankind was determined and decreed before man was even created. The plan of salvation originated in eternity past with God.[46]

And since it is impossible for God to say anything that is untruthful (Num. 23:19) since He Himself is Truth and the source of Truth (John 14:6, 17), His promises can be trusted with absolute assurance and confidence. Also, the Greek word used for "hope," which is *elpidi*, means "trust, confidence, expectation of what is sure or certain." The certainty of our eternal life was promised to us as His elect by God Himself Who cannot lie before even the foundations of the world and is entirely certain to be seen.

Heading into the book of Hebrews, we will get to see a lot more on this. In chapter 2, there is a passage that we looked at in the last chapter, but I want to dissect one more part of it specifically for this chapter. In verse 10, we read, "For it was fitting that He, for Whom and by Whom all things exist, in bringing many sons to glory, should make the Founder of their salvation perfect through suffering."

> What God did through the humiliation of Jesus Christ was perfectly consistent with His sovereign righteousness and holiness. Without Christ's humiliation and suffering, there could be no redemption. Without redemption, there could be no glorification (cf. Rom. 8:18, 29–30). In His divine nature, Christ was already perfect. However, His human nature was perfected through obedience, including suffering in order that He might be an understanding High Priest, an example for believers (cf. Heb. 5:8–9, 7:25–28; Phil. 2:8; 1 Pet. 2:21), and establish the perfect righteousness (Matt. 3:15) to be imputed to believers (2 Cor. 5:21; Phil. 3:8).[47]

Being brought to glory, as is mentioned here in this verse "bringing many sons to glory," refers to our glorification, which is the final culmination of the trifold act of salvation when we will be fully glorified into the image of Christ and we will be forever transformed to be exactly like Him (1 John 3:2; cf. Rom. 8:29–30; 2 Cor. 3:18; Phil. 3:21; 2 Pet. 1:4), and there is no possible way that we can do this in ourselves. This is entirely an act of God. This is entirely a divine and gracious act of the One Who is the Founder and Author of our salvation and faith (Phil. 1:6; Heb. 12:2). He brings us to glory by and through His Own will. He founded our salvation, and He will bring it to completion.

Following this up with verse 11, "For He Who sanctifies and those who are sanctified all have one source," we see again all three aspects of salvation being portrayed here in these passages. We see Jesus being named as the Founder of our salvation in verse 10, which speaks of our justification; verse 11 details His sanctification work in us, and as we just mentioned, being brought to glory speaks of our passively received final glorification. So this is another one of those beautiful passages that include and describe all three aspects.

In chapter 6, we see a section discussing the certainty of God's promise. Starting in verse 13, we read, "For when God made a promise to Abraham, since He had no one greater by whom to swear, He swore by Himself, saying, 'Surely I will bless you and multiply you.' And thus Abraham, having patiently waited, obtained the promise."

We just discussed this eternal and irrevocable covenant a little bit ago when we were looking into chapter 11 of Romans. God made and swore this unilateral oath and promise to Abraham strictly upon His Own name as there is no one greater than Himself to swear the oath. Continuing into verse 16:

> For people swear by something greater than themselves, and in all their disputes, an oath is final for confirmation. So when God desired to show more convincingly to the heirs of the promise the unchangeable character of His purpose, He guaranteed it with an oath so that by two unchangeable things, in which it is impossible for God to lie, we who have fled for refuge might have strong encouragement to hold fast to the hope set before us. We have this as a sure and steadfast anchor of the soul, a hope that enters into the inner place behind the curtain, where Jesus has gone as a forerunner on our behalf, having become a High Priest forever after the order of Melchizedek.

> God's Word does not need any confirmation from someone else. It is reliable because God Himself is faithful. People confirm their promises by appealing to someone greater (especially to God) as witness. Since no one is greater than God, He could only provide an oath from Himself. By doing so, He is willingly (v. 17)

> accommodating Himself to human beings who
> desire the confirmation because of the character-
> istic unreliability of human promises. The fact
> that God had said it assured its fulfillment. Hope
> for the fulfillment of God's salvation promises
> is the "anchor for the soul" keeping the believer
> secure during the times of trouble and turmoil.
> Our hope is embodied in Christ Himself, Who
> has entered into God's presence in the Heavenly
> Most Holy Place on our behalf.[48]

Since "it is impossible for God to lie," and due to His "unchange-
able character," what He promises is absolutely certain. Once we are
adopted as His sons (Rom. 8:15–17), we are and forever will be "heirs
of the promise" and may hold fast with the strongest of encouragement with the surest and most steadfast anchor of hope that Jesus
will bring us to completion (cf. John 6:37–40, 44, 47, 10:28–29,
17:12, 15, 24; Phil. 1:6; Heb. 12:2). Also, as we have mentioned
before, the word used here for "hope" is *eplidos*, which means "trust,
confidence, expectation of what is sure or certain." In the Greek,
it signifies an absolute assurance and confidence and expectancy of
what is certain. It does not carry a possible sense of uncertainty or
unfulfillment like it might in English context.

In chapter 7, we see this starting in verse 23:

> The former priests were many in number,
> because they were prevented by death from con-
> tinuing in office, but He holds His priesthood
> permanently, because He continues forever.
> Consequently, He is able to save to the uttermost
> those who draw near to God through Him, since
> He always lives to make intercession for them.

Since this verse refers to Jesus's present intercession for us, the
word *save* in this verse is referring to our sanctification, which is the
continuing process by which we are freed from the power of sin. This

continuing process of salvation will eventually be completed in our glorification when we are saved from the presence of sin. The word *uttermost* is referring to this glorification. We also see here again that it is Christ Who constantly "lives to make intercession for" us (cf. Rom. 8:34). The term used here for "draw near" is *proserchomenous*; it means "to approach, draw near, come to" and is in the present tense passive verb form, which indicates that Jesus continues to save those who, through the intercessory work of the Spirit dwelling within us, keep drawing near to Him.

Our justification is a once-for-all event accomplished on the cross, but our sanctification is an ongoing process. We also see here an example of the paradoxical duality of God's divine sovereignty and man's responsibility again. We must continue to draw near to God, but it is Jesus and the Spirit Who save us and intercede for us, and as we have seen elsewhere, He and the Spirit are the One Who sanctifies us and empowers us with an irrevocable attitude of perseverance (cf Jer. 32:40; Rom. 8:29–30, 38–39; 1 Cor. 1:8–9; 2 Cor. 5:17; Phil. 1:6, 2:11–13; Heb. 12:2; 1 Pet. 1:5; Jude 24).

In chapter 10, we see more on our sanctification. In verse 10, we read, "And by that will we have been sanctified through the offering of the body of Jesus Christ once for all." And in verse 14, "For by a single offering [namely Himself] He has perfected for all time those who are being sanctified." These two verses together show two different aspects of sanctification.

> Sanctify means to "make holy," to be set apart from sin for God. When Christ fulfilled the will of God, He provided for the believer a continuing, permanent condition of holiness (Eph. 4:24; 1 Thess. 3:13). This is the believer's positional sanctification as opposed to the progressive sanctification that results from daily walking by the will of God.[49]

Verse 10 speaks of our positional sanctification, which in the Greek for "have been sanctified" is *hegiasmenoi*, which is a past perfect verb tense, which means it is a completed action with continuing present results. Our sanctification (positional) has been completed, and as verse 14 states, we have already been perfected. We have been made holy. When God looks at us, He sees Christ's perfect, holy, and righteous sacrifice imputed to us. "Has perfected" is also found in the past perfect verb tense in the Greek. We have been set apart from sin because Jesus paid the price for all of it. It has all been washed away, never to be seen again, and so positionally, we have been sanctified and set apart.

In verse 14, we are told we are "being sanctified." In the Greek, it is *hagiazomenous*, which this time is a present tense verb; therefore, a progressive or continuous action. This refers to our progressive sanctification which is the ongoing action of the Spirit within us maturing and growing us so that our outward actions and habits look more and more like Christ and less and less like our old self prior to surrendering to Jesus. Both of these verses confirm and show that we have once for all been made holy and set apart from sin and "perfected for all time," yet in the flesh, the Spirit works to transform our fleshly image into the image of Christ. And all of this so that we may rest in full assurance of our security.

Continuing on in verse 15:

> And the Holy Spirit also bears witness to us; for after saying, "This is the covenant that I will make with them after those days, declares the Lord: I will put My laws on their hearts, and write them on their minds," He then adds, "I will remember their sins and their lawless deeds no more." Where there is forgiveness of these, there is no longer any offering for sin. Therefore, brothers, since we have confidence to enter the Holy Places by the blood of Jesus, by the new and living way that He opened for us through the curtain, that is, through His flesh, and since we have a great Priest over the House of God, let us draw near with a true heart in full assurance of faith,

> with our hearts sprinkled clean from any evil con-
> science and our bodies washed with pure water.
> Let us hold fast the confession of our hope with-
> out wavering, for He Who promised is faithful.

First of all, being "washed with pure water" is not referring to Christian baptism. It is instead referring to the purifying of a person's life by the means of the Holy Spirit and of the Word of God (cf. John 7:38–39, 15:3; Eph. 5:26; Ti. 3:5). Secondly, throughout verses 15–23, we are given many references to the full assurance we possess in our perseverance because "He Who promised is faithful." He has written His laws on our hearts and minds, and He will remember our sins no more! He has forgiven us completely, He has perfected us, and He works our sanctification that we may shine in His image. "Let us draw near with a true heart in full assurance of faith." And this is perfectly mirrored a little bit later in chapter 12 verse 2, which describes Jesus as "the Founder and Perfecter of our faith." He created our faith and He will perfect it, "sanctify it," unto its completion. "He Who began a good work in you will bring it to completion at the Day of Jesus Christ" (Phil. 1:6).

In chapter 13, verse 5, we see a quote taken from earlier in Joshua chapter 1. "Keep your life free from the love of money, and be content with what you have, for He has said, 'I will never leave you nor forsake you.'" This was one of the many statements made in the early Old Testament speaking of God's provision and security of His people. And since God is immutable and unchanging (Mal. 3:6; Heb. 1:12, 13:8; Jas. 1:17), those promises still hold true to His children today. Just as Christ prayed to the Father to hold them and keep them from evil and sanctify them unto eternal life (John 17), God will bring His Own to completion (Phil. 1:6; Heb. 12:2).

Going back into a couple spots in Hebrews, we see a few verses that may trip a few people up on this issue of eternal security or perseverance of the saints. First of all, in chapter 6, starting at verse 4, we read:

> For it is impossible, in the case of those who
> have once been enlightened, who have tasted the

Heavenly gift, and have shared in the Holy Spirit, and have tasted in the goodness of the Word of God and the powers of the age to come, and then have fallen away, to restore them again to repentance, since they are crucifying once again the Son of God to their own harm and holding Him up to contempt.

A proper interpretation of Hebrews requires the recognition that it addresses three distinct groups of Jews: (1) believers; (2) unbelievers who were intellectually convinced of the Gospel; and (3) unbelievers who were attracted by the Gospel and the Person of Christ but who had reached no final conviction about Him. Failure to acknowledge these groups leads to interpretations inconsistent with the rest of Scripture. In 6:4–6, the phrase "once been enlightened" is often taken to refer to Christians, and the accompanying warning taken to indicate the danger of losing their salvation if they "have fallen away" and "are crucifying once again the Son of God." But there is no mention of their being saved and they are not described with any terms that apply only to believers (such as holy, born again, righteous, or saints).

This problem arises from inaccurately identifying the spiritual condition of the ones being addressed. In this case, they were unbelievers who had been exposed to God's redemptive truth, and perhaps made a profession of faith, but had not exercised genuine saving faith. They had received instruction in Biblical truth, which was accompanied by intellectual perception, but understanding the Gospel is not the equivalent of salvation. In John 1:9–12, it is clear that enlightening is not the equivalent of salvation. All men experience the goodness of God, but that does not mean that they are all saved (cf. Matt. 5:45; Acts 17:25). Many Jews, during the Lord's earthly ministry, experienced the blessings from Heaven that He brought, whether that gift refers to Christ or the Holy Spirit, experiencing either one was not the equivalent of salvation (cf. John 6:66; Acts 7:51). These Hebrews had not yet been regenerated in spite of all they had heard and seen (cf. Matt. 13:3–9; John 6:60–66). They were repeating the sins of those who died in the wilderness after seeing the miracles performed through Moses and Aaron and hearing the voice of God at Sinai. The Greek term for "having fallen away," *parapipto*, was used to translate terms for severe unfaithfulness and apostasy. It is equivalent to the apostasy seen in Ezekiel 18:24 and in Hebrews 3:12.

The former, apparent righteousness was not genuine (cf. 1 John 2:19), and God did not remember it as a valid expression of faith. The seriousness of this unfaithfulness is seen in the severe description of rejection within this verse: they re-crucify Christ and treat Him contemptuously. Those who sinned against Christ in such a way had no hope of restoration or forgiveness (cf. 2:2–3, 10:26–27, 12:25). The reason is they had rejected Him with full knowledge and conscious experience. With full revelation they rejected the truth, concluding the opposite of the truth about Christ, and thus had no hope of being saved. They can never have more knowledge than they had when they rejected it. They have concluded that Jesus should have been crucified, and they stand with His enemies. There is no possibility of these verses referring to losing salvation. Those who want to make this verse mean that believers can lose salvation will have to admit that it would then also say that one could never get it back again. Those who hear the Gospel message and respond in faith are blessed; those who hear and reject it are cursed (Matt. 13:18–23).[50]

We see this same concept all the way back in the Old Testament as well back in 1 Chronicles 28 verse 9:

And you, Solomon my son, know the God of your father and serve Him with a whole heart and with a willing mind, for the Lord searches all hearts and understands every plan and thought. If you seek Him, He will be found by you, but if you forsake Him, He will cast you off forever.

As we are looking at throughout this chapter, once you belong to God, you will persevere, and you may have complete assurance of your security because God holds you, but for those who refute this and want to say that believers can lose their salvation through free will would then also have to admit that if lost, that person could never come back again. If the belief of losing salvation was held, then you would also have to hold that if lost, it would be lost forever and could never be gained again because if "you forsake Him, He will cast you off forever." This is also mirrored in Matthew 10:32–33.

One last thing in this passage in Hebrews 6, the word for "tasted" used here:

[I]s the same Greek word that is used in Matthew 27:34 regarding Jesus's tasting the wine mixed with gall during His crucifixion. After tasting what was being offered to Him, He refused to drink it. Perhaps the use of this word in this passage (vv. 4–6) refers to those who superficially 'tasted' the Gospel and outwardly appeared to embrace the Christian experience, but inwardly never committed in full surrender to Christ. In this case, the act of "falling away" was simply the public expression of their true position and their rejection of Jesus as Messiah regardless of the evidence.[51]

Moving back into chapter 10, we see a bit more of this. Starting in verse 26:

> For if we go on sinning deliberately after receiving the knowledge of the truth, there no longer remains a sacrifice for sins, but a fearful expectation of judgment, and a fury of fire that will consume the adversaries. Anyone who has set aside the law of Moses dies without mercy on the evidence of two or three witnesses. How much worse punishment, do you think, will be deserved by the one who has spurned the Son of God, and has profaned the blood of the covenant by which he was sanctified, and has outraged the Spirit of grace? For we know Him Who said, "Vengeance is Mine; I will repay." And again, "The Lord will judge His people." It is a fearful thing to fall into the hands of the living God. But recall the former days when, after you were enlightened, you endured a hard struggle with sufferings, sometimes being publicly exposed to reproach and affliction, and sometimes being partners with those so treated. For you had compassion for those in prison, and you joyfully accepted the plunder of your property, since you knew that you yourselves had a better possession and an abiding one. Therefore do not throw away your confidence, which has a great reward. For you have need of endurance, so that when

you have done the will of God you may receive what is promised. For, "Yet a little while, and the coming One will come and will not delay; but My righteous one shall live by faith, and if he shrinks back, My soul has no pleasure in him."

The warnings found here in 10:26–38 deal with the sin of apostasy, an intentional falling away, or defection. In verse 26, the reference once again is to apostate Christians, not to genuine believers who are often incorrectly thought to lose their salvation because of their sins. Apostates are those who move toward Christ, hear and understand His Gospel, and are on the verge of saving belief, but then rebel and turn away. This warning against apostasy is one of the most serious warnings in all of Scripture. Not all of the Hebrews would respond to the gentle invitation of 10:19–25. Regarding the "we" in verse 26, the author of Hebrews is speaking rhetorically. In verse 39, he excludes himself and genuine believers from this category. The Greek phrase for "sinning deliberately" or "if we willingly indeed sin" is "*hekousios gar hamartanonton hemon*" which carries the idea of deliberate intention that is habitual. The sin is rejecting Christ deliberately. The Greek term for knowledge denotes specific knowledge, not general spiritual knowledge (cf. Heb. 6:4; 1 Tim. 2:4). Though the knowledge was not defective or incomplete, the application of the knowledge was certainly flawed. The apostate is beyond salvation because he has rejected the only sacrifice that can cleanse him from sin and bring him into God's presence. To turn away from that sacrifice leaves him with no saving alternative (Matt. 12:31). And we see in verse 38, it is faith which pleases

God. The individual that draws back from the knowledge of the Gospel and faith will prove his apostasy.[52]

But then we read in verse 39, "But we are not those who shrink back and are destroyed, but of those who have faith and preserve their souls."

> The writer expresses confidence that believing readers ("we") will not be counted among "those" who fall away to destruction. Apostates will draw back from Christ but there are some who are near to believing who can be pulled "out of the fire" (cf. Jude 23). Preservation from eschatological, or final, destruction is the concept of "preserve" in this context.[53]

Hanging on 10:38 for just a bit longer, we see again a paraphrase of Habakkuk 2:4, "The just shall live by faith."

> This expression emphasizes that true faith is not a single event, but a way of life—it endures. That endurance is called the Perseverance of the Saints (cf. Col. 1:22–23; Heb. 3:12–14). One central theme of the story of Job is that no matter what satan does, saving faith cannot be destroyed (cf. Rom. 8:31–39).[54]

> satan was tempting God to cause something to happen in the life of Job that would destroy his faith. But no matter what happened in the life of Job, nothing could destroy that faith, because that faith was designed by God to endure. God would have had to have broken His hold on Job. And the point of the book of Job is that when God has someone that belongs to Him, nothing

can change that, nothing. satan can tempt God to act against Job or anybody else; God has no capacity to succumb to that temptation. In the book of Revelation, chapter 12 verse 10, it says that satan is before the throne of God, day and night, accusing the brethren. he's doing exactly what he did against Job, only he's doing it *constantly*; and he's doing it now as I'm speaking. he will do it until the events of Revelation 12 take place in the future, the end of the age, and he's accusing the brethren.

Do you think he has some accusations that are legitimate? Of course. he is basically trying to get God to turn on us. he's tempting God to forsake a people who are less than perfect. he's saying things to God like, "They're not faithful. They don't love You like they should. They don't serve You like they should. They don't love each other like they should. They don't worship You like they should. They don't give like they should. They sin like they shouldn't." satan constantly is in the very place of God, His throne room, accusing believers, tempting God with the diatribe against us, to break His hold on us.

And how does God respond to that? In Job's case, the faith was unbreakable because God held it firm. But listen to God's word through Paul in Romans 8: "If God is for us, who is against us? Who will bring a charge against God's elect?" Well, satan. Will it succeed? "God is the One Who justified; who is the one who condemns? Christ Jesus is He Who died, yes, rather Who was raised, Who is at the right hand of God, Who also intercedes for us. Who will separate us from the love of Christ? Will tribulation, or distress, or persecution, or famine, or nakedness, or peril, or sword? No. In all these things we over-whelmingly conquer. I am convinced that nei-ther death, nor life, nor angels, nor principalities, nor things present, nor things to come, nor pow-ers, nor height, nor depth, nor any other created thing, will be able to separate us from the love of God, which is in Christ Jesus our Lord." Who is bringing a charge against God's elect? satan is. Who is he that condemns? satan is. Who is the one who would want to separate us from the love of Christ? satan is, and he's before the throne of God relentlessly telling God to let us go because of our unfaithfulness, tempting God to throw away His children because of their failure. Would God ever do that? Let me tell you something: if you could lose your salvation, then God is a sin-ner and has fallen to a temptation from satan. That is a profound thought. If a person can lose their salvation, then satan has triumphed over God, satan has broken God's holiness, and God is not holy.[55]

Also, one last thing on Habakkuk 2:4:

> When, for instance, we are told four times in our Bibles (Hab. 2:4; Rom. 1:17; Gal. 3:11; Heb. 10:38) that "the just shall live by faith," it is not simply that we live in a spirit of optimism, a faith or hope that everything will come out all right at last. And when we speak of the doctrine of justification by faith, it is not to say that he who maintains a courageous heart will thereby be declared righteous. Faith is not the savior. Faith is the hand that lays hold of Him Who does save. Therefore, the folly is of talking of weak faith as opposed to strong faith. The feeblest faith in

Christ is saving faith. The strongest faith in self,
or something other than Christ, is but a delusion
and a snare, and will leave the soul at last unsaved
and forever forlorn.[56]

There is another verse that seems to cause some a bit of similar
confusion. Peter's second letter, chapter 2, verse 20. "For if, after they
have escaped the defilements of the world through the knowledge of
our Lord and Savior Jesus Christ, they are again entangled in them
and overcome, the last state has become worse for them than the
first." This, again, is not referring to someone losing their salvation.

"Defilements" has the idea of putrid and
poisonous vapors. Morally, the world gives off a
deadly influence. Peter notes that at some point
in time, these false teachers and their followers wanted to escape the moral contamination
of the world system and sought religion, even
Jesus Christ (on their own terms, not His). Peter
described false teachers in detail in this chapter
so that Christians would always recognize their
characteristics and methods. The greatest sin of
Christ-rejecters and the most damning work of
satan is misrepresentation of the Truth and its
consequent deception. Nothing is more wicked
than for someone to claim to speak for God to
the salvation of souls when in reality he speaks
for satan to the damnation of souls (cf. Deut.
13:1–18, 18:20; Jer. 23; Ezek. 13; Matt. 7:15,
23:1–36, 24:4–5; Rom. 16:17; 2 Cor. 11:13–14;
2 Tim. 4:3–4).

Peter's point is that satan has always endeav-
ored to infiltrate groups of believers with the
deceptions of false teachers (cf. John 8:44). Since
Eve, he has been in the deceit business (cf. 2 Cor.
11:3–4). These false teachers parade themselves

as Christian pastors, teachers and evangelists,
but these false teachers had never genuinely been
converted to Christ. They heard the true Gospel
and moved toward it, but then rejected the Christ
of that Gospel. That is apostasy, like the people
of Hebrews 10:26–27. Their last end is far worse
than the first (cf. Luke 11:24–26).[57]

A very helpful passage for us to look at concerning this topic
of apostasy is shown to us in 1 John, chapter 2, verse 19. "They
went out from us, but they were not of us; for if they had been of
us, they would have continued with us. But they went out, that it
might become plain that they all are not of us." This verse shows to
us that it is those who were not genuinely born again that are the
ones who "fall away" because they did not ever possess a genuine
faith to begin with, and therefore were never truly saved to begin
with. It is not an issue of losing their salvation, they never had it!
They didn't fall away; they may have drawn close, but they then
turned back away.

The first characteristics of antichrists, i.e.,
false teachers and deceivers, is that they depart
from the faithful. They arise from within the
church and depart from true fellowship and
lead people out with them. This verse also places
emphasis on the doctrine of the Perseverance of
the Saints. Those genuinely born again endure
in faith and fellowship and the Truth (1 Cor.
11:19; 2 Tim. 2:12). The ultimate test of true
Christianity is endurance (Mark 13:13; Heb.
3:14). The departure of people from the Truth
and the Church is their unmasking.[58]

The departure of those who "fall away" proves of their unregenerate heart. They were not regenerate and then became unregenerate

once again; they were and remained unregenerate in the first place. Being born-again, you cannot become unborn.

> Salvation is forever. Those who's faith is genuine will never totally or finally fall away from Christ. They will persevere in grace unto the very end. Even if they fall into grievous sins or continue in sin for a time, they will never abandon the faith completely. God preserves His people through their perseverance. True believers *will* persevere. Professing Christians who turn against the Lord only prove that they were never truly saved (1 John 2:19). No matter how convincing a person's testimony may seem, once that person becomes apostate, he or she demonstrates irrefutably that the testimony was hypocritical and the professed salvation was spurious. God *will* keep His Own (Jude 24; also cf. 2 Tim. 2:19).[59]

> Believers who persevere give evidence of the genuineness of their faith. God, as part of His saving work, secures our perseverance. True believers 'are being guarded through faith for a salvation' (1 Peter 1:5). Those who do fall away give proof that they were never truly believers to begin with (1 John 2:19). God is the One that keeps you from stumbling (Jude 24; also cf. 1 Cor. 1:7–8, Phil. 1:6). For Paul, perseverance in the faith is essential evidence that faith is real. If a person ultimately and finally falls away from the faith, it proves that person never really was redeemed to begin with.[60]

The book of James is often seen as a guide to wise and godly living. We have already seen a few lessons pulled from this book, but here we will look at a couple lessons on this Perseverance of the

Saints that we mentioned early in and throughout our chapter here. Chapter 1, verse 12 says this, "Blessed is the man who remains steadfast under trial, for when he has stood the test he will receive the crown of life, which God has promised to those who love Him."

This passage speaks of the believer who successfully endures and perseveres unto eternal life and Heavenly reward. Such a person will never relinquish his or her saving faith in God, no matter the trial, just as we have seen in the last couple paragraphs. God has promised this reward to those who love Him and persevere in the saving faith that has been gifted to them (Eph. 2:8–9), and this perseverance lays evidence of the genuineness of their saving faith. "The perseverance of the saints is the human response to the predestinating work of God. You reveal you are kept by God if you don't abandon your faith in the midst of a trial."[61]

We also see this same endurance mentioned in chapter 5, verse 11, "Behold, we consider those blessed who remained steadfast. You have heard of the steadfastness of Job, and you have seen the purpose of the Lord, how the Lord is compassionate and merciful."

"Job is the classic example of a man who patiently endured suffering and was blessed by God for his persevering faith."[62] No matter what satan threw at Job, no matter what he inflicted him with, Job's true and genuine saving faith in God persevered through his many painful and toughest trials until the end, and God blessed him for it.

First Peter also mentions this same truth in its first chapter, verses 6 and 7:

> In this you rejoice, though now for a little while, if necessary, you have been grieved by various trials, so that the tested genuineness of your faith…may be found to result in praise and glory and honor at the revelation of Jesus Christ.

We see here again that the trials we endure are meant to test the genuineness of the faith within us. And just as was taught to us in James 1:2–4, we are to rejoice in these trials because they strengthen us and produce and strengthen our steadfastness, which leads to our maturation and reveals the genuineness of our saving faith in Jesus Christ's finished work.

Moving into Peter's first letter, we read in chapter 1, starting at verse 3:

> Blessed be the God and Father of our Lord Jesus Christ! According to His great mercy, He has caused us to be born again to a living hope through the resurrection of Jesus Christ from the dead, to an inheritance that is imperishable, undefiled, and unfading, kept in Heaven for you, who by God's power are being guarded through faith for a salvation ready to be revealed in the last time.

As a quick recap here, we see that it is God Who is the One that originally causes and initiates us to be born again. This goes back to God's grace in His sovereignty of beginning our new life in Him. But then taking the rest of this verse, we also see that we are born again to a living hope, which again, the word for hope, *elpida* in the Greek, carries with it a sense of "expectation of what is sure and certain." It is absolute. There is no sense of a possible negative failure or lack of fulfillment as there may be in the English sense of the word *hope*. We also see a beautifully descriptive image of what we are living in hope/*elpida* of.

Peter describes the inheritance that awaits us in Heaven with such profound words as imperishable, undefiled, and unfading! A trifecta of adjectives that absolutely denies the possibility that we will not receive them! I guarantee you that there will not be a single inheritance that is left unaccounted for in some remote corner of Heaven because someone who once believed and was truly saved, then lost his/her salvation or decided to walk away from Christ by his/her own free will. God Himself causes us to be born again from the very beginning and we live in absolute assurance and hope of an inheritance that will never disappear or decay or fade away, that is divinely secured for us, "kept in Heaven for you!"

Nothing can take this away from you! Not even our own free will because God Himself, with His infinite and sovereign power, is guarding and keeping and protecting us through a genuine and salvational faith that will persevere until the end! Our endurance is eternally secure in Him! Our perseverance is eternally secure in Him! Our inheritance is eternally secure in Him! Our hope is absolutely assured through Christ's finished work!

> Supreme power, omniscience, omnipotence, and sovereignty not only keep the inheritance, but also keep the believer secure. No one can steal the Christian's treasure, and no one can disqualify him from receiving it (cf. Rom. 8:31–39). The Christian's response to God's election and the Spirit's conviction is faith, but even faith is empowered by God (cf. Eph. 2:8–9). Moreover, the Christian's continued faith in God is the evidence of God's keeping power. At the time of salvation, God energizes faith, and continues to preserve it. Saving faith is permanent; it never dies.[63]

And the result of this saving faith is spoken of in verse 9, "Obtaining the outcome of your faith, the salvation of your souls," this speaks of the final aspect of our salvation, that of glorification. We also see a continuance of this teaching just a few verses later in verse 23. "Since you have been born again, not of perishable seed but of imperishable, through the living and abiding Word of God."

First of all, the verb "having been born again" is *anagegennemenoi* in the Greek which is a passive form verb which means it is something that is done to us, not something that we do in ourselves. Secondly:

> All seed (plant, animal, and human) is corruptible, but so is our own human flesh (1 Cor. 15:53) and, indeed "the whole of Creation" (Rom. 8:22). However, we have been redeemed

> by the incorruptible blood of Christ (1:19) to an
> incorruptible inheritance (1:4), an incorruptible
> body (1 Cor. 15:53), and an incorruptible crown
> (1 Cor. 9:25), to serve an incorruptible King (1
> Tim. 1:17), all revealed and activated through
> the incorruptible, eternal Word of God (1:23).[64]

We have been reborn of "imperishable seed," which by definition means it will never perish! We are not reborn of "imperishable-as-long-as-you…" seed. We are redeemed, we are secure, we will persevere, we are already made perfect (Rom. 8:30), and we are forever imperishable!

We have looked at a few things in John's first letter already but there are two more verses I want us to look at. Chapter 2, verses 1 and 2: "My little children, I am writing these things to you so that you may not sin. But if anyone does sin, we have an Advocate with the Father, Jesus Christ the righteous. He is the propitiation for our sins, and not for ours only but also for the sins of the whole world."

> Lest anyone regard the promises of 1 John
> 1:7 and 9 as a license to sin, John stresses that
> these very promises should keep them from
> a lifestyle of sin. That is, the sacrificial love of
> their Savior, providing full forgiveness and free
> salvation, should by all rights lead them to hate
> sin and constrain them to a life of holiness. This
> provision is not applicable to a life of habitual
> sin, which would indicate that the sinner has
> not yet truly been born again (cf. 3:6). Christ,
> our Advocate and propitiation, offered Himself
> as our sacrifice. The value of Christ's blood was
> infinite and sufficient to cover all of the sins of all
> the men of every age of history, though it offers
> eternal salvation only for the elect, only and all of
> those who believe on Him. This does not mean
> however that its power is in any way limited.[65]

The short epistle of Jude is the only New Testament book exclusively devoted to confronting "apostasy," and therefore offers a couple more lessons on this subject. In the first verse, we read, "Jude, a servant of Jesus Christ and brother of James, to those who are called, beloved in God the Father and kept for Jesus Christ."

The word for "kept" in the Greek is *teteremenois* which means "having been kept, maintained, preserved, spiritually guarded" and is in a passive verb form, which again means that it is something being done to us or for us, not something we do to or for ourselves. God the Father holds us infinitely and eternally secure through His great omnipotence, all for the sake of His Son Jesus Christ. God not only originates and initiates our faith and salvation, but He also completes it and brings it to its end for and through Christ (Eph. 2:8–9; Phil. 1:6; Heb. 12:2), therefore preserving and keeping the believer secure for eternal life (cf. John 6:37–44, 10:28–30, 17:11, 15; Rom. 8:31–39; 2 Tim. 4:18; Heb. 7:25, 9:24; 1 Pet. 1:3–5).

We also see this continued and expanded upon in verses 24–25:

> Now to Him Who is able to keep you from stumbling and to present you blameless before the presence of His glory with great joy, to the only God, our Savior, through Jesus Christ our Lord, be glory, majesty, dominion, and authority, before all time and now and forever. Amen.

Here we see the phrase "able to keep" you, and this time, in the Greek, we read it "*dynameno phylaxai*," which means, "I Am powerful, I Am able, empowered or enabled by God" to "guard, protect, preserve by having an eye on, or to keep what is entrusted."

This time, it is an aorist (simple past tense) active verb form, and its subject is God Himself, again meaning that it is His doing, not ours. God Himself holds and keeps us eternally secure by His Own omnipotent power, and He alone is able to keep us and prevent us from stumbling, preserving us until the end, where He Himself will present us holy, righteous, and blameless, faultless, and without a single blemish! Isn't that glorious news? He does this all for the sake of

His Own Son and for His Own glory. This is all His work, not ours. He holds us eternally and securely until the end, entirely innocent and guiltless through the finished work of His Son for His Own glory.

Moving into the final book of God's Word, we see comfort and encouragement being given in 13:10 and 14:12. In both verses, it tells us, "Here is a call for the endurance of the saints," and in chapter 14, it continues, "those who keep the commandments of God and their faith in Jesus." In the context, it is an encouragement to withstand, to persevere, and endure through the persecution that will come with full assurance and confidence that God will ultimately deliver us.

> These verses are excellent Scriptural support for the doctrine of Perseverance of the Saints, which assures all true believers in Christ that they will never lose their faith. The regenerate will continually endure, right to the end, in obedience to the Truth, no matter what may come against them (cf. Jer. 32:40; Matt. 24:13; John 6:35–40, 10:27–30; Rom. 8:31–39; Phil. 1:6; 1 John 5:4, 11–13, 20).[66]

There is one more beautiful picture and aspect from Scripture that I want to illustrate before starting to wrap this chapter up. Going back to Luke 15, we see the parable of the Prodigal Son in verses 11–32. Jesus told us, "There was a man who had two sons. And the younger of them said to his father, 'Father, give me the share of property that is coming to me.'"

First of all, the significance of this is that in requesting this from his father, the boy was in essence saying he wished his father were dead, seeing as you do not receive an inheritance until postmortem. He was basically telling his father, "Dad, I wish you were dead! I just want your stuff!" However:

> [T]he father graciously fulfilled the request, giving him his full share, which would have been one third of the *entire* estate—because the right

of the firstborn (Deut. 21:17) gave the elder
brother a double portion. This act pictures all
sinners (related to God the Father by creation)
who waste their potential privileges and refuse
any relationship with Him, choosing instead a
life of sinful self-indulgence.[67]

Shortly after this, the son left his father's house and wandered
off to a distant land, again showing the level of contempt that he
had for his father by moving so far away. "There he squandered his
property in reckless living." This was not just "merely wasteful extrav-
agance, but also wanton immorality (vs 30). The Greek word for
'reckless' means 'dissolute' or 'wasteful' and conveys the idea of an
utterly debauched lifestyle."[68]

After spending some time in this manner, he eventually wasted
everything that he had and began to be in need. He hired himself
out as a servant feeding pigs, which was entirely detestable to the
Jews, yet he was so desperate and needy he longed to eat the pig slop
that he was feeding them. But when he came to his senses he said to
himself:

> "How many of my father's hired servants
> have more than enough bread, but I perish here
> with hunger! I will arise and go to my father, and
> I will say to him, 'Father, I have sinned against
> Heaven and before you. I am no longer worthy
> to be called your son. Treat me as one of your
> hired servants.'" And he arose and came to his
> father.

This is where we really begin to see the boundlessness of the
Father's love, mercy, and grace for us. Continuing in verse 20, "While
he was still a long ways off, his father saw him and felt compassion
and ran and embraced him and kissed him." The first thing we see
here is that if the father saw him while he was still a long ways away,
that means the father was intently waiting and watching for his son

to return. If he was busy working or attending to his affairs, he would not have even noticed him coming back.

Secondly, when his father saw him, he felt compassion for his son. He wasn't angry. He wasn't anticipating giving him the scolding or the beating of a lifetime for wasting away a third of his entire estate. He felt true loving compassion. And third, when he saw his son returning, he RAN to him! There is quite a significance to this! First of all, this is the only spot in the entirety of Scripture where God is pictured as being in a hurry! God knows all and is in control of all and is never caught off guard or rushed, but when we acknowledge Him and come to Him in true repentance and confession, He runs to us! The next thing I want to dissect is this:

> I have always pictured this scene of the prodigal son returning to his father, with a distant hill, and then the son having to walk down a long countryside-style driveway, toward his father's massive farmhouse, set back quite a ways from the nearest main road, much like an old style plantation in the Old South. However, Jesus taught us this parable in the cultural context of Palestine. The father's house was a part of a village, and as the son returned he would have had to pass through the surrounding farmer's fields to get to his father's, and word would have spread throughout the entire village. The whole village would have known the situation and the circumstance that surrounded the family, and no doubt the shame and disgust they would have had for such a disrespectful, rebellious, foolish and reckless son would have been more than visible upon him as he passed through the village. The father could have allowed his son to make the long torturous walk-of-shame through the village, while they all scowled at him, but instead the father sacrificially RAN toward his son, embraced him

and kissed him, and then walked back the entire distance to the house, through the village, alongside of him, to save him, protect him and/or to bear the shame for him, and then threw him a gigantic party and feast to celebrate his return.[69]

Our Heavenly Father never asks us to come groveling to Him because of what we have done. He never exposes us to public shame. But He does ask us to make an effort to step out of the pigpen and head home, admitting we need help. God's Son was nailed to the cross so we would not have to be impaled on the agony of our addictions. He was publicly humiliated and shamed so that we could be free from shame.[70]

Jesus not only accomplished everything that needed to be done for our salvation and reconciliation to the Father (John 19:30), but He also bore our shame so that we wouldn't have to! He suffered horrendous torture, ridicule, abuse, and shame during His persecution so that He may shield us from ours. Just like everything else, we continue to look at self and bear our guilt and shame, even to the point of becoming frozen by it, but this is entirely unwarranted and unnecessary because Christ took all of that upon Himself as well and buried it! Shame was included in His victorious words, "It is finished!" Shame is meant as a weapon from the enemy to beat us down, drag us down, hold us down, and keep us focused on ourselves instead of looking at, worshipping, praising, and glorifying the finished work of Christ and living in correlation with His free gift offered to us through His substitution for us.

Shame is unhealthy and need not be present; conviction, on the other hand, is healthy, from the Spirit within us, and ultimately draws us back to and closer to God! In verses 17–19, we see conviction in the son's heart as he determines to return to his father, and as we looked at in chapter 6, that is our part of the equation. True heartfelt conviction leads to a repentant and surrendered heart and leads us to confess and ask God for forgiveness (v. 21). And when we turn our eyes and heart to God in true repentance, He sees us, runs to us, embraces us, shields our shame, and brings us into His Kingdom forever. We were dead and are now alive; we were lost, and now are found (vv. 24, 32). And as we have seen in this chapter, that heart of flesh (Ezek. 11:19, 36:26) which leads to repentance is gifted to us (Rom. 3:24, 6:23) when Christ raises us from the dead (Rom. 5:6, 8, 10; Eph. 2:5) and brings us back to life.

The doctrine of "the perseverance of the saints," also known as "preservation of the saints," "eternal security," "held by God," or "once saved, always saved," is that which:

> [T]he Bible teaches that those who are born again will continue trusting in Christ forever. God, by His Own power through the indwelling presence of the Holy Spirit, keeps or preserves the believer forever. This wonderful truth is seen in Ephesians 1:13–14, where we see that believers are "sealed with the Holy Spirit of promise, Who is the guarantee of our inheritance." When we are born again, we receive the promised indwelling presence of the Holy Spirit that is God's guarantee that He Who began a good work in us will complete it (Phil. 1:6). In order for us to lose our salvation after receiving the promised Holy Spirit, God would have to break His promise or renege on His "guarantee," which He cannot do. Therefore, the believer is eternally secure because God is eternally faithful. One of the misconceptions about the doctrine of the perseverance of the saints is that it will lead to "carnal Christians" who believe that since they are eternally secure, they can live whatever licentious lifestyle they wish and still be saved. But that is a misunderstanding of the doctrine and what the Bible teaches. A person who believes he can live any way he wants because he has professed

Christ is not demonstrating true saving faith (1 John 2:3–4). Our eternal security rests on the Biblical teaching that those whom God justifies, He will also glorify (Rom. 8:29–30). Those who are saved will indeed be conformed to the image of Christ through the process of sanctification (1 Cor. 6:11). When a person is saved, the Holy Spirit breaks the bondage of sin and gives the believer a new heart and a desire to seek holiness. Therefore, a true Christian will desire to be obedient to God and will be convicted by the Holy Spirit when he sins. True Christians will never "live any way they want" because such behavior is impossible for someone who has been given a new nature (2 Cor. 5:17). Clearly, the doctrine of the Perseverance of the Saints does accurately represent what the Bible teaches on this important subject. If someone is truly saved, he has been made alive by the Holy Spirit and has a new heart with new desires. There is no way that one who has been "born again" can later be "unborn." Because of His unique love for His children, God will keep all of His children safe from harm, and Jesus has promised that He would lose none of His sheep (John 10:27–30). The doctrine of the Perseverance of the Saints recognizes that true Christians will always persevere and are eternally secure because God keeps them that way. It is based on the fact that Jesus, the "Author and Perfecter of our faith" (Heb. 12:2), is able to completely save those whom the Father has given Him (Heb. 7:25) and to keep them saved through all eternity. The Bible is clear that the true believer cannot lose his/her salvation because we are saved by God (Romans 8:30), sealed by the Holy Spirit (Eph. 1:13–14), and kept by God until the day of redemption (Eph. 4:30). Just as once we are born, we cannot be made unborn, we have been made new creatures in Christ (2 Cor. 5:17), and we cannot be made old again by any means.[71]

I have never met a Christian who had lost his salvation. However, I have met plenty who had lost their assurance. Our security rests in the hands of an unconditionally loving Heavenly Father. One Who gave His best to insure our fellowship with Him forever. Our assurance rests in understanding and acceptance of these glorious truths. Placing the responsibility for maintaining salvation on the believer is adding works to grace. Salvation would no longer be a gift. It would become a trade—our faithfulness for His faithfulness. The salvation spoken of by Jesus and Paul takes place at one moment in time yet seals the believer for all time. This faith moves the Judge not only to forgive and pardon the sinner, but to adopt him into His Own Family as well. As we contemplate all that has been offered to us through Christ, we are forced to wonder why. Why the mercy? Why the kindness? The only answer is love—love of such magnitude that all human illustrations fall short, love that is unconditional at its core with no hidden agendas and no fine print. God's love is such that He accepts us just the way we are but refuses to leave us there.[72]

Doctor, pastor, and theologian, Tom Ascol, has this to say:

The only way that ungodly people receive God's justification is through faith, but be careful, faith does not justify! God justifies you through faith! The faith that brings justification

turns from sin, it repents, but repentance doesn't
justify you, God justifies you through the faith
that does indeed repent. We need to be very careful not to suggest, not to think that God rewards
our faith by granting us righteousness. Faith itself
is no work. Faith is the means through which we
lay claim to the work Jesus has done to justify
sinners. God justifies the ungodly. God doesn't
require you to change in order for Him to justify
you, God changes you by granting you the salvation that has at its very heart justification. God
has done everything necessary to make us right
with Him. You can't add to that. You can't detract
from that. Your righteousness comes to you from
Christ. God loves you for Christ's sake, and no
matter how well you perform you are not going
to cause Him to love you more, you are not going
to cause Him to accept you further, but it's also
true that on your worst day, your standing before
God is still secure. When you're looking at the
ash heap of your sin, your failures, your thoughts,
your actions, your inactions, and you think how
can I be so stupid, how can I be right back here
again? How could I live this way? And you don't
want to lift your eyes to Heaven because you
think *God is angry with me, God hates me, I can't
believe in God's love.* God justifies ungodly people (Rom. 5:6, 8, 10). It's not your actions. Your
sin cannot cause you to lose God's acceptance.
Your sin needs to be put to death, it needs to be
acknowledged, it needs to be hated, it needs to be
fought, but my brothers and sisters, believe this
Gospel, the relationship you have with God is
not sustained by your effort, it's sustained by His
grace and by what Jesus has already, once-for-all,
accomplished. Even though you're a great sinner,

> God shows great grace through all that He has
> done in His Son, the Lord Jesus.[73]

This does not give us free rein to sin as we please, but our sins are entirely covered by God's grace all the more. As it says in Romans 5:20–21, "where sin increased, grace abounded all the more, so that, as sin reigned in death, even so grace would reign through righteousness to eternal life through Jesus Christ our Lord." Again, this does not mean sin as much as you please; we should fight against our sin and repent of it, but the more sin is present, the more grace prevails.

In the New Covenant, when Jesus Christ died on the cross, the veil of the temple was rent from top to bottom (Matt. 27:51; Mark 15:38; Luke 23:45), and the Holy Place in the Temple in Jerusalem was exposed. The Holy of Holies was exposed to everyone, and God was by graphic illustration saying that all those who believe in My Son now can come directly into My presence. We all enjoy intimacy; we all have access.

This is a good illustration that the New Covenant had changed things. Unlike the strict rituals and laws and traditions of the Old Covenant, in which only the high priest could enter into the presence of God in the Holy of Holies, once a year, and only after strict cleansing and sacrificial ceremonies had taken place, it was now open and available for all to see and enter in, without any need of rituals, ceremonies, sacraments, or even sacrifices. Jesus Christ was now the "once and for all" sacrifice that covered all and brought direct and personal access to God.

> John 19:30 says, "When Jesus therefore had received the sour wine, He said, 'It is finished!'" The Greek expression is only one word—*tetelestai*. It was not the groan or curse of a victim; it was the proclamation of a victor. It was a shout of triumph: "IT IS FINISHED!"
> The wealth of meaning in that phrase is surely impossible for the human mind to fathom. What was finished? His earthly life? Yes, but far

more. Every detail of redemptive prophecy? Certainly, but not that alone.

The work of redemption was done. All that the law of God required, full atonement for sins, everything the symbolism of ceremonial law foreshadowed—the work that the Father had given Him to do—everything was done. Nothing was left. The ransom was paid. The wages of sin were settled. Divine justice was satisfied. The work of Christ was thus accomplished in total. The Lamb of God had taken away the sins of the world (John 1:29). There was nothing more on earth for Him to do except die so that He might rise again.

Here it is appropriate to add a crucial footnote: when Jesus said, "It is finished," He meant it! Nothing can be added to what He did. Many people believe they must supplement His work with good deeds of their own. They believe they must facilitate their own redemption through baptism, other sacraments and religious rituals, benevolent deeds, or whatever else they can accomplish through their own efforts. But NO works of human righteousness can expand on what Jesus accomplished for us. "He saved us, not on the basis of deeds which we have done in righteousness, but according to His mercy" (Ti. 3:5). The beginning and the end of our salvation was consummated by Jesus Christ, and we can contribute nothing!

What would you think if I took a felt-tipped pen and tried to add more features to the Mona Lisa? What if I got a hammer and chisel and offered to refine Michelangelo's Moses? That would be a travesty. They are masterpieces! No one needs to add to them.

In an infinitely greater way, that is true of Jesus's atoning work. He has paid the full price of our sins. He has purchased our redemption. He offers a salvation from sin that is complete in every sense. "It is finished!" Nothing we can do would in any way add to what He accomplished on our behalf.

Having finished His work, our Lord "bowed His head, and gave up His spirit" (John 19:30). There was no jerk, no sudden slump. He bowed His head. The Greek word evokes the picture of gently placing one's head on a pillow. In the truest sense, no man took Jesus's life from Him. He laid it down on His Own accord (cf. John 10:17–18). He simply and quietly yielded up His spirit, commending Himself into the Father's hands (Luke 23:46).

Only the omnipotent God Who is Lord of all could do that. Death could not claim Jesus apart from His Own will. He died in complete control of all that was happening to Him. Even in His death, He was Lord.

To the human eye Jesus looked like a pathetic casualty, powerless in the hands of mighty men. But the opposite was true. He was the One in charge. He proved it a few days later by forever bursting the bonds of death when He rose from the grave (1 Cor. 15:20–57).

And He is still in charge. "For to this end Christ died and lived again, that He might be Lord both of the dead and of the living" (Rom. 14:9).

This, then, is the Gospel our Lord sends us forth to proclaim: That Jesus Christ, Who is God incarnate, humbled Himself to die on our behalf. Thus He became the sinless sacrifice to pay the penalty of our guilt. He rose from the dead to declare with power that He is Lord over all, and He offers eternal life freely to sinners who will surrender to Him in humble, repentant faith. This gospel promises nothing to the haughty rebel, but for broken, penitent sinners, it graciously offers everything that pertains to life and godliness (2 Pet. 1:3). [74]

In Rome, when a man would be judged guilty of a crime, he would be put in prison. A certificate of debt would be placed on his prison door. After he had done his time and paid the penalty for his crime and had satisfied the demands of the law, a word would be written across the certificate of debt. The word was "tetelestai," which means literally, "It is finished" or "It is paid in full." Because this debt to society was paid, it meant that the man would never have to come into double jeopardy; he'd never be judged for that crime again. It is the same for you and me. If you belong to Jesus Christ, that is, if you have accepted the payment He made for sin on the cross and acknowledged that He is Lord of your life, you are "saved." Your debt is tetelestai. You cannot get lost after you are saved, because if you could (which you can't), Jesus would have to die again to save you. When Jesus said, "It is finished," we can take Him at His word. If you know that you gave your life to Him, determine today that you will never again wonder whether Jesus has the power to forgive all of your sin, past, present, and future, that He might bring you to God. [75]

Before we leave this chapter, I want to add a few responses to a few possible rebuttals.

> You say, "Well wait a minute. Isn't Scripture full of warnings to people not to fall away, such as we read in Hebrews 6:4–6, not to fall away and put Christ to an open shame? Such as we read in 1 Timothy chapter 1, those people who made shipwreck of the faith, aren't they warned about that? Those who have been delivered over to satan to learn not to blaspheme, aren't there warnings?"
>
> Yes, of course, and those are warnings to false believers. Those are warnings to people who are uncommitted. Those are warnings to people who have come close to the Gospel and made a superficial acknowledgment of the Gospel but not a real one. And so it's very crucial for us to understand that the doctrine of the perseverance of the saints does not mean that people who pray a prayer or quote/unquote accept Jesus or make a decision for Jesus in some emotional experience are necessarily secure and can live any way they want to live. No. If they have really come to Christ, there will be in them an enduring faith that will be characterized by a love for righteousness, a love for Christ and a hatred of sin. It will not be perfection but it will indicate direction in the way of righteousness.[76]

Also, you might ask:

> "But must I not hold on to the end if I would be saved at last?"
>
> May I, without irreverence, venture to recast a Bible story? If the account of Noah and

the flood went something like this, what would
you think of it? Suppose that after the ark was
completed God said unto Noah, "Now, get eight
great spikes of iron and drive them into the side
of the ark." And Noah procured the spikes and
did as he was bidden. Then the word came unto
him, "Come thou and all thy house and hang
onto these spikes." And Noah and his wife, and
his three sons and their wives, each held onto
a spike. And the rains descended and the flood
came, and as the ark was borne up on the waters
their muscles were strained to the utmost as they
clung to the spikes. Imagine God saying to them,
"If you hang on until the deluge is over you will
be saved!" Can you even think of such a thing as
anyone of them going safely through?

But oh, how different the simple Bible story.
"And the Lord said unto Noah, 'Come thou and
all thy house into the ark'" (Gen. 7:1). Ah, that is
a very different thing than holding on! Inside the
ark, they were safe as long as the ark endured the
storm. And every believer is in Christ and is as
safe as God can make him. Look away then from
all self-effort and trust in Him alone. Rest in the
ark and rejoice in God's great salvation.

And be sure to remember that it is Christ
Who holds you, not you who hold Him. He has
said, "I will never leave thee, nor forsake thee"
(Deut. 31:6; Heb. 13:5). "For if, when we were
enemies, we were reconciled to God by the death
of His Son, much more, being reconciled, we
shall be saved by His life" (Rom. 5:10). He Who
died for you now lives at God's right hand to
keep you, and the Father sees you in Him. "He
hath made us accepted in the beloved" (Eph.
1:6). Could anything be more sure?[77]

Might I add, we also see in Genesis 7:16 that it was the Lord that shut them into the ark and closed it to secure it and to secure them safely within the ark until He brought the ark to rest over a year later and told them to depart from the ark. They did not have to hang on. They did not have to secure themselves. They endured until the end because God secured them! And so will you if you truly believe in Christ as Savior! For "if the Son shall set you free, you shall be free indeed" (John 8:36).

If I may offer one more picture before we close this chapter, let us return to our analogous courtroom.

> We are sitting in the courtroom, as the prosecutor stands and presents the case against us. He begins by pulling down a screen, and shows a video of our entire life—focusing on every disgusting sordid detail. We sit hanging our head in total shame as he concludes by saying, "This man's life is littered with endless failures, violations, dissensions, wickedness, sin, and addictions, and had said numerous times he was going to stop his behavior. Look at how often he promised to change—but he lied!"
>
> The defense attorney stands to present our case. He declares, "Everything the prosecution has shown you is true. Every detail is correct. All except one. He left out a key ingredient. Everything this man has done was paid for." Then our Defense Attorney stands up, pulls off His shirt and shows the scars on His back and asks that they be entered as evidence. He shows His hands, His feet, and His side and proclaims, "I don't deny that My child has done what he has done. But it has already been paid for."[78]

In the words of an anonymous believer, "If anyone is ever to be kept out of Heaven for my sins, it will have to be Jesus, for He took them all upon Himself and made Himself responsible for them. But He is in Heaven already, never to be turned out, so now that I know that I am secure!"[79]

9

Unnecessary Works/Acts

As we have seen throughout this book, our salvation is entirely dependent upon Jesus Christ, beginning to end. He foreknew us, predestined us, chose us, elected us, called us, justified us, sanctifies us, holds us, secures us, intercedes for us, prays for us, fights for us, glorifies us, and brings us safely to fulfillment and eternal salvation and imperishable inheritance through His finished work (John 17, 19:30; Rom. 8:29–30; Phil. 1:6; Heb. 12:2). We add nothing to this nor could we take anything away from it. We must accept His innocent substitution in our place and place our entire faith for salvation upon Him and surrender entirely to Him as Lord and Savior; but even our knowledge of Him, our desire to seek Him, and our faith in Him is a gracious gift granted to us by Him (John 3:27, 6:44–45, 14:26; Eph. 2:8–9). We do not deserve it, and we certainly cannot earn it.

We could never be "good enough" or obey well enough to merit it. We are inherently sinful from birth, "sinful from the time my mother conceived me" (Ps. 51:5) and dead enemies of God (Rom. 5:6, 8, 10; Eph. 2:5). "No one is righteous, no not one" (Ps. 14:1–3, 53:1–3). Nothing we can do, apart from the work of Jesus Christ, can bring us back from the dead. Dead men cannot bring themselves to life. "No one can come to [Jesus] unless the Father Who sent [Jesus] draws him (John 6:44); unless it is granted him by the Father (John 6:65)." Our works do not save us (Rom. 3:20), our obedience does not save us, our rituals, legalism, sacrifices, practices, sacraments (Rom. 3:21, 27–28)—none of that saves us.

This is not to take a purely Calvinistic view, though. We do have a responsibility in this. Our responsibility is this: full acceptance of Jesus Christ as our Savior and complete surrender to Him as Lord and Savior (Rom. 10:9–10). And this full acceptance and complete surrender, by definition, would and does include both confession and repentance, but it is only through His work and none of our own. Zero self-righteousness or merit. We must accept that it is only by His innocent substitution in our place that we can receive redemption and salvation and reconciliation to God.

We do not nor can we do anything nor perform anything nor obey perfectly enough in order to earn nor deserve nor receive His mercy and grace and eternal gifts and coinheritance. It is only by acknowledging and accepting His gracious gifts given out of His infinite and eternal love for us all to the praise and worship of His glory! Faith is our necessary component, but it is not the faith in Him that saves us; faith is our connection to Christ alone Who saves us.

But once again, the great and divine paradox comes into play, even our knowledge of Him and our faith in Him is a gracious gift granted to us by Him (Eph. 2:8–9). And in that, we must simply admit that our minds are entirely inferior to God's, and even though we cannot seem to understand how these two truths dwell together, we see that they are both Biblically taught and true without apology throughout the whole of Scripture, so we rest in God's Word and give Him all the glory.

Sadly, however, there are those out there, certain denominations and churches that teach a works-based salvation, that which is dependent upon man's achievements or accomplishments or obedience and is therefore earned, deserved and/or merited, or at least is some form of even partially works-based salvation, instead of giving all rightful glory to God. Many of them believe that there are certain things they must do or perform in order to earn, deserve or receive, lay hold of, or be granted salvation, or that they must fulfill some set of requirements in order to reach Heavenly achievement. They may think that they have to complete some checklist or "be good" enough in obedience in order to deserve or receive entrance into Heaven. They may think that it is being done through God's grace or that their ability to do so is through the grace of God, but the bottom line is that it is still based on human performance or completion, instead of simply human acceptance and surrender to Christ alone.

Many times, they will try to base their beliefs upon Scripture; however, it is all too often out of context and contradictory to the whole of Scripture. There are far too many of these examples to tackle all of them in this one chapter or even this one book, but we will try to go through a couple as an example of the many and apply it to Scripture as to prepare you for further inspection of some of the others on your own.

When a doctrine is formed around a verse or set of verses in order to dictate and teach a certain doctrinal stance, but that stance seems to be in contradiction or dispute against other verses in Scripture, you need to dig deeper and cross reference and use Scripture to interpret Scripture and look at context in order to determine the truth because God's Word never contradicts itself. "All Scripture is inspired by God and profitable for teaching, for reproof, for correction, for training in righteousness" (2 Tim. 3:16). God is not a liar (Num. 23:19; 1 Sam. 15:29; Ti. 1:2; Heb. 6:18) and is not divided against Himself (Mark 3:24–25; 1 Cor. 1:13; 2 Tim. 2:13), so if a doctrine taught seems to contradict other parts of Scripture, immediate analysis is necessary in order to prevent further incorrect teaching because one part of Scripture will never contradict another. As mentioned, there are several doctrinal differences taught between various denominations and churches, but since we have been focusing on salvation and the grace of God throughout this book, we will only look at some of the teachings that deal specifically with salvational issues and God's grace.

The first and main one that I will inspect in this chapter is known as baptismal regeneration or baptismal salvation.

> Baptismal regeneration is the belief that baptism is necessary for salvation, or, more precisely, that regeneration does not occur until a person is water baptized. Baptismal regeneration

is a tenant of numerous Christian denominations, (including Roman Catholic, Orthodox, Lutheran, and Anglican) but is most strenuously promoted by churches in the Restoration Movement, specifically the Church of Christ and the International Church of Christ. Advocates of baptismal regeneration typically have a four-part formula for how salvation is received. They believe that a person must believe, repent, confess and be baptized in order to be saved. They believe this way because there are Biblical passages that seem to indicate that each of these actions is necessary for salvation. Repentance, understood Biblically, is required for salvation. Repentance is a change of mind. Repentance, in relation to salvation, is changing your mind from rejection of Christ to acceptance of Christ. It is not a separate step from saving faith. Rather, it is an essential aspect of saving faith. One cannot receive Jesus Christ as Savior, by grace through faith, without a change of mind about Who He is and what He did. Confession, understood Biblically, is a demonstration of faith. If a person has truly received Jesus Christ as Savior, proclaiming that faith to others will be a result. If a person is ashamed of Christ and/or ashamed of the message of the Gospel, it is highly unlikely that the person has understood the Gospel or experienced the salvation that Christ provides. Baptism, understood Biblically, is an identification with Christ. Christian baptism illustrates a believer's identification with Christ's death, burial and resurrection (Rom. 6:3–4). As with confession, if a person is unwilling to be baptized—unwilling to identify his/her life as being redeemed by Jesus Christ—that person has very likely not been made a new creation (2 Cor. 5:17) through faith in Jesus Christ. Those who contend for baptismal regeneration and/or this four-part formula for receiving salvation do not view these actions as meritorious works that earn salvation. Repenting, confessing, etc., do not make a person worthy of salvation. Rather, the official view is that faith, repentance, confession and baptism are "works of obedience," things a person must do before God grants salvation. While the standard Protestant understanding is that faith is the one thing God requires before salvation is granted, those of the baptismal regeneration persuasion believe that baptism—and, for some, repentance and confession—are additional things God requires before He grants salvation. The problem with this viewpoint is that there are Biblical passages that clearly and explicitly declare faith to be the only requirement for salvation. John 3:16 states, "For God so loved the world that He gave His one and only Son, that whoever believes in Him shall not perish but have eternal life." In Acts 16:30, the Philippian jailer asks the apostle Paul, "What must I do to be saved?" If ever there was an opportunity for Paul to present a four-part formula, this was it. Paul's response was simple: "Believe in the Lord Jesus Christ and you will be saved (Acts 16:31)." No baptism, no confession, just faith. Advocates of baptismal regeneration point to certain Scripture verses for Biblical support, however, there are Biblically and contextually sound interpretations of those verses that do not support baptismal regeneration. There are literally dozens of verses in the New Testament that attribute salvation to faith/belief with no other requirement mentioned in

the context. If baptism, or anything else, is necessary for salvation, all of these verses are wrong,
and the Bible contains errors and is therefore no
longer worthy of our trust. Receiving salvation is
not a process or a multi-step formula. Salvation
is a finished product, not a recipe. What must we
do to be saved? Believe in the Lord Jesus Christ,
and we will be saved.[1]

There are about a dozen verses of Scripture that advocates of
baptismal regeneration will often quote to try and promote or teach
this doctrine versus several dozen verses that teach the doctrine of
"by grace through faith alone." As stated before, if any Scripture
seems to contradict any other Scripture, and more so dozens of other
Scriptures throughout the Bible, which we have already studied
throughout the earlier portions of this book, immediate analysis and
contextual interpretation is necessary and must be performed. First
of all, there are many more passages that contradict the belief of baptismal regeneration than there are that seem to support it.

Secondly, there are many straightforward passages throughout
Scripture that state entirely plainly that true, authentic, fully surren-
dered faith is our one and only responsibility in receiving salvation.
Habakkuk 2:4, John 3:16, John 11:25–26, Acts 2:21, Acts 16:31,
Romans 1:16–17, Romans 10:9–10, Galatians 2:16, Ephesians
2:8—just to name a quick few.

Going through in canonical order, the first passage that is used
by advocates of baptismal regeneration is Matthew 28:18–20, which
reads:

Jesus came and said to them, "All authority
in Heaven and on earth has been given to Me.
Therefore, go and make disciples of all nations,
baptizing them in the name of the Father and of
the Son and of the Holy Spirit, teaching them
to observe all that I have commanded you. And

behold, I Am with you always, til the end of the age."

This passage is known as The Great Commission. First of all, this passage doesn't even specifically mention salvation, so means of salvation should not wholly be taught from this passage; however, we do see order and pattern is established.

> The participles take the force of the command to make disciples: Go, make disciples, baptize, teach. The order is informative as it previews the obedient work of the apostles in Acts. First, they made disciples, next they baptized, then they taught and provided a means for the perpetuity of instruction in the churches thus established. Jesus's command gives an explicit order that His disciples have no right to alter.[2]

Luke also accords with Christ's missionary commission in expressing this order and pattern in Acts 18:8, which tells us, "Many of the Corinthians who heard him believed and were baptized." One first becomes a disciple and follower of Christ, a believer in Christ, and then as a believer is baptized. Therefore, though this passage offers this pattern—reaching, learning/believing, baptizing, teaching—and also offers a direct commission from Jesus that all Christians should be baptized and how to be baptized in the name of the Triune God, it is completely inadequate in teaching baptismal regeneration. And also, to those who hold to the teachings of believe, repent, confess, and be baptized, in order to be saved, this passage doesn't even include repentance or confession.

Now, as we continue into this, don't get me wrong; baptism is absolutely necessary as a Christian as it is here commissioned by Jesus Himself, but it does not preexist or lead to salvation. Baptism, as we shall begin to see, is an obedient act of an already saved believer and follower of Christ. It is an outward public declaration of an already existing inward spiritual truth. Baptism is done out of the obedience of a saved life.

The next passage we will look at which baptismal regeneration advocates use to teach this doctrine is Mark 16:16, which reads, "Whoever believes and is baptized will be saved, but whoever does not believe will be condemned." First of all, there is much debate between theologians and Biblical historians on whether or not this section of Scripture was inspired and/or was part of the original text.

> The external evidence strongly suggests that these verses (9–20) were not originally part of Mark's Gospel. While the majority of Greek manuscripts contain these verses, the earliest and most reliable do not. Further, some that include the passage note that it was missing from older Greek manuscripts, while others have scribal marks indicating the passage was considered spurious. The fourth century church fathers Eusebius and Jerome noted that almost all Greek manuscripts available to them lacked verses 9–20.[3]

Not only does this group of twelve verses remain absent from important early manuscripts, but it also displays certain peculiarities of vocabulary, style, and theological content that are unlike the rest of Mark. The transition from verse 8 into verse 9 is abrupt and awkward compositionally and contextually. The substance of the narratives and appearances of Jesus in 9–20 seem to carry a different feel to them from that of the previous verses. There are also a significant number of Greek words that are present in these verses that are found nowhere else in Mark's Gospel, which argues the possibility that Mark did not write this final section.

However, since it is possible to be wrong on this issue, despite these considerations of the possible unreliability of this section, we will still consider what we see in this passage, although possibly with reservation. Even if used, these are also some of Jesus's last words before ascending to Heaven as it is with the last passage we looked at in Matthew, but if you compare this to Jesus's last words in the end of Luke chapter 24, verse 47 doesn't even include the mention of baptism but only that repentance and remission of sins should be preached in His name. Luke, whose authenticity is not disputed, says this starting at verse 44:

> Then He said to them, "These are My words that I spoke to you while I was still with you, that everything written about Me in the Law of Moses and the Prophets and the Psalms must be fulfilled." Then He opened their minds to understand the Scriptures and said to them, "Thus it is written, that the Christ should suffer and on the third day rise from the dead, and that repentance and forgiveness of sins should be proclaimed in His name to all nations, beginning from Jerusalem. You are witnesses of these things. And behold, I Am sending the promise of My Father upon you." He then led them out of town, blessed them, and then ascended into Heaven as they praised Him.

Now, to look more specifically at Mark 16:16 itself, in light of the baptismal regeneration doctrine, we see that this text actually teaches the opposite. Yes, the first part of the verse says, "Whoever believes and is baptized will be saved," but it does not end there. The verse continues by saying, "but whoever does not believe will be condemned." To only look at the beginning of this verse, you could justifiably say that baptism may be a necessary component of salvation, but to use the whole verse, we see that belief is the key ingredient here. There is kind of a four-possibility matrix or quadrant or two by two graph that could be made here. Belief: yes or no; and baptized: yes or no—forming four possible outcomes.

Do you believe and are you baptized? Do you believe but are not baptized? Do you not believe but are baptized? Or are you neither a believer nor baptized? The first part of the verse covers possibility number one. The second part of the verse basically covers the last two possibilities as it does not specify whether or not the person is baptized. The one possibility that this verse absolutely does not touch on is a believer who is not baptized. You see, back in these early days, following the Great Commission, it was basically entirely foreign to think of a believer who was not baptized. They were almost, in a sense, synonymous in that every person who came to Christ was almost immediately baptized as seen throughout the book of Acts.

Usually, at the very moment of conversion, a current disciple or apostle who was present, and probably the one that led them through their conversion, would immediately say something like, "Can anyone withhold water for baptizing these people, who have received the Holy Spirit just as we have" (Acts 10:47)? And they would be baptized right away.

As this verse plainly shows us, and as is the norm throughout Acts, they had received the Holy Spirit already, prior to being baptized in water, and therefore were saved prior to being baptized in water. Baptism was the immediate and first act of obedience of the converted and saved believer, declaring his submission and identification with Christ. If anyone were to refuse this act of obedience, being unwilling to announce his identification with Christ, it was analogous to the continuance of an unregenerate heart of someone who remained lost and dead—the unconverted. So, though saved and baptized were somewhat viewed as synonymous, the latter does not precede or make possible the former, but the saved will and should always be baptized.

> The first command for every Christian is baptism. The apostles sometimes included baptism in the call to faith (Acts 2:38; cf. Mark 16:16). Baptism is not a condition of salvation but an initial step of obedience for the Christian. Conversion is complete before baptism occurs; baptism is only an external sign that testifies to what has occurred in the sinner's heart. Baptism is a ritual, and it is precisely the kind of 'work'

Paul states cannot be meritorious (cf. Rom. 4:10–11). Nevertheless, one can hardly read the New Testament without noticing the heavy stress the early church placed on baptism. They simply assumed that every genuine believer would embark on a life of obedience and discipleship. That was nonnegotiable. Therefore, they viewed baptism as the turning point. Only those who were baptized were considered Christians. That is why the Ethiopian eunuch was so eager to be baptized (Acts 8:36–39).[4]

Charles Spurgeon wrote, "If the professed convert distinctly and deliberately declares that he knows the Lord's will, but does not mean to attend to it, you are not to pamper his presumptions, but it is your duty to assure him that he is not saved."[5]

Continuing on in Mark 16:16, the latter half of the verse says, "whoever does not believe will be condemned." It simply does not matter whether you are baptized or not, if you do not believe, you will be condemned. Belief is the key here, not baptism. Yes, they can be linked together intimately, but the latter does not make the former possible. If you do not believe, you will be condemned. Period. If you do believe, then you will be saved and there is no reason whatsoever as to why you should not be baptized. It is commanded that all believers be baptized by Jesus Himself in the Great Commission. However, salvation is not dependent upon baptism.

Nowhere in the Bible does it say, "He that is not baptized is/will be condemned;" however, it does say in several spots, "He who does not believe is/will be condemned" (Ps. 78:21–22; Matt. 10:33; Mark 16:16; Luke 8:12; John 3:18, 36, 5:38, 8:24; 2 Thess. 2:12; 1 John 2:23, 5:10; Jude 4–5; Rev. 21:8). Plus, there are a few stories in the Bible that talk of people who were saved with no mention of being baptized (Matt. 9:2—paralytic; Luke 7:47–50—penitent woman; Luke 18:10–14—publican; Luke 23:42–43—thief on the cross; John 4:39–42—many Samaritans believe, and baptism is not mentioned; John 17:3).

Plus, there is no written record of any of the apostles being baptized (which would kind of be a big deal if baptism were necessary for salvation), other than Paul in Acts 9, but still, he also clearly received the Holy Spirit prior to being baptized (vv. 17–18). Belief is the determining factor of salvation, not belief and baptism married together as prerequisites leading to salvation. Baptism is instead a commanded first act of obedience of all converted and saved believers.

Another passage that is used to teach this doctrine is John 3:5. This passage comes from the discussion when Nicodemus the pharisee approached Jesus. It reads, "Jesus answered, 'Truly, truly, I say to you, unless one is born of water and the Spirit, he cannot enter the Kingdom of God.'"

> Jesus referred not to literal water here but to the need for "cleansing" (e.g., Ezek. 36:24–27). When water is used figuratively in the Old Testament, it habitually refers to renewal or spiritual cleansing, especially when used in conjunction with "spirit" (Isa. 44:3–4, 55:1–3; Jer. 2:13; Joel 2:28–29; remember that at the time of Jesus their entirety of Scripture was only that of the Old Testament—the New Testament hadn't been written yet; they were in the process of living it). Thus, Jesus made reference to the spiritual washing or purification of the soul accomplished by the Holy Spirit through the Word of God at the moment of salvation (cf. Eph. 5:26; Ti. 3:5) required for belonging to His Kingdom.[6]

To assume that just because the word *water* is being used here that it automatically assumes reference to the sacrament of water baptism and that the sacrament of water baptism is necessary in order to receive salvation is entirely presumptuous.

There are several verses throughout Scripture that have water references that are entirely non-baptismal in substance. It is very often referring to either the Word of God or the Holy Spirit or the spiritual cleansing made possible by Christ, not the physical sacrament of water baptism, and it further does not define baptism as necessary for salvation.

In John 4:14, Jesus says, "Whoever drinks <u>the water I give</u> shall never thirst. The <u>water that I give</u> him will become in him a <u>spring of water welling up to eternal life</u>." This passage is referring to Christ Himself as the Living Water Who is the source of eternal life which is mediated by the Holy Spirit. It clearly does not refer to baptism.

John 7:38–39 gives us these words from Jesus, "He *that believes on Me*, out of his belly shall flow <u>rivers of living water</u>. (But <u>this He spoke of the Spirit</u>, which they *that believe on Him should receive*.)" First of all, notice here that at the beginning and the end of this verse, it confirms the fact that it is only through believing in Jesus that we shall be saved and filled with the Holy Spirit. It has nothing to do with a mandate to baptism. Also, the reference to water here is specifically defined in this passage itself, "This He spoke of the Spirit." The Spirit is the substance of the reference to "water."

We see another reference to water in Ephesians 5:26, which we will look at deeper later in this chapter. "[H]aving cleansed her by the washing of water by the Word." This passage also defines the use of the word *water* right inside the verse itself. The "water" is referring to the Word, not the physical act of baptism. The Word refers to Jesus Christ (John 1:1–4, 14). Jesus alone is the source of salvation.

To put salvation or the reception of salvation or obtainment of salvation on anything other than Jesus Himself and Jesus alone is heresy and leads to self-righteousness and works-based religiosity. Other verses confirm this also, using these same analogies. In John 15:3, Jesus tells us, "Already you are clean because of the Word that I have spoken to you."

James 1:21 tells us, "Receive with meekness the implanted Word, which is able to save your souls."

First Peter 1:23 teaches us this, "You have been born again… through the living and abiding Word of God."

All of these passages are referring to salvation and new life in Christ and link that salvation to the Word of God, Jesus Himself, and/or the Spirit, not to a physical sacrament of water baptism.

Those who believe in some sort of baptismal efficacy quote verses such as John 3:5 and Titus 3:5, etc., as referring to baptism's relation to salvation. I don't believe that this assumption can bear scrutiny. In short, water and cleansing in these contexts refer to the efficacy of the Spirit-empowered Word of God to apply Christ's completed work to cleanse the entire person of sin (its culpability, its corrupting power, and its reign). When Jesus spoke of living water as flowing from our innermost being, He referred to the cleansing power of the Spirit (John 7:39). Paul spoke of Jesus's giving Himself up for the church, "to make her holy, cleansing her by the washing with water through the Word" (Eph. 5:26). James, focusing on the Word, wrote, "He chose to give us birth through the Word of Truth, that we might be a kind of firstfruits of all He created" (James 1:18). Paul describes salvation in a monergistic context: "[God] saved us, not because of righteous things we had done, but because of His mercy. He saved us through the washing of rebirth and renewal by the Holy Spirit, Whom He poured out on us generously through Jesus Christ our Savior" (Ti. 3:5–6). Paul carefully constructs this presentation to exclude any act of human obedience, even relating justification in the next verse not to faith but to grace, "so that being justified by His grace we might become heirs according to the hope of eternal life" (Ti. 3:7). These texts, along with others, show that the references to washing refer to the reality of spiritual cleansing as opposed to the Old Testament ritual washings. These washings are fulfilled through the perfect, once-for-all sacrificial death of Jesus Christ by which He reconciled His people to God, thus gaining for them the Spirit's operations of calling, union with Christ, sanctification, and persevering grace. The washing of our body with pure water, being born of water and the Spirit, the washing of regeneration, the washing of water with the Word point not to baptism but to the reality of the Spirit's powerful application of the Word for salvation.[7]

John MacArthur has much to add on this dialogue between Jesus and Nicodemus in John 3. In his book, *The Gospel According to Jesus*, he writes:

> When Nicodemus heard Christ talking about a new birth, his head must have been a bog. He had always believed that salvation was to be earned by good works. He probably even expected Christ to commend him for his strict legalism! Instead, Jesus confronted him with the futility of his religion. What a let down! Unlike religious works, being born again was something Nicodemus could not do himself.
>
> Nicodemus's reply has often been misunderstood: "How can a man be born when he is old? He cannot enter a second time into his mother's womb and be born, can he" (John 3:4)? Nicodemus was not speaking in literal terms. We must give him credit for a little common sense. Surely he was not so feeble-minded as to think Jesus was really talking about reentering the womb and literally being born again. A teacher himself, Nicodemus understood the rabbinical method of figurative language to teach Spiritual

truth, and he was merely picking up Jesus's symbolism. He was really saying, "I can't start all over. It's too late. I've gone too far in my religious system to start over. There's no hope for me if I must begin from the beginning."

Jesus was demanding that Nicodemus forsake everything that he stood for, and Nicodemus knew it. Far from offering this man an easy conversion, Christ was challenging him with the most difficult demand He could make. Nicodemus would gladly have given money, fasted, or performed any ritual Jesus could have prescribed. But to call him to a Spiritual rebirth was asking him to acknowledge his own insufficiency and turn away from everything he was committed to.

Jesus merely reiterated, "Truly, truly, I say to you, unless one is born of water and the Spirit, he cannot enter into the Kingdom of God" (John 3:5). Some people say that means literal water—H2O. It doesn't. This has nothing to do with water or baptism. Salvation cannot be accomplished by a bath. John 4:2 says Jesus baptized no one. If baptism were a condition of salvation, He would've been baptizing people; after all, He came to seek and to save the lost (Luke 19:10). The water Jesus is speaking of is merely symbolic—as it was in the Old Testament—of purification.

Nicodemus would have understood this reference to the Old Testament water of purification, which was sprinkled on the altar and sacrifices in most of the rituals. Being a scholar, Nicodemus no doubt remembered Ezekiel 36:25 and the promise of the New Covenant: "Then I will sprinkle clean water on you." Two verses later is the promise, "I will put My Spirit within you" (v.

27). Those statements, bringing the ideas of the water and the Spirit together, sandwich another promise, "I will give you a new heart, and put a new spirit within you; and I will remove the heart of stone from your flesh and give you a heart of flesh" (v. 26). That is the Old Testament promise of regeneration by water and the Spirit.

The only baptism mentioned here is the baptism of the Holy Spirit. John the Baptist said, "He Who sent me to baptize in water said to me, 'He upon Whom you see the Spirit descending and remaining upon Him, this is the One Who baptizes in the Holy Spirit'" (John 1:33). Spirit baptism takes place at salvation, when the Lord places the believer into the body of Christ by means of the Holy Spirit (1 Cor. 12:13), and purifies the believer by the water of the Word (Eph. 5:26; cf. John 15:3). Paul refers to this as "the washing of regeneration, and renewing by the Holy Spirit" (Ti. 3:5), almost perfectly echoing Jesus's words in John 3:5: "Unless one is born of water [the washing of regeneration] and the Spirit [and renewing by the Holy Spirit], he cannot enter into the Kingdom of God."

Thus, Jesus was saying to Nicodemus, "You need to be spiritually purified and spiritually reborn." The whole point was that law and religious rituals—including baptism—cannot give eternal life. We can assume Nicodemus got the message, because it jarred him fiercely.[8]

Pastor John also has this to add from a sermon he preached called Becoming a Better You.

I love the encounter between Jesus and Nicodemus because Nicodemus says, "What do I need to do to be born again?" Now, he understands that this is an analogical discussion with spiritual realities in view. He's not stupid. He knows he's talking to The Teacher in Israel. And when Jesus says to him, "You need to be born again," he knows He's not talking about going back in the womb and being reborn. But he speaks back in analogies, "How do I do this? How can I be born again?" That is such a basic question. "How do I do that?" And Jesus says this, "Well that which is born of the flesh is flesh, and that which is born of the Spirit is spirit. Don't be amazed that I said to you, 'You must be born again.'"

But as far as how you do that, "The wind blows where it wishes and you hear the sound of it. You don't know where it comes from, where it's going, so is everyone who's born of the Spirit." What? What is His answer? His answer is, you can't do anything! Anymore than you can control the wind! You can't control the Holy Spirit. But you have been, if you are born again, regenerated by the power of God, and the will of God, and the purpose of God. How does it happen though? Isn't there a context in which it happens? Yes. First Peter 1:20–23, "You're begotten again by the Word of Truth." The hearing of the Gospel, as we heard from Micah earlier. Faith comes by hearing the Word of Christ. The hearing of the Gospel, and at that moment the marvelous regenerating power of the Spirit of God, because He wills to do it, gives us life. And this is the means that produces in us a living hope. That is a hope that never dies. We are not like all men, most miserable, because we have a hope that dies. Look, all the hope you have in this world will die. If it's all in this world, if all your hope is here it will die, if it hasn't died it will die, but we have a hope that will not die. A living hope, given to us because we have been given life, regenerated. We now have eternal life. And for us to die is merely gain, to enter into the fullness of that life. The source is God. The motive is mercy. The means is regeneration.[9]

Not physical water baptism.

Pastor John also adds this in a devotional called *An Old Testament Illustration of Salvation*:

"As Moses lifted up the serpent in the wilderness, even so must the Son of Man be lifted up; so that whoever believes will in Him have eternal life" (John 3:14–15). To emphasize for Nicodemus that there was no excuse for him to be ignorant of the way of salvation, Jesus appealed to a familiar incident in the Old Testament (Num. 21:5–9). The event took place during Israel's forty years of wilderness wandering after leaving Egypt and before entering the Promised Land. As a judgment on the people's incessant complaining, the Lord sent venomous snakes to infest their camp. In desperation, the Israelites begged Moses to intercede on their behalf. And God answered Moses' prayerful petition by showing mercy to His rebellious people. He instructed Moses to make a bronze replica of a snake and raise it above the camp on a pole. Those who were bitten would be healed if they but looked at it, thereby acknowledging their guilt and expressing faith in God's forgiveness and healing power. The point of Jesus's analogy is that just "as Moses lifted up the serpent in the wilderness, even so must the Son of Man be lifted up" (crucified; cf.

8:28; 12:32, 34). The term *must* emphasizes that Christ's death was a necessary part of God's plan of salvation. He had to die as a substitute for sinners. The stricken Israelites were cured by obediently looking to the elevated serpent, apart from any works or righteousness of their own, in complete hope and dependence on God's Word. In the same way, whoever looks in faith alone to the crucified Christ will be cured from sin's deadly bite and "will in Him have eternal life."[10]

In the book of Acts, we find a couple passages that baptismal salvation adherents use to teach this doctrine. Before we get into those specific verses, though, I feel that we should touch on a few things first. First of all, the book of John was actually written after Acts. It was the latest written of the gospel accounts. Prior to John writing his account in the Gospel of John, Luke had already written his second book, the book of Acts. John appears in the Bible first as it parallels the eyewitness gospel accounts of Jesus's ministry here on earth in the flesh in Matthew, Mark, and Luke, but it was written by John 20–30 years after Acts had already been written. If water baptism was absolutely necessary for salvation, why is it barely talked about in John, other than (possibly) just that one verse (although not literally) in 3:5? Plus, throughout his Gospel, John referred to himself as "the one whom Jesus loved." He was one of the chief apostles, so you would think that if baptism was absolutely necessary for salvation, that John, being so close to Jesus, would've made a much more clear and indicative case for its absolute necessity.

Not to mention, why wouldn't Jesus Himself have made a more clear case for its necessity? If it is of utter importance, why wouldn't John—and Jesus, for that matter—spend much more time making certain that it was taught in fullness so that no one may misinterpret? Adherents may say that the one passage in John 3:5, along with the others we looked at in the gospels, is all you need and that it doesn't need to be hammered to death, but when Jesus and John, and later Paul and Peter, all made far more statements of faith and salvation without mention to physical water baptism as necessity, the question still holds. Plus, we have already seen that the other couple of verses in the gospel accounts don't exactly teach a solid and proof-positive doctrine.

Secondly, some who hold to the teachings of baptismal regeneration also tend to hold to the school of belief that Acts is a foundational book that the structure and practice of the entire New Covenant church should be based off of (The Restoration Movement is based on trying to restore today's church to that of the New Testament church of Acts). This should not be the case for a couple reasons.

Acts presents a **transitional period** where God's focus turns from Israel to the Church. The events recorded in Acts are not always normative and can't be seen as the exact pattern that is to follow forever after. Many devout Jews found it hard to make the transition rapidly, even Paul; therefore, parts of Acts deal with these situations, while other portions deal with the Gentiles being led to Christ and receiving the same gift that the Jews had received. Each situation is dealt with uniquely and isn't always the same as some of the others.

For example: Samaritans and Gentiles (Cornelius) waiting to receive the Holy Spirit until the Jews were there to witness it so as to dissolve any dichotomy that would've remained if the Jews had not physically witnessed the indwelling. There is simply a difference in the way things were being done during Acts since it is a book of transition, so how can you make a structured and permanent practice when things differ from one chapter to another?

Compare these two passages to see some of the differences in practice. Acts 8:15–17 shows us the account of Peter and John ministering to some Samaritans:

> Peter and John, who came down and prayed for them that they might receive the Holy Spirit, for He had not yet fallen on any of them, but they had only been baptized in the name of the Lord Jesus. Then they laid their hands on them and they received the Holy Spirit.

And then in Acts 10:44–48, we see a very different operation:

> While Peter was still saying these things, the Holy Spirit fell on all who heard the Word. And the believers from among the circumcised who had come with Peter were amazed, because the gift of the Holy Spirit was poured out even on the Gentiles. For they were hearing them speaking in tongues and extolling God. Then Peter declared, "Can anyone withhold water for baptizing these people, who have received the Holy Spirit just as we have?" And he commanded them to be baptized in the name of Jesus Christ. Then they asked him to remain for some days.

And, yes, both of these passages mention baptism, but neither one shows any legitimacy to baptismal regeneration. Plus, the two passages show completely opposite sequences, and one shows laying on of hands, and the other does not. Again, Acts is a transitional book. You cannot take the experiences of the people in Acts and make it the structural norm for the Church as a whole for the rest of succeeding history. They are not meant as commands or explicit statements; they are merely historical experiences extracted out of a transitional period, and what happens during a transition does not necessarily set the pattern.

> If we're going to take the book of Acts as normative, then we must take the book of Acts in its total as normative and we're going to have some immensely difficult issues to deal with. The fact of the matter is that Acts was never intended to be the primary basis for teaching doctrine to the church. The book of Acts records only the earliest days of the church age and shows the church in tradition coming out of the old age and into the new. Coming out as it were,

the Old Testament into the New Testament. The apostolic healings and miracles and signs and wonders evident in the book of Acts were not even common to all believers even in those days, but were uniquely restricted to the apostles and those who worked alongside of them. They were exceptional events, each with specific purposes, and always associated with the ministry of the apostles and their frequency can be seen decreasing dramatically even from the beginning of the book of Acts to the end. Acts covers a crucial period that started at the beginning of the church at Pentecost and ended about thirty years later with Paul in prison following his third missionary journey. Transitions are seen from beginning to end in the book of Acts, changes come in almost every chapter as the Old Covenant fades away and the New Covenant comes in all its fullness. In the book of Acts, we are in a transition which moves from the synagogue to the church. We are in a transition which moves away from an order of law into an order of grace. The Church has transformed from a group of Jewish believers to a body made up of Jews and Gentiles united in Christ. Believers at the beginning of Acts were related to God under an old pattern. By the end, all believers were in Christ, living under a new pattern, indwelt by the Holy Spirit in a new and unique relationship. Acts, therefore, covers an extraordinary time in history, a time of transition from the old to the new, and the transition it records, listen carefully, is never to be repeated. There is only one time frame in which you move from the old to the new. That history does not come again, never will come again. And those elements that are true of that transition are not repeatable. For the transition itself needs not repetition. Therefore, we must say, the only teachings in the book of Acts which can be called normative for the church are those that are explicitly taught elsewhere in Scripture.[11]

So we see that we should not exactly base doctrinal formation off of the book of Acts as it is a transitional book and at times shows differences in sequences when referring to the salvational processes being done in its timeline, but we may use the book of Acts to solidify a doctrine or teaching if it indeed mirrors the rest of Scripture on an issue. Taking this into consideration, there are three passages in the book of Acts that teachers of the baptismal regeneration doctrine use to teach this doctrine, so we will look at each of these and compare them to the rest of Scripture to see if they do indeed mirror or part from the teachings found throughout the rest of Scripture.

The first is found in Acts 2:38, and is probably the most influential for this doctrine of baptismal regeneration. In this section of Scripture, Peter is giving his famous and unapologetic sermon at Pentecost to all of those, from many different areas, about the Gospel of Christ Jesus Who had recently been crucified, but then rose from the dead, was witnessed alive by many, and then ascended into Heaven. The Holy Spirit had just come in a powerful and overwhelming presence, just as Christ had promised, and the Spirit filled all of the believers in Christ and indwelt them and they all started praising God in different languages.

There were many others in the area that heard this going on and came to investigate. After Peter's sermon and telling of the Gospel message, many were convicted and asked, "What shall we do?"

Verse 38 reads, "And Peter said to them, 'Repent and be baptized every one of you in the name of Jesus Christ for the forgiveness of your sins, and you will receive the gift of the Holy Spirit.'"

Those who teach baptismal regeneration use this passage as one of their main go-to passages for this doctrine as it plainly states in most English translations similar wording to, "Repent and be baptized...for the remission of sins" or "for the forgiveness of your sins," and it seems to plainly teach that we must both repent and be baptized in order to become forgiven of our sins, which are two of the main components that they believe are necessary for salvation to be realized and effected.

Quickly in regard to that, might I express that belief and confession are not included in this passage, which are the other two components held in their four-part formula for how salvation is received. So would that mean that in using this passage to teach this doctrine it either negates these two components or is wholly inadequate by itself to base doctrine off of? But also, in interpreting this passage in this way, it seems to contradict everything else that we have already looked at as far as salvation being received or credited to our account. So we must dig deeper and cross reference with the rest of Scripture.

First of all, when Peter says, "Repent," he is referring to:

> [A] change of mind and purpose that turns an individual from sin to God (1 Thess. 1:9). Such change involves more than fearing the consequences of God's judgment. Genuine repentance knows that the evil of sin must be forsaken and the Person and work of Christ totally and singularly embraced. Peter exhorted his hearers to repent, otherwise they would not experience true conversion. This is no mere academic change of mind, nor mere regret or remorse. John the Baptist spoke of repentance as a radical turning from sin that inevitably became manifest in the fruit of righteousness. True repentance cannot occur apart from genuine sorrow over one's sin (2 Cor. 7:10). Repentance belongs to the realm or sphere of salvation. Repentance is at the very heart of and proves one's salvation. All true repentance is produced by God's sovereign grace, and without such grace human effort to change is futile (cf. Jer. 13:23). When God, by grace, grants saving faith (Eph. 2:8–9), it includes

the granting of repentance from sin. Neither is a human work.[12]

Repentance is a necessary component, but it is not a separate component. True repentance is a necessary and essential aspect of true and saving faith. It is a radical turning from sin which finds its authorship and effectual position from fully surrendered faith and trust in Jesus Christ as the only One Who could redeem us from those sins.

"Repentance toward God and faith toward Christ are like two sides of the same coin, each of which implies and requires the other."[13]

True repentance is to view all sin as an afterthought. To see sin as a past activity and to move forward ahead of it as to not return. It is to reject your old way of life in sin, and in turn to seek God's purpose for your life. Repentance is at the very heart of and proves one's salvation, and this attitude of their hearts was apparent in verse 37 which states, "When they heard this, they were pierced to the heart, and said to Peter and the rest of the apostles, 'Brothers, what shall we do'" (NASB)? Repentance also demonstrates new behavior that proves a change of heart, and a conscious decision to turn away from sin.

Peter also includes "be baptized." In the Greek, the word used here is *baptizo* and simply means "to immerse fully" into something. Full submersion, fully engulfed immersion. It can mean in water, but isn't always necessarily implied. First Corinthians 10:2 states, "All were baptized into Moses." The word used here is taken from the root word *baptizo*, and it simply means that they were immersed into Moses' teachings and following God the way he was leading them and had absolutely nothing to do with water. However, here in this passage in Acts, Peter was referring to and:

[O]beying Christ's command from Matt. 28:19 and urging the people who repented and turned to the Lord Christ for salvation to identify, through the waters of baptism, with His death, burial and resurrection. This is the first time the apostles publicly enjoined people to obey that ceremony. Prior to this, many Jews had experienced the baptism of John the Baptist, and were also familiar with the baptism of Gentile converts to Judaism (proselytes). For the new believer, this was a crucial but costly identification to accept "in the name of Jesus Christ."[14]

To keep progressing through this verse, Peter continues, "Be baptized every one of you in the name of Jesus Christ;"

> [T]hat is, firmly believe the doctrine of Christ, and submit to His grace and government; and make an open solemn profession of this, and come under an engagement to abide by it, by submitting to the ordinance of baptism; be proselyted to Christ and to His holy religion, and renounce your infidelity. Take Jesus for your King, and by baptism swear allegiance to Him; take Him for your Prophet, and hear Him; take Him for your Priest, to make atonement for you.[15]

We are to be baptized believing and relying fully in the name of Jesus Christ as the prophesied Messiah, being a truly repentant confessant, denouncing all sin as a past occurrence, and swearing our eternal commitment, loyalty, and dedication to Him. The word *baptized* or *baptizo* used here is reflective of Christ's command of immersion in water, but it more fully meant complete immersion into Christ Himself. "Baptism, more than any other symbol, conveys our communion with Jesus. It expresses that our lives are irrevocably wrapped up with Jesus Christ."[16]

Early Christian theologian and philosopher, St. Augustine of Hippo, called baptism "a visible sign of an invisible grace." And let's not forget that Christ commissioned us to go and make disciples of all nations and baptize them but to link the sacrament of baptism in water as a necessary component leading to salvation still lies in contrast to much of Scripture, even though on the surface it looks like it's pretty straightforward, "Be baptized every one of you in the name of Jesus Christ for the remission of sins, and you will receive the gift of the Holy Spirit." So we must continue to dig deeper.

First of all, jumping back into the gospels a bit, we read a few passages that help lay ground here. In Mark 1:4 we read, "John baptized…proclaiming a baptism of repentance for the remission of sins." We also see a very similar phrase in Luke 3:3, "proclaiming a baptism of repentance for the forgiveness of sins." Almost the same wording as we see in Acts 2:38, but slightly different and very telling. This is:

> [A] baptism resulting from true repentance. John's ministry was to call Israel to repentance in preparation for the coming of Messiah. Baptism did not produce repentance, but was its result (cf. Matt. 3:7–8). Far more than a mere change of mind or remorse, repentance involves a turning from sin to God (cf. 1 Thess. 1:9), which results in righteous living. Genuine repentance is a work of God in the human heart, as we see in Acts 11:18, which tells us, "God has granted to the Gentiles also the repentance that leads to life." John's rite of baptism did not produce forgiveness of sins; it was only the outward confession and illustration of the true repentance that results in forgiveness. This baptism was to symbolize and testify of the forgiveness already received upon repentance. The symbolism of John's baptism likely had its roots in OT purification rituals (cf. Lev. 15:13). Baptism had also long been administered to Gentile proselytes coming into Judaism. The baptism of John thus powerfully and dramatically symbolized repentance. The meaning of John's baptism differs somewhat

from Christian baptism (cf. Acts 18:25, 19:1–5). Actually, Christian baptism altered the significance of the ritual, symbolizing the believer's identification with Christ in His death, burial and resurrection.[17]

John acknowledged this difference also, as did some of the other apostles. In Matthew 3:11, we read John the Baptist's words, "I baptize you with water for repentance, but He [Jesus] will baptize you with the Holy Spirit and with fire" (also stated in Mark 1:8; Luke 3:16; John 1:26, 31, 33; Acts 1:5, 11:16). This passage in Matthew and the one in Luke add "and with fire" to the text, which speaks of Christ's baptism of judgment upon the unrepentant, but all of these verses clearly show that there is a difference between John's baptism and Christian baptism in the name of Jesus Christ receiving the Holy Spirit.

There is clearly a distinction being made between being baptized in water and being baptized with the Holy Spirit. The only time the phrase "baptized with water" is used anywhere in Scripture is in correlation with John's baptism, not in the baptism of the Holy Spirit. The water is not needed for the baptism of the Holy Spirit to be effective. The Complete Jewish Bible translation reads Luke 3:16 like this:

> Yochanan (John) answered them all, "I am immersing you in water, but He Who is coming is more powerful than I... He will immerse you in the Ruach Hakodesh (Holy Spirit) and in fire."

And we see this clearly as there are cases where someone had clearly received the Holy Spirit prior to being baptized in water (Acts 9:17–18, 10:44–48, 16:14). We also see several cases of receiving forgiveness of sins and salvation with no mention of baptism at all (Matt. 9:2; Luke 7:47–50, 18:10–14, 23:42–43; John 4:39–42, 17). The thief on the cross is the prime example. He was nailed to a cross next to Jesus and pleaded with Jesus to remember him when He entered into His Kingdom, and Jesus said, "Truly, I say to you, today you will be with Me in Paradise" (Luke 23:42–43). This man was in his last hours. He did not get baptized before his legs were broken and he succumbed to his death while hanging from a cross. His faith and trust in Jesus was, and is also for us, his only necessary component for accepting and receiving Jesus's free gift of being in His direct presence in Paradise for all of eternity.

I once had a proponent of baptismal regeneration tell me that this example of the thief on the cross is excluded because it was before the New Covenant was confirmed since Christ had not yet died, which meant that they were still residents of the Old Covenant. This simply does not stand, though, since we have seen that throughout all of Scripture God's plan of redemption has never changed. It simply doesn't matter whether before or after Christ's death, before or after Pentecost, from Genesis to Revelation, it has always been salvation by faith alone in Christ alone (or for those of the Old Testament, faith in the coming Messiah) as far as the human responsibility constituent is concerned.

The *Thayer's Greek Lexicon*, speaking of John's baptism, explains it as:

> [T]hat purification rite by which men on confessing their sins were bound to spiritual reformation, obtained the pardon of their past sins and became qualified for the benefits of the Messiah's Kingdom soon to be set up. This was valid Christian baptism, *as this was the only baptism the apostles received and it is not recorded anywhere that they were ever re-baptized after Pentecost*.[18]

There isn't a single written record of the apostles even being baptized other than Paul in Acts 9, but still, even then, he clearly received the Holy Spirit prior to being baptized in water (Acts 9:18). Also in the story of Apollos (Acts 18:24–28), there is also not a reference to him being re-baptized in water. He had received John's baptism, but once Priscilla and Aquila explained the Way of God more adequately to him, it never mentions him being rebaptized.

Getting back to Acts 2:38, we also see just a few verses earlier in Acts chapter 2, at verse 21, Peter in his sermon quotes from Joel 2:32, "And it shall come to pass that everyone who calls upon the name of the Lord shall be saved." And this exactly mirrors what we saw in Romans 10:9–10 and 13:

> If you confess with your mouth that Jesus is Lord and believe in your heart that God raised Him from the dead, you will be saved. For with the heart one believes and is justified, and with the mouth one confesses and is saved... For everyone who calls on the name of the Lord will be saved.

> Peter's message was climaxed with essentially the same exhortation as that preached by John the Baptist—"the baptism of repentance for the remission of sins" (Luke 3:3). The difference is that now—and ever since—both repentance and baptism are to be "in the name of Jesus Christ." This, of course, implies faith in Christ as the only One Who can provide remission of sins. The full meaning of baptism in water also now had become evident, testifying of the baptism of the Spirit, as well as the death and resurrection of Christ. It is not that baptism is required for remission of sins (note, for example, the thief on the cross), but rather that baptism is always inseparably associated in Scripture with true repentance and faith.[19]

> Baptism does not produce forgiveness and cleansing from sin. The reality of forgiveness precedes the rite of baptism (Acts 2:41). Genuine

repentance brings from God the forgiveness of sins (cf. Eph. 1:7), and because of that the new believer was to be baptized. Baptism, however, was to be the ever-present act of obedience, so that it became synonymous with salvation. Thus, to say one is baptized for forgiveness was the same as saying one was saved. Every believer enjoys the complete forgiveness of sins, and the gift of the Holy Spirit.[20]

Then Peter finishes up his sermon by saying, in verse 39, "For the promise is for you and for your children and for all who are far off, everyone whom the Lord our God calls to Himself." So we see here again, as we discussed earlier in the book regarding God's divine sovereignty, it is only those who God calls to Himself who receive this promise of salvation. Salvation is ultimately from the Lord, as we have seen through the earlier portions of this book and all the Scripture that we referenced to it, so Peter is not saying here that there is now a new component needed in order to receive salvational status. Ultimately, it is still all God's work within us as we use to be dead and wretched sinners and enemies of God (Rom. 5:6, 8, 10; Eph. 2:5), and He has made us alive anew.

Yes, Peter was referencing the sacrament of water baptism and calling out for them to partake in it, but he was not saying the sacrament of water baptism is necessary in order to be forgiven of all our sins and therefore to be saved, but in the salvational sense, he was saying that "baptizo," full immersion, "in the name of Jesus Christ" is what brings about remission of sins. Full immersion into Christ is synonymous with saving faith. Not the water. Not just simple head knowledge but truly calling on the name of Christ as our only means of salvation and immersing ourselves fully into His truth which is the only thing we can and must do for remission of sins to take place. "Baptism is a public representation of that which actually saves the believer—one's personal faith in the death, burial and resurrection of Jesus the Messiah."[21]

In Matthew 26:28, we received these words from Jesus, "This is My blood of the covenant...for the forgiveness of sins."

"Covenants were ratified with the blood of a sacrifice. The blood of the new covenant is not an animal's blood, but Christ's Own blood, shed for the remission of sins."[22] The blood is what saves us; the water is merely a symbol of what already has taken place.

One of the biggest and most favorable benefits that this verse has for the baptismal regeneration doctrine is that it uses the English phrasing, "Repent and be baptized...for the forgiveness of sins." As we've stated, on the surface, that looks pretty straightforward, but as we also have seen, it contradicts many other portions of Scripture, and we've also shown that it doesn't exactly mean what it initially looks like at quick glance. Peter is being reflective of the sacrament of water baptism, following the command of Jesus in Matthew 28:19, but not in a salvation sense; the salvational assimilation being taught is that of full and complete immersion into Christ Himself and reception of the Holy Spirit through Him.

We are able to shine much more light on this by going further into this passage and deeper into the original Greek text. The Greek preposition *eis*, which is the word that is translated into the English word *for*, has several different meanings. "Because of," "in view of," "in response to," "in order to obtain," "for the purpose of." Baptismal regeneration proponents would love to use the last couple of those choices, in essence making it a forward-looking action; however, many theologians have stated that there are several different usages of this word, *eis*, but have failed to find anything stating that it always means a forward-looking action, and have failed to find any Greek scholar saying that it always means "in order to obtain" as the only meaning.

Eis cannot and simply does not always mean a forward-looking action in order to obtain. Even in English, if I were to say, "Take this aspirin for a headache," I am not saying, "Take this aspirin in order to obtain a headache." I am saying, "Take this aspirin because of or in response to a headache."

The Holman Christian Standard Version adds to this by saying:

> *For* could have two meanings. If you saw a poster saying "Jesse James Wanted for Robbery," *for* could mean Jesse is wanted so he can commit a robbery or is wanted because he has already committed a robbery. The latter sense is the correct one. So too in this passage, the word *for* signifies an action in the past. Otherwise, it would violate the entire tenor of the New Testament teaching on salvation by grace and not by works.

Taking all of this into consideration, this verse might be better translated by saying "because of the forgiveness of sins."

> A comparison of Peter's message in Acts 10:34–43 makes it clear that "remission of sins" comes to "whoever believes." Believers are baptized in view of God's work of forgiveness, not in order to receive that forgiveness. God's forgiveness in Christ gives baptism it's significance. Baptism is a public declaration that a person's sins have been forgiven because of the finished work of Christ on the cross.[23]

Baptism does not produce forgiveness of sins. The consummation and reality of forgiveness precedes the religious sacrament of water baptism (Acts 2:41, 9:18, 10:44–48). Acts 3:19 and 2 Corinthians 7:10 show us that genuine repentance brings from God the forgiveness of sins (also cf. Ps. 32:5; Prov. 28:13; Eph. 1:7; 1 John 1:9), and because of that preexistent truth, the new believer was to be baptized. However, baptism was to be the ever-present and immediate act of obedience once a salvational relationship with Christ was established so that it became synonymous with salvation, in a sense. The Amplified Holy Bible translation reads like this:

> Repent [change your old way of thinking, turn from your sinful ways, accept and follow Jesus as the Messiah] and be baptized, each of you, in the name of Jesus Christ because of the forgiveness of your sins; and you will receive the gift of the Holy Spirit.

Peter's sermon in Acts 2:

> [W]as a clarion call to repentance. The message penetrated his listener's hearts, and they asked Peter what response was expected of them. Peter said plainly, "Repent, and let each of you be baptized in the name of Jesus Christ for the forgiveness of your sins." Note that he made no mention of faith. That was implied in the call to repentance. Peter was not making baptism a condition of their salvation; he simply outlined the first step of obedience that should follow their repentance (cf. 10:43–48). Peter's audience, familiar with the ministry of John the Baptist— understood baptism as an external corroboration of sincere repentance (cf. Matt. 3:5–8). Peter was not asking them to perform a meritorious act, and the whole of Biblical teaching makes that clear. But the message he gave them that day was a straightforward command to repent. As the context of Acts 2 shows, the people who heard Peter understood that he was demanding unconditional surrender to the Lord Jesus Christ.[24]

The second of the three passages in Acts that is used to teach baptismal regeneration is found in Acts chapter 10. In this account, a Gentile man named Cornelius called for Peter to come and teach him and his family everything about God, so Peter also preached the Gospel message to this group of people, and upon learning everything about Christ, and believing in Him, the Holy Spirit came upon them.

The verse we are focusing on is verse 47, which reads, "Can anyone withhold water for baptizing these people, who have received the Holy Spirit just as we have?" What is confusing about baptismal regeneration proponents using this verse to teach that baptism is a necessary component in receiving salvation is that it plainly demonstrates and teaches the exact opposite. It is plainly made and stated apparent that the Holy Spirit was received prior to the administering of the sacrament and even the presence of water.

In context, this section starts in verse 44 and reads:

> While Peter was still saying these things, the Holy Spirit fell on all who heard the Word. And the believers from among the circumcised who had come with Peter were amazed, because the gift of the Holy Spirit was poured out even on the Gentiles. For they were hearing them speaking in tongues and extolling God. Then Peter declared, "Can anyone withhold water for baptizing these people, who have received the Holy Spirit just as we have?" And he commanded them to be baptized in the name of Jesus Christ.

First of all, going back just one more verse to 43, as we have looked at earlier, it says, "To Him [Jesus] all the prophets bear witness that everyone who believes in Him receives forgiveness of sins through His name." So this verse right here shows what is truly necessary for forgiveness of sins; it couldn't be laid out any simpler, and it coincides with the rest and entirety of Scripture—belief alone in the name of Christ alone brings about forgiveness of sins and therefore salvation. And as always, this is always a wholehearted fully surrendered faith in Christ as Savior, not just simple head knowledge.

Stepping back into this passage, though, and looking at the context of verses 44–48, it is plainly observed that "the Holy Spirit fell on all who heard the Word."

"These people, who have received the Spirit just as we have" were shown to have all the evidence of a redeemed and saved life. They were filled with the Holy Spirit, speaking in tongues and extolling, praising, glorifying, and exalting God's name! They were believers! They were redeemed! They were reborn! They were indwelt with the Holy Spirit, "the guarantee of our inheritance" (2 Cor. 1:22, 5:5; Eph. 1:14). They were at this moment saved and reborn and regenerated, fully immersed into Christ, and now children of God. And they had yet to be baptized in water, as is plainly seen as Peter asks, "Can anyone withhold water for baptizing these people, who have received the Holy Spirit just as we have?"

"Willingness to be baptized is the consistent response in the book of Acts of all who placed their faith in Christ. It is the appropriate response (Matt. 28:19–20) of a regenerated heart" (Acts 2:36–38).[25]

Immediately after this, into chapter 11, Peter returns to Jerusalem and reports back to the church, and initially they started to criticize Peter for going into a Gentile house and eating with them, for this was against their customs and practices as they saw these people as very dirty. Peter then proceeded to recount the entire testimony of what happened and that he received a vision and was sent by God. He also told of their family's conversion and how they received the Holy Spirit just as they themselves had received the Spirit and said, "Who am I to stand in God's way?"

To which all of the other apostles and disciples were silenced and accepted God's sovereignty (cf. Acts 11:1–18). The point I make here is that in recounting this testimony to the rest of the church in Jerusalem, Peter seems to negate the mention of their being baptized in water, and no one seemed to ask, "Well, did you baptize them? Did they get saved? Did they go all the way?"

For one, the sacrament of baptism wasn't the key ingredient. It's not a salvational step. They knew that these people were saved apart from the water because they received the Holy Spirit. And secondly, as we have stated baptism was an immediate response of obedience upon the salvational effect of regenerate new believers. It did not save them, but the church would've assumed that that would have been the immediate action taken after the fact.

The last of the three verses found in Acts that is used for the teaching of baptismal regeneration is found in Acts 22:16, which reads, "And now why do you wait? Rise, and be baptized, and wash away your sins, calling on the name of the Lord."

In this account, we see Paul recounting his conversion along the road to Damascus when Jesus Himself appeared to Paul. Once again, you can at least see how this may be misinterpreted to understand baptism as necessary for the forgiveness of sins, but as we have seen throughout our study, that contradicts the rest of Scripture, so we must look closer. First of all, again, the New Testament was not written in English but in Greek, which did not use punctuation marks until several centuries after Christ, so where the commas and periods are is irrelevant, so for this verse to hold to the entire rest of Scripture, it has to read with the main clause "wash away your sins" being connected to "by calling on His name" and not washing away your sins by baptism.

Corresponding to this, as we see then looking into the Greek text, grammatically speaking, the Greek aorist participle, *epikalesamenos*, translated here in the English, "calling on His name," refers either to an action that is simultaneous with or before that of the main verb, "be baptized." Here, Paul's calling on Christ's name for salvation preceded his water baptism. The participle, therefore, may be translated "having called on His name," which makes more sense as it would clearly indicate the order of events and agrees with the rest of Scripture as we have seen in Acts 2:21, "And it shall come to pass that everyone that calls upon the name of the Lord shall be saved" and Romans 10:13, "For everyone who calls on the name of the Lord will be saved."

Also, in Galatians 1:11–12, we see that Paul received the Gospel by direct revelation from Jesus, and in Acts 9:17–18, he clearly receives the Holy Spirit prior to baptism, and when recounting his entire story of conversion in Acts 26:12–18, he reiterates Christ's direct revelation to him and his conversion and doesn't even mention his own baptism, which you think he would mention if it was a salvational component and which also kind of corresponds with a couple peculiar statements from Paul in 1 Corinthians chapter 1, if indeed baptism were a necessary component to receiving forgiveness of sins and salvation.

In verses 14–16, we read Paul saying, "I thank God that I baptized none of you except Crispus and Gaius, so that no one may say that you were baptized in my name (I did baptize also the house of Stephanas. Beyond that, I do not know whether I baptized anyone else.)." Now, taking this verse into consideration, if baptism were necessary in order to receive salvation, in essence, Paul would be saying here that he thanks God that he saved none of them except for a handful of people, which would be an incredibly horrible thought. If baptism is a necessary component leading to salvation, then Paul is stating that he is thankful that he did not lead more to salvation. That's absurd!

The main point here is found in the next verse, 17, "For Christ did not send me to baptize but to preach the Gospel, and not with words of eloquent wisdom, lest the cross of Christ be emptied of its power." Again, if baptism was indeed necessary, he would essentially be saying here that Christ did not send him to save people. That is ludicrous!

Baptism is not the key here. Preaching the Gospel is the saving component, which brings people into a relationship with Christ and teaching them His Word so that they may believe and trust Him fully and be surrendered in true faith. Verse 17 directly states that it is the preaching of the Gospel that is the importance, not baptism; otherwise, the cross of Christ would be wholly ineffective. If baptism is necessary, then the cross of Christ was entirely insufficient.

Before we move on, on this same note, in John 4:2, it says that Jesus did not baptize any, so in this same line of thinking as with Paul in 1 Corinthians, if baptism is necessary for salvation, it would mean that Jesus did not save any. Pretty humorous, huh?

Moving into Romans, we see another passage that is used by those who teach baptismal regeneration in verses 3–4 of chapter 6:

> Do you not know that all of us who have been baptized into Christ Jesus were baptized into His death? We were buried therefore with Him by baptism into death, in order that, just as Christ was raised from the dead by the glory of the Father, we too might walk in newness of life.

Again, we see that at least on the surface it could be misread as referring to the sacrament of water baptism; however, again, if taught that way, it stands in contrast with all the rest of what Scripture has shown us, so we must continue to look deeper yet again. As we saw back in our discussion with Acts 2:38, the Greek term used here is *baptizo*, which merely means "immersed into."

> So the phrase "baptized into Christ Jesus… baptized into His death" used here has nothing to do with water baptism. Paul was using the expression "baptize" in the same way he employed it in 1 Corinthians 10:2, where he spoke of the Israelites as having been "baptized into Moses."
>
> "Baptized into," in that sense means "identified with" or "linked to." In Galatians 3:27, Paul said, "All of you who were baptized into Christ have clothed yourself with Christ." Again, he was speaking of union with Christ: "The one who joins himself to the Lord is one in spirit with Him" (1 Cor. 6:17).[26]

The sacrament of water baptism certainly does picture this beautiful reality that we die to the old and rise up to the new; however, it is simply an external symbol (1 Pet. 3:21) recognizing the already existent internal salvational truth and is not the saving work itself or even the moment when the saving miracle comes to fullness. By placing truly surrendered saving faith in Jesus Christ, we have all become spiritually immersed, "baptizo," into the Person of Christ and are wholly and indefinitely united with Him and eternally and infinitely identified with Him. Just as here in Romans 6:3–4, 1 Corinthians 10:2 and 12:13, and Galatians 3:27, "baptized" simply means "immersed into."

The nation of Israel was "immersed into Moses," indicating their oneness, solidarity, with him as their leader, just as we are "immersed into Christ," indicating our oneness and our solidarity with Him as our Lord and Savior.

> We are actually in union with Christ and to Him. You cannot have read the New Testament even cursorily without noticing this constantly repeated phrase—"in Christ"—"in Christ Jesus." The apostles go on repeating it and it is one of the most significant and glorious statements in the entire realm and range of truth. It means that we are joined to the Lord Jesus Christ; we have become a part of Him. We are in Him. We belong to Him. We are members of His body. And the teaching is that God regards us as such; and this, of course, means that now, in this relationship, we are sharers in, and partakers of, everything that is true of the Lord Jesus Christ Himself.[27]

Isn't that such a beautiful and mind-blowing truth? Ninety times in the New Testament, we are told that we are "in Christ," "in Jesus Christ," "in Christ Jesus." We are immersed into Him! Continuing on into verses 5–6 of chapter 6, we read:

> For since we have been united with Him in a death like His, we shall certainly be united with Him in a resurrection like His. We know that our old self was crucified with Him in order that the

body of sin might be brought to nothing, so that
we would no longer be enslaved to sin.

This speaks of a spiritual crucifixion on our part, not a literal,
just like verses 3–4 are speaking of a spiritual baptism, not a literal.
Plus, this speaks of being forever washed clean, never to be dirty
again. The water only offers an outer and temporary cleansing. Also,
to take a broader look at the systematic and orderly book of Romans
in regards to this passage in view:

> In Romans chapters 1–5, Paul deals with
> sin and salvation, and baptism is never men-
> tioned. Baptism is not mentioned until you get
> to chapter 6, which begins the section on sanc-
> tification of the Christian life. Baptism does not
> belong on the salvation side, baptism belongs on
> the Christian life side. Obedience after you're a
> Christian, not obedience to become a Christian.[28]

Moving into Paul's first letter to the Corinthians, we see another
passage that proponents of baptismal regeneration use in their teaching, located in chapter 12, verse 13. It reads, "For in one Spirit we
were all baptized into one body—Jews or Greeks, slaves or free—and
all were made to drink of one Spirit." This is found in a section of
Scripture where Paul is utilizing a metaphor describing each individual believer and child of God as being unique and separate members
but all of one whole body. He is referring to the spiritual body of
Christ and the entirety of His church made up of His followers.

Not everyone can be an eye or an ear, a foot, or a hand; each
member has its own unique role and purpose, but we are all combined
into one whole body. This passage is speaking of being immersed
deeply, *baptizo*, into Christ and into union with all other believers,
by the Spirit, as one whole body. We see the very same symbolism
being used in 1 Corinthians 6:17, "He who is joined to the Lord
becomes one Spirit with Him." There is absolutely no actual water

being used or referenced in this verse; neither is this verse making any direct reference to the salvational process anyways.

We also see this exact same symbolism in Paul's letter to the Galatians. In chapter 3, verse 27, as it reads, "For as many of you as were baptized into Christ have put on Christ." Once again teachers of baptismal regeneration will use this verse in their lessons; however, once again, there is no literal water being used here. This is again speaking of being immersed into Christ, *baptizo*, and here it adds a bit more to the analogy and metaphorical picture of putting on Christ as if we were to wear Him as a garment, as our spiritual clothing, fully clothed and engulfed by Him.

This is the same analogous picture and the exact same verb in the Greek, *endyo*, that we are given in Ephesians chapter 6 when we are told to "put on" the armor of God, which is the Lord and Spirit Himself. We are to wear Him as a spiritual garment of protection against all things that are not of God. He is our protection; He is our new life. Water baptism, which is not mentioned here in Galatians, does not save. It is the being immersed into the spiritual union with Christ that happens at the moment of salvation, through faith, by the Holy Spirit that saves. We are fully found in Him, and He is fully found on us.

We also see here, though, in the context of this verse, many statements that add to this. Stepping back into chapter 2, verse 16, we read:

> Yet we know that a person is not justified
> by works of the law but through faith in Jesus
> Christ, so we also have believed in Christ Jesus,
> in order to be justified by faith in Jesus Christ
> and not by works of the law, because by works of
> the law no one will be justified.

We have looked at these verses in an earlier chapter, but we review them as it is the context of this verse in 3:27. Works would refer to any acts of obedience that we would have to do on our own part, including baptism. We are saved by the blood of Christ, and this is facilitated on our part through faith alone. Paul spends the end of chapter 2 and all of chapter 3 on this subject: justification by faith alone, not by works.

> I have been crucified with Christ. It is no longer I who live, but Christ Who lives in me. And the life I now live in the flesh I live by faith in the Son of God, Who loved me and gave Himself for me. I do not nullify the grace of God, for if righteousness were through the law, then Christ died for no purpose. (vv. 2:20–21)

Paul also says here that he was crucified with Christ. This is not literal. This is a spiritual association with Christ through Christ's crucifixion in our place. Just as these verses we are looking at refer to a spiritual baptism, immersion into Christ, which is then followed in the obedience of a saved life by a physical sacrament making an outward public statement of an already present inward reality.

Continuing on with the context of chapter 3:

> Abraham believed God, and it was counted to him as righteousness…it is those of faith who are the sons of Abraham… God would justify the Gentiles by faith…those who are of faith are blessed…all who rely on works of the law are under a curse…no one is justified before God by the law, "for the righteous shall live by faith." Christ redeemed us from the curse of the law by becoming a curse for us…so that we might receive the promised Spirit through faith…so that the promise by faith in Jesus Christ might be given to those who believe…in order that we might be justified by faith. But now that faith has come, we are no longer under a guardian, for in Jesus Christ you are all sons of God, through faith. For as many of you as were baptized into

Christ have put on Christ. There is neither Jew
nor Greek, there is neither slave nor free, there
is neither male or female, for you are all one in
Christ Jesus. (vv. 6–14, 22, 24–28)

Paul just hammered away on the issue of salvation by faith alone,
and he certainly did not just upend it all with one verse but that we
are, through faith, entirely, infinitely, eternally, fully immersed into
spiritual union with Christ Himself, and we are wholly engulfed by
Him, all of which happens at the very moment of salvation, which
is by grace through faith, done by the Holy Spirit because of the
finished work of Christ. This is certainly not referring to one act of
obedience leading to the reception of salvation.

Baptism is not an offer made by man
to God, but an offer made by Christ to man.
Baptism is essentially passive—being baptized,
suffering the call of Christ. Baptism therefore
betokens a breach. This breach is not effected by
man's tearing off his own chains through some
unquenchable longing for a new life of freedom.
The breach has been effected by Christ long since,
and in baptism it is effected in our own lives. He
belongs to Christ alone, and his relationship with
the world is mediated through Him. This death
is a passive event. He can only die in, through
and with Christ. Christ is his death. He receives
his death as a gift. This death is a gift of grace:
a man can never accomplish it by himself. He
who becomes Christ's Own possession must submit to his cross, and suffer and die with Him. It
is a death full of grace. Baptismal (immersion)
death means justification from sin. The sinner
must die that he may be delivered from his sin.
If a man dies he is justified from sin (Rom. 6:7;
Col. 2:20). Sin has no further claim on him, for

death's demand has been met, and its account settled. Justification from sin can only happen through death. The only reason why a sinner's death can bring justification and not condemnation is that this death is a sharing of the death of Christ. It is baptism, immersion, into the death of Christ which effects the forgiveness of sin and justification, and completes our separation from sin. When He called men to follow Him, Jesus was summoning them to a visible act of obedience. To follow Jesus was a public act. Baptism is similarly a public event, for it is the visual means whereby a member is grafted on to the visible body of Christ (Gal. 3:27ff; 1 Cor. 12:13). The breach with the world which has been effected in Christ can no longer remain hidden; it must come out into the open through membership of the Church and participation in its life and worship. Everything necessary for salvation has been accomplished. The baptized live by a constant renewal of their faith in the death of Christ as His act of grace in us. The source of their faith lies in the once-and-for-all-ness of Christ's death. The sacrament should be administered only where there is a firm faith present which remembers Christ's deed of salvation wrought for us once and for all.[29]

In Paul's letter to the Ephesians, there is another passage that is sometimes used by some churches who teach baptismal regeneration. In Ephesians 4:5, we read, "One Lord, one faith, one baptism." To understand that this automatically means water baptism is unwarranted, and even more so, completely unwarranted to understand that it necessarily leads to salvation. John the Baptist, Jesus, and Peter talked about baptism with water and baptism with the Holy Spirit and baptism with fire in Matthew 3:11, Mark 1:8, Luke 3:16, and

John 1:33; and then baptism with water and baptism with the Holy Spirit in John 1:26, 31 and Acts 1:5, 11:16.

However:

> [T]his probably does refer to the water baptism following salvation, which is a believer's public confession of faith in Jesus Christ. Spiritual baptism, by which all believers are placed into the body of Christ, is implied in Eph. 4:4, "There is one body and one Spirit."[30]

But also note that this verse says nothing about baptism leading to salvation. Also, cross referencing Luke 12:50, we see Jesus say these words, "But I have a baptism to be baptized with" in the KJV or in the NIV, "But I have a baptism to undergo." He was not talking about His baptism; He was talking about His crucifixion! He was talking about being immersed into suffering! We also see in Matthew 20:22 (KJV and NKJV), Jesus says, "Are you able...to be baptized with the baptism that I am baptized with?" which the NIV and other translations omit out of the text, also being omitted in verse 23. Neither of these verses are talking about water baptism; they are talking about His crucifixion; they are talking about His immersion into suffering, which we are baptized/immersed (*baptizo* = immersed) into upon belief and faith in Jesus Christ as our Lord and Savior.

There is one other verse in Ephesians that is also used to teach baptismal regeneration, and it is found in Ephesians chapter 5, verses 25–27. It reads:

> Husbands, love your wives, as Christ loved the church and gave Himself up for her, that He might sanctify her, having cleansed her by the washing of water with the Word, so that He might present the church to Himself in splendor, without spot or wrinkle or any such thing, that she might be holy and without blemish.

So we see here the phrase "the washing of water." We have already looked at the reference to water and cleansing earlier in this chapter during our discussion on John 3:5, but we will add more here.

> The assumption that the "washing or rebirth" (Tit. 3:5) refers to baptism is purely gratuitous. This text and several others that mention washing, cleansing, and water (e.g., Eph. 5:26; John 3:3–8) form a part of every sacramentalist's discussion of the operations of grace within baptism. None of them, however, even mention baptism. The reference to water and cleansing is much more easily understood in its canonical context of the use of water as a symbol of purification in the ceremonial law. These types of purification are then fulfilled in the personal work of the Holy Spirit in regeneration. Thus, the "washing of rebirth" should be read as "the washing which is rebirth, even the renewal of the Holy Spirit." This is a fulfillment of the prophecy of Ezekiel 36:25–27: "I will sprinkle clean water on you, and you will be clean; I will cleanse you from all of your impurities and from all your idols. I will give you a new heart and put a new spirit in you; and I will put My Spirit in you and move you to follow My decrees."
>
> This prophecy in turn gives the spiritual reality behind the series of ritual cleanings required of the cleansed leper in Leviticus 14:7–9, as well as other ceremonial cleansings. The fulfillment of such cleansings is not baptism but the reality of the operations of the Spirit in regeneration and sanctification.[31]

Looking into the Greek, we see that the word used for "washing" is *loutron*, which means "a laver or a bath" (referring to a large brass bowl for the ritual ablutions of Jewish priests) and "is used metaphorically of the Word of God, as an instrument of spiritual cleansing, Ephesians 5:26; and in Titus 3:5, of 'the washing of regeneration.'"[32]

It simply is unwarranted to assume that the use of the word *washing* or *water* used here refers to the sacrament of water baptism, especially when it is explained in this very same passage as being "with the Word" (ESV, AMP, NASB), "by the Word" (KJV, NKJV), "through the Word" (NIV), and in the Greek, the preposition used is *en*, which could mean "in, by, with, among, at, on, through."

The point is that the main source of the cleansing is the Word, not a forced implication of the sacrament of water baptism. It is all done by the Word. In John 15:3, we read, "You are clean through the Word." In John 17:17, "Sanctify them in the truth; Your Word is truth." In 2 Thessalonians 2:13, "Through sanctification by the Spirit and belief in the truth." In James 1:21 "The Word...which can save you." And in 1 Peter 1:23, "Born again...by the Word of God."

The main ingredient being used here is that of the Word of God, which is Christ (John 1:1, 14), that cleanses and saves, which is exactly in line with everything that we have seen throughout Scripture. To interpret baptism as necessary in order to receive salvation distorts the several passages being used in favor of this teaching and challenges numerous other passages in Scripture which plainly teach salvation by grace alone through faith alone in Christ alone. This verse simply does not speak of literal and physical water baptism. It is speaking of the inward spiritual truth made possible only by the action of Christ and the Spirit.

The next passage that baptismal regeneration adherents will use in this doctrine is found in Colossians 2:12, but in order to get the full perspective, we will look at the context along with it. Starting in verse 6:

> Therefore, as you received Christ Jesus the
> Lord, so walk in Him, rooted and built up in
> Him and established in the faith, just as you

were taught, abounding in thanksgiving. See to it that no one takes you captive by philosophy and empty deceit, according to human tradition, according to the elemental spirits of the world, and not according to Christ. For in Him the whole fullness of Deity dwells bodily, and you have been filled in Him, Who is the head of all rule and authority. In Him also you were circumcised with a circumcision made without hands, by putting off the body of the flesh, by the circumcision of Christ, having been buried with Him in baptism, in which you were also raised with Him through faith in the powerful working of God, Who raised Him from the dead. And you, who were dead in your trespasses and the uncircumcision of your flesh, God made alive together with Him, having forgiven us all our trespasses, by cancelling the record of debt that stood against us with its legal demands. This He set aside, nailing it to the cross. He disarmed the rulers and authorities and put them to open shame, by triumphing over them in Him.

This entire section of Scripture is speaking of spiritual realities being done for us and within us, not external acts or performances or obedience on our part leading to the reception of our salvation. This passage mentions that we have been buried with Him in baptism, but again, this entire section speaks of inward spiritual activity being done by God Himself within us through the completed work of Christ and the indwelling of the Spirit, all of which is facilitated simply by our faith in Him, not by actions done by us. And as we have seen in past sections of Scripture, the Greek being used here simply means "immersion" and here is specifically being related to immersion into the death and resurrection of Christ.

Just as "a circumcision made without hands" is referring to the spiritual significance, so too is the reference to baptism. Just as we see in Luke 12:50, Jesus states, "I have a baptism to be baptized with," He is certainly not talking about physical water at all. He is speaking of "a baptism of suffering. He was referring to His death. Christian baptism *symbolizes* identification with Him in death, burial and resurrection."[33]

Neither of these passages are saying that the partaking of physically being baptized in water is necessary in order to receive salvation as our passage here directly says "raised with Him through faith," and that this is all the powerful workings of God Himself within us, making us alive together with Him (dead men cannot raise themselves from the dead), forgiving all of our sins and cancelling our entire sin debt by nailing it to the cross.

> Baptism is the symbol of the believer's association with Christ's death on the cross. Water baptism itself does not bring forgiveness of sins, but Paul uses the rite to help explain the work of the Spirit. The early church would never have understood the idea of an unbaptized Christian. Baptism and faith were considered to be the outward and inward realities of being a Christian (see Acts 2:21, 38, 10:43, 47–48, 16:31–33; Rom. 6:3–5). Some have highlighted Paul's close association of baptism and circumcision in this passage as an indication that water baptism is a sign of the New Covenant, just as circumcision was a sign of the Abrahamic Covenant.[34]

> The rite of male circumcision was specifically a sign of identity with the earthly people of God; similarly, baptism has now become the symbolic rite (not a saving act) of all God's people, whether male or female, Jew or Greek, into the Heavenly family of God. It also, like circumcision, symbolizes separation from sin and unto God, but in a different and more meaningful way

than circumcision could do. It symbolically identifies the believer with the death, burial and resurrection of Christ, as we are "buried with Him"
in baptismal waters, then "risen with Him" to a
new life.[35]

Since this verse directly relates circumcision and baptism, I
would like to take a second to look deeper at the connection.

Circumcision symbolized man's need for
cleansing of the heart (cf. Deut. 10:16, 30:6; Jer.
4:4; Rom. 2:29) and was the outward sign of
that cleansing of sin that comes by faith in God
(Rom. 4:11; Phil. 3:3). At salvation believers
undergo a spiritual "circumcision" by putting off
the sins of the flesh (cf. Rom. 6:6; 2 Cor. 5:17;
Phil. 3:3). This is the new birth, the new creation
in conversion. The outward affirmation of the
already accomplished inner transformation is
now the believer's baptism by water. This work of
God in the innermost being of the individual is
the true salvation that grants a new will to obey
Him in place of the former spiritual insensitivity
and stubbornness. This new heart will allow the
believer to love the Lord wholeheartedly, and is
the essential feature of the New Covenant (see Jer.
31:31–34, 32:37–42; Ezek. 11:19, 36:25–28).
We are called to cut away all the sin in our hearts,
as circumcision surgery cuts away the skin. This
leaves us with a clean relationship to God.[36]

Circumcision, just like baptism, was an act of obedience toward
God immediately upon accepting Him as Lord, making public declaration that you are now a member of God's people. It symbolized cutting away the old sin of the flesh and living new in God.
Circumcision itself did not save people, and neither does baptism.

It boils down to a matter of the heart, not the outward acts of obedience or deeds or works. As we saw in the earlier chapters of this book, obedience never saves. And we see this symbolism several places throughout Scripture.

In Deuteronomy 10:16, we read, "Circumcise therefore the foreskin of your *heart*." Real physical circumcision involves the male reproductive organ, which literally did nothing at all as far as forgiveness of sins, but here we see the true spiritual significance in that the real matter involved the heart. We see this also mirrored in a few other places.

Deuteronomy chapter 30, verse 6, "The Lord your God will circumcise your heart." Jeremiah says in chapter 4, verse 4, "Circumcise yourselves to the Lord; remove the foreskins of your hearts." And then later in Jeremiah, chapter 9, verse 26, "For all the nations are uncircumcised, and all the house of Israel are uncircumcised of heart." And in Romans chapter 2, verse 29, we plainly read, "Circumcision is a matter of the heart." Not the external organ. It is an internal reality which always precedes the external obedience.

> Trusting circumcision for salvation was a waste of time. That was not the way to find acceptance in Christ. Anyone who was circumcised for salvation was adding works to faith, thus demonstrating a lack of faith in the sufficiency of Christ's death. The act of circumcision was not the problem. It was the bad theology attached to the act that concerned Paul (cf. Acts 16:3; Gal. 5:2–3). Besides, you can't just pick and choose which parts of the law you want to keep and which parts you want to dispose of. If you think salvation comes from the law, you better keep the whole thing. It was all or nothing. Combining Christ and the law wouldn't work because they were two entirely different systems. Law and grace don't mix. A gift is not a gift if you have to do something to get it.[37]

We also see that in the Jerusalem council that took place in Acts chapter 15, the church even argued about the necessity of circumcision as a necessary means of salvation. In verse 1, it says:

> Some men came down from Judea and were teaching the brothers, "Unless you are circumcised according to the custom of Moses, you cannot be saved." And after Paul and Barnabas had no small dissension and debate with them, Paul and Barnabas and some of the others were appointed to go up to Jerusalem to the apostles and the elders about this question."

And then in verse 5 we read, "Some believers who belonged to the party of the Pharisees rose up and said, 'It is necessary to circumcise them and to order them to keep the law of Moses.'"

After there had been much debate, Peter stood up and spoke to the council recounting his encounter with Cornelius back in chapter 10 when the Gentiles heard the Word of God through Peter's mouth and believed, and that God Who knew their hearts gave them the Holy Spirit and made no distinction between the Gentiles and the Jews, and that He cleansed their heart *by faith*. Then Peter continues in verse 10:

> Now, therefore, why are you putting God to the test by placing a yoke on the neck of the disciples that neither our fathers nor we have been able to bear? But we believe that we will be saved through the grace of the Lord Jesus, just as they will.

Circumcision was not necessary for salvation, and neither is baptism. Circumcision was, and baptism is now, an outward symbol (1 Pet. 3:21) of the inward reality that has already taken place in the heart of the believer, through the providence of God, the completed work of Christ, and the indwelling of the Spirit, leading to the obedience of the act of the sacrament being publicly performed. In Romans chapter 2, we see in verses 25–29 that the religious circumcision rites, no matter how much God-given, contain no properties of salvation, "For circumcision indeed is of no value if you obey the law, but if you break the law, your circumcision becomes uncircumcision" (2:25; also cf. 1 Cor. 7:19). It boils down to the heart, for "circumcision is a matter of the heart" (Rom. 2:29), not any outward acts of obedience or deeds or works.

And then in Romans chapter 4, we see a very telling piece of Scripture from verses 9–12:

> Is this blessing then only for the circumcised, or also for the uncircumcised? We say that faith was counted to Abraham as righteousness. How then was it counted to him? Was it before or after he had been circumcised? It was not after, but before he was circumcised. He received the sign of circumcision as a seal of the righteousness that he had by faith while he was still uncircumcised. The purpose was to make him the father of all who believe without being circumcised, so that the righteousness would be counted to them as well, and to make him the father of the circumcised who are not merely circumcised but who also walk in the footsteps of the faith that our father Abraham had before he was circumcised.

As we have looked at in depth earlier throughout this book, salvation on our part simply comes through faith. It is not in the partaking of any religious rituals or sacraments or obedience or good works, leading to the receiving of salvation.

> Most Jews in New Testament times were thoroughly convinced that circumcision was the unique mark that set them apart as God's chosen people. They also believed it was the means by

which they became acceptable to God. In fact, circumcision was considered such a mark of God's favor that many rabbis taught that no Jew could be sent to hell unless God first reversed his circumcision. Genesis 17:10–14 records God's instructions that circumcision was to be a mark of God's covenant with Abraham and his descendants. On the basis of that passage the rabbis taught that circumcision itself was the means of getting right with God. But as Paul carefully points out, Abraham was not made righteous by his circumcision. When God commanded him to be circumcised, he had already been declared righteous (Rom. 4:9–12). The chronology of Genesis proves that Abraham was declared righteous long before he ever observed God's command to be circumcised. At Abraham's circumcision he was ninety-nine years old and Ishmael was thirteen (Gen. 17:24–25). But when Abraham was justified (15:6), Ishmael had not even been conceived (16:2–4). At Ishmael's birth Abraham was eighty-six (16:16). So Abraham was justified at least fourteen years before his circumcision. When Abraham was declared righteous, he was actually no different than an uncircumcised Gentile.

Circumcision and other external rituals— including baptism, penance, holy orders, marriage, celibacy, extreme unction, fasting, prayer, or whatever—are no means to justification. Abraham was in God's covenant and under His grace long before he was circumcised, whereas Ishmael, although circumcised, was never in the covenant. Circumcision, a sign for man's need for spiritual cleansing, was only a mark of the covenant relationship between God and His people. Paul already stated in Romans 2:28–29, "For he is not a Jew who is one outwardly; neither is circumcision that which is outward in the flesh. But he is a Jew who is one inwardly; and circumcision is that which is of the heart, by the Spirit, not by the letter; and his praise is not from men, but from God." Only justification by faith makes someone a son of Abraham (4:12).[38]

We also see in Paul's letter to the Galatians in the beginning of chapter 5:

> For freedom Christ has set us free; stand firm therefore, and do not submit again to a yoke of slavery... If you accept circumcision, Christ will be of no advantage to you. I testify again to every man who accepts circumcision that he is obligated to keep the whole law.

And the same could be said for baptism today. If you submit to baptism as a necessary means of salvation, then you are obligated to keep the whole law, and Christ is of no advantage to you. Verse 4:

> You are severed from Christ, you who would be justified by the law; you have fallen away from grace. For through the Spirit, by faith, we ourselves eagerly wait for the hope of righteousness. For in Christ Jesus neither circumcision nor uncircumcision counts for anything, but only faith working through love.

And then in verse 11, "If I, brothers, still preach circumcision... the offense of the cross has been removed." It is absolutely not dependent upon our obedience to the law, which would fully include partaking in the sacraments, that leads to our righteousness, but it is entirely and only through our faith by the grace of God. To add anything else to it nullifies the work of the cross and subjects us to the entirety of the law, which we cannot fulfill.

> It is those who want to make a good showing in the flesh who would force you to be circumcised, and only in order that they may not be persecuted for the cross of Christ. For even those who are circumcised do not themselves keep the law, but they desire to have you circumcised that they may boast in your flesh. But far be it from me to boast except for the cross of our Lord Jesus Christ, by which the world has been crucified to me, and I to the world. For neither circumcision counts for anything, nor uncircumcision, but a new creation. (Gal. 6:12–15)

There is a verse in 1 Corinthians that seems to parallel this but also paradoxically contrasts it at the same time; however, we know that Scripture never contradicts itself, so let's take a look. It is found in chapter 7, verse 19. It says, "Circumcision is nothing, and uncircumcision is nothing," which agrees with everything we've just discussed, but then it goes on to express, "but what matters is the keeping of the commandments of God."

The second half of that verse seems to contradict what we just learned from Romans and Galatians on this specific topic, and we will dive into the obedience side of things much deeper later on in chapter 10, but what Paul is saying in this verse is that:

> "Christ has fulfilled the old Levitical Law, so it is no longer binding," and is referring to the "commandments found in Matthew 22:36–40 and that they can only be kept by the believer understanding that all power and strength comes through the cross, which must ever be the object of our faith. That gives the Holy Spirit latitude

to work in our lives, helping us to do that which needs to be done."[39]

Again, we will get a much deeper look into the role of obedience later on in chapter 10, but this verse is not deviating from what we already established. For one, this specific verse, in context, is referring to those who already belong to the Church and thus are already saved, not unbelievers who are coming to faith. It is also, therefore, not directly linking obedience to the commandments with that of receiving or obtaining salvation. We will look at and apply the role of obedience later on, but here we see again that the ritual or sacrament is said to be of no benefit and worthy of nothing.

Listen to this point made that Thomas Nettles, professor of church history, has to say. This is such a strong and true point.

> Paul raged against a heresy that sought to add something of religious ceremony (circumcision) to the completed work of Christ in order to complete salvation (cf. Gal. 3:1–5, 5:1–6). He insisted that from the cross of Christ flow all the blessings of eternal life and life in the Spirit (cf. 2:20, 3:13–14, 5:11, 6:14–15). Hearing and believing the message of the cross unleashes all the blessings stored in it. How strange would it be that Paul introduces a new ceremony by which Christ's saving work becomes effectual? Could he really be saying, "Reject the heretical formula of hearing plus believing plus circumcision; instead replace it with hearing plus believing plus baptism?" That interpretation of baptism would run counter to Paul's purpose of Galatians. Their baptism gave a physical presentation of the spiritual certainties involved in faith. Faith is not empty but engages us with the resurrected Christ in His present status of living to make intercession for us. Thus, when by faith we are clothed with Christ,

baptism illustrates the transaction that actually has taken place. As a divinely ordained manner of expressing an existing confidence, baptism is spoken of as the thing itself. When Paul refers to Galatians' baptism as being "clothed...with Christ," he encourages them to remember that Christ's death alone, and no human ritual, bears to them spiritual life.[40]

It is heresy to think that we need to add something or do something in order to receive the "free gift" (Rom. 5 and 6) that Christ made possible for us when He proclaimed, "It is finished!" Paul raged against the heretical formula of hearing plus believing plus circumcision, so he certainly would not have just followed that up and instead replace it with the heretical formula of hearing plus believing plus (physical water) baptism! Baptism, used here in Colossians 2:12, is simply referring to the reality of spiritual "immersion" into Christ's death, burial, and resurrection, which is symbolized by the after-the-fact outward proclamation of the already existent inward conversion. It is the evidence and response of a new life, not the means of obtaining a new life or even the moment when the new life is finally attained.

The next passage used to teach this doctrine is found in Titus 3:5. Once again, we will start by looking at the surrounding context. Starting at verse 4:

> But when the goodness and loving kindness of God our Savior appeared, He saved us, not because of works done by us in righteousness, but according to His Own mercy, by the washing of regeneration and renewal of the Holy Spirit, Whom He poured out on us richly through Jesus Christ our Savior, so that being justified by His grace, we might become heirs according to the hope of eternal life.

Once again, we see that it is ALL God's work within us and "not because of any works done by us." Salvation has NEVER been by deeds, obedience, or works. It is always all done by God's grace.

> He saved us…according to His Own mercy, by the washing of regeneration and renewal of the Holy Spirit, Whom God poured out on us richly through Jesus Christ our Savior…being justified by His grace… Not because of any works of our own.

First of all, there is no water in this passage. To assume that "the washing of regeneration" automatically means that physical water baptism is necessary for salvation is entirely presumptuous. It is instead speaking of the spiritual cleansing of the Holy Spirit referred to in-depth in Ezekiel 36:25–29, which we touched on in our look at Ephesians 5:26–27 just a couple pages back. But to look closer at this Ezekiel passage:

> I will sprinkle clean water on you, and you shall be clean from all your uncleanness, and from all your idols I will cleanse you. And I will give you a new heart, and a new spirit I will put within you. And I will remove the heart of stone from your flesh and give you a heart of flesh. And I will put My Spirit within you, and cause you to walk in My statutes and be careful to obey my rules… I will deliver you from your uncleanness.

This is the washing referenced here and throughout Scripture, and again, it refers to a spiritual truth, not an external physical rite. We see it referenced in Psalm 51:7 and 10 and Hebrews 10:22; this is the same washing that Paul writes about in Ephesians 5:26 and here in Titus 3:5; it's also the same promise that Jesus had in mind in John 3:5. This is a spiritual truth, not an external ritual.

In the same way, Scripture also talks about the sprinkling of ashes and blood (throughout the Old Testament ceremonial sacrifices in Exodus, Leviticus, Numbers, Kings, Chronicles; Heb. 9:3, 12:24; 1 Pet. 1:2), which also always refers to the existence of a spiritual truth only evidenced by the external symbol. Even so, when used externally, as in the Old Testament ceremonial washings and baptism of the New Testament, the water is merely an external symbol of the internal truth of the heart, all of which is done by God Himself. The water does not actually touch the heart; only the Spirit can! It is His work in us, not what we do on the outside. Nor is the moment of the external, the corresponding reception of the internal.

God Himself pledges to us this spiritual renewal. God is the One Who cleanses us from our sin, gives us this new heart of flesh, and removes our heart of stone, grants us a new spirit or disposition which is inclined to worship Him, and indwells us with His Holy Spirit Who enables us to even walk in obedience to His Word.

> Salvation brings divine cleansing from sin and the gift of a new, Spirit-generated, Spirit-empowered, and Spirit-protected life as God's Own children and heirs (Titus 3:7). This is the new birth (cf. John 3:5; 1 John 2:29, 3:9, 4:7, 5:1). And the Spirit is the agent of this "washing of regeneration."[41]

Although it is not an external practice but an internal truth accomplished prior to and which leads to the following in our obedience in the external rite. "God our Savior...poured out His Holy Spirit unto us richly through Jesus Christ...it is God Who saved us...according to His Own mercy...so that we are justified by His grace."

> The central truth of salvation is justification by grace through faith alone (Eph. 2:8–9). When a sinner repents and places his faith in Jesus Christ, God declares him just (Rom. 10:9–10),

imputes the righteousness of Christ to him (Rom. 3:22; 2 Cor. 5:21), and gives him eternal life by virtue of the substitutionary death of Christ as the penalty for that sinner's iniquity (John 3:16; Gal. 3:13; Phil. 3:8–9).[42]

Some passages deal with aspects of the immediate operations of God in salvation (e.g., 2 Tim. 1:9). In such passages we see three different aspects of the divine causation: God in His purpose and grace is the ultimate cause; Christ by His death and righteousness is the meritorious cause; and the Spirit by His calling and regeneration is the effectual cause. A second class deals with the appropriate and congruent human means and responses connected with salvation (e.g., "It is with your mouth that you confess and are saved" [Rom. 10:10]; "Whoever turns a sinner from the error of his way will save him from death" [James 5:20]). The third level concerns those reminders instituted by the Lord Himself that all of our salvation resides in Him and provides an ongoing testimony in the church of this reality. When our enactment of the ordinance reflects its reality, by metaphor it is said to save us: "This cup is the new covenant in My blood" (Luke 22:20), which is "poured out for many for the forgiveness of sins' (Matt. 26:28). Of this same sort is Peter's phrase, 'baptism that now saves you also" (1 Pet. 3:21).[43]

This leads us into the last passage that baptismal regeneration adherents will use to teach this doctrine. In 1 Peter chapter 3, verses 20–21, we read:

The ark…in which a few, that is, eight persons, were brought safely through water. Baptism, which corresponds to this, now saves you, not as a removal of dirt from the body but as an appeal to God for a good conscience, through the resurrection of Jesus Christ.

In this passage, Peter is speaking of Noah's Ark in which Noah and his family:

[H]ad been rescued in spite of the water, not because of the water. Here, water was the agent of God's judgment, not the means of salvation. Peter is teaching that the fact that 8 people were in an ark and went through the whole judgment, and yet were unharmed, is analogous of the Christian's experience in salvation by being in Christ, the Ark of one's salvation. He is not at all referring to water baptism here, but rather a spiritual immersion, *baptisma*, into union with Christ as an ark of safety from the judgment of God. The resurrection of Christ demonstrates God's acceptance of Christ's substitutionary death for the sins of those who believe. Judgment fell on Christ just as the judgment of the flood waters fell on the ark. The believer who is in Christ is thus in the ark of safety that will sail over the waters of judgment into eternal glory. To be sure he is not misunderstood, Peter clearly says he is not speaking of water baptism, "not the putting away of the filth from the flesh." In Noah's flood, they were kept out of the water while those who went into the water were destroyed. Being in the ark and thus saved from God's judgment on the world prefigures being in Christ and thus saved from eternal damnation. The word for "appeal" in verse 21 has the idea of a pledge, agreeing to certain conditions of a covenant (the New Covenant) with God. What saves a person plagued by sin and a guilty conscience is not some external rite, but the agreement with God to get in the ark of safety, the Lord Jesus, by faith in His death and resurrection.[44]

Therefore:

> [B]oth the flood, with its ark of safety, and baptism, with its emergence from the waters of "burial," are "like figures" or "symbols" of the wonderful reality of the death and resurrection of Christ, as well as the death to sin and new life of the believer. Baptism in and of itself would at most only be a bath for washing off the filth of the flesh (v. 21), but it becomes the "answer of (or better, 'appeal for') a good conscience toward God" when experienced as a testimony of ones saving faith in the atoning death and justifying resurrection of the Lord Jesus secured forever by Christ's resurrection.[45]

This passage simply is not equating physical water baptism to the moment of attained salvational regeneration as it states that that type of act would only result in a removal of dirt from the body. This passage is saying that the physical act of water baptism is merely an external "symbol (NIV)," "picture (NLT)," "like figure (KJV)," "antitype (NKJV)," or in the original Greek, *antitupon*, which means "representative, counterpart" and simply "corresponds (ESV, NASB, AMP)" to the internal truth, the "appeal to God for a good conscience" (v. 21).

When we cross reference this with a couple places in Scripture, we find more depth to this. In Hebrews 11:7, we read:

> By faith, Noah, being warned by God concerning the events as yet unseen, in reverent fear constructed an ark for the saving of his household. By this he condemned the world and became an heir of the righteousness that comes by faith.

Noah and his family were saved by faith, not the water. Twice, this passage mentions faith and never water. He was saved by the ark, a symbol of Jesus Christ, from the water, which symbolized and realistically became the judgment. "The earth was formed out of the water and through the water by the Word of God, and that by means of these the world that then existed was deluged with water and perished" (2 Pet. 3:6). Noah and his family were not saved by or through the water, but, in fact, it became the judgment in which the entire rest of the world was destroyed by it. The water did not save them, nor does it save us now.

We also see some beautiful imagery when we go back to Genesis and look at the original text. In Genesis 6:14, we see the account of God first instructing Noah in the building of the ark. God Himself instructs Noah to "cover it [the ark] inside and out with pitch." The Hebrew word used here for "pitch," which was some type of tar that essentially waterproofed the ark keeping it completely safe from the destruction outside, is *kopher* or *kaphar*, and is also translated to mean "atonement," "reconciliation," "propitiate," "expiate," "to cover over," or "ransom."

In providing a protective covering against the waters of judgment, it thus becomes a beautiful picture of Christ. They were saved from destruction when they were found covered by Christ, "baptisma (Greek)" or "immersed" in Christ, not immersed in the water. They were in fact kept out of the water by being confined to the ark, the symbol of the Savior, Jesus Christ. Just as the ark covered them and spared them from the judgment, Christ covers us and is our atonement, our propitiation, our reconciliation, and ransoms us away from the judgment and to the Father. Immersion into Christ is what saves you, not baptism into water.

If someone was still to ask, "Must I not first be baptized before I can know that I am saved?" theologian H. A. Ironside has this to say:

> It is right and proper that you should be baptized. But baptism cannot affect the salvation of your soul. It is, as Peter tells us (1 Pet. 3:21), a figure of salvation, just as the deliverance of Noah in the ark of old. But we are told distinctly, "By grace are you saved through faith; and that not of yourselves: it is the gift of God" (Eph. 2:8). To the inquiring jailer at Philippi, who asked the definite question, "What must I do to be saved?" there came the definite answer, "Believe on the Lord Jesus Christ, and thou shalt be saved" (Acts 16:30–31). Baptism followed believing. It was the God-ordained way of confessing Christ as Savior and Lord. Many have been saved who could not possibly be baptized. Consider again the case of the penitent thief, and **be assured that God has never had two ways of saving sinners**. The same grace that saved him will save you, when you trust in Jesus Whose blood alone cleanses from all sin. There are a number of passages relating to baptism that may seem a little confusing. But rest your soul on the clear, *definite statement concerning salvation by grace* and as you study your Bible the perplexing portions will become clearer under the Holy Spirit's guidance. It is Christ's baptism of judgment that is the basis of our deliverance from death.

Lord Jesus, we remember
The travail of Thy soul;
When in Thy love's deep pity
The waves did o'er Thee roll.
Baptized in death's dark waters,
For us Thy blood was shed;
For us Thou Lord of glory
Wast numbered with the dead.[46]

In the end it is Jesus Who saves. Obedience is any step taken in a response to a salvation offered, not an effort at salvation earned. In the end, God has the right to save any heart, for He and only He alone sees the heart. Would you wanna marry someone who wanted to keep the marriage a secret? Baptism is a sacred vow of the believer to follow Jesus Christ. It celebrates the union of sinner with Savior. A vow to be faithful to the end. It is not the act that saves us, but it is the act that symbolizes how we are saved. We are never told to be baptized and then believe, but to come to belief, to trusting faith, then display that decision by associating ourselves with Christian baptism. The work of salvation is a finished work of Christ on the cross.[47]

So "baptism is then like a wedding ring. The ring does not make you married. If you take it off are you still married? Of course. It is merely a symbol of the covenant that was taken."[48]

The biblical message is that salvation occurs at the moment of genuine faith. Salvation is received by grace alone, through faith alone, in Christ alone. Good works and obedience to God's Word, including baptism, are inevitable *results of salvation*, not *requirements for salva-*

tion. So, defining baptism as a different type of work does not change the fact that it is a work. Baptism is something we must actively participate in. Salvation is a gift we simply receive from God's gracious and merciful hands. The Bible verses that link salvation and baptism do so because baptism identifies conversion; it is the declaration that salvation *has occurred*. The idea of an un-baptized believer was anathema to the New Testament writers. If a person claimed to believe in Christ, but was ashamed to proclaim that faith in public, it would be an indication that the person's faith was not genuine. Baptism is not necessary for salvation. Baptism is an important step of obedience that every Christian should take. Baptism is a public declaration of faith in Christ. Baptism is an identification of an old life dying with Christ and a new life being resurrected as a new creation (1 Cor. 5:17). So, while baptism is very important, it is not a requirement for salvation. To make baptism a requirement for salvation is an attack on the perfection and sufficiency of God's provision of salvation through Jesus Christ.[49]

A baby does not suddenly come to life at birth. Birth does not bestow or initiate life. Birth is the result of life that began at conception. Birth is a confirmation of what has been taking place in the womb and an initiation of the life into a different environment, but it does not make non-life into life. Spiritual life is initiated when the sinner begins to believe the Gospel. With the first assenting faith, a person becomes a disciple of Christ—a learner. Being begotten, or conceived, by the Gospel, a person's faith should continue to develop to the stage of obedience. If the person dies on the way to the baptistry, he dies a disciple, and there is assurance that God will receive that life. Baptism does not give life. The life begins with the conception. Baptism confirms the changes that have been working in the individual in that life process. It becomes a public declaration of the saving faith of the disciple, and the Spirit given as a seal or witness. Baptism is an initiation into a new environment and relationship. But baptism does not initiate the life. Salvation is by faith which is accepting and obedient. In both physical and spiritual realms, life begins at conception rather than birth. Birth does not give life.[50]

If I accept Christ as my Lord and Savior, repent of my sins, and confess that I need Jesus to be my substitution in order to be received into God's eternal Kingdom, and I immediately head to church in order to be obedient and be baptized, but then get slaughtered by a semi on the way to church, would I then end up in hell for not being baptized?

I once had a baptismal regeneration proponent say to me as I asked him that question, "Well, it's unsure. That's kind of a gray area. Only God knows the heart and can make that call."

NO! God doesn't deal with gray areas! It's true that only God knows the heart, but you can be assured that if you truly accept Christ as your Savior, and even if you die on the way to the baptistry, you will be saved and redeemed of your sins and enter into Heaven because of Christ's propitiatory work in your place, despite having never been baptized because baptism is not the saving act or the moment of receiving the saving effect.

Since the Bible does not contradict itself, any interpretation of a specific passage that contradicts the general teaching of the Bible is to be rejected. Every treatment of salvation in the Bible makes clear that it is by grace through faith plus or minus nothing. Baptism is simply the demonstrator of real faith and real transformation which issues obedience. Baptism is the immediate and inseparable indicator of salvation because salvation produces obedience. It is an outward confession of the inward spiritual occurrence. It's a required, commanded New Testament ordinance for believers. An initiatory rite demonstrating your union with Christ in His death, burial and resurrection. Baptism gives a spiritual truth, physical form. The moment you put your faith in Christ you become a Christian. By a supernatural, sovereign, divine, spiritual miracle, God puts you in Christ and you die at the cross and you arise to walk in newness of life. Believing is what saves, confessing is what affirms the reality of belief, paying identification to Christ publicly. The relationship of water baptism to salvation is the relationship of obedience to salvation. If you are reluctant to be baptized there is question about your willingness to be obedient, and an unwilling heart in the manner of obedience may well reveal an unregenerate person because Jesus said, "If you love Me, then keep My commandments" (John 14:15), and it starts with this simple command. A good example of a baptismal confession would be: "I hereby confess in my willing submission to this divinely appointed ordinance, my glad obedience to the command of my Lord and Savior. In this symbolic way, I show my identification with the One Who bore my sins, took my place, died in my stead, was buried and rose again for my justification. As Christ went through the reality of suffering and death to secure my salvation, so by my immersion in water and coming out I thus publicly declare my identification with my Lord in His death, burial and resurrection on my behalf with the intention to walk with Him in newness of life."[51]

Scripture represents all spiritual obedience as subsequent to and consequent on the new birth. One cannot see the Kingdom unless he is born again (John 3:3); that is, one cannot have his eyes opened to understand and embrace the realities of God's merciful action in establishing a Kingdom of the redeemed apart from the new birth. Since this is true, one cannot believe with the intent of obeying without having already experienced the new birth. Apart from the consummated operation of regeneration, therefore, one wouldn't even desire to come to the baptismal waters as an expression of faith in Christ and dependence on His redemptive work.

The Apostle John, in both his Gospel and first letter, regularly represents the new birth as precedent to all Christians virtue, love, obedience, and faith: "If you know that He is righteous, you know that everyone who does what is right has been born of Him" (1 John 2:29). The practice of righteousness is the evidence of, not the cause of or the occasion of, the new birth. "No one who is born of God will continue to sin, because God's seed remains in him; he cannot go on sinning, because he has been born of God" (1 John 3:9). Christians have an intrinsic revolt against sin and detestation of it and are no longer under its reign because of the new birth. The new birth caused their abhorrence of sin; their abhorrence of sin was not the cause or occasion of the new birth: "Everyone who loves has been born of God and knows God" (1 John 4:7). Our love for God is not the cause or occasion of the new birth. Rather, the new birth precedes, and this constitutes the source and cause of our love to God: "Everyone who believes that Jesus is the Christ is born of God…for everyone born of God overcomes the world. This is the victory that has overcome the world, even our faith" (1 John 5:1, 4). Our faith that grasps the glory of Christ above all things in the world and that counts the world's applause and threats as nothing compared to the excellency of Christ Jesus manifests the presence of the new birth. Our faith is neither the cause nor the occasion of the new birth; rather, the new birth gives rise to faith.

For this reason, baptism follows regeneration, follows faith, and does not form a constituent element in either. All faith flows from regeneration; all obedience flows from faith. Baptism is an act of obedience to Christ that testifies to the prior existence of the regenerating work of the Spirit that has produced faith in Christ.[52]

So throughout this chapter, we have looked at each of the passages that proponents of the baptismal regeneration doctrine use to teach this doctrine and cross referenced them with the rest of Scripture in an attempt to discard any contradictions that a certain interpretation might have with the whole of Scripture. There are perfectly Biblical and contextually sound interpretations of these verses that do not support the baptismal regeneration doctrine, which also coincide naturally with the rest of Scripture which teaches that salvation is by grace alone through faith alone in Christ alone.

It all rests in Christ's finished work on the cross (John 19:30) and is offered to us as a free gift (Rom. 6:23), and we simply accept it as truth and commit in full surrendered faith in the glorious fact that Jesus Christ is our Lord and Savior (Rom. 10:9–10) and that only by His work, His sacrificial substitution in our place, and His Spirit within us are we brought to justification and redemption and reconciliation to God and saved from death. It is not by any work or obedience of our own (Ti. 3:5). Our faith neither is the saving agent but the relationship that connects us to the saving agent, that of Christ. To add any other thing to the reception of our salvation is to nullify the Gospel of Christ and the power of His sacrifice on the cross, and His words, "It is finished," become insufficient.

As stated in the beginning of this chapter, there are far too many examples of doctrinal misinterpretations to tackle all of them in this one chapter or even this one book, so here we simply tried to go through some passages as an example of the many, some of which at least on the surface appear to be pretty straightforward, but nonetheless contradict the rest of Scripture if so taught that proponents of a certain doctrine have misinterpreted and cross-referenced them with the rest of Scripture and dug deeper in order to conjoin the whole of God's Word. In so doing, we tackled one large Scriptural interpretive contradiction as to prepare you for further inspection of some of the others on your own.

Contextual and doctrinal contradictions in Scripture are just one of the many discreet ways that the enemy will use to try and corrupt our full and uninhibited trust and reliance and certainty in God's infallible and inerrant Word (Ps. 12:6, 19:7, 119:89; Prov. 30:5; John 6:68; 2 Tim. 3:16; 1 Pet. 1:21). satan even tried to use God's Word to tempt God Himself! When Jesus was led by the Spirit into the wilderness to be tempted by the devil (Matt. 4; Mark 1; Luke 4), the devil even tried to use Scripture to tempt Jesus, The Word Himself (John 1:1, 14). In Matthew 4:6 and Luke 4:10–11, we see the devil quoting Psalm 91:11–12 when he said to Jesus:

> If You are the Son of God, throw Yourself down, for it is written, "He will command His angels concerning You, to guard You" and "On their hands they will bear You up, lest You strike Your foot against a stone."

But when you look at the text, we see that satan completely twisted it's meaning and used a passage instructing us to trust God and tried to justify it as a way to test God. Jesus knew full well this interpretation of Scripture was false and contradictory to the rest of Scripture, so Jesus cross-referenced Scripture with Scripture and rebutted using Scripture and quoted from Deuteronomy 6:16 and said in Matthew 4:7 and Luke 4:12, "Again it is written, 'You shall not put the Lord your God to the test.'"

So just as Jesus has so perfectly modeled for us here in these passages, when we happen to come across a teaching or doctrinal stance that seems to contradict a separate portion of Scripture, it is imperative that we need to dig deeper and cross-reference and use Scripture to interpret Scripture and look at context in order to determine the truth, as we did here, because God's Word will never contradict itself; and if a doctrine is found that seems to contradict other parts of Scripture, immediate analysis is necessary in order to prevent further incorrect teaching.

One last thing I want to add before leaving this chapter, while we are on the subject of the temptation of Christ, this starts a great point. Whether you are at the beginning or the end of your experience of life, you're going to be in the same battle. In Luke 22:44, Jesus is so in anguish He is sweating drops of blood. Throughout your entire Christian life, satan will never give up and stop tempting and tormenting you. In fact, it will get harder toward the end. It didn't get easier for Jesus either toward the end. satan intensified his attempts the closer Christ got to the cross and His goals and mission! And so it will be with you.

I once had an old friend of mine express this to me as he was nearing his passage from this life to the next. I had asked him how he was doing/feeling. He said to me, "I've never felt more persecuted in my life!" I asked what he meant. "Well, the enemy knows that I've basically got one foot in the ground, and he has been relentless at trying to get me to crack before I die and meet Jesus." My friend persevered until the end, like we studied throughout chapter 8, and I find great solace knowing he has been established with Christ in eternal glory!

James 1:2–4 tells us to embrace our trials, struggles, persecutions, etc. because they test our faith and build in us steadfastness and lead us into deeper communion and greater trust in Christ.

And on that note, God promises us in 1 Corinthians 10:13 that "God is faithful, and He will not let you be tempted beyond your ability, but with the temptation He will also provide the way of escape, that you may be able to endure it."

Have you ever thought, *Why is this happening? I can't handle this! God this is too hard, too much!* This is our weakness talking. God promises that He will not allow us to be tempted beyond our ability, and this goes back to the perseverance of the saints. He will not allow us to be pushed beyond what we can handle, past our breaking point, because the faith He gives us is a faith that perseveres, and He also promises to provide us with the way of escape. So next time you feel like you're drowning and can't handle everything going on, remember God will not allow you to be tempted beyond your ability. Think of it instead this way: *Wow, God must think I'm a total rock star! He must see me as a lot stronger than I see myself, if He is allowing this to happen and knows that I can handle this!*

After all, He does know you better than you know yourself! He created you! In these situations, the best thing you can do is follow Jesus's model, "It is written." Turn to Scripture and respond to the assaults of hell with the Word of God (2 Tim. 3:16).

10

Good Works/Obedience/Proof of Salvation/Fruits of the Spirit

In this chapter, we will finally get to the role of obedience and to the purpose and function of good works. Up until now, we have talked about how our obedience does nothing to save us. Nothing we do, nothing we complete, nothing we act on or participate in can lead to our salvation or to the receiving of that salvation. It is not by any righteousness of our own; it is not fulfilled and realized by the completion of some checklist, obtained by saying a certain prayer, or accomplished, achieved, earned, deserved, nor merited by any of our own means in any way, shape, or form whatsoever. It is absolutely, entirely, and solely done, fulfilled, and accomplished by Christ's finished work and our faith in His Word and work, which includes total surrender to Him as Lord and Savior, reliance entirely on His sacrifice for our substitution, and acceptance of His gracious gift given to us, free of charge, out of His infinite love for us.

All of this is eternally fulfilled by grace alone (God's initiative) through faith alone (our ingredient) in Christ alone (the ultimate price and fulfillment). We are conceived and born into sin, redeemed entirely and solely by Christ, raised from the dead, reborn, and reconciled to God all by His completed work, all while we were dead in sin (Eph. 2:5). He brings our dead souls back to life, and being enlightened by His Spirit, we accept His sacrificial gift as our redemption and justification. We are deemed holy, righteous, and true by acknowledging His suffering and substitution in our place as the only means possible for ourselves to be able to approach the infinite and eternal holy and righteous God.

He endured what we deserved so that we may inherit what He deserves. And it is only by acknowledging and accepting this glorious truth that we receive and attain this gift and privilege of new life together as one with our holy and righteous Triune God. There is literally zero ability and/or opportunity for us to earn it, deserve it, merit it to our account, obey well enough, or be good enough by any other means whatsoever—ever!

What's sad is that so many people, churches, denominations, unbelievers, even Christians nowadays believe that you have to be obedient to be saved, that you have to be a good person and do good things to deserve entrance into Heaven, that you have to obey the Ten Commandments or the commandments and teachings of Christ or the more than 600 laws of the Levitical Covenant or obey a certain set of guidelines and rituals and sacraments in order to be found not guilty and/or "good enough" so as to be deemed worthy to enter into Heaven. And as we have spent the majority of this book discussing already, that is simply not true.

We were all born into sin, and you cannot obey your way out of death! You cannot make up for the sin nature that is already inherent in all of us. We all deserve death, and nothing we do, say, or act on makes up for everything already done. It still demands a response of justice! It is only by accepting Jesus's claim and substitution in our place that we receive salvation, and our entire sin debt is eternally erased from our account because Christ secured it and paid it on His account.

As we saw in the last chapter, "obedience is any step taken in a response to a salvation offered, not an effort at salvation earned." For the purpose of this book, works are any deed or performance or action executed in obedience to a command or law. So, then, where does obedience and good works come into play in all of this? Simply put, they become the evidence and proof of a saved and redeemed life. We foreshadowed this just a little bit back in chapter 3, and just to take a quick excerpt from there, obedience comes from a life redeemed (Rom. 1:5–6, 6:17, 7:4, 15:18, 16:26; Eph. 2:10; Ti. 2:11–12). Obedience is fruit of the Spirit in the life of the reborn. Obedience comes from a converted, thankful, and repentant heart that finally understands what was desperately lost, what has been found, what price has been paid, by what extreme sacrifice, at what extreme cost, without any self-input, all as a gracious and merciful and free gift (Rom. 5:15, 16, 17, 6:23) from an infinitely loving Father and Creator Who was previously unknown to us (Rom. 5:6, 8, 10; Eph. 2:4–5).

Any and all obedience, any and all good works only become manifested in and upon a redeemed life. Before and without Christ's work and the Holy Spirit within us "all our [so-called] righteous deeds are like filthy rags" (Isa. 64:6 AMP). For we do not even know what to pray for without the presence of the Spirit within us (Rom. 8:26). And furthermore, we are even told in 1 Corinthians 12:3 that "No one can say 'Jesus is Lord' except in the Holy Spirit." We can't even acknowledge Jesus as Lord if the Spirit does not already dwell within us.

Hebrews 11, verse 6, also tells us that, "without faith it is impossible to please Him, for whoever would draw near to God must believe that He exists and that He rewards those who seek Him." If we do not have faith in God and believe that He is real and that He redeems those who come to Him, then we simply cannot please Him in any way whatsoever. Prior to a redeemed life, we are ignorantly incompetent (in fact, we are dead), unqualified, and simply incapable of doing anything right and good on our own. So it is only upon being redeemed, reborn, and cleansed from our sin and death that we are able to respond to God in an obedient and godly manner. All so-called good deeds previous to this are out of selfish pride, not from a saved and regenerate heart that wants to glorify its Savior. We must be brought back to life, and the sinful fog of our vision must be fully cleansed before we can ever approach, look upon and acknowledge, and respond to the great and amazing glory of God and, therefore, accept His propitiation for us. "Works have a place—but as a demonstration of having received God's forgiveness, not as a badge of merit of having earned it."[1]

> The crucifixion of Christ was a one-time historical fact with continuing results into eternity. Christ's sacrificial death provides eternal payment for the believer's sins, and does not need to be supplemented by any human works. The notion that sinful, weak, fallen human nature could improve on the saving work of the Holy Spirit was ludicrous to Paul. An inheritance by definition is something granted, not worked for. In salvation, the initiating will is God's, not man's. Man's will participates in response to God's promptings.[2]

Salvation is achieved entirely by the finished work of Christ and was not, is not, cannot be, nor ever will be supplemented by anything we do. God's initiating will prompts and fulfills this glorious gift and reality, and it is our newly redeemed and cleansed will that responds to God, but "to say that good works must be present BEFORE a person is saved is to make salvation dependent on our obedience, which is works-salvation, not salvation by grace alone, through faith alone, in Christ alone. As Titus 3:5 declares, 'He saved us—*not by works of righteousness that we had done*, but according to His mercy, through the washing of regeneration and renewal by the Holy Spirit.'"[3]

Jesus Himself elaborates on this in John 15:16 when He says, "You did not choose Me, but I chose you and appointed you that you should go and bear fruit and that your fruit should abide." Jesus was stating to His disciples, and still to us today, that He sovereignly chooses us to be with Him, not vice versa. As we touched on in earlier chapters, we are to have entirely zero spiritual pride in the fact that we are His and He is ours. He did the choosing, not us. And He did this for this purpose: that we go and bear our fruit. This is our good works, our obedience, fruit of the Spirit (Gal. 5:22–23), and any righteous deeds that are now pleasing to God (cf. Isa. 64:6), and this is how we are now to walk in our reborn and redeemed lives. This all comes as a product of our salvation and redeemed lives; it is not a prerequisite to our redeemed lives.

Paul backs this up also in his letter to the Ephesians when he says in chapter 2, verse 10, "For we are His workmanship, created in Christ Jesus for good works, which God prepared beforehand, that we should walk in them." This refers all the way back to eternity past. God created us in Christ before the foundations of the world (cf. Eph. 1:3–14) for the purpose of good works that we should walk in them. We are created and redeemed for good works, not redeemed by good works. We become one with Christ, thus resulting in the walking in and doing of good works. And to step back just a couple verses, we have already looked at these two verses in-depth, but verses 8–9 prelude this by saying, "For it is by grace you have been saved through faith. And this is not of your own doing, it is the gift of God, not as a result of works, so that no one may boast."

We are not saved by works; we are saved entirely by God's grace and free gift. Our part is simply relying on this truth in faith, and we are saved and created in Christ for the purpose of good works, and God prepared all of this in eternity past so that we have absolutely zero ability or entitlement to boast or be prideful.

> It is the nature of the Christian to produce fruit (Eph. 2:10). The inevitable result of genuine salvation is good works. We are not saved by works, but works are the only proof that faith is genuine, vibrant, and alive (Jas. 2:17). Fruit is the only possible validation that a branch is abiding in the true vine (Matt. 7:16–17). If someone's faith is genuine, that person's life will bear good fruit.[4]

Early twentieth century New Testament scholar and educator J. Gresham Machen explains it like this:

> Faith is the acceptance of a gift at the hands of Christ. It is a very wonderful thing: it involves a change of the whole nature of man; it involves a new hatred of sin and a new hunger and thirst after righteousness. Such a wonderful change is not the work of man; faith itself is given us by the Spirit of God. Christians never make themselves Christians; but they are made Christians by God. It is quite inconceivable that a man should be given this faith in Christ, that he should accept this gift which Christ offers, and still go on contentedly in sin. For the very thing which Christ offers us is salvation from sin—not only salvation from the guilt of sin. The very first thing that the Christian does, therefore, is to keep the law of God: he keeps it no longer as a way of earning his salvation—for salvation has been given him freely by God—but he keeps it joyously as a central part of salvation itself. The faith of which Paul speaks is, as Paul himself says, a faith that works through love; and love is the fulfilling of the whole law. The faith that Paul means when he speaks of justification by faith alone is a faith that works.[5]

This is repeatedly shown to us throughout Scripture that good works and obedience are the glorious result of salvation, not a prerequisite. In Acts chapter 6, we are shown in verse 7 that, "the Word of God continued to increase, and the number of the disciples multiplied greatly in Jerusalem, and a great many of the priests became obedient to the faith."

"True saving faith always produces obedience and submission to the Lordship of Jesus Christ."[6]

Paul also takes this phrase and builds on the concept of "the obedience of faith" a couple of times in Romans. In chapter 1, verses 5–6, we read, "Jesus Christ our Lord, through Whom we have received grace and apostleship to bring about the obedience of faith for the sake of His name among all the nations, including you who are called to belong to Jesus Christ." He also mentions it later on in chapter 16, verse 26, "according to the command of the eternal God, to bring about the obedience of faith."

As we continue to see, obedience, though always linked with faith, never preempts faith. Obedience is never something done leading to faith and, therefore, salvation. Obedience, almost as if it were married to faith, is first found in us upon the saving presence of the birth of faith in us when we who are called to belong to Jesus receive His grace and are made to be His disciples, all to the praise and glory of His name. It is the obedience of faith, not the faith of obedience. It is the obedience belonging to our existing faith, not our faith which comes from our obedience.

Paul continues to say in Romans chapter 6, verse 17, "But thanks be to God, that you who were once slaves of sin have become obedient with all your heart to the standard of teaching to which you were committed, and, having been set free from sin, have become slaves of righteousness."

True saving faith leads to a wholehearted obedience to God out of a thankfulness for what He has done in us. We were slaves of sin, and He has made us into slaves of righteousness. To obey God wholeheartedly means to give yourself fully over to Him, to love Him "with all your heart and with all your soul and with all your mind (Matt. 22:37)."

Now to be honest and transparent, are any of us perfect disciples at fulfilling this? Not by a long shot! But through God's grace, and our saving faith in Him, He indwells us with His Holy Spirit, and we are made redeemed and righteous, and through Him, we now possess the power and ability to do so. Though, because we are still trapped in this sinful flesh, we all still stumble to one degree or another, even as Paul confessed in Romans 7, "I do not do the good I want, but the evil I do not want is what I keep on doing. Now if I do what I do not want, it is no longer I who do it, but sin that dwells within me. O wretched man that I am! Who will save me from this body of death" (15–17, 24)?

This is Paul speaking! This is the greatest apostle that ever lived, and the man who penned half of the New Testament! And he penned this after he was saved and converted! If he suffered in this way after his redemption, how much more impossible would it have been prior to his conversion? We simply are incapable of any form of righteous obedience prior to our redeemed lives (Isa. 64:6). We are redeemed to the obedience of faith. We become obedient in our faith; we are not in faith because of our obedience. "After a man is justified by faith, then that true and living faith works by love (Gal. 5:6), and good works always follow justifying faith, and are most certainly found together with it."[7]

"It's not what we do that determines who we are; it's who we are and what we believe that determines what we do."[8]

Once again, this also is the work of God, as Paul confesses in Romans 15 verses 17–19, "In Christ Jesus, then, I have reason to be proud of my work for God. For I will not venture to speak of anything except what Christ has accomplished through me to bring the Gentiles to obedience—by word and deed, by the power of signs and wonders, by the power of the Spirit of God." Paul accepts none of the credit for bringing the Gentiles to faith and obedience but boasts only in the accomplished work of the Lord and the Spirit through himself.

He does the same thing again in 1 Corinthians 15:10, "But by the grace of God I am what I am, and His grace toward me was not in vain. On the contrary, I worked harder than any of them, though it was not I, but the grace of God that is with me." Paul again is giving all credit to God Who works all good things through him. Any good works that we do or any righteous obedience done is only accomplished through the presence and work of God's Spirit within us. Apart from Him, we can do nothing good (Isa. 64:6, Jas. 1:17).

Paul once more reiterates this in Philippians chapter 2, verses 12–13:

> Therefore, my beloved, as you have always
> obeyed, so now, not only in my presence but

> much more in my absence, work out your own
> salvation with fear and trembling, for it is God
> Who works in you, both to will and to work for
> His good pleasure.

Once again, Paul is pointing out that it is God Who produces in us any and all good works, obedience, and spiritual fruit. He does this by creating in our redeemed hearts a desire to obey Him through the presence and working of His indwelling Spirit, all for His glory, and we are told to live out that which God is doing within us.

Just so no one gets confused with the phrase "work out your own:"

> [W]e are not told to work for our salvation,
> but to work it out in practice in our lives. Our
> salvation is received entirely by grace through
> faith, not of works (Eph. 2:8–9). Works can no
> more retain salvation for us than they can achieve
> it in the first place, but they are the visual evi-
> dence of salvation. We have been created to do
> good works (Eph. 2:10) if we are truly saved. In
> fact, we are assured here that God is now working
> in us through His indwelling Holy Spirit.[9]

> I love the apparent contradiction in this
> passage. Paul says in one breath, "Work out your
> own salvation," and in the next, "It is God Who
> works in you." The both-ness here doesn't allow
> us to escape with a simple conclusion. Yes, it is
> God who works in you. And, yes, there is work
> for you to do. Yes, the Spirit empowers you to
> do the work. And, yes, you do the work. Like
> many things in life, there really isn't a sew-it-
> all-up solution. And I love that. God is big and
> mysterious enough that we cannot simply put
> a label on this process and move on. It requires

> continual engagement and wrestling and discovering how to live a Spirit-filled life today. Not ten years from now. Not tomorrow. But right now, in the particular time and place He has put us. As we "work out our salvation" and as "God works in us." Let us keep in step.[10]

However, this ability to do so and the desire to do so come as part of a redeemed life. God has never come across someone who was "working out his own salvation" and then realized He needed to bring this person to salvation or has come to the conclusion that "Oh, here's someone who has done all the right things and deserves to be saved!" Salvation comes first by the grace of God in Christ's finished work, through our faith, and then comes the working and the obeying, made available by the presence of the Holy Spirit within us.

> Let me say as clearly as possible right now that salvation is by God's sovereign grace and grace alone. Nothing a lost, degenerate, spiritually dead sinner can do will in any way contribute to salvation. *[Romans 5:8]* Saving faith, repentance, commitment, and obedience are all divine works, wrought by the Holy Spirit in the heart of everyone who is saved. I have never taught that some pre-salvation works of righteousness are necessary to, or part of, salvation. But I do believe without apology that real salvation cannot, and will not, fail to produce works of righteousness in the life of a true believer. There are no human works in the saving act, but God's work of salvation includes a change of intent, will, desire, and attitude that inevitably produces the fruit of the Spirit. The very essence of God's saving work is the transformation of the will, resulting in a love for God. Salvation thus establishes the root that will surely produce the fruit.[11]

Faith and obedience is something that God effects in us. It changes us, and we are reborn from God. It is impossible, indeed, to separate works from faith, just as it is impossible to separate heat and light from fire.

Many of the early reformers had much to say about this also. John Calvin puts it like this"

> Faith alone justifies, but the faith that justifies is never alone. We dream not of a faith which is devoid of good works, nor of a justification which can exist without them... Would you then obtain justification in Christ? You must previously possess Christ. But you cannot possess Him without being made a partaker of His sanctification: for Christ cannot be divided... Thus, it appears how true it is that we are justified not without, and yet not by works. We deny that good works have any share in justification, but we claim full authority for them in the lives of the righteous... It is obvious that gratuitous [grace-wrought] righteousness is necessarily connected with regeneration. Therefore, if you would duly understand how inseparable faith and works are, look to Christ, Who, as the apostle teaches (1 Cor. 1:30), has been given to us for justification and for sanctification. Wherever, therefore, that righteousness of faith, which we maintain to be gratuitous, is, there too Christ is, and where Christ is, there too is the Spirit of holiness, Who regenerates the soul to newness of life.[12]

The late preacher Charles Spurgeon states, "Although we are sure that men are not saved for the sake of their works, yet we are equally sure that no man will be saved without them."[13]

Professor, theologian, priest, monk, and seminal figure in the Protestant Reformation, Martin Luther, had this to say:

> When we have thus taught faith in Christ, then do we teach also good works. Because thou hast thus laid hold upon Christ by faith, through Whom thou art made righteous, begin now to work well. Love God and thy neighbour, call upon God, give thanks unto Him, praise Him, confess Him. Do good to thy neighbour and serve Him: fulfill thine office. These are good works indeed, which flow out of this faith.[14]

Luther also preached on this extensively. In one of his sermons, he stated regarding the relationship with justification by faith and that of good works:

> True faith, of which we speak, cannot be manufactured by our own thoughts, for it is solely a work of God in us, without any assistance on our part. As Paul says to the Romans, it is God's gift and grace, obtained by one Man, Christ. Therefore, faith is something very powerful, active, restless, effective, which at once renews a person and again regenerates him, and leads him altogether into a new manner and character of life, so that it is impossible not to do good without ceasing.
>
> For just as natural as it is for the tree to produce fruit, so natural is it for faith to produce good works. And just as it is quite unnecessary to command the tree to bear fruit, so there is no command given to the believer, as Paul says (1 Thess. 4:9), nor is urging necessary for him to do good, for he does it of himself, freely and unconstrained; just as he of himself without command

sleeps, eats, drinks, puts on his clothes, hears, speaks, goes and comes.

Whoever has not this faith talks but vainly about faith and works, and does not himself know what he says or whither it tends. He has not received it. He juggles with lies and applies the Scriptures where they speak of faith and works to his own dreams and false thoughts, which is purely a human work, whereas the Scriptures attribute both faith and good works not to ourselves, but to God alone.

Is not this a perverted and blind people? They teach we cannot do a good deed of ourselves, and then in their presumption got to work and arrogate to themselves the highest of all the works of God, namely faith, to manufacture it themselves out of their own perverted thoughts. Wherefore I have said that we should despair of ourselves and pray to God for faith as the apostles did in Luke 17:5. When we have faith we need nothing more; for it brings with it the Holy Spirit, Who then teaches us not only all things, but also establishes us firmly in it, and leads us through death and hell to Heaven.

Now observe, we have given these answers, that the Scriptures have such passages concerning works, on account of such dreamers and self-invented faith; not that man should become good by works, but that man should thereby prove and see the difference between false and true faith. For wherever faith is right it does good. If it does no good, it is then certainly a dream and a false idea of faith. So, just as the fruit on the tree does not make the tree good, but nevertheless outwardly proves and testifies that the tree is good, as Christ says, "By their fruits ye shall know them" (Matt.

7:16). Thus we should also learn to know faith by its fruits.

From this you see, there is a great difference between being good, and to be known as good; or to become good and to prove and show that you are good. Faith makes good, but works prove the faith and goodness to be right. Thus the Scriptures speak plainly, which prevails among the common people, as when a father says unto his son, "Go and be merciful, good and friendly to this or to that person." He does not command him to be merciful, good and friendly, but because he is already good and merciful, he requires that he should also show and prove it outwardly toward the poor by his act, in order that the goodness which he has in himself may also be known to others and be helpful to them.

You should explain all passages of Scripture referring to works, that God thereby desires to let the goodness received in faith express and prove itself, and become a benefit to others, so that false faith may become known and rooted out of the heart. God gives no one His grace that it may remain inactive and accomplish nothing good, but in order that it may bear interest, and by being publicly known and proved externally, draw everyone to God, as Christ says: "Let your light so shine before men, that they may see your good works, and glorify your Father Who is in Heaven" (Matt. 5:16). Otherwise it would be but a buried treasure and a hidden light. But what profit is there in either? Yea, goodness does not only thereby become known to others, but we ourselves also become certain that we are honest, as Peter says: "Wherefore, brethren, give the more diligence to make your calling and election sure" (2 Pet. 1:10). Where works do not follow, a man cannot know whether his faith is right; yea, he may be certain that his faith is a dream, and not right as it should be. Thus Abraham became certain of his faith, and that he feared God, when he offered up his son. As God by the angel said to Abraham: "Now I know, that is, it is manifest, that thou fearest God, seeing thou hast not with-held thy son, thine only son, from Me" (Gen. 22:12).

Then abide by the truth, that man is inter-nally, in spirit before God, justified by faith alone without works, but externally and publicly before men and himself, he is justified by works, that he is at heart an honest believer and pious. The one you may call a public or outward justification, the other an inner justification, yet in the sense that the public or external justification is only the fruit, the result and proof of the justification in the heart, that a man does not become just thereby before God, but must previously be just before Him. So you may call the fruit of the tree the public or outward good of the tree, which is only the result and proof of its inner and natural goodness.

This is what James means when he says in his Epistle: "Faith without works is dead" (James 2:26). That is, as the works do not follow, it is a sure sign that there is no faith there; but only an empty thought and dream, which they falsely call faith.

[I]nasmuch as works naturally follow faith, as I said, it is not necessary to command them, for it is impossible for faith not to do them without being commanded, in order that we may learn to distinguish the false from the true faith. [15]

The Augsburg Confession of 1530 stated:

> Moreover, ours teach that it is necessary to do good works; not that we may trust that we deserve grace by them, but because it is the will of God that we should do them. By faith alone is apprehended remission of sins and grace. And because the Holy Spirit is received by faith, our hearts are now renewed, and so put on new affections, so that they are able to bring forth good works. For thus saith Ambrose: "Faith is the begetter of a good will and of good actions."

The Belgic Confession of 1561 had this to say:

> We believe that this true faith, being wrought in man by the hearing of the Word of God and the operation of the Holy Ghost, doth regenerate and make him a new man, causing him to live a new life, and freeing him from the bondage of sin… Therefore, it is impossible that this holy faith can be unfruitful in man.

> If salvation is truly a work of God, it cannot be deficient. It cannot fail to impact an individual's behavior. It cannot leave his desires unchanged or his conduct unaltered. It cannot result in a fruitless life. It is the work of God and will continue steadfastly from its inception to ultimate perfection (Phil. 1:6; Heb. 12:2). [16]

So as we continue to see, out of a redeemed life comes obedience and good works. We are not saved and redeemed because of good works and obedience, but they become the product and resulting evidence of a redeemed life. It becomes the evidence and the visible proof of a life that has been redeemed from its fallenness. We are told in Titus 2:11–12:

> For the grace of God has appeared, bringing salvation for all people, training us to renounce ungodliness and worldly passions, and to live self-controlled, upright, and godly lives in the present age, waiting for our blessed hope, the appearing of the glory of our great God and Savior Jesus Christ, Who gave Himself for us to redeem us from all lawlessness and to purify for Himself a people for His Own possession who are zealous for good works.

Through our newly redeemed life, which has been created and granted to us by God alone, our new heart of flesh (Ezek. 36:26) yearns for good works and putting aside the ungodly things of the world that ruled our pasts. We are regenerated and now strive to live a more self-controlled and upright life out of thankfulness to Him Who purified us and our obedience and fruit testify to the proof of this heart change. W. E. Vine, author of the *Vine's Expository Dictionary*, puts it like this, "When a man obeys God he gives the only possible evidence that in his heart he believes God."[17]

This leads us into a section of Scripture that has led some to misinterpret this. James chapter 2, verses 14–26, when looked at by itself superficially and not paired with the rest of Scripture, can possibly lead someone to an incorrect interpretation and doctrine on this topic. This portion of Scripture states:

> What good is it, my brothers, if someone says he has faith but does not have works? Can that faith save him? If a brother or sister is poorly clothed and lacking in daily food, and one of you says to them, "Go in peace, be warmed and filled," without giving them the things needed for the body, what good is that? So also faith by itself,

if it does not have works, is dead. But someone will say, "You have faith and I have works." Show me your faith apart from your works, and I will show you my faith by my works. You believe that God is One; you do well. Even the demons believe—and shudder! Do you want to be shown, you foolish person, that faith apart from works is useless? Was not Abraham our father justified by works when he offered up his son Isaac on the altar? You see that faith was active along with his works, and faith was completed by his works; and the Scripture was fulfilled that says, "Abraham believed God, and it was counted to him as righteousness"—and he was called a friend of God. You see that a person is justified by works and not by faith alone. And in the same way was not also Rahab the prostitute justified by works when she received the messengers and sent them out by another way? For as the body apart from the spirit is dead, so also faith apart from works is dead.

So we see here that there are a couple verses that, at least on the surface, seem to present and verify that we are "justified by works and not by faith alone" as it so directly states in verse 24 and also similarly states in a few other spots. However, if taken superficially, it directly contradicts other portions of Scripture which say the exact opposite, like Galatians 2:16 that directly states:

> Yet we know that a person is not justified by works of the law but through faith in Jesus Christ, so we also have believed in Christ Jesus, in order to be justified by faith in Christ and not by works of the law, because by works of the law no one will be justified.

So these two passages seem to directly contradict each other! They are seemingly almost the exact opposite phraseology, but how can that be since God's Word never contradicts itself and can never be in error? Isn't God's Word inerrant and infallible? Rest assured it is! These are not contradictions, unless taken superficially and, might I say, out of context. This portion of Scripture actually perfectly affirms exactly what we have been discussing so far in this chapter. Or I would better say that this portion of Scripture is exactly the point that we have been trying to make in our discussion of this chapter. I would rather say that we are affirming it's point instead of saying that it is affirming our point. This is exactly what we have been discussing so far, and we are able to confirm this stance with this portion of Scripture. Just like the early reformers stated, "We are justified by faith alone, but justifying faith is never alone."

> James' point is not that a person is saved by works, for he has already strongly and clearly asserted that salvation is a gracious gift from God (1:17–18), but that there is a kind of apparent faith that is dead and does not save (2:14, 17, 20, 26). James is not disputing the importance of faith, rather he is opposing the notion that saving faith can be a mere intellectual exercise void of a commitment to active obedience. The kind of faith that is without works is mere empty profession, not genuine saving faith. The only possible evidence of true saving faith is works (cf. 2 Pet. 1:3–11). James is not contrasting two methods of salvation (faith versus works), instead he contrasts two kinds of faith: living faith that saves and dead faith that does not (cf. 1 John 3:7–10).[18]

> A person who has genuinely received salvation will produce good fruit. Good works are the inevitable result of salvation (Eph. 2:10). What differentiates a "living faith" from a "dead faith"

in James 2:14–26 is the presence of good works. One would be right to denounce churches that teach intellectual assent to the facts of the Gospel as sufficient for salvation. It is also right to reject the idea that a dead faith, a faith that produces no good works, could save a person. Faith/trust in Christ as the Savior is what saves a person, but this faith is a living faith that always results in and produces good works.[19]

Thomas Manton, who was a prominent and prolific English Puritan clergyman who lived and preached during the 1600s and was a huge influence to the late and much more currently well-known preacher, Charles Spurgeon, wrote in his commentary to the book of James (published in 1693):

> Works are an evidence of true faith. Graces are not dead, useless habits; they will have some effects and operations when they are weakest and in their infancy... This is the evidence by which we must judge, and this is the evidence by which Christ will judge... Works are not a ground of confidence, but an evidence; not the foundation of faith, but the encouragements of assurance. Comfort may be increased by the sight of good works, but it is not built upon them; they are seeds of hope, not props of confidence; sweet evidences of election, not causes; happy presages and beginnings of glory; in short, they can manifest an interest, but not merit it.[20]

Throughout this portion of James, we see that this point is confirmed to be true instead of being contradictory to the truth. These passages are teaching us that works themselves, along with obedience, do not save us but are those that evidence a true and saving faith. A "so-called" faith that does not evidence itself with that of good works is a dead faith; that which is not a true faith at all! In verse 14, when it says, "If someone says that he has faith," that is, merely giving lip service, "but does not have works," which would be the evidence or lack thereof of a true and saving faith, that dead faith will not save him. Which is exactly what verse 17 says, "faith by itself, if it does not have works, is dead," and therefore is not true and would not save. Verse 18 clearly states this point by saying that "I will show you (demonstrate, evidence) my faith by my works."

> Genuine faith in Christ for salvation inevitably produces works that demonstrate its reality. James never says that works produce salvation, nor even that faith plus works can save, but that good works always accompany true saving faith.[21]

> The clue to the understanding of this section is the fact (very often ignored) that in verse 14...the author has not said, "If a man have faith," but "If a man say he hath faith." This fact should be allowed to control our interpretation of the whole paragraph... The burden of this section is not (as is often supposed) that we are saved through faith plus works, but that we are saved through genuine, as opposed to counterfeit, faith.[22]

Verse 19 makes another very critical point, "Even the demons believe—and shudder." Mere intellectual faith or belief will not save you just as it does not save the demons and fallen angels. They know the truth about God! They spent some time in Heaven before being cast out of Heaven for their pride and rebellious activities and attempts at insurrection. They know Who God is! They certainly believe and know that He is real and is Who He says He is; however, they rebel against Him and despise Who He is and, therefore, do not count Him as their Savior but instead live eternally opposed to Him. So their simple intellectual belief in Him is not enough to save because it is not a true and genuine saving faith in Christ as their Lord and Savior. It is instead a wretched and dead knowledge and belief in Him. And again, verse 20 states, "Faith apart from works is useless." Faith that is not evidenced by works is a dead and useless faith that will not save anyone. Mere intellectual belief is not enough.

James is expressly teaching that real faith will no doubt produce righteous behavior. The true character of saving faith may be examined in light of the believer's works. One enters into salvation by grace through faith (Eph. 2:8–9). Faith is by Nature turned and toned toward obedience (Acts 5:32; Rom. 1:5, 2:8, 16:26), so good works are inevitable in the life of one who truly believes. These works have no part in bringing about salvation (Eph. 2:9; Rom. 3:20, 24, 4:5; Ti. 3:5), but they show that salvation is indeed present (Eph. 2:10, 5:9; 1 John 2:5). James wrote, "Prove yourselves doers of the Word, and not merely hearers who delude themselves" (1:22). James uses a substantive (*poietai* in the Greek) "doers of the Word" or "Word-doers" instead of a straightforward imperative ("do the Word"). He is describing characteristic behavior, not occasional activity. It is one thing to fight; it is something else to be a soldier. It is one thing to build a shed; it is something else to be a builder. James is not merely challenging his readers to *do the Word*; he is telling them real Christians are *doers of the Word*. That describes the basic disposition of those who believe unto salvation. Hearing is important, as James has emphasized in 1:19–21. Faith comes from hearing (Rom. 10:17). However, actual faith must be something more than mere hearing. Hearing is a means, not an end. The end is faith, which results in obedience.[23]

In verse 21, when the Scripture asks, "Was not Abraham our father justified by works?" it answers its own question with more confirmation of this same substance. His "faith was active along with his works, and faith was completed by his works." His faith showed active proof of his true and genuine saving faith and was completed or fulfilled and demonstrated, reaching its maturity, not its conception, by the visual evidence of his works.

> At first glance, this first statement in verse 21 does seem to be contradicted by Paul in Romans 4:2, when he denied that Abraham was justified by works. Actually, there is no conflict between the two. James certainly taught that the works of the law could not save (2:10, 4:17), and Paul taught clearly that genuine faith would produce good works (Eph. 2:10). It is simply a semantic matter of emphasis. Salvation must be of grace, accepted by faith, since no one can earn it, but only God can know the heart and the reality of a profession of faith. But the reality of that faith can only be demonstrated to others by good works. The point is that Abraham was justified by faith in the sight of God, as testified in Genesis 15:6, but he was justified in the sight of men (even in his own estimation) when he demonstrated the reality of his faith (Gen. 22:18) in his obedience to God's command to offer up Isaac.[24]

And before returning back to verse 24, we are first instructed by verse 23 which states, "Abraham believed God, and it was counted to him as righteousness." It is entirely Abraham's faith which credits Abraham as being righteous in the eyes of God, and it is merely, following into verses 24–26, the works that evidence his saving faith and distinguish it apart from a dead faith.

> Salvation has nothing to do with my performance. If I'm truly saved, then my actions are

going to show. All through the New Testament
a person's faith is shown through his actions.
New Testament teachings are clear that someone
who loves God and doesn't obey God is a liar,
and the truth is not in him (1 John 2:4; also cf.
John 14:15, 21–24, 15:10–14; 1 John 4:19–20,
5:2–3; 2 John 1:6).[25]

It has often been imagined that Paul's view
of justification differed from James's, because Paul
wrote, "For we maintain that a man is justified
by faith apart from the works of the Law" (Rom.
3:28); while James wrote, "You see that a man is
justified by works, and not by faith alone" (James
2:24). But there is no contradiction. Paul was saying that human works cannot earn favor with God,
and James was saying that true faith must always
result in good works. Paul was denouncing the
notion that the unregenerate can but merit with
God through works. James was condemning the
idea that the true believer might fail to produce
good works. The saving faith described by the apostle Paul is a dynamic force that inevitably produces
practical righteousness. He did not accept dead,
lifeless "faith" entirely devoid of good works.[26]

And neither did James.
Calvin said:

Those who are justified by true faith prove
their justification by obedience and good works,
not by a bare and imaginary semblance of faith...
The justification of believers shall be operative.
And as Paul contends that men are justified without the aid of works, so James will not allow any
to be regarded as justified who are destitute of

good works. An empty phantom of faith does not justify, yet the believer manifests his justification by good works.[27]

In 2 Peter chapter 1, we see a beautiful portion of Scripture which shows us a bit of framework and progression of the redeemed Christian life along with some assurance and also warning about our spiritual development. Starting in verse 3, we read:

> His divine power has granted to us *(which is past tense, by the way)* all things that pertain to life and godliness, through the knowledge of Him Who called us to His Own glory and excellence, by which He has granted to us His precious and very great promises, so that through them you may become partakers of the divine nature, having escaped from the corruption that is in the world because of sinful desire.

We have already touched on these two verses back in chapter 7, but we will look at them again as they are relevant to this chapter as well. We see that the verb in the beginning of this portion of Scripture is in the past tense. We have already received all things, all of these gracious and blessed gifts from God in full, absolutely everything pertaining to our righteousness and living our newly transformed lives of righteousness when He called us and made us His Own, when we surrendered and put our trusting faith in Him and became partakers of His divine nature and escaped the clutches of sin and death. We did not have these things beforehand.

Continuing on with verse 5, we see a "succession of seven attributes to be added to one's saving faith which should be understood as natural developments of true faith rather than as arbitrary additions."[28]

> For this very reason, make every effort to supplement your faith with virtue, and virtue

with knowledge, and knowledge with self-control, and self-control with steadfastness, and
steadfastness with godliness, and godliness with
brotherly affection, and brotherly affection with
love.

Peter is describing the responsibilities that result from possessing the godly resources described in verses 1–4.

> People are not saved by their efforts. But, on
> the other hand, grace saves no one to make him
> like a log of wood or a block of stone. Grace makes
> people active. God has been diligently at work
> with us; now we must diligently work together
> with Him. It is not our will that accomplishes
> our salvation, yet it is not accomplished without
> our will. As we have seen a mason take up first
> one stone and then another and then gradually
> build a house, so are we Christians to take first
> one virtue and then another and then another,
> piling up these stones of grace upon one another
> until we have built a palace for the indwelling of
> the Holy Spirit.[29]

> Because of all the God-given blessings in
> verses 3–4, the believer cannot be indifferent or
> self-satisfied. Such an abundance of divine grace
> calls for total dedication. That is, making maxi-
> mum effort. The Christian life is not lived to the
> honor of God without effort. Even though God
> has poured His divine power into the believer, the
> Christian himself is required to make every disci-
> plined effort alongside of what God has done.[30]

We also see that this beautiful succession of the Christian life
then culminates in verse 7 with love, which is the single word impact

or lesson of the entire New Testament. Reading 1 John chapters 3 and 4 drives this subject home wonderfully, and in 1 John 3:19, it tells us that "by this we shall know that we are of the truth and reassure our heart before Him." All of these attributes, all of our "good deeds," our "acts of obedience," and the love that flows through us toward others as a result of this inner transformation being done within us act as the assurance of our salvation.

We are also given a bit of a constructive warning here too, starting in verse 8.

> For if these qualities are yours and are increasing, they keep you from being ineffective or unfruitful in the knowledge of our Lord Jesus Christ. For whoever lacks these qualities is so nearsighted that he is blind, having forgot that he was cleansed from his former sins.

First of all, I want to point out that lacking these qualities does not necessarily mean one is not saved, which forces the point that it is not those qualities which make a true and saved Christian. Your good works, these beautiful attributes, don't make you a true and saved follower of Christ. Your salvation does not depend on them. Verse 9 plainly states that even those who (are saved but) lack these qualities have still been cleansed of their former sins. They are still saved; they just aren't evidently proving it yet with the outpouring of these gifts and attributes.

First Corinthians speaks into this same exact principle in chapter 3, verse 15, which speaks of the final judgment and the testing of each person's deeds on earth. "If anyone's work is burned up, he will suffer loss, though he himself will be saved, but only as through fire." A saved believer in Christ may not exhibit an abundance of good works or divine attributes or Christlike virtues, he may not accomplish much for the purpose of God here on earth, his works may prove to be stubble (v. 12) and be burned up (vv. 13, 15) in the fire of God's judgment, but he is still a saved believer (v. 15), and will not ever lose his salvation.

The works, the virtues, the divine attributes do not make the person; the saved child of God, through the presence of the indwelling Holy Spirit, is granted and exhibits these qualities, revealing the evidence of the Spirit in his or her saved life. And if these qualities are possessed by the child of God and growing in intensity, they guard against inactivity for God's purpose, ineffectiveness, and unfruitfulness. Verse 10, back in 2 Peter:

> Therefore, brothers, be all the more diligent to make your calling and election sure, for if you practice these qualities you will never fall. For in this way there will be richly provided for you an entrance into the eternal Kingdom of our Lord and Savior Jesus Christ.

> This expresses the bulls-eye Peter has been shooting at in verses 5–9. Though God is sure who His elect are and has given them an eternally secure salvation, the Christian might not always have assurance of his salvation. Security is the Holy Spirit revealed fact that salvation is forever. Assurance is one's confidence that he possesses that eternal salvation. In other words, the believer that pursues the spiritual qualities mentioned above guarantees to himself by spiritual fruit that he was called and chosen by God to salvation. As the Christian pursues the qualities and sees that his life is useful and fruitful, he will not stumble into doubt, despair, fear or questioning, but enjoy assurance that he is saved.[31]

None of this is saying that the absence of these qualities will prevent your salvation or that the presence of the qualities will birth your salvation, nor is any of this saying that the absence of these qualities may lead to the loss of your salvation; this whole section is speaking of assurance. "Peter is distinguishing between a just-barely-made-it entrance into the eternal Kingdom and a richly abundant one. The Scripture indicates that fruitful and faithful living here will be rewarded by greater privileges and rewards in glory (cf. Rev. 22:12)."[32]

"Peter's point is that a Christian who pursues the listed virtues (vv. 5–7) will not only enjoy assurance in the present, but a full, rich reward in the future life (1 Cor. 4:5, Rev. 22:12)."[33]

Some may try to use Hebrews 5:9 as a rebuttal to some of this, saying that obedience is necessary for salvation. It reads, "And being made perfect, He became the source of eternal salvation to all who obey Him." This verse is obviously talking about Jesus being our sacrifice and our Redeemer, but to use this text to state that our salvation is based on obedience is unwarranted, especially after all that we have already looked at. This verse is simply labeling those or naming those as the ones who obey Him. He became the source of eternal salvation to all of His children, the believers, the chosen, the elect, those who have faith in Him, those who are evidenced as possessing His gifts and the presence of the Holy Spirit within displaying obedience and virtue. "True salvation evidences itself in obedience to Christ, from the initial obedience to the Gospel command to repent and believe to a life pattern of obedience to the Word."[34]

Some may also try to use 1 Peter 1:22 as a rebuttal to this as well. It reads, "Having purified your souls by your obedience to the truth for a sincere brotherly love." This is merely a fault of translations. Several translations are worded very similar to this but damagingly leave out an important addition to the phrase. The term that is excluded is "through the Spirit." Taken from the original Greek, it should read "Having purified your souls in the obedience of the truth through the Spirit to the unpretended brotherly love." So we immediately see, once again, that it is certainly not our own power to purify ourselves or even to live in obedience without the presence of the Spirit through us.

Matthew Henry has this to add on this verse in his Commentary on the Whole Bible:

> Peter supposes that the Gospel had already
> had such an effect upon them as to purify their

souls while they obeyed it through the Spirit, and that it had produced at least an *unfeigned love of the brethren*; and thence he argues with them to proceed to a higher degree of affection, to love one another with a pure heart fervently, 1 Pet. 1:22. Learn, (1) It is not to be doubted but that every sincere Christian purifies his soul. The apostle takes this for granted: *Seeing you have*, etc. To purify the soul supposes some great uncleanness and defilement which had polluted it, and that this defilement is removed. Neither the Levitical purifications under the law, nor the hypocritical purifications of the outward man, can effect this. (2) The Word of God is the great instrument of a sinner's purification: *Seeing you have purified your souls in obeying the Truth*. The Gospel is called Truth, in opposition to types and shadows, to error and falsehood. This Truth is effectual to purify the soul, if it be obeyed, John 17:17. Many hear the Truth, but are never purified by It, because they will not submit to It nor obey It. (3) The Spirit of God is the great Agent in the purification of man's soul. The Spirit convinces the soul of its impurities, furnishes those virtues and graces that both adorn and purify, such as faith (Acts 15:9), hope (1 John 3:3), the fear of God (Ps. 34:9), and the love of Jesus Christ. The Spirit excites our endeavours, and makes them successful. The aid of the Spirit does not supersede our own industry; these people purified their own souls, but it was through the Spirit. (4) The souls of Christians must be purified before they can so much as love one another unfeignedly. There are such lusts and partialities in man's nature that without divine grace we can neither love God nor one another as we ought to do; there is no charity but out of a pure heart. (5) It is the duty of all Christians sincerely and fervently to love one another. Our affection to one another must be sincere and real, and it must be fervent, constant, and extensive.

So as works, virtues and obedience become the visual and evidential proof of a true and saving faith within us along with the presence and the work of the Holy Spirit versus that of a dead faith and offers us the assurance of our life in Christ, there also becomes a much greater and significant purpose for the visual evidence of our works, and that is to bring glory to God. And this is made evident in numerous places throughout the New Testament.

Matthew 5:16 tells us plainly, "Let your light shine before others, so that they may see your good works and give glory to your Father Who is in Heaven." When we shine the light of our new and "Godly life it gives convincing testimony to the saving power of God. And that brings Him glory!"[35]

"By this My Father is glorified, that you bear much fruit and so prove to be My disciples" (John 15:8).

"Likewise, my brothers, you also were made to die to the law through the body of Christ, so that you may belong to another, to Him Who has been raised from the dead, in order that we may bear fruit for God" (Rom. 7:4).

Our actions, good works, obedience, and our fruit all put God's glory on display for all to see.

> They will glorify God because of your submission flowing from your confession of the Gospel of Christ and the generosity of your contribution for them and for all others while they long for you and pray for you, because of the surpassing grace of God upon you. (2 Cor. 9:13–14)

> And it is my prayer that your love may abound more and more, with knowledge and all

> discernment, so that you may approve what is
> excellent, and so be pure and blameless for the
> day of Christ, filled with the fruit of righteous-
> ness that comes through Jesus Christ, to the glory
> and praise of God. (Phil. 1:9–11)

Our submission, our confession, our generosity, our contribution, our love, our purity—it is all evidence of our righteousness in
Christ along with His ongoing work within us through His Spirit,
and it is all manifested and granted to us by the grace of God, through
Christ, and it is all for the praise and glory due to God alone! This is
reiterated in Philemon 6, "I pray that the sharing of your faith may
become effective for the full knowledge of every good thing that is in
us for the sake of Christ." Every good thing being effected within us
and our outward evidences of this true and saving faith is all meant
for the glory of Christ.

First Peter 2:12 elaborates on this a bit more, "Keep your conduct among the Gentiles honorable, so that when they speak against
you as evildoers, they may see your good deeds and glorify God on
the day of visitation." We are to live our newly redeemed lives in
respectable manners so that even unbelievers will see His glory.

> Peter is teaching that when the grace of God
> visits the heart of an unbeliever, he will respond
> with saving faith and glorify God because he
> remembers the testimony of believers he had
> observed. Those who don't believe will expe-
> rience the visitation of His wrath in the final
> judgment.[36]

There's one last verse I want to add to this discussion. It is found
in Titus chapter 1, verses 15 and 16. Paul is raging on about many
different evil and wretched types of people, and then writes this:

> To the pure, all things are pure, but to the
> defiled and unbelieving, nothing is pure; but both

their minds and their consciences are defiled.
They profess to know God, but they deny Him
by their works. They are detestable, disobedient,
unfit for any good work.

Once again, Paul is affirming the teaching that works are not
the source of salvation but instead the evidence of a saving relationship with God; this time, though, in the negative sense. He is
expressing that these vile people who even though they may profess
to know God clearly evidence themselves as liars by their less-than-
stellar works. They are proclaiming their fallenness by the absence of
good works and by the presence of negative works. He also continues
his attack on them by calling them flat out repulsive and that they are
purely unfit to even perform a single good deed.

These are clearly an unsaved people, and they are wholly inadequate to even execute one good deed, work, or virtue in their fallen
state. They are entirely incapable without the presence of the Spirit
and an already redeemed life. Works do not get you there; works are
only possible once you are there. And getting there is only possible
through the One and only One that has paid the price, redeemed
us, and reconciled us to His Father; the One Who victoriously proclaimed, "It is finished!" It is only through Christ and only by His
grace, acknowledged upon us through our faith.

I'd like to think for example of the thief on
the cross. A lifetime of sin. All he did was sin for
what, 40 years? He's dying, he may begin with
cursing, like we heard from John... BAM! The
Spirit blew, where It wills, no explanation! This
man's repenting, he's crying out for mercy, and
Jesus says, "See ya in paradise today!" That man
will experience the judgment according to works.
What will he have? Not many. Half an hours
worth? But they're sweet! And they're real! So the
file will be opened, the books and the book, we
got the book of life, and the books. These books

are really thick! Everything you've ever done, every idle word. Jesus says, everything, they're all written down. So this man's file is gonna be picked up like this, and just everyone is F. His grades are all F! Pick them up, and throw them out. He's gotta a little bitty teeny file at the back. And in it is, "Heart was broken for his sin. Recognized Savior. Lovingly exhorted his comrade in evil. Died." And the Lord will hold this up to the whole universe, "HE WAS REAL! He trusted My Son! This is the evidence!" So that had he ever read a commandment in the Bible that says, "You will not enter into the Kingdom without a work," he'd know how to interpret it. The work isn't the ground of his acceptance, the work was the fruit of this amazing opening of his heart, believing in Jesus, being justified, and the fruit for 15 minutes, half an hour, an hour, and that gets written down.[37]

Summary

So as we come to a close, when we take a look at everything that we have seen throughout the course of this book, tying everything in to Scripture, our salvation is entirely dependent upon Jesus Christ, beginning to end. From before time even began, before the foundations of the world, before anything was ever created, He foreknew us, predestined us, chose us, and elected us to be His children (Rom. 8:29; Eph. 1:4–5; 2 Thess. 2:13; 2 Tim. 1:9; Ti. 1:2). He knew us and called us before we were ever conceived (Ps. 22:9–10, 71:6; Isa. 44:2, 24; Jer. 1:5; Gal. 1:15). He justified us, sanctifies us, secures us, glorifies us, and brings us safely to fulfillment and eternal salvation and imperishable inheritance through His finished work (John 17:22, 19:30; Rom. 8:29–30; 1 Cor. 6:11; Eph. 1:4–14; Phil. 1:6; Heb. 12:2; 1 Pet. 1:2–5).

He holds us, intercedes for us, prays for us, and fights for us (John 6:37–40, 44–47, 10:28–30, 17; Rom. 8:34; Heb. 7:25, 9:24; 1 John 2:1), and all of this out of His infinite, sacrificial, agape love for us (John 3:16; Rom. 5:6–11; Eph. 2:4–7; 2 Thess. 2:16; 1 John 3:1, 16, 4:9–10). We add nothing to this (Rom. 3:20; Gal. 2:16) nor could we take anything away from it. We do not deserve it, and we certainly cannot earn it. We could never be "good enough" or obey well enough to merit it. We are inherently sinful and totally depraved from birth, "sinful from the time my mother conceived me" (Ps. 51:5); we are conceived and born with the inherent sin nature, and therefore dead enemies of God (Rom. 5:6, 8, 10; Eph. 2:5). "No one is righteous, no not one" (Ps. 14:1–3, 53:1–3), and "the wages of sin is death" (Rom. 6:23), and that is exactly what we all deserve.

God is holy, righteous, true and just, and must uphold justice to the millennia of evil that this world has succumbed to. Nothing we can do in ourselves can bring us back from the dead or erase our sin or our debt to justice. Dead men cannot bring themselves to life. "No one can come to [Jesus] unless the Father Who sent Him draws him (John 6:44)…unless it is granted him by the Father (John 6:65)." Our works do not save us (Rom. 3:20), our obedience does not save us, our rituals, legalism, sacrifices, practices, sacraments (Rom. 3:21, 27–28)—none of that saves us.

Our faith, which is our only ingredient in this salvational formula, is not what saves us either, however, but it is the link and relationship that connects us to Christ Who is our Savior. God sovereignly chose us as His Own, before the beginning of time, He predestined us to know Him and come to Him, to believe in Him and to surrender to Him, but paradoxically (to us), we do have a responsibility in this also.

Our responsibility is this: full acceptance of Jesus Christ as our Savior and complete surrender to Him as Lord. We must accept His innocent substitution in our place, and place our entire faith for salvation upon Him and surrender entirely to Him as Lord and Savior (Matt. 16:24, 19:27; Mark 8:34–38, 10:29; Luke 9:23, 14:25–35; John 6:68–69, 20:31; Rom. 1:16, 10:9–10, 13; 1 John 2:15–17), but even our knowledge of Him and our faith in Him is a gracious gift granted to us by Him (John 3:27, 6:44–45, 14:26; Eph. 2:8–9). This baffles our feeble minds, but we are fallen, and God is holy, infinite, and supreme! Also, this full acceptance and complete surrender on our parts include both repentance and confession, a turning away from our old way of life and walking in a new way of life in a progressively maturing likeness of Christ, but it is only through His work and none of our own. Zero self-righteousness or merit; boasting or pride is entirely unjustified.

We must accept that it is only by His innocent substitution in our place that we can receive redemption and salvation and reconciliation to God along with our ongoing sanctification. We do not nor can we do anything or perform anything or obey perfectly enough in order to earn or deserve or receive His mercy and grace and eternal gifts and imperishable and undefiled co-inheritance. If you think you can earn it, then you don't understand it. And at least sometimes, I might even be so bold as to say you don't have it. It is only by acknowledging and accepting His gracious gifts given out of His infinite and eternal love for us, all to the praise and worship of His glory!

But once again, the great and divine paradox comes into play, even our knowledge of Him and our faith in Him is a gracious gift granted to us by Him (Eph. 2:8–9). Our obedience and works do not save us; instead, they are manifest in us upon a redeemed life (Eph. 2:10) and act as the outward evidence of our new internal reality and offer us assurance of this blessed reality of our newly redeemed and reconciled life in Christ and also finally become a light to the world that His name may be glorified and that His presence may be evident and known and that our witness and testimonies may help lead others to seek Him and find relationship with Him as that is Christ's command to us in the Great Commission (Matt. 28:19–20) and the highest priority of a follower of God.

> This, then, is the Gospel our Lord sends us forth to proclaim: That Jesus Christ, Who is God incarnate, humbled Himself to die on our behalf. Thus, He became the sinless sacrifice to pay the penalty of our guilt. He rose from the dead to declare with power that He is Lord over all, and He offers eternal life freely to sinners who will surrender to Him in humble, repentant faith. This Gospel promises nothing to the haughty rebel, but for broken, penitent sinners, it graciously offers everything that pertains to life and godliness (2 Pet. 1:3).[1]

> Our expression of faith places us into an unconditional relationship with our Heavenly Father. He makes this offer to all people everywhere. Some will choose to accept it by faith,

others will reject it. But the offer remains. Such is the nature of His love.

Sure, there are those who will abuse such an offer. But so pure is His love that even then He will not go back on His word. He remains faithful to the faithless. Nothing can separate us from His love. No one can snatch us from His hand. Where sin abounds, grace superabounds. Anything less would be less than unconditional.

Yet even with all this God has not abandoned the concept of justice. For within His plan of salvation there are special rewards for those who respond to Him in like kind. Great is their reward in Heaven. Eternity will not be the same for every believer. We will all stand and give an account of our lives. We will be judged according to our deeds, whether good or bad. Our rank in His future Kingdom is being decided each and every day of our lives.

For those who have as their ambition to be pleasing to the Lord, this comes as great news. For those who are seeking to have their cake and eat it too, this is rather disheartening. And so it should be. God is not one to be mocked. There are no loopholes in His economy. Even within the context of His grace, we will still reap what we sow. But that sword cuts both ways. For those who sow seeds of faithfulness and obedience, their crop will yield enduring fruit. For those who sow seeds of disobedience and selfishness, their crop will fail to endure the fiery judgment. They will have nothing to show for their lives. They will be poor in the Kingdom of Heaven.

God has gone to great lengths to make our relationship with Him possible. Doing so cost Him His Son. But the sacrifice of His Son did far more than merely provide us with the possibility of such a relationship; it guaranteed the permanency of that relationship as well.

Your salvation is secure. My prayer is that you would experience the assurance of this precious and costly gift.[2]

So what do we do with all this? What are we to do? What is our role? There is a devotional by John MacArthur that I think perfectly sums up our relational and redeemed spiritual reality in Him and what should be our loving response to His overall providence and sovereignty and calling in our lives called "Matching Your Practice to Your Position."[3]

"God chose us 'that we should be holy and blameless before Him'" (Eph. 1:4).

The challenge of Christian living is to increasingly match your practice to your position.

God chose you in Christ to make you holy and blameless in His sight. To be "holy" is to be separated from sin and devoted to righteousness. To be "blameless" is to be pure without spot or blemish—like Jesus, the Lamb of God (1 Pet. 1:19).

Ephesians 1:4 is a positional statement. That is, Paul describes how God views us "in Christ." He sees us as holy and blameless because Christ our Savior is holy and blameless. His purity is credited to our spiritual bank account. That's because God made Christ "Who knew no sin to be sin on our behalf, that we might become the righteousness of God in Him" (2 Cor. 5:21).

Despite our exalted position in God's sight, our practice often falls short of His holy standard. Therefore the challenge of Christian living is to increasingly match our practice to our position, realizing that sinless perfection won't come until we are in Heaven fully glorified (Rom. 8:23).

How do we meet that challenge? By prayer, Bible study, and yielding your life to the Spirit's control. Commit yourself to those priorities today as you seek to fulfill the great purpose to which you've been called: "good works, which God prepared beforehand, that we should walk in them" (Eph. 2:10).

Thank God that He does not expect us to earn our own righteousness but has provided it in His Son. Ask His Spirit to search your heart and reveal any sin that might hinder your growth in holiness. Confess that sin and take any steps necessary to eliminate it from your life.

Once redeemed by Christ and indwelt by the Spirit, we are now reborn and renewed, and as the Spirit continues to work on us, perfecting us and bringing us toward glory, we are to run the race as if to win. First Corinthians tells us in chapter 9, starting at verse 23:

> I do it all for the sake of the Gospel, that I may share with them in its blessings. Do you not know that in a race all the runners run, but only one receives the prize? So run that you may obtain it. Every athlete exercises self-control in all things. They do it to receive a perishable wreath, but we an imperishable. So I do not run aimlessly; I do not box as one beating the air. But I discipline my body and keep it under control.

Now having the revealed Savior in our lives, we are to run the race as if to win, disciplining ourselves in godly living and a Christlike image, made possible through the presence and guidance of the Holy Spirit.

Paul also adds in Philippians:

> For to me to live is Christ, and to die is gain. My desire is to depart and be with Christ, for that is far better. But to remain in the flesh is more necessary on your account. Convinced of this, I know that I will remain and continue with you all, for your progress and joy in the faith, so that in me you may have ample cause to glory in Christ Jesus. (1:21, 23–26)

Finally, though we strive to be with Christ, we are to live as beacons for God's glory, for the world to see that He may use our lives to reveal Himself to others and lead them to Him.

As a closing statement I will simply quote Paul once more as he is the best model of a fallen sinner who has taken hold of the majestic Gospel of our Lord and Savior, Jesus Christ. Starting in Philippians chapter 3, verse 7:

> But whatever gain I had, I counted as loss for the sake of Christ. Indeed, I count everything as loss because of the surpassing worth of knowing Christ Jesus my Lord. For His sake I have suffered the loss of all things and count them as rubbish, in order that I may gain Christ and be found in Him, not having a righteousness of my own that comes from the law, but that which comes through faith in Christ, the righteousness from God that depends on faith—that I may know Him and the power of His resurrection, and may share His sufferings, becoming like Him in His death, that by any means possible I may attain the resurrection from the dead. Not that I have already obtained this or am already perfect, but I press on to make it my own, because Christ Jesus has made me His Own. Brothers, I do not

consider that I have made it my own. But one thing I do: forgetting what lies behind and straining forward to what lies ahead, I press on toward the goal for the prize of the upward call of God in Christ Jesus. Our citizenship is in Heaven, and from it we await a Savior, the Lord Jesus Christ, Who will transform our lowly body to be like His glorious body, by the power that enables Him even to subject all things to Himself. Stand firm thus in the Lord. Rejoice in the Lord always; again I will say rejoice. Let your reasonableness be known to everyone. The Lord is at hand; do not be anxious about anything, but in everything by prayer and supplication with thanksgiving let your requests be made known to God. And the peace of God which surpasses all understanding, will guard your hearts and your minds in Christ Jesus. Finally brothers, whatever is true, whatever is honorable, whatever is just, whatever is pure, whatever is lovely, whatever is commendable; if there is any excellence, if there is anything worthy of praise, think about these things. What you have learned and received and heard and seen in me—practice these things, and the God of Peace will be with you. I rejoiced in the Lord greatly. I have learned in whatever situation I am to be content. In any and every circumstance, I have learned the secret of facing plenty and hunger, abundance and need. I can do all things through Christ Who gives me strength. And my God will supply every need of yours according to His riches in glory in Christ Jesus. To our God and Father be glory forever and ever. Amen.

List of Scriptures w/ Page Numbers

Gen 3:15-21	238
Gen 3:16-19	34
Gen 3:21	34,200,329
Gen 3:22-24	35
Gen 3:23-24	35
Gen 4	200
Gen 5:21-24	201
Gen 5:22,24	202
Gen 6:5	37
Gen 6:8	318
Gen 6:8-13	37
Gen 6:9	38,202
Gen 6:14	503
Gen 6:17-19	38
Gen 7:1	38,435
Gen 7:16	436
Gen 8:21	38
Gen 12:1-4	203
Gen 14:18-19	201
Gen 15	238,384
Gen 15:1,3-6	204-205
Gen 15:6	157,158,173,185,200,215,493,536
Gen 16:16	493
Gen 17:10-14	493
Gen 17:15-16,19,21	205
Gen 17:17	206
Gen 17:24-25	493
Gen 18:11-12	206
Gen 21:1-3	205-206
Gen 22:1-4	207
Gen 22:5	207

2 Sam 12:21-23	53-54
Kings	499
1 Kings 3:12	39
1 Kings 8:46	38,39
1 Kings 8:56	197
1 Kings 19:18	275
1 Kings 21:6-16	393
2 Kings 14:6	51
Chron	499
1 Chron 28:9	111,408
2 Chron 6:36	39
2 Chron 7:14	111
2 Chron 15:2	111
2 Chron 20:15,29	336
2 Chron 25:4	51
Neh 4:20	336
Est 8:8-12	393
Job 1:1	39
Job 1:21	240
Job 4:7	39
Job 4:17	39
Job 5:19	337
Job 14:1	51
Job 14:1-2,4	39

John 17:12,15,24	402
John 17:13-14	365
John 17:15	306,366,387,397
John 17:16-19	366
John 17:17	486,543
John 17:19-21	154
John 17:20	370
John 17:20-21	367
John 17:21	387
John 17:22	373,549
John 17:22-23	368
John 17:24	375-376,387
John 17:24-26	368-369
John 17:26	305
John 18:9	92,365,369,370
John 19:28	135
John 19:30	135,141,142,144,156,175,182, 222,226,241,312,315,339,359, 371,377,425,430,431,432,433, 438,497,510,511,546,549
John 20:27-29	154
John 20:29	198-199
John 20:30-31	161
John 20:31	116,550
Acts 1:5	466,484
Acts 1:8	298
Acts 2	259,472
Acts 2:4	367
Acts 2:21	110,111,114,159,443,448,475
Acts 2:21,38	488

Rom 1:5	535
Rom 1:5-6	72,516,520
Rom 1:6-7	93
Rom 1:16	550
Rom 1:16-17	170,171,443
Rom 1:17	159,160,171,197-198,413
Rom 1:18-23	183
Rom 1:18-25	19,102
Rom 1:18-32	86
Rom 1:18-3:20	171
Rom 1:19-20	20
Rom 1:26-32	20
Rom 2:1-5	20-21
Rom 2:4	264
Rom 2:8	535
Rom 2:8-9,11	21
Rom 2:15-16	21
Rom 2:17-24	25-26
Rom 2:19-20	158
Rom 2:25	492
Rom 2:25-29	27,492
Rom 2:28-29	493-494
Rom 2:29	489,490,492
Rom 3:1-19	257
Rom 3:9	28
Rom 3:10-18	28
Rom 3:11	49,81,240,293
Rom 3:19-20	60
Rom 3:20	28,57,61,63,71,115,438,549,550
Rom 3:20,24	535
Rom 3:20,28	158

Endnotes

Chapter 1

1 A. W. Tozer, *The Knowledge of the Holy*, pp. 1–2.
2 www.hebrew4christians.com/Names_of_G-d/Elohim/elohim.html.
3 www.hebrew-streams.org/works/monotheism/context-elohim.html.
4 A. W. Tozer, *The Knowledge of the Holy*, pp. 17, 19.
5 Ibid., pp. 22–23.
6 Ibid., p. 9.
7 A. W. Tozer, *The Knowledge of the Holy*, p. 9.
8 Ibid., pp. 8–9.
9 Ibid., pp. 44–47
10 Quoted by A. W. Tozer in *The Knowledge of the Holy*, p. 44.

Chapter 2

1 Excerpted from Chuck Missler's *24-hour Commentary on the Book of Romans.*
2 Dietrich Bonhoeffer, *The Cost of Discipleship*, 143–144.
3 Ibid., pp. 147–148.
4 http://www.gotquestions.org/religion-spirituality.html.
5 Sermon: Alistair Begg, Eph. 1:1–6:24, "Introducing Ephesians," January 18, 2016.
6 Excerpted from Chuck Missler's *24-hour Commentary on the Book of Romans.*
7 Dictionary.
8 MacArthur Study Bible footnotes.
9 Ibid.
10 Sermon: John MacArthur, "Becoming a Better You," 1 Peter 1:3–5, March 26, 2010.
11 A neat little writing about this can be found at www.yashanet.com/studies/judaism101/sidebars/ohr.htm.
12 J. C. Ryle, *Holiness* (James Clark, Cambridge, 1952), p. 1.

13 Ken Willig, *The Free Gift*, p. 11. Copies of this book can be attained from tfgbook.com.

14 MacArthur Study Bible footnotes.

15 Ibid.

16 Ibid.

17 Henry Morris Study Bible footnotes.

18 MacArthur Study Bible footnotes.

19 Henry Morris Study Bible footnotes.

20 Tim Campbell, Grace Church, Lakeland FL, "You Must Be Born Again," John 3:1–8, February 21, 2016.

21 An excellent clip that helps explain this can be found at https://anchorednorth. org/do–aborted–babies–go–to–heaven/.

22 http://www.gotquestions.org/age-of-accountability.html.

23 John MacArthur, "Prophecy, Eternity and Preparing for Christ's Coming," May 14, 2016.

24 Also, for more on this subject check out the book, *Safe in the Arms of God* by John MacArthur.

Chapter 3

1 http://www.gotquestions.org/Mosaic–Law.html.

2 http://www.gotquestions.org/Levitical–Law.html.

3 Ken Willig, *The Free Gift*, pp. 20–21.

4 Ray Pritchard, *An Anchor for the Soul*, p. 116.

5 Sermon: John MacArthur, "Becoming a Better You," 1 Peter 1:3–5, March 26, 2010.

6 MacArthur Study Bible footnotes.

7 Sermon: John Piper, "Can You Begin by the Spirit and Be Completed by the Flesh?, Gal. 3:1–5, March 13, 1983.

8 Footnotes from the Amplified Holy Bible for Galatians 2:16.

9 Kris Langham, "Romans 4–8 Explained | I'm Saved. Now How Do I Stop Sinning," YouVersion Bible App, Day 4.

10 Ken Willig, *The Free Gift*, pp. 27–28

Chapter 4

1 Sermon: Alistair Begg, "Introducing Ephesians, Eph. 1:1–6:24," January 18, 2016.

2 Sermon: John MacArthur, "Election: Christ's Honor and Our Blessing," 2 Thess. 2:13–17, June 9, 2019.

3 Ibid.

4 John MacArthur, Drawing Near, January 17.

5 MacArthur Study Bible footnotes.

6 Ibid.

7 Ibid.

8 Sermon: Alistair Begg, Chosen in Him, Eph. 1:3–6, January 17, 2016.

9 Ibid.

10 MacArthur Study Bible footnotes.

11 Enhanced Strong's Dictionary.

12 Dietrich Bonhoeffer, *The Cost of Discipleship*, p. 215.

13 Henry Morris Study Bible footnotes.

14 Sermon: John MacArthur, "Election: Christ's Honor and Our Blessing," 2 Thess. 2:13–17, June 9, 2019.

15 MacArthur Study Bible footnotes

16 Sermon: John MacArthur, "Election: Christ's Honor and Our Blessing," 2 Thess. 2:13–17, June 9, 2019

17 Sermon: John MacArthur, "The Lord's Greatest Prayer, Part 3," John 17:6–10, January 10, 2016,

18 Quoted from Biblical Commentator Chuck Missler.

19 Sermon: John MacArthur, "Election: Christ's Honor and Our Blessing," 2 Thess. 2:13–17, June 9, 2019.

20 Sermon: Alistair Begg, "Chosen in Him," Eph. 1:3–6, January 17, 2016.

Chapter 5

1 Sermon: Alistair Begg, "Chosen in Him," Eph. 1:3–6, Jan 17, 2016.

2 Sermon: John MacArthur, "Twin Truths: God's Sovereignty and Man's Responsibility," John 3:11–21, February 17, 2013.

3 John MacArthur, *Saved without a Doubt*, p. 173.

4 http://www.gotquestions.org/Calvinism–vs–Arminianism.html.

5 A. W. Tozer, *The Knowledge of the Holy*, p. 36.

Chapter 6

1 https://bible.org/question/what–does–greek–word–tetelestai–mean.

2 John MacArthur, *The Gospel According to Jesus*, p. 87.

3 Sermon: Stephen Davey, "I Long to See You."

4 Oswald Chambers, My Utmost for His Highest, "Have You Come to 'When' Yet?," June 20.

5 MacArthur Study Bible footnotes to Phil. 3:9.

6 John MacArthur, *The Gospel According to the Apostles*, p. 30.

7 John MacArthur, *The Gospel According to Jesus*, p. 116.

8 John MacArthur, "An Old Testament Illustration of Salvation," September 26, *Daily Readings from the Life of Christ*.

9 MacArthur Study Bible footnotes.

10 Ibid.

11 Ibid.

12 Ibid.

13 John MacArthur, *The Gospel According to Jesus*, p. 55–56.

14 MacArthur Study Bible footnotes.

15 Ibid.

16 Joshua Harris, *Sex Is Not the Problem, Lust Is*, p. 49–50.

17 MacArthur Study Bible footnotes.

18 Kris Langham, "Romans 4–8 Explained | I'm Saved. Now How Do I Stop Sinning," YouVersion Bible App, Day 2.

19 MacArthur Study Bible footnotes.

20 Ibid.

21 Ibid.

22 There's an interesting visual lesson done by RC Sproul of this image found at http://youtu.be/mSN2r_BpxdY.

23 MacArthur Study Bible footnotes.

24 Ibid.

25 Ibid.

26 Henry Morris Study Bible footnotes.

27 MacArthur Study Bible footnotes.

28 Ibid.

29 Francis Chan, *Crazy Love*, p. 114.

30 MacArthur Study Bible footnotes.

31 Ibid.

32 Clement of Rome, First Epistle to the Corinthians 32:4.

33 Polycarp of Smyrna, Epistle to the Philippians 1:2–3.

34 R.C. Sproul quoted from John MacArthur, *The Gospel According to the Apostles*, p. 87.

35 John MacArthur, *The Gospel According to the Apostles*, pp. 23–25.

36 John MacArthur, *The Gospel According to Jesus*, p. 87.

Chapter 7

1 A. W. Tozer, *The Knowledge of the Holy*, pp. 93, 95.

2 John MacArthur, *The Gospel According to Jesus*, p. 196.

3 Dietrich Bonhoeffer, *The Cost of Discipleship*, pp. 313–314.

4 John MacArthur, *The Gospel According to the Apostles*, p. 90.

5 John Calvin, *Institutes of the Christian Religion*, 2:99.

6 J.C. Ryle, *Holiness*, pp. 29–30.

7 John MacArthur, *The Gospel According to the Apostles*, p. 91.

8 MacArthur Study Bible footnotes to Eph. 4:7.

9 John MacArthur, *The Truth about Grace*, pp. 104–105.

10 MacArthur Study Bible footnotes.

11 Dietrich Bonhoeffer, *The Cost of Discipleship*, p. 306–307.

[12] *Strong's Expanded Exhaustive Concordance of the Bible.*

[13] John MacArthur, *The Gospel According to Jesus*, pp. 86–87.

[14] MacArthur Study Bible footnotes.

[15] Ravi Zacharias quoted in *Case for Faith* by Lee Strobel, p. 219–220.

[16] MacArthur Study Bible footnotes.

[17] Ibid.

[18] H. A. Ironside, *Full Assurance*, pp. 116–117.

[19] MacArthur Study Bible footnotes.

[20] D. Martyn Lloyd–Jones, *Studies in the Sermon on the Mount*, 2:248.

[21] John MacArthur, *The Gospel According to Jesus*, pp. 178–179.

[22] John MacArthur, *The Gospel According to the Apostles*, p. 98.

[23] MacArthur Study Bible footnotes.

[24] John MacArthur, *The Gospel According to the Apostles*, pp. 103–104.

[25] MacArthur Study Bible footnotes.

[26] Ken Willig, *The Free Gift*, pp. 9–10.

[27] John MacArthur, *Saved Without a Doubt*, p. 60.

[28] Ibid.

[29] MacArthur Study Bible footnotes.

[30] John MacArthur, *Remember and Return*, pp. 84–85.

[31] John MacArthur, *The Gospel According to Jesus*, p. 116.

[32] MacArthur Study Bible footnotes.

[33] Dietrich Bonhoeffer, *The Cost of Discipleship*, pp. 308–309, 311.

[34] John MacArthur, *The Gospel According to the Apostles*, pgs. 88–90.

[35] John MacArthur, Remember and Return, p. 37.

[36] Quoted from Chuck Missler's *24-hour Commentary on the Book of Romans*, in Session 9, on Romans 8.

[37] John MacArthur, "The Body Formed in Eternity Past, Part 2;" Ephesians 1:4–6, January 5, 1978.

[38] *Devotional from Future Grace*, by John Piper, January 15.

[39] John MacArthur, *The Gospel According to Jesus*, pp. 188–189.

[40] MacArthur Study Bible footnotes.

[41] Ibid.

[42] Ibid.

[43] John Piper, *Fifty Reasons Why Jesus Came to Die*, p. 49.

[44] MacArthur Study Bible footnotes.

[45] Dietrich Bonhoeffer, *The Cost of Discipleship*, p. 312.

[46] MacArthur Study Bible footnotes.

[47] Ibid.

[48] John MacArthur, *The Gospel According to Jesus*, p. 86.

[49] MacArthur Study Bible footnotes.

[50] Ibid.

[51] Ibid.

[52] Joseph Alleine (1672).

53 There is a cute but beautiful illustration of this in a video called "The Good–O–Meter" which can be found at https://youtu.be/XrLzYw6ULYw.

54 https://www.facebook.com/secretchurch/videos/10156443009661204?sfns=mo.

55 Ken Willig, *The Free Gift*, p. 21.

56 A. W. Tozer, *Evenings with Tozer, Daily Devotional Readings Compiled by Gerald B. Smith*, January 16.

57 Sermon: Kevin Donoho, "Say What? Grace," May 13, 2018.

58 Excerpted from a Dave Peters sermon, Grace, April 13, 2018.

Chapter 8

1 John MacArthur sermon: "The Perseverance of the Saints, Part 1," August 29, 2004. This whole sermon is remarkable! If you'd like to listen to all of it, you can find it at www.gty.org/library/sermons–library/90–270/the–perseverance–of–the–saints–part–1.

2 John MacArthur, *The Gospel According to Jesus*, pp. 114–115.

3 H. A. Ironside, *Full Assurance*, pp. 30–32.

4 MacArthur Study Bible footnotes.

5 Matthew Henry's Commentary on the Whole Bible.

6 John Piper, *Fifty Reasons Why Jesus Came to Die*, p. 47.

7 Matthew Henry's Commentary on the Whole Bible.

8 Charles Stanley, *Eternal Security. Can You Be Sure?*, p. 4.

9 Excerpt from *Saved Without a Doubt* by John MacArthur.

10 MacArthur Study Bible footnotes.

11 www.truth4freedom.wordpress.com/faqs–and–helpful–links/once–saved–always–saved/.

12 Charles Stanley, *Eternal Security. Can You Be Sure?*, pp. 3–4.

13 MacArthur Study Bible footnotes.

14 Ibid.

15 Ibid.

16 Ibid.

17 Sermon: John MacArthur, "The Lord's Greatest Prayer, Part 3," John 17:6–10, January 10, 2016.

18 Ibid.

19 MacArthur Study Bible footnotes.

20 Ibid.

21 Ibid.

22 John MacArthur sermon: "The Perseverance of the Saints, Part 1," August 29, 2004.

23 Excerpted from Chuck Missler's *24-hour Commentary on the Book of Romans*.

24 MacArthur Study Bible footnotes.

25 Ibid.

26 Theologian Louis Berkhof, *Systematic Theology*, page 546.

27 MacArthur Study Bible footnotes.

28 *Strong's Expanded Exhaustive Concordance of the Bible.*

29 MacArthur Study Bible footnotes.

30 Ibid.

31 Ibid.

32 Ibid.

33 Excerpted from Chuck Missler's *24-hour Commentary on the Book of Romans.*

34 http://www.zianet.com/maxey/reflx171.htm.

35 MacArthur Study Bible footnotes.

36 Ibid.

37 Ibid.

38 Charles Stanley, *Eternal Security*, p. 121.

39 MacArthur Study Bible footnotes.

40 *Strong's Expanded Exhaustive Concordance of the Bible.*

41 MacArthur Study Bible footnotes.

42 Ibid.

43 Ibid.

44 There is an extensive twelve-page list entitled "The Sufferings of Paul" that can be found at www.biblecharts.org/apostlepaulcharts/15 percent20–percent20 The percent20Sufferings percent20of percent20Paul.pdf.

45 MacArthur Study Bible footnotes.

46 Ibid.

47 Ibid.

48 Ibid.

49 Ibid.

50 Ibid.

51 Amplified Holy Bible footnotes.

52 MacArthur Study Bible footnotes.

53 Ibid.

54 Ibid.

55 Sermon: John MacArthur, "Taking Sin Seriously at the Lord's Table," February 18, 2018, James 1:13–17.

56 H. A. Ironside, *Full Assurance*, pp. 38–39.

57 MacArthur Study Bible footnotes.

58 Ibid.

59 John MacArthur, *The Gospel According to Jesus*, p. 109.

60 MacArthur Study Bible footnotes.

61 John MacArthur, *Saved Without a Doubt*, p. 173.

62 MacArthur Study Bible footnotes.

63 Ibid.

64 Henry Morris Study Bible footnotes.

65 Ibid.

66 MacArthur Study Bible footnotes.

67 Ibid.

68 Ibid.

69 69.Paraphrased from Ted Roberts, *Pure Desire*, p. 105.

70 Ibid., p. 106.

71 www.gotquestions.org/perseverance–saints.html.

72 Charles Stanley, *Eternal Security*, p. 192.

73 Sermon: Dr. Tom Ascol, "Justification by Faith."

74 John MacArthur, *The Gospel According to Jesus*, p. 240–241.

75 Adrian Rogers, *Love Worth Finding Devotional*, April 8, 2020, www.lwf.org/daily–devotions/the–cross–once–and–for–all.

76 Sermon: "John MacArthur, The Perseverance of the Saints, Part 1," August 29, 2004.

77 H. A. Ironside, *Full Assurance*, pp. 102–103.

78 Paraphrased from Ted Roberts, *Pure Desire*, p. 111.

79 Excerpted from *Saved Without a Doubt* by John MacArthur, p. 115.

Chapter 9

1 www.gotquestions.org/baptismal–regeneration.html.

2 Thomas J. Nettles, *Understanding Four Views on Baptism*, pp. 33–34.

3 MacArthur Study Bible footnotes.

4 John MacArthur, *The Gospel According to the Apostles*, pp. 207–208.

5 Charles Spurgeon, *The Soul Winner*, p. 38.

6 MacArthur Study Bible footnotes.

7 Thomas J. Nettles, *Understanding Four Views on Baptism*, p. 147–148.

8 John MacArthur, *The Gospel According to Jesus*, pp. 53–55.

9 Sermon: John MacArthur, "Becoming A Better You," March 26, 2010, 1 Peter 1:3–5.

10 John MacArthur, *Daily Readings from the Life of Christ*, September 26.

11 Sermon: John MacArthur, "What Was Happening in the Early Church?," September 8, 1991.

12 MacArthur Study Bible footnotes.

13 Henry Morris Study Bible footnotes.

14 MacArthur Study Bible footnotes.

15 Matthew Henry's Commentary on the Whole Bible.

16 Alistair Begg, Blog Archive, TruthForLife.org, March 19, 2013.

17 MacArthur Study Bible footnotes.

18 Joseph Thayer, *Thayer's Greek Lexicon*, also Larry Pierce, *Outline of Bible Usage*; for Strong's NT #908, *baptisma*.

19 Henry Morris Study Bible footnotes.

20 MacArthur Study Bible footnotes.

21 Footnotes from the Amplified Holy Bible for 1 Peter 3:21.

[22] MacArthur Study Bible footnotes.

[23] Thomas Nelson NKJV Study Bible footnotes.

[24] John MacArthur, *The Gospel According to the Apostles*, p. 83.

[25] Thomas Nelson NKJV Study Bible footnotes.

[26] John MacArthur, *The Truth about Grace*, p. 89.

[27] D. Martyn Lloyd–Jones, *Sanctified Through the Truth: The Assurance of Our Salvation*, 116–117.

[28]

[29] Dietrich Bonhoeffer, *The Cost of Discipleship*, pp. 256–261.

[30] MacArthur Study Bible footnotes.

[31] Thomas J. Nettles, *Understanding Four Views on Baptism*, p. 74.

[32] *Strong's Expanded Exhaustive Concordance of the Bible.*

[33] MacArthur Study Bible footnotes.

[34] Thomas Nelson NKJV Study Bible footnotes.

[35] Henry Morris Study Bible footnotes.

[36] MacArthur Study Bible footnotes.

[37] Charles Stanley, *Eternal Security*, pg139.

[38] John MacArthur, *The Gospel According to the Apostles*, pp. 101–102.

[39] The Expositor's Study Bible footnotes.

[40] Thomas J. Nettles, *Understanding Four Views on Baptism*, p. 32–33.

[41] MacArthur Study Bible footnotes.

[42] Ibid.

[43] Thomas J. Nettles, *Understanding Four Views on Baptism*, p. 148.

[44] MacArthur Study Bible footnotes.

[45] Henry Morris Study Bible footnotes.

[46] H. A. Ironside, *Full Assurance*, pp. 118–119.

[47] Max Lucado, https://maxlucado.com/baptism–the–demonstration–of–devotion/.

[48] Robert Morey, "Salvation through Water Baptism?" YouTube series.

[49] http://www.compellingtruth.org/baptism–salvation.html.

[50] Cecil Hook, *Free to Change*, p. 161–163.

[51] Sermon: John MacArthur, "Understanding Baptism," January 29, 1989.

[52] Thomas J. Nettles, *Understanding Four Views on Baptism*, p. 146–147.

Chapter 10

[1] Quoted by Ravi Zacharias in *Case for Faith* by Lee Strobel, p. 224.

[2] Footnotes from Gal. 3:1, 3, 18; 1 Thess. 1:4, MacArthur Study Bible.

[3] https://www.gotquestions.org/Church–of–Christ.html.

[4] John MacArthur, *The Gospel According to Jesus*, p. 169.

[5] J. Gresham Machen, *What Is Faith?*, pp. 203–204.

[6] MacArthur Study Bible footnotes.

[7] Schaff, *The Creeds of Christendom*, 3:117–118.

[8] Neil Anderson, *The Bondage Breaker*.

9   Henry Morris Study Bible footnotes.

10 Francis Chan, *Crazy Love*, pp. 204–205.

11 John MacArthur, *The Gospel According to Jesus*, p. 15.

12 Ibid., p. 259.

13 Charles Spurgeon, *The New Park Street Pulpit*, 4:265.

14 John Dillenberger, *Martin Luther*, pp. 111–112.

15 Martin Luther, "Justification of Faith," *Classic Sermons on Faith and Doubt*, ed. Warren W. Wiersbe, 78–83.

16 John MacArthur, *The Gospel According to Jesus*, p. 86.

17 W. E. Vine, *Vine's Expository Dictionary of Old and New Testament Words*, 3:124.

18 MacArthur Study Bible footnotes.

19 https://www.gotquestions.org/Church–of–Christ.html.

20 Thomas Manton, *A Commentary on James*, p. 239.

21 Henry Morris Study Bible footnotes.

22 C. E. B. Cranfield, "The Message of James," *The Scottish Journal of Theology*, 18/3 September 1965, p. 338.

23 John MacArthur, *The Gospel According to the Apostles*, p. 142.

24 Henry Morris Study Bible footnotes.

25 Francis Chan, *Crazy Love*, p. 183.

26 John MacArthur, *The Gospel According to Jesus*, pp. 246–247.

27 John Calvin, *Institutes of the Christian Religion*, 2:115.

28 Henry Morris Study Bible footnotes.

29 The Spurgeon Study Bible footnotes.

30 MacArthur Study Bible footnotes.

31 Ibid.

32 Thomas Nelson NKJV Study Bible footnotes.

33 MacArthur Study Bible footnotes.

34 Ibid.

35 Ibid.

36 Ibid.

37 John Piper, www.facebook.com/TogetherfortheGospel/videos/440569583487014/.

Summary

1   John MacArthur, *The Gospel According to Jesus*, p. 241.

2   Charles Stanley, *Eternal Security*, p. 193–194.

3   John MacArthur, *Drawing Near*, January 8.

About the Author

My name is Chad Staerkel. First and foremost, I am a redeemed child of God, though I miss the mark and fail My Lord and Savior daily. Anything and everything good in me is from God, the only thing I have ever personally accomplished is putting Christ on the cross. But thanks be to God, He has redeemed me, He is transforming me and He has reconciled me back to Himself, and calls me His child. I hold no official formal training or theological degree; however, I am a devoted follower of God who felt led to take on the project of this book, and sincerely feel God has guided and helped me through the entire process, has drawn me closer to Himself and taught me so much more through the studying and research and writing of this book. The process of this book was an immense blessing to myself, and I pray it will be also to those who read it, and will also draw them closer to God as well.

Professionally, I am a skydiving instructor near Chicago IL. I pastor a small church composed of skydivers during the skydiving season, and attend a local church during the offseason, in which I have served for several years in both the youth ministry and worship teams. I also have a huge heart for missions, and have served on several short-term mission trips; a few to Bolivia, one to Thailand, and one to Honduras, with prayers to serve on many more in the future, and the definite possibility of a long-term position if led by God to do so.

I was born and raised in a loving Lutheran home in Oshkosh, Wisconsin, and went to Lutheran schools all the way up through high school. I no longer hold specifically to a certain denomination;

I am simply a child of God and a follower of Christ. By the Grace of God, as far back as my memory takes me, I have always known Christ as my Savior. I have never been an atheist. During my college years I started to dig and study on my own to make sure what I believed was the Truth, and in so doing learned a bit about other religions (though I do not consider Christianity a "religion," and this book will explain why), and dove deep into the Scriptures, all of which firmly solidified my devotion to the One and only Triune God, our Lord, Savior and King, The Way, The Truth and The Life, Jesus Christ! I am nothing without Him! To God be ALL the glory!

Lightning Source UK Ltd.
Milton Keynes UK
UKHW010717070223
416609UK00001B/24